Studies in Modern Chinese Economy

The series aims to look through all key issues around China's development since the reform and open-up, involving topics of economic growth, institutional reform, reform of state-owned enterprises, income distribution and balanced development, movement of population and regional economic development, rural economic development, innovation and economic incentive polices and local governance etc. The authors are all first-class economists in China. It's helpful to understand the history as well as the status quo of China's path in development.

More information about this series at https://link.springer.com/bookseries/16588

Miaojie Yu

China's Miracle in Foreign Trade

格致出版社
Truth & Wisdom Press

Springer

Miaojie Yu
National School of Development
Peking University
Beijing, China

ISSN 2730-5376 ISSN 2730-5384 (electronic)
Studies in Modern Chinese Economy
ISBN 978-981-16-6029-0 ISBN 978-981-16-6030-6 (eBook)
https://doi.org/10.1007/978-981-16-6030-6

Jointly published with Truth and Wisdom Press
The print edition is not for sale in China (Mainland). Customers from China (Mainland) please order the print book from: Truth and Wisdom Press.
ISBN of the Co-Publisher's edition: 978-7-5432-2946-4

This Springer imprint is published by the registered company Springer Nature Singapore Pte Ltd.
The registered company address is: 152 Beach Road, #21-01/04 Gateway East, Singapore 189721, Singapore

Dedicated to my darling, Wei Tian

& my son, Yushen Yu

Preface

China began its era of reform and opening-up around four decades ago, which profoundly changed China and has significantly influenced the world. As a result of its opening-up policies, China has become the largest country in the world in goods trade and the second-largest country in services trade, registering with goods trade of USD 4.58 trillion and services trade of USD 784 billion in 2019. Partially because of this amazing achievement, the growth of China's foreign trade since 1979 is described as "China's Miracle of Foreign Trade."

How China realize this splendid achievement within such a short time? This is a very natural question that comes to our mind. Chapter 1 hence provides a possible answer to this question. Briefly, China's opening-up since 1979 has experienced three stages: the extensive margin, the intensive margin, and all-around opening-up. Before China's access to the World Trade Organization (WTO) in 2001, China's foreign trade exhibits a feature of a rapid expansion in the extensive margin which is due, in large part, to China's low labour cost based on its labour abundant factor endowment. It is important to stress processing trade, especially in this stage, that plays an important role to contribute China's miracle of international trade. After China's accession to the WTO, the development of China's foreign trade is featured with the deepening intensive margin. The main driving force of China's incremental international trade became the realization of scale economies with the large international market. After global financial crisis in 2008, because of increasing labour costs and an expanding China's domestic market, weak foreign demand and trade protectionism in some developed countries, and cheap labour costs in other developing countries, the Chinese government has proposed an all-around opening-up as the next major phase, especially since 2013. The new driving force of China's international trade will be the dividends of institutional reform achieved by expanding imports, expanding market access for foreign firms, strengthening IP rights protection, and nurturing innovation.

Turning to the development strategy of China's foreign trade, it is evident to see that China started with the adoption of import substitution after gaining its political independence in 1949. Chapter 2 aims to understand how import substitution, along with other policy instruments, helped China to establish its own complete industrial system. Particularly, Chap. 2 extends the Sah-Stiglitz "Economics of Price Scissor" model by extending their model to an open economy and allowing agricultural rationing and estimate its key structural parameters in China's government welfare objective function using a province-level panel data before China's economic reform. It turns out that the weight of peasants in the government's welfare objective function is smaller than the weight of workers. In addition, the weight of current consumption is also smaller than that of future investment. Such findings were consistent with the reality of Chinese economy before the era of economic reform.

Chapter 3 takes a step forward to consider how import protection affects an importing sector's relative size. This is an important question indeed for both academic researchers and policymakers. Trade theory has no clear prediction on how import protection affects an importing sector's relative size. It is also important for policymakers to understand the effectiveness of industrial protection. In Chap. 3 we estimate the impact of trade protection on industrial production relative size based on a translog GDP functional system. Using an industrial panel data set and controlling for factor endowments and technology improvement, we find empirical evidence that trade protection does not help much increase a sector's relative size. Such findings are also robust to both the inclusion of the role of political economy and the coverage of various non-tariff measures as proxies of industrial protection.

Export-led development strategy is one of the most important driving forces to boost China's foreign trade, particularly, in the last three decades in the 20th century. The key interesting questions are how China proceeds its export-led development strategy, and consequently, how such policy designs affect firm productivity given that manufacturing firms are the most fundamental microeconomic individual to support the whole-country's macroeconomic development. Section 3 picks up this task and covers four chapters from Chaps. 4 to 7 provide an answer to this important question.

Chapter 4 starts with a firm-level investigation on China's processing trade, with a particular focus on size, trends, characteristics, and key features. We begin to analyze why processing trade has developed rapidly in China since 1979. China's opening-up policy, particularly the establishment of special export zones, has played a significant role in the rapid growth of processing trade. We use transaction-level trade data (2000–2006) from China to investigate various factors affecting processing trade. These include origin and destination countries, leading import and export commodities, transport modes, firm ownership, leading ports and their trade volume, and top cities and provinces where producers and consumers are located.

Since China's opening-up, China has become the world factory. Needless to say, it is essential to understand Chinese manufacturing firms' productivity if one wants to understand the Chinese economy. Yet how productivity is and should be estimated remains an area of active research. Chapter 5 reviews some state-of-the-art methods for estimating productivity. We apply these methods to Chinese manufacturing data in the new century. We estimate dozens of different specifications for hundreds production function estimates and compare the strengths and pitfalls of each Total Factor Productivity (TFP) estimation approach.

Since China's opening-up in late 1970s, China set up a variety of industrial parks including Special Economic Zones (SEZs), economic development zones, export processing zones, and high-tech industrial zones. How does the establishment of industrial zones affect firm productivity? Chap. 6 provides an analysis for us to enrich the understanding of this question. In Chap. 6, we investigate the effect of the place-based industrial policy on firm productivity in China using the responses of Chinese medium and large firms to the establishment of state-level SEZs in the first decade of the new century. Evidence shows that SEZs improve productivity and generate positive spillovers. The productivity premium of firms located in industrial parks is mainly attributed to the better business environment (lower taxes) in SEZs. On average, the establishment of a SEZ leads to a productivity gain of 19%.

Chapter 7 takes a step further to examine how firms adjust their extensive margin measured by firm's export scope in response to trade liberalization. Chapter 7 provides a theoretical and empirical analysis of the effects of market competition and market expansion on firms' product line decisions. The theoretical model explicitly incorporates cost of management. Firms are heterogeneous in terms of managerial efficiency. We use import tariff cut as a proxy for increased market competition and export tariff reduction as a proxy for market expansion. The theoretical analysis predicts that the home country's tariff cut reduces all home firms' export product line, whereas in response to the foreign country's tariff reductions, firms with high managerial efficiency expand export product lines whereas firm with low managerial efficiency reduces export product lines. These predictions are supported by Chinese firm-level data.

Since 1990s, China experiences a rapid trade liberalization by cutting import tariffs. Such policy reforms have significant impact on Chinese economy. Thus Sect. 4 includes two chapters (i.e., Chaps. 8 and 9) to examine how trade liberalization affects Chinese firm productivity.

Chapter 8 developed a Mincer (1974)-type approach to investigate the impact of input trade liberalization on firms' wage inequality between skilled and unskilled workers (or skill premium). When controlling for product market tariffs in a firm's industry, we find robust evidence that reduced input tariffs in a firm's industry are associated with a higher skill premium at firms with more skilled workforces. This effect is more pronounced at ordinary (non-processing) firms. We also provide evidence that reduced input tariffs in a firm's industry are associated with higher value added and profits at firms with more skilled workforces.

Chapter 9 instead examines how input liberalization affects firm import behaviour. By using comprehensive production and trade data of Chinese firms, we show that import sources of Chinese firms switch from developing countries to developed countries as input tariffs fall in China. This is evident for both import value and import scope. The observation still exists after we exclude the possible influence of reducing processing trade. We further demonstrate that the mechanism can be attributed to quality upgrading and innovation led by input cost reductions. We also carefully handle the possible endogeneity problem and the findings are robust and significant to different empirical methodologies and measurements.

Contents

List of Figures

List of Tables

Part I
Overview

Chapter 1
China's Opening-Up Policies: Achievements and Prospects

China began its era of reform and opening up in 1978, which profoundly changed China and has deeply influenced the world. As a result of its opening-up policies, China has become the largest country in the world in goods trade and the second-largest country in services trade. Both inward and outward foreign direct investment (FDI) flow grew fast, reaching US$134.97 billion and US$143.04 billion, respectively, in 2018. Those figures represent 13.3% and 14.1% of the world FDI flow. Over the past four decades, China's volume of trade in foreign goods has increased 204-fold, whereas its GDP has increased only 34-fold. In this respect, China has successfully pulled off a miracle in foreign trade. This chapter reviews the major practices and achievements of and lessons learned from China's opening-up policy and forwards policy suggestions for China's continued opening in the future.

1.1 Introduction

China's opening-up process can be regarded as having occurred in three stages: a stage characterized by expanding the extensive margin of opening, that is, a stage focused on increasing the quantity of resources, labor, or production, where "margin" denotes the range (before 2001); a stage of expanding the intensive margin of opening, which focused on improving the quality or output per unit of resource or labor (2001–2017); and a general opening (since 2017) after the Chinese Communist Party (CCP) announced a new era of all-around opening up in China at its Nineteenth National Congress.

Before opening, China had followed an import substitution strategy, which was characterized by a lesser reliance on imports and exports. China had also implemented a heavy industry–oriented development strategy, which entailed lowering interest rates, depreciating the renminbi, and distorting the prices of labor, raw materials,

This chapter is coauthored with Zhongtenglong and originally published in D. Dollar, Y. Huang, Y. Yao (eds.), China 2049, Chapter 12, Brookings Institution Press, Washington, D.C., 2020.

M. Yu, *China's Miracle in Foreign Trade*, Studies in Modern Chinese Economy,
https://doi.org/10.1007/978-981-16-6030-6_1

and even agricultural products—all to support the development of heavy industry. This strategy led to surplus labor, low incomes, and hence slow economic growth.

After 1978, the Chinese government abandoned the heavy industry–oriented development strategy and began to employ an export-oriented strategy, which lasted until the global financial crisis of 2008–2009. Before China's entry into the World Trade Organization (WTO) in 2001, the major force driving export growth was a comparative advantage based on the country's factor endowment. China is a labor-abundant country and its labor costs are relatively cheap. Accordingly, China exported labor-intensive products and served as the largest "world factory."

Since China's accession to the WTO, however, the cost of labor has increased significantly, and China no longer realizes a cost-saving advantage compared with such countries as Vietnam and other East Asian countries. Indeed, the fundamental force driving China's export boom today is the country's increased market size.

The global financial crisis that began in 2008 had significant negative impacts on the global economy, especially in developed economies. In the context of weakening demand from the developed countries, China's reliance on exports to drive economic growth was no longer tenable. China has begun switching from labor cost advantages to quality, brand, and service to drive exports.

At the Nineteenth National Congress of the CCP, held in October 2017, the State Council made it clear that China's economy was in the process of shifting from a focus on accelerating growth to a focus on high-quality development. As a result, improving the quality of export goods and services has become a top priority. At the same time, trade protectionism and antiglobalization sentiments are on the rise around the world. Against this background, the Chinese government has proposed implementing a new strategy that features opening up across the board, with the twin goal of promoting the development of both the Chinese economy and the global economy.

What's more, the China-U.S. trade conflict provoked by the United States has been escalating since the beginning of 2018. This conflict has had negative effects on both the Chinese and the U.S. economy and contributes to uncertainty about global economic development. Therefore, the external environment China faces has become increasingly complex. China intends to deal with the challenges calmly and confidently. Even as China must fight back against the attacks launched by the United States, the country plans to further open up to the world by broadening market access, improving the investment environment for foreign investors, strengthening the protection of intellectual property (IP) rights, and expanding imports, among other steps.

This chapter explores the historical development of the extensive margin of the opening-up process, reviews the dynamic evolution of the intensive margin of opening up, considers the recent development of the generalized opening up announced by the State Council, and offers a set of policy recommendations.

1.2 Expanding the Extensive Margin of Opening, 1978–2000

China's opening-up strategy before its accession to the WTO included the following important actions: setting up special economic zones and industrial parks, relaxing market access for foreign investors, reducing tariffs on imports, and encouraging processing trade. The following discussion elaborates on each of these four aspects, with comments particularly on China's expanding the extensive margin during the opening-up process.

1.2.1 Setting Up Open Economic Zones and Industrial Parks

China's establishment of open economic zones was one of the most important changes resulting from the opening-up policy. Before 2000, the establishment of open economic zones can be thought of as occurring in three waves. The first wave, also known as the "point" phase, entailed the adoption of four cities in 1981 as the special economic zones (SEZs): Shenzhen, Zhuhai, and Shantou in Guangdong province and Xiamen in Fujian province. Shenzhen was chosen because of its excellent geographic location; it is a small village near Hong Kong. A similar rationale applied to the selection of Zhuhai, a small town on the western Pearl River near Macau. Shantou was chosen because of its strong network of connections with Chinese immigrants in East Asian countries. Similarly, Xiamen was chosen because it is close to Taiwan province.

The second wave of the establishment of open economic zones brought in many coastal cities, from Dalian, a northern coastal city in Liaoning province, to Beihai, a southern coastal city in Guangxi province. The cities are connected along a "line" and are called coastal open cities. The third wave of open economic zones extended to include zones and parks from the cities along the east coast to the central and western provinces. In particular, the government set up twenty-five high-tech industrial development zones in Shenyang, Tianjin, Wuhan, and Nanjing. Thus, by 1992 China had established six SEZs (the original four point zones, plus Hainan, and Pudong in Shanghai), fourteen coastal open cities, fifty-four national-level economic and development zones, fifty-three high-tech industrial parks, and fifteen tariff-free zones (Naughton 2018).

All of these zones—SEZs, coastal open cities, economic and development zones, and even high-tech development zones—had very similar policy designs. In particular, foreign firms located in the zones were exempt from corporate tax in their first three years. In their fourth and fifth years, they had to pay a corporate tax rate of only 17%, which was half the tax rate levied on Chinese domestic firms. This policy lasted for around three decades. After 2007, foreign firms had to pay the same 25% corporate tax rate as domestic firms. In addition, wholly owned foreign firms and subsidiaries were permitted in all types of zones.

1.2.2 Relaxing Market Access for Foreign Direct Investment

After 1978, the Chinese government began gradually relaxing access to the Chinese market for foreign investment. In 1979 the Sino-Foreign Equity Joint Venture Law was promulgated, making foreign-invested enterprises legal economic organizations. Later on, more laws and regulations were issued, all of which provided a legal basis for the supervision of foreign investment and protected the rights and interests of foreign investors. Foreign investment grew from almost nothing in 1978 to a cumulative amount of US$23.4 billion in 1991.

In 1992, at the Fourteenth Congress of the CCP, China's leadership announced a market economy would be set up, which markedly improved the willingness of foreign companies and individuals to invest in China. The open areas were extended from the cities along the east coast to the central and even western provinces. To facilitate foreign investors and improve the quality of foreign investment, the Chinese government released its *Catalogue for the Guidance of Industries for Foreign Investment* in 1995. The catalogue assigns all industries to one of four categories: encouraging, allowing, limiting, and forbidding foreign investment. China began to open some service sectors to foreign investment, including its retail, financial, freight, and software industries. After 1992, foreign investment flowed quickly into China, reaching a new high of US$38.9 billion in 1993. From 1994 to 1999, foreign investment topped US$40 billion each year.

1.2.3 Reducing Import Tariffs

Before the economic reforms of 1978, China adopted the import substitution strategy by setting high import tariffs and other nontariff barriers against foreign products. In 1992, at the Fourteenth Congress of the CCP, the State Council announced it would set up a market economy. Thereafter China began actively cutting its import tariffs. The simple import tariff, still 42% in early 1992, was reduced to 35% in 1994 during the Uruguay round of WTO negotiations. During the next three years, China cut its import tariffs another 50% or so. At the end of 1997, the simple import tariff was reduced to around 17%. The most important reason for taking such a major step in opening up was that China hoped to accede to the WTO as soon as possible; in 1994, China was still only an observer, rather than a formal member, of the WTO. After its accession to the WTO, China's simple import tariff was reduced from around 17% to around 10% in 2006. Since 2006, China's import tariff rate has remained stable.

Trade liberalization has been significant for the Chinese economy. To understand the country's economic development, it is essential to understand the realization of firm productivity, since "productivity is not everything, but almost everything," as Paul Krugman has said. It is widely accepted that trade liberalization fosters firm productivity. Yu (2015) finds that trade liberalization has contributed to around 14.5% of Chinese firm productivity growth in the twenty-first century.

1.2.4 Encouraging the Processing Trade

The processing trade is a key for understanding China's trade development over the past four decades. "Processing trade" denotes the process by which a domestic firm initially obtains raw materials or intermediate inputs from abroad and, after local processing, exports the value-added final goods (Feenstra and Hanson 2005). As Dai et al. (2016) note, the iPhone is a perfect example of China's processing trade. Foxconn, a famous iPhone assembler in Shenzhen, imports 155 intermediate components of smart phones from Japan, Korea, and the United States. After producing the final products domestically, Foxconn exports back to the United States and other foreign markets. Governments typically encourage processing trade by offering tariff reductions or even exemptions on the processing of intermediate goods.

Processing imports and exports developed quickly after 1978, especially after 1992, when at the Fourteenth Congress of the CCP it was announced that the state would set up a market economy. Just before China's accession to the WTO, the government decided to establish export processing zones (EPZs) to promote processing trade. Since then, China has set up more than sixty EPZs. Different from the earlier open economic zones and industrial parks, such EPZs are spread across the country. They are located not only in eastern coastal cities but also in western inland cities, such as Urumchi in Xinjiang province. Only processing firms are allowed to enter the EPZs. They also enjoy special tariff treatment. In particular, firms in the EPZs are treated as "inside the territory but outside the customs," as they are exempted from import duty.

Figure 1.1 shows China's export revenues by trade regimes (including ordinary export, processing export, and other exports) after 1978. As can be seen, export revenues in processing regimes increased to US$137.65 billion in 2000 from $1.13 billion in 1981. Processing export revenues increased to $675.1 billion in 2008 from $147.4 billion in 2001, with an annual average growth rate of 29%, far outpacing the annual average growth (12.3%) during 1992 and 2001. Processing export revenues exceeded ordinary export revenues in 1993, and this situation held until 2010.

Figure 1.1 also shows China's import revenues by trade regimes (including ordinary import, processing import, and other imports) after 1978. Import revenues in processing regimes increased to US$92.56 billion in 2000 from $1.5 billion in 1981. Processing import revenues increased to $378.4 billion in 2008 from $93.9 billion in 2001, with an annual average growth rate of 24.6%, also far outpacing the annual average growth (16.1%) during 1992 and 2001. Both lines were close before ordinary import revenues began to increase quickly after 2007.

Industries that are intensively engaged in the processing trade are also labor-intensive. The processing trade thus absorbs many workers. In particular, the four major processing industries are household appliances; toys; clothing, footwear, and hats; and leather goods. The four industries employed 13.2 million workers in 2009 and 16.2 million workers in 2014, accounting for more 10% of all employment in manufacturing. The processing trade has also contributed to China's deep integration into global value chains. Accordingly, China has functioned as a nonsubstitutable

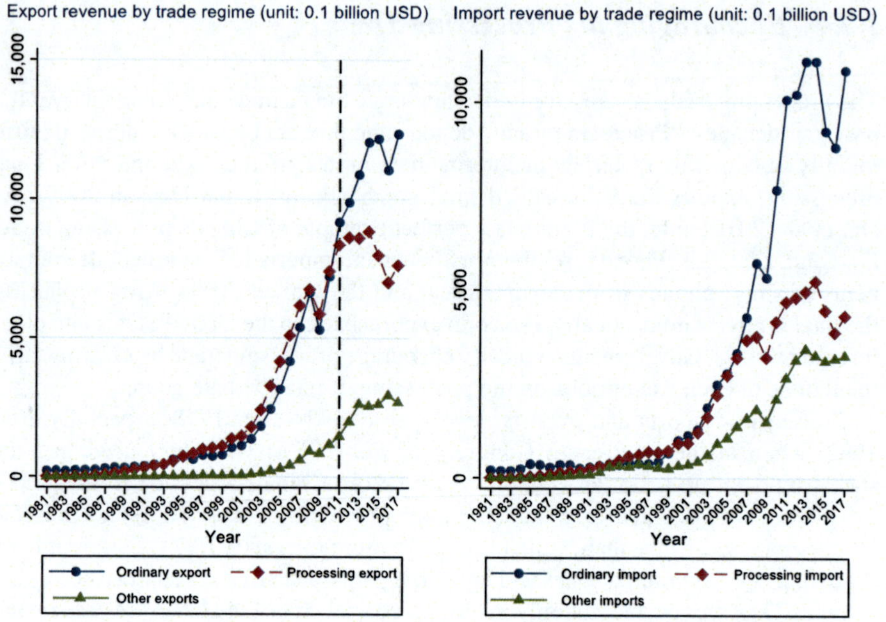

Fig. 1.1 China's export and import revenue by trade regimes, 1981–2017. *Source* Data from *China's Customs Statistics Yearbook* (various years)

"world factory." Of course, this also implies that China has naturally maintained a high global trade surplus. Indeed, around two-thirds of China's trade surplus is generated from its processing trade.

1.2.5 Comments on the Stage of Extensive-Margin Opening

Before the era of economic reforms, China had adopted a heavy industry–oriented strategy and import substitution strategy. These strategies led to a surplus agricultural labor force, a low urbanization rate, and low resident income. All these factors laid a strong foundation for the export-oriented strategy implemented after the start of the reforms and opening-up policy.

As one of the most important steps in opening up, China gradually established a series of open economic zones and industrial parks between 1978 and 2000, providing preferential terms for firms locating within the zones or parks and promoting export growth. Meanwhile, the Chinese government also relaxed market access for FDI. With an abundant and cheap labor force but lacking in technological know-how and equipment, China's choice of the processing trade as a way to participate in global trade was almost inevitable. The processing trade increased rapidly, and China became a new "world factory." During this period, China applied to join the General

Agreement on Tariffs and Trade (GATT) in 1986, and, beginning in 1992, started actively cutting import tariffs., which decreased by nearly 60% between 1992 and 1997. This move shows China's determination to expand its opening up.

However, China was not a member of the WTO during the stage of extensive-margin opening, which posed a serious threat to China's international trade. As an example, the United States granted China only temporary normal trade relations (temporary NTR) status. The U.S. Congress reviews that status annually. Chinese exporters would have faced the punishing non-NTR tariffs had the NTR status not been renewed. Therefore, China's exports still faced great uncertainty. China hoped that accession to the WTO would solve the problem.

1.3 Focusing on the Intensive Margin of Opening, 2001–2017

Since the turn of the twenty-first century, China has focused more on opening intensively than extensively, as exemplified by the expansion of various open economic zones or industrial parks. In the twenty-first century, before the Nineteenth Party Congress of the CCP, five important events characterized the features of the intensive margin: accession to the WTO, expanding market access for FDI, the relaxation of outward FDI, establishment of free trade pilot zones, and new-economy pilot cities. This section introduces each of the above five actions and comments on the intensive margin of opening up.

1.3.1 Accession to the WTO

Meeting the Tariff Reduction Commitment. As one of the conditions of joining the WTO, China committed to reducing its import tariffs to a certain level before 2006; the highest tariff rate China could set was known as the bound tariff rate. From 2001 to 2006, the applied average tariff rate was always less than the bound average tariff rate set in 2001. In other words, China met its tariff reduction commitment.

Removal of Export Trade Policy Uncertainty. The nominal value of Chinese exports increased more than 16-fold between 1992 and 2008. An obvious acceleration of export growth took place around 2001, when China officially entered the WTO. Before WTO accession, from 1992 to 2001, the annual nominal export growth rate was about 14.1%, whereas after accession to the WTO, from 2002 to 2008, the annual nominal export growth rate reached as high as 27.3%.

A substantial proportion of the soaring Chinese exports could be attributed to the elimination of the high tariff threat after its WTO accession. According to U.S. law, imports from nonmarket economies such as China are subject to relatively high tariff rates originally set under the Smoot-Hawley Tariff Act of 1930. These rates, known as "non-NTR" or "column 2" tariffs, are typically substantially larger than the "MFN" (most favored nation) or "column 1" rates the United States offers fellow members of the WTO.

When China joined the WTO on December 11, 2001, the United States effectively assigned China permanent NTR status on January 1, 2002, which completely removed Chinese exporters' concern over possible sudden tariff spikes (Pierce and Schott 2016).

Elimination of Nontariff Measures. China issues nontariff measures (NTMs) mainly focusing on ensuring food safety, human and animal health, product quality and safety, and environmental protection, which together account for about 90% of the total NTMs taken.

China is actively following good international practices such as International Organization for Standardization (ISO) and International Electrotechnical Commission (IEC) standards in preparing its own national standards. Of the 1,448 mandatory standards related to NTMs, 555 standards (about 38%) are directly adopted from ISO, IEC, and standards promulgated by other international organizations. China is putting increasing effort into streamlining its national standards with international best practices and seeking international cooperation in the standardization process. Especially with China's new Standardization Law, China intends to foster trade, economic, and social development by reducing restrictions.

There are in total 2,071 NTMs identified by the General Administration of Quality Supervision, Inspection and Quarantine (AQSIQ). Of these 2,071 NTMs, only 646 measures apply unilaterally to all countries around the world. The remaining 1,425 measures (about 69%) apply bilaterally or plurilaterally to only a certain group of countries. Specifically, 896 (around 63%) measures out of the total measures that are bilaterally or plurilaterally applied by AQSIQ were implemented after 2010. This shows that over the years, China is increasingly moving from a unilateral relationship with countries—that is, one in which it applies the same measure to all countries—to a bilateral relationship.

1.3.2 Expanding Market Access for FDI

After the *Catalogue for the Guidance of Industries for Foreign Investment* was first issued in 1995, it has been updated seven times, in 1997, 2002, 2004, 2007, 2011, 2015, and 2017. The number of encouraged categories increased from 115 in 1995 to 153 in 2017; the number of restricted categories decreased from fifty-six in 1995 to seven in 2017; and the number of prohibited categories decreased from ten in 1995 to seven today. This shows that the market access for foreign investment has been constantly expanding. And foreign investment could be guided to the industries China prioritizes for development. For example, foreign investment was expanded from labor-intensive industries to capital- and technology-intensive industries.

Meanwhile, the Chinese government has also introduced preferential policies to encourage more FDI in Central and Western China. In addition, at this point almost

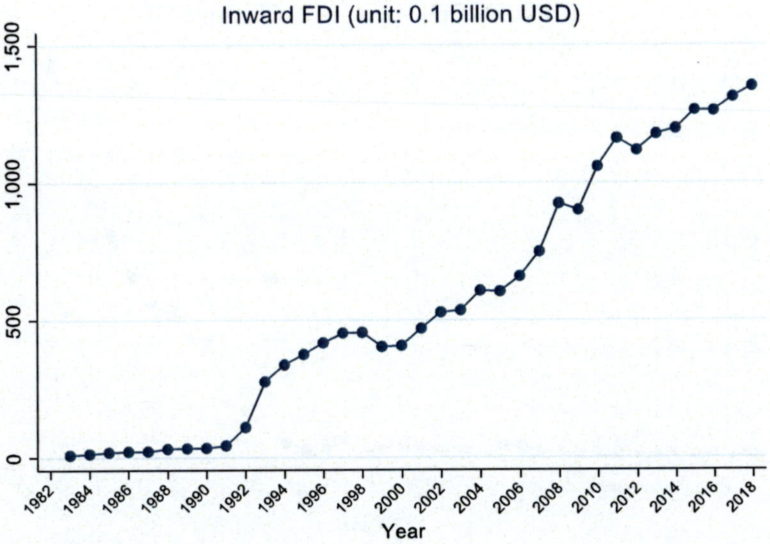

Fig. 1.2 China's annual utilized inward FDI, 1982–2018. *Source* Data from *China's Customs Statistical Yearbook* (various years)

all service sectors are accessible by foreign investors. Some of them have a limitation of holding ratio. Thanks to this policy, China's import in services also grew quickly, from US$248 billion in 2011 to US$514 billion in 2018, for an annual growth rate of 11.4%.

Figure 1.2 plots China's annual utilized inward FDI from 1983 to 2018. FDI grew to US$134.9 billion in 2018 from US$40.7 billion in 2000, with an average annual growth rate of 7%. It is worth noting that the growth rate has slowed in recent years. Specifically, the average annual growth rate was only 3% between 2011 and 2018.

1.3.3 *Relaxation of Outward FDI*

Before 1991, only state-owned enterprises were allowed to invest abroad, and case-by-case approval was required, regardless of the investment amount (Voss et al. 2008). In the 1990s, China's foreign reserve holdings increased fast as a result of trade surpluses and high FDI inflow, which promoted outward FDI (OFDI). But OFDI was still stringently restricted in this period by the government issuing the "Opinions on Strengthening the Management of Overseas Investment Projects" in 1991. As can be seen from Fig. 1.3, China's OFDI had remained at a very low level from 1982 to 1999. The average OFDI from 1982 to 1999 was US$1.5 billion.

In the twenty-first century, the government's policy with respect to OFDI has switched from restriction to relaxation. In 2000 the Chinese government proposed the "Going Out" strategy for the first time. OFDI increased dramatically, to US$6.9

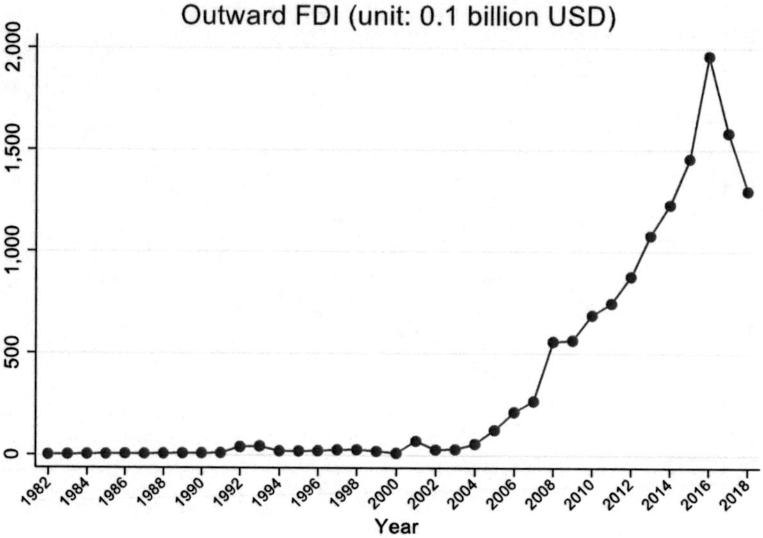

Fig. 1.3 China's annual flow of outward FDI, 1982–2018. *Source* Data from Ministry of Commerce of China; UNCTAD statistics

billion in 2001 from US$1 billion in 2000, but fell back in the following three years. In 2004, many implementing rules were introduced by the government, such as the "Decision on Reforming the Investment Systems," issued by the State Council, corresponding detailed policies to simplify the approval procedures, delegate approval authority, and increase approval efficiency promulgated by the National Development and Reform Commission (NDRC) and the Ministry of Commerce (MOFCOM). As a response, China's OFDI more than doubled, to US$12.3 billion in 2005 from US$5 billion in 2004, and grew continuously in the next years.

As a result of the 2008 global financial crisis, global FDI inflows fell by 14% in 2008 (UNCTAD 2009), while China's 2008 OFDI flow was double that in 2007. The Chinese government further encouraged OFDI by raising the approval threshold to more than US$300 million for resource development projects and more than US$100 million for other projects.

In 2014, China's OFDI entered a new stage of "registration-based and approval-supplemented" FDI. In this stage, only projects involving sensitive industries or with a value of more than US$1 billion are required to obtain official approval in advance. All other projects need only register with the provincial Development and Reform Commission (DRC). Established Chinese overseas enterprises are exempt from the approval and registration procedures. As a result, China's OFDI increased further, to US$196 billion in 2016 from US$73 billion in 2014. Afterward, China's OFDI fell in the ensuing two years because of escalating trade protectionism and antiglobalization behavior.

1.3.4 Establishment of Pilot Free Trade Zones

In 2013, the government set up a pilot free trade zone (FTZ) in Shanghai. The area of the pilot is not large (its initial area is only around 29 square kilometers), but its economic impact is potentially huge. The whole landscape of the establishment of the pilot FTZ can be summarized as $1 + 3 + 7$, achieved in three steps. First, the government set up the first pilot FTZ in Shanghai in September 2013. Second, the pilot was extended to three other FTZs in large coastal provinces in April 2015: Guangdong, Tianjin, and Fujian. Third, in September 2016, the government set up seven more coastal and inland pilot FTZs, in Liaoning, Shaanxi, Henan, Hubei, Chongqing, Sichuan, and Zhejiang provinces. The objective of setting up the pilot FTZs is to replicate them in other non-FTZ places if those places are ready for the reform.

Drawing on the country's earlier experiment with SEZs, the government decided on four roles for the pilot FTZs. First, the pilot FTZs aim to promote further trade and investment facilitation. This goal is consistent with the development of EPZs. For goods within the pilot FTZs, the government requires "release the first line, but hold up the second line." The idea is that the imported intermediate goods used in the FTZs will be exempt from tariffs (that is, released from the first line), but the final products that use such intermediate inputs cannot be sold outside the zones to China's domestic market (hold up the second line).

Second, the pilot FTZs are intended to promote China's "negative list" investment mode. Differing from the previous "positive list," the new negative list investment mode has fewer regulations or restrictions on foreign investment in China. If the products or sectors are listed, foreigners are not allowed to invest in those areas. In other words, foreigners may invest in anything that does not appear on the list. This gives foreign investors huge room to invest in new industries or sectors. It turns out that this policy design has been the most successful policy reform. And because it was so successful in all eleven FTZs, in 2018 the Chinese government decided to expand the policy to the whole country.

Third, the pilot FTZs are intended to give a further push to China's financial reform. In particular, the FTZs aim to promote financial innovation with convertible capital projects and by offering more financial services. This reform so far has had only limited effects. Its limited impact is not difficult to understand, as FTZs make up only a tiny proportion of China's area. Unlike the trade reform, the financial reform cannot be clearly applied separately to entities located inside FTZs but not outside them. It is difficult to undertake a financial experiment in a small area and then apply it to the rest of the country.

Fourth, the pilot FTZs require local governments to reduce bureaucratic procedures and simplify the process of doing business within the zones. Specifically, the FTZs emphasize after-event supervision rather than before-event approval.

1.3.5 New-Economy Pilot Cities Experiment

Different from the establishment of the pilot FTZs, the opening up via the new-economy pilots in twelve cities is less well known. In 2015 the government decided to choose twelve cities located in five city groups, as well as some coastal cities, to experiment with the so-called "new-economy pilot." Jinan, the capital of Shandong province, is the largest of the twelve cities. Zhangzhou, a coastal city in Fujian province, was chosen mainly because of its strong connections with Taiwan province. Fangchenggang, a coastal city in Guangxi province, was chosen because it neighbors one of the SEZs in Vietnam. The government hopes to develop a bilateral border trade by setting up this new-economy zone.

The other eight cities are located around China's five major metropolitan areas. Dalian, in Liaoning, and Tangshan, in Hebei, are the two northern cities closest to the Beijing-Tianjin-Hebei metropolitan area. Xian was chosen because it is the largest city in Northwestern China. Chongqing was chosen because it is one of the core cities among the Chengdu-Chongqing megacities. Wuhan and Nanhang were chosen because they are two large cities in Central China. Finally, Pudong, in Shanghai, and Suzhou, in Jiangsu, are connected to the Yangtze River Delta economic belt.

The experiment of these new-economy zones focuses on six areas. First, it aims at exploring the new management mode of the government. Second, it aims at exploring the coordination of various industrial parks. Third, it hopes to explore new ways to encourage FDI. Fourth, it aims at promoting high-quality exports of domestic products. Fifth, it seeks significant improvement of financial services. Sixth, the zones should focus on promoting all-around opening-up in the regions.

After three years of the experiment, the independent evaluation panel, led by the National School of Development at Peking University, expressed satisfaction with the twelve cities' new-economy reforms. Particularly, the panel recognized that the reforms have successfully improved local economic development and been helpful in the supply-side structural reform.

1.3.6 Comments on the Stage of Intensive Margin of Opening Up

After accession to the WTO, China realized its commitment to reduce import tariffs, and the trade policy uncertainty faced by Chinese exporters was drastically reduced. These moves facilitated the rapid growth of imports and exports. As shown in Fig. 12.4, China's foreign trade dependence ratio, which is the ratio of total international trade volume to GDP, rose quickly between 2001 (38.1%) and 2006 (63.95%). This means that the contribution of foreign trade to GDP growth increased significantly. Meanwhile, China further expanded market access for FDI and relaxed restrictions on OFDI, both of which also increased quickly during this period.

After the financial crisis broke out in 2008, foreign markets were badly shocked, facing weak demand and trade protectionism. Since the turn of the twenty-first century, and especially after 2004, the cost of labor in China has increased dramatically and the country's population dividend has shrunk fast. Compared with many East Asian countries, China no longer has a significant comparative advantage on the labor-intensive margin. A not small part of China's foreign markets has been taken over by countries such as Vietnam and Bangladesh. Thus strategies that continue to rely on a simple processing trade to promote China's exports are no longer feasible. Indeed, both processing import and export volumes decreased dramatically after the global financial crisis broke out (see Fig. 12.1).

At the Eighteenth National Congress of the CCP, China's leadership proposed deepening the reform of China's foreign trade system, promoting openness through institutional reform, and fostering new competitive advantages in foreign trade. To this end, the Chinese government began to establish pilot FTZs in 2013 and to implement the new-economy pilot cities experiment in 2016. These two policy initiatives have succeeded in improving local economic development and have been helpful in the supply-side structural reform (Fig. 1.4).

At the Nineteenth Party Congress, held in 2017, it was emphasized that China's economy has shifted from a high-speed, increasing-volume stage to a high-quality development stage. The Chinese government has proposed the next step, an all-around opening up, that would promote the development of both the Chinese economy and the global economy. The specific measures to implement an all-around opening up are discussed in the next section.

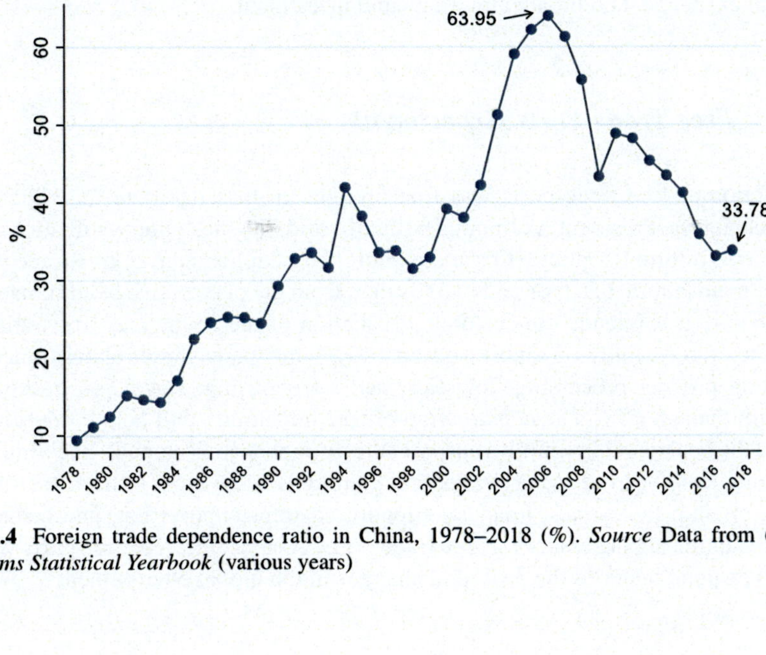

Fig. 1.4 Foreign trade dependence ratio in China, 1978–2018 (%). *Source* Data from *China's Customs Statistical Yearbook* (various years)

1.4 Features of the All-Around Opening Up

China's strategy of an all-around opening up heavily relies on rolling out the Belt and Road Initiative (BRI), and developing China's free trade ports and the Guangdong–Hong Kong–Macau Greater Bay Area.

1.4.1 Belt and Road Initiative

The BRI, which was initiated by the Chinese government in 2013, is devoted to improving regional connectivity on a transcontinental scale. The initiative aims to strengthen infrastructure, trade, and investment links between China and other countries through which the BRI will pass. Currently, sixty-four countries are actively involved in the BRI. These include ten ASEAN countries, eighteen countries in Western Asia, eight in South Asia, five in Central Asia, seven in the Commonwealth of Independent States, and sixteen in Central and Eastern Europe. The scope of the initiative is still taking shape—recently, the BRI has been interpreted as open to all countries as well as to international and regional organizations.

In addition to trade and FDI, the BRI also concentrates on infrastructure projects. As one of the largest infrastructures and investment projects in history, the BRI addresses the "infrastructure gap" and thus has the potential to accelerate economic growth across the involved countries. The initiative calls for integration of the countries into a cohesive economic area through building infrastructure, increasing cultural exchange, and broadening trade and investment.

1.4.2 Free Trade Ports Experiment

The notion of free trade ports was first brought up in a report to the Nineteenth Party Congress. President Xi Jinping explicitly said that the country will allow more freedom to reform the pilot FTZs and explore the establishment of free trade ports.

The main feature of a free trade port is that, from the perspective of administrative supervision, it is outside the customs jurisdiction of the country. A free trade port combines the features of a port and an FTZ, with many trade-related functions, including product processing, logistics, and warehousing. But it is a more open platform than an FTZ. The construction of free trade ports will help FTZs advance toward the goal of being a more transparent institutional environment, like Singapore and Hong Kong (China). Meanwhile, breakthroughs in the areas of trade facilitation measures, ship fuel prices, financial support, customs supervision, and inspection and quarantine are necessary for free trade ports. As a result, free trade ports will be able to respond better to the profound changes in the global environment.

1.4.3 Greater Bay Area

The construction of the Guangdong–Hong Kong–Macau Greater Bay Area (GBA) is one of the most urgent tasks facing China in its opening-up process. The GBA includes nine municipal areas and the Special Administrative Regions of Hong Kong and Macau. The nine municipal cities are on the east and west banks of the Pearl River: Shenzhen, Dongguan, Huizhou, Guangzhou, Foshan, Jiangmen, Zhaoqing, Zhongshan, and Zhuhai. In this way the GBA coincides with the Pearl River Delta, which is a top economic development zone (EDZ) in China, along with the Yangtze River Delta.

The development of the GBA should focus on the following perspectives. First, to build the GBA, the real economy and the financial economy should be combined, focusing on the real economy. The services industry can play an auxiliary role to boost the GBA economy. The second goal in constructing the GBA is to facilitate innovation. China is transforming from a manufacturing power to an innovation power. The GBA should play a key role in the formation of an innovative country. The third objective is to achieve institutional innovation. Fourth, the GBA should pay more attention to its ecological environment.

Other all-around opening measures include (1) further widening market access, (2) improving the investment environment for foreign investors, (3) strengthening protection of IP rights, and (4) taking the initiative to expand imports.

1.4.4 Policy Recommendations

This chapter has reviewed the practices and achievements of China's liberalization of international trade and investment and the country's integration into the international economy since 1978. China has done well so far. However, the internal and external environments in which China must operate have become increasingly complex, with rising labor costs, an aging population, and, in the international arena, accelerating unilateralism and the China-U.S. trade conflict. As emphasized by President Xi, China's opening door will not be closed and will only open even wider. Below are listed several concrete policy recommendations to promote China's continued opening in the future.

Support Multilateralism and Contribute to the Reform of the WTO. Unilateralism and protectionism are on the rise around the world, posing a challenge to the authority and effectiveness of the multilateral trading system. In this context, China should actively participate in WTO reforms. Specifically, China should reinforce the role of the WTO Dispute Settlement Committee and seek to gain a seat on the committee.

Consolidate Existing Regional Free Trade Agreements (FTAs) and Actively Promote New FTAs. To date, China has concluded seventeen FTAs with twenty-five partners in Europe, Asia, Oceania, South America, and Africa. China could deepen its cooperation with these partners in various fields such as trade, investment, and cultural exchange. Thirteen other regional FTAs are in the negotiations stage. The most important of these is the Regional Comprehensive Economics Partnership (RCEP). Since 2012, there have been twenty-two rounds of negotiations on establishing the RCEP. China has been actively communicating with the negotiating parties during the current critical round, hoping to address major disagreements and conclude negotiations sometime in late 2019. In addition, China could also consider participating in the Comprehensive Progressive Trans-Pacific Partnership (CPTPP), which is now led by Japan, after the United States dropped out. There are two important reasons for China to participate. First, the CPTPP has lower requirements for openness than the TPP, ones similar to China's existing policies for openness. Second, joining the CPTPP would expand China's circle of friends and offset the negative impacts on China's economy caused by China-U.S. trade frictions.

Deal with the China-U.S. Trade Conflicts by Further Opening Up and Pursuing High-Quality Development. China will be obliged to respond to the attacks launched by the United States by setting high tariff and nontariff barriers for U.S. exports. The Chinese government should provide necessary subsidies for industries and workers who bear the brunt of the costs of this trade conflict. China's GDP is approaching that of the United States and is expected to surpass it by 2027, when the effects of the China–U.S. trade frictions peak. Once China's GDP is 1.5 times that of the United States, the United States may accept China's rise, and China-U.S. relations are expected to shift from competition to cooperation. However, the competition between China and the United States will exist for a long time, potentially for the next thirty years. The Chinese government and Chinese people should be psychologically prepared and concentrate on doing their own jobs well.

Expand Market Access and Improve the Quality of Openness. The Chinese government should try to expand market access for foreign countries by encouraging more foreign investments and imports. Specifically, the negative investment list system should be implemented nationwide, and all companies registered in China should be treated equally. The convenience of doing business in China should also be improved. For example, a secure and effective electronic customs clearance system would speed up the integration of customs and simplify the agency's procedures. Furthermore, developing a better living environment and better services for businesspersons and international talent is a necessary step for China to improve the movement of personnel as well as the ability to attract talent.

China should also strengthen and enforce protections for IP rights. IP rights protection is required by foreign enterprises and should be required by Chinese enterprises. It would provide the biggest boost to the competitiveness of the Chinese economy. To reduce China's technological dependence on foreign countries, the Chinese government should set up special funds to encourage enterprises to develop core technologies.

At present, China has a deficit in its trade in services, which is consistent with China's current stage of economic development. However, in the future, China should vigorously develop the service industry and service trade, making service trade another engine of China's economic growth.

1.5 Conclusion

This chapter has described China's international trade and investment development and opening-up policies the four decades since the country began its economic reform. Overall, the opening-up policy has occurred in three waves: expanding the extensive margin, increasing the intensive margin, and an all-around opening up.

International trade is a major focus of China's opening-up policy. China's growing role in international trade before the country's accession to the WTO was driven mainly by the country's cheap labor pool, which gave it a comparative advantage. This was especially useful for labor-intensive industries, where the cost of labor is one of the most important input factors. Moreover, cheap labor to some extent affected the incremental exports of machinery and transport equipment. This is because China's foreign trade in machinery and transport equipment is mainly conducted through its processing trade, which takes advantage of the low cost of labor.

After China's accession to the WTO, the main driving force of China's incremental international trade became the realization of scale economies with the large international market, according to the increasing returns-to-scale theory. One piece of evidence of this is that the share of the processing trade keeps decreasing, whereas total trade volume is increasing (see Fig. 12.1). This phenomenon is not accounted for in traditional comparative advantage theory.

In recent years, because of increasing labor costs and an expanding domestic market in China, weak foreign demand and trade protectionism in developed countries, and cheap labor costs in other developing countries and their increasing presence in global trade, China's economy has pivoted toward high-quality development and away from high-volume production and the processing trade. In international trade, China is striving to shift from a trader of quantity to a trader of quality. The Chinese government has proposed an all-around opening up as the next major phase. The new driving force of China's international trade will be the dividends of institutional reform achieved by expanding imports, expanding market access for foreign firms, strengthening IP rights protection, and nurturing innovation.

Policy recommendations to ensure China's continuing sustainable and high-quality opening up include (1) supporting multilateralism and contributing to the WTO reform; (2) consolidating existing FTAs and actively promoting new ones; (3) dealing with the China-U.S. trade conflicts reasonably, calmly, and confidentially; and (4) further expanding market access and improving the quality of openness.

Part II
Import Substitution and Trade Protection

Chapter 2
The Economics of Price Scissors: An Empirical Investigation for China

The Sah-Stiglitz "Economics of Price Scissor" model, concerning the political economy of price scissors, formulates the optimal terms of trade against peasants. In the present paper, by extending their model to an open economy and allowing agricultural rationing, we first check whether their model stands up to China's data and, if so, estimate its key structural parameters. Using a province-level panel data over the years 1949–1992, we find that the weight of peasants in the government's welfare objective function is smaller than the weight of workers. In addition, the weight of current consumption is also smaller than that of future investment. Such findings are consistent with China's reality.

2.1 Introduction

As initiated by Preobrahensky (1926), the term of "price scissors" mentions that the government in developing countries, especially socialist countries, sets an appropriate terms of trade against peasants to extract profits from peasants in the rural sector to subsidize workers in the urban sector. As a result, the government in such countries could increase capital accumulation using the price scissors. Later, Sah and Stiglitz (1984) (henceforth S–S) deliver an elegant theoretical model to formalize the optimal terms of trade against peasants by analyzing the government's social welfare function. Perhaps because of the paper's simple but powerful theoretical structure, it has soon been applied in a variety of subsequent theoretical analysis. For instance, Carter (1986) extends the model in the S–S from a closed-economy to an open-economy setup. Blomqvist (1986) also examines a case with an indirect taxation from agricultural goods in socialist countries. All of these works have recognized that the price-scissors is an important policy in socialist countries such as former Soviet Union and China.

This chapter is coauthored with Justin Yifu Lin at Peking University.

M. Yu, *China's Miracle in Foreign Trade*, Studies in Modern Chinese Economy,
https://doi.org/10.1007/978-981-16-6030-6_2

More importantly, traditional wisdom believes that governments in socialist countries have given more attentions on investment than on consumption, and more weights on workers than on peasants. However, this view is taken as a priori. In this study we therefore investigate whether the view is supported by China's data. And if so, to what extent, the government put a heavy weight on industrial development compared to the agricultural development? And a heavy weight on future investment relative to current consumption?

To the purpose of our estimations, we develop a theoretical setup from the S–S (1984) due, in large part, to its clear-cut empirical predictions for the structural parameters. In order to explore the optimal terms of trade against peasants, the S–S (1984) used the Bergson-Samuelson social welfare function to assign a relative weight between current consumption and future investment. In the model, welfares from both urban workers and peasants are taken equivalently in the mind of the social planner. Such a simplification is helpful for us to estimate the two relative weights: the weight of current consumption relative to future investment and the one of peasants' welfare relative to workers' welfare.

Based on a theoretical model, we therefore estimate related structural parameters to investigate the relative importance for both agricultural and industrial sectors, and the relative importance for both future investment and current consumption in the social planner's mind, by using China's province-level panel data over years 1949–1992. We tailor and extend the S–S (1984)'s theoretical model to fit with the case in China by allowing international trade and agricultural rationing. Indeed, China had a low openness ratio but had never been a close economy even before its economic reform since 1978.[1] Moreover, different from the S–S (1984) by restricting the weight for welfares between peasants and workers, we also allow it to show its own flexibility and let data predict its magnitude.

In the present paper we also estimate the relative agricultural price elasticity of wage since such data, though essential, are unavailable for our key structural estimations for the relative weight between current consumption and future investment. The estimations for such elasticities certainly may suffer from usual measurement error problem due to data quality, or are sensitive by different estimation methods. One may be worried that such a measurement error would create an endogeneity problem for our structural estimations. We therefore address this problem using appropriate instrument variables.

Our paper joins a small set of the related literature. Strikingly enough, very few studies have performed the related empirical investigation on the price scissors though the S–S (1984) also has clear-cut empirical predictions. One exception is Li and Tsui (1990). Different from other theoretical studies which treat the former Soviet Union as a work-horse, they use China as a sample of developing countries to test the Preobrazhensky's First Proposition. They find evidence that the agricultural relative price is positively, but not negatively, correlated with the capital accumulation. They then explain this unexpected result using the efficiency wage hypothesis. After that,

[1] As pointed out by Naughton (2005), before 1979, China's total trade/GDP ratio is around 10%. It reached its minimum level of 5% in 1970–1971.

Knight (1995, 1999) also provides some interesting empirical findings to discuss the rural–urban divide in China.

Our findings are important because we are able to identify the relative magnitudes between current consumption and future investment in China's government objective function. In addition, we also calculate the weight of peasants' welfare relative to urban workers. It is understood that governments in socialist countries favor future investment over current consumption, and care benefits of workers more than those of peasants. However, to the best of our knowledge, very few previous studies had examined their relative quantitative magnitudes.

One potential limitation of our current approach is that we do not have feasible data on both disaggregated province-level agricultural trade and price elasticity of wage. To fully explore effects of price scissors on agricultural trade, it is a plus to run regressions using panel data. Unfortunately, we cannot access the disaggregated province level data on agricultural trade for years 1949–1992. Inspired by the gravity model in trade theory, we therefore seek for estimating the share of manufacturing trade relative to whole trade volume by allowing the heterogeneous foreign demand behavior across provinces.

The remainder of the paper is organized as follows. Section 2.2 is an introduction on price scissors in China. Section 2.3 delivers our theoretical framework based on the S–S model. Section 2.4 specifies the econometric methods. Section 2.5 describes the data, shows the empirical findings, and checks its robustness. Section 2.6 concludes.

2.2 Price Scissors in China

Before the economic reform, prices of all commodities in China were set by the government. As pointed out by Lin (2003, 2005, 2007), China, like many other less developed countries (LDC), adopted a heavy-industry-oriented development strategy after gaining its political independence in 1949. Heavy industries were capital-intensive. The projects in heavy industries required huge capital inputs and long gestation. However, China was a capital- scarce agrarian economy at that time. Moreover, China's political leaders also emphasized the importance of self-reliance to raise such capital. Therefore, the only way left for the government was to squeeze agricultural surplus for investments in heavy industries by lowering agricultural prices paid to peasants while raising the price of industrial products sold to the peasants. In a nutshell, under this strategy, it is natural for the government to select the price scissors against peasants in favor of industrial investment.

Figure 2.1 is helpful for us to understand the essence of price scissors. Without the government's intervention, the agricultural relative price is determined by the market directly, yields the level $(p_A/p_I)_0$. In order to squeeze benefits of agricultural peasants for its future investment, the government sets a lower agricultural relative price $(p_A/p_I)_1$, which yields an excess demand of agricultural goods. In the absence of price adjustment, the government has to import agricultural goods to clear the market. But this is infeasible since the relative price of agricultural good is lower than the

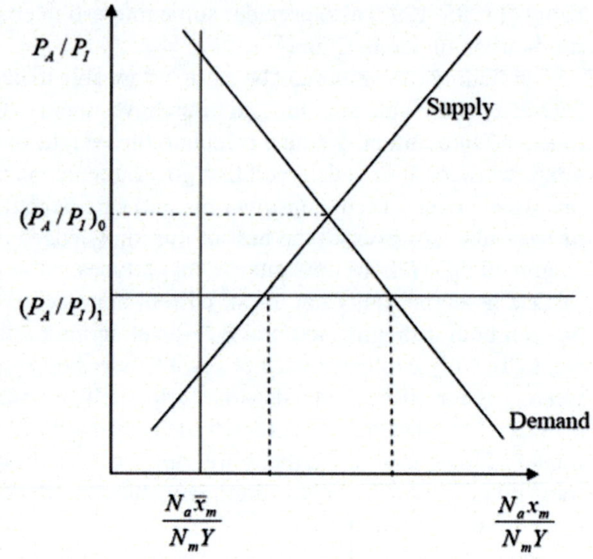

Fig. 2.1 Price scissors against peasants and agricultural rationing. *Notes* When the government sets a price scissor $\left(\frac{P_A}{P_I}\right)_1$ against the peasants, the market has excess demand for agricultural good. Therefore, the country has import demand pressure on agricultural goods. However, the agricultural rationing for urban workers, as shown in the vertical line for the agricultural relative demand, $\frac{N_a\bar{x}_m}{N_mY}$ not only offsets such import demand but also makes the country export agricultural goods

world level, which suggests exports of agricultural goods. Therefore, the only way left for the government was that it had to ration its agricultural goods. Put another way, the demand curve is regulated into a vertical one. By rationing agricultural goods, not only the government did not have to import agricultural goods but also could export its agricultural goods to earn scarce foreign exchanges.

Following previous works like Lardy (1983), we define price scissors (p) as the relative ratio between the purchasing price index of farm products (p_A) and rural retail price index of industrial products (p_I). That is, $p \equiv p_A/p_I$.[2] Figure 2.2 shows that the agricultural relative price index keeps a pretty stable constant level before 1985. In contrast, the agricultural relative price index increases after 1985.[3] However, such an increase is not attributable to the price scissors against peasants since prices of goods are not fully set by the government after 1985.

China began its price reform in 1978. Instead of adopting a shock therapy, China implemented a dual-track gradual reform in its transition to a market economy. As discussed by Lin et al. (1996), such a dual-track price system includes two stages. In the first stage, from 1978 to 1984, the government merely focused on adjusting agricultural prices relative to industrial prices.

In contrast, in the second stage, from 1985 to 1992, the government aimed at introducing a market track paralled to the planned track. In this stage, some key

[2] As discussed by Li and Tsui (1990), the price ratio would also be measured by an alternative index $p_A/\overline{p}_I$ where $\overline{p}_I$ is the ex-factory price index of industrial goods. In this paper we measure the price scissors using index p_A/p_I since there are many missing data for the other index.

[3] Note that, for some years, the relative agricultural price ratios are higher than one. But since various price indices here are calculated using the Laspeyres formula, a ratio which is higher than one does not imply that agricultural price level is higher than industrial price level.

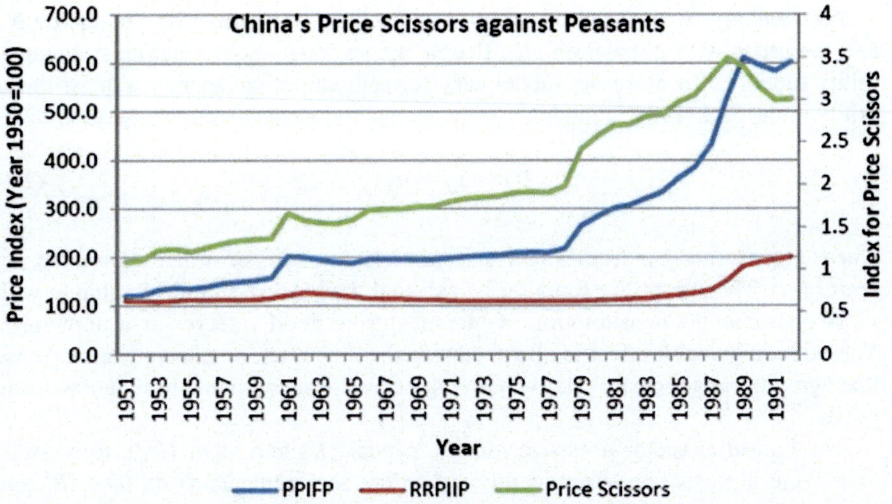

Fig. 2.2 China's various price indices. *Notes* The price scissors are defined as the relative ratio between purchasing price index of farm products (PPIFP) and rural retail price index of industrial products (RRPIIP). Sources for such data are from "China Compendium of Statistics, 1949–2004" by China Statistics Press, 2006

commodities were still included within various national plans, of which prices were set by the government as it did before the economic reform. For those commodities excluded from the national plans, their prices were determined by the market directly. Accordingly, there are three types of prices setting during this stage: fixed stated-regulated price, state guiding price, and market-determined price. In particular, in 1992 when China government officially adopted a marketing economy, the whole weights of both fixed stated-regulated price and state guiding price only accounted for 7.1% in the whole economy.[4] It decreased to less than 5% in year 1999. Put another way, 95% of commodity prices were determined by the market forces by 1999.[5]

2.3 The Theoretical Framework

Our theoretical model is based on the S–S (1984). To keep our model fit with China's case, we extend their model by allowing both international trade and agricultural rationing. In addition, consumers' utility functions in the S–S (1984) are also tailored to be suitable for empirical estimations.

[4] *Source* State Planning Commission, Price Administration Bureau; "The Weights and Changes of Three Patterns of Price," *Price in China*, 1997, No. 12.

[5] *Source* Official web site of China's Ambassy in New Zealand.

An economy is consisted of two different sectors, the rural with population N_a and the urban with population N_m. People are sector-immobile but have identical utility function. To make the model easy for estimation, we specify a quasi-linear utility in the S–S (1984)'s model:

$$U_j = y_j + u(x_j), \tag{2.1}$$

where a consumer j is from either agricultural sector (a) or urban manufacturing sector (m). The sub-utility function is, as usual, increasing and differentiable with x_j. A consumer j's consumption of manufacturing good y serves as a numeraire. Therefore, all wealth effect is absorbed into the manufacturing sector, in the sense that agricultural goods are relatively living necessities, compared to manufacturing goods.

The industrial sector uses two factors, capital (K) and labor (L_m), to produce manufacturing products whereas the agriculture sectors depends on land (R) and labor (L_a). Note that L_m and L_a measures the hours worked by each worker, which are immobile in this setup. This is exactly consistent with China's reality: people are not easily to relocate freely due to the severe residency control. Technologies in both industries are constant returns to scale. The agricultural price relative to the industrial price is p, which is chosen by the government in socialism countries. A higher relative price implies a lower scissor. A peasant's budget constraint is as follows:

$$px_a + y_a = pX(R/N_a, L_a). \tag{2.2}$$

A representative peasant's indirect utility function, V_a, is:

$$V_a(p, N_a) = \max_{x_a} pX(R/N_a, L_a) - px_a + u(x_a). \tag{2.3}$$

From the envelope theorem, we have:

$$\partial V_a/\partial p = X - x_a \equiv S_a, \tag{2.4}$$

where the residual rural surplus, S_a, is defined as $X - x_a$. Similarly, the wage rate (w), which is set by the authority, is the unique source of income for urban workers.[6] This suggests the budget constraint for an urban worker as follows:

$$px_m + y_m = wL_m. \tag{2.5}$$

By the same token, applying the envelope theorem for a representative worker's indirect utility function, V_m, we obtain:

[6] Note that workers in socialist countries do not have capital endowment explicitly. According to the laws in such countries, all capital endowment directly belongs to the state.

$$\partial V_m/\partial p = -x_m;\ \partial V_m/\partial w = L_m. \tag{2.6}$$

Different from the S–S (1984)'s model, we allow the country to have some foreign trade (Carter 1986). To the very least, China is never a close economy after 1949. Even before its economic reform in 1978, it still traded with some other socialist countries by exporting agricultural products (Naughton 2005). Given the depressed agricultural relative price, one would expect countries like China with the adoption of price-scissors should import agricultural product to balance its excess demand. However, the government in China simultaneously had the rationing on agricultural goods for urban workers. Therefore, the balance equation for agricultural goods is:

$$E = N_a S_a - N_m \overline{x}_m, \tag{2.7}$$

where E is the agricultural export and $\overline{x}_m$ is the consumption ration for an urban worker imposed by the government. Note that, as demonstrated in Fig. 2.1, the agricultural demand for urban worker $\overline{x}_m$ with rationing is less than its demand without rationing x_m: $\overline{x}_m < x_m$. Due to the agricultural ration, the country not only did not import but also could export its agricultural goods.

The government exports the agricultural goods at a given world level (p^w) which is higher than the domestic agricultural price due to the price depression at home. The markup ($\epsilon \equiv p^w - p$) is collected as a part of the government surplus. Therefore, we have governmental surplus (G) as follows:

$$G = N_m[Y(K/N_m, L_m) - wL_m] + \epsilon E. \tag{2.8}$$

That is, the government can obtain the surplus from two sources: the industrial surplus and net agricultural trade surplus. The industrial surplus is measured by the profit retained in the industrial sector. The last term of the RHS is the agricultural trade surplus. Different from the usual tariff setup, we don't model the markup as a function of domestic agricultural price here since such a price difference between domestic and world price is much more random and irregular since the domestic price is set up by home government arbitrarily.[7]

The government maximizes its aggregate welfare by choosing the optimal relative price.

Following the S–S (1984), we use a Bergson-Samuelson social welfare utility function:

$$\Omega = N_a V_a + \beta N_m V_m + \delta G. \tag{2.9}$$

The first term of the RHS in (2.9) measures the aggregate welfare from the agricultural sector while $N_m V_m$ is the aggregate welfare from the industrial sector. The coefficient β measures the weight between the agricultural sector and the industrial

[7] Of course, a possible extension is to consider a trade markup is a non-linear function of agricultural price.

sector in this social welfare function. Note that the government also has surplus from the two sectors (*G*). The coefficient δ measures the social value of the marginal investment, which could be treated as a weight between people's consumers' surplus (consumption) and investment. The objective of the present paper, again, is to estimate these two weights β and δ in the government's objective function.

Substituting (2.8) into (2.9), we obtain:

$$\Omega = N_a V_a + \beta N_m V_m + \delta N_m [Y(K/N_m, L_m) - wL_m] + \delta \epsilon E. \quad (2.10)$$

To determine the optimal terms of trade against peasants, we take the partial derivative of the government's social welfare function Ω with respect to *p*, and set it zero:

$$\frac{\partial \Omega}{\partial p} = \frac{\partial \Omega}{\partial p} + \frac{\partial \Omega}{\partial w}\frac{\partial w}{\partial p} = 0. \quad (2.11)$$

With some algebra manipulation as shown in Appendix, we obtain the equilibrium condition as follows:

$$\beta \cdot pN_m x_m - pE + (\delta - \beta)(N_m w L_m)\eta - N_m p\overline{x}_m = 0. \quad (2.12)$$

Note that the first term of (2.12), $pN_m x_m$, is aggregate agricultural consumption from urban workers. The second term, pE, is agricultural trade value. The third term is the product of the aggregate urban wage level ($N_m wL_m$) and the agricultural relative price elasticity of wage (η) which is defined as $\eta \equiv (dw/dp) \cdot p/w$. Finally, the last term measures the exogenous urban agricultural demand under rationing.

2.4 The Econometric Model

Equation (2.12) sheds light on the essence of our empirical specification. The provincial local governments are expected to have the same government objective function as the central authority since, under the planning economy system in China, the local government is directly controlled by the central government. Hence, our empirical specification relies on a province-level panal data set. However, it has no particular directional guidance for the entrance of an error term of the econometric model. We therefore first consider a specification as follow:

$$C_{it} = 1/\beta \cdot A_{it} + (\beta - \delta)/\beta \cdot \eta W_{it} - N_m p\overline{x}_m/\beta \quad (2.13)$$

$$= \gamma_1 \cdot A_{it} + \gamma_2 \cdot \eta W_{it} + \zeta_i + \phi_t + \mu_{it}, \quad (2.14)$$

where the regressand is the agricultural consumption from urban workers ($C \equiv pN_m x_m$). It is mainly affected by the value of agricultural export ($A \equiv pE$), the urban wage level ($W \equiv N_m w L_m$), and the relative agricultural price elasticity of wage (η). The last term $N_m p\overline{x}_m/\beta$ is captured by both the province-specific fixed effects ζ_i and year-specific fixed effects ϕ_t since the agricultural ration is directly determined by the government exogenously. The idiosyncratic term, μ, which bridges a gap between our theoretical framework above and the empirical specification, captures any other factors that affect the agricultural urban consumption volume but not considered in the original trade model. The subscript i denotes province and t denotes year. Our main interests of the present paper are to estimate the structural parameters $\widehat{\gamma}_1 = 1/\beta$ and $\widehat{\gamma}_2 = (\beta - \delta)/\beta$.

Without a doubt, such a specification is not a unique one to estimate (2.12). One could consider, at least, two other optional empirical specifications. The first one is to move the agricultural export (A_{it}) to the LHS as a regressand. In this way, the other two terms C_{it} and ηW_{it} are its regressors. Alternatively, one can also estimate the effect of agricultural export and urban agricultural consumption on the product of wage bills and elasticity, ηW_{it}. If so, which specification is the most suitable one? Herein we adopt Specification (2.14) for following reasons.

First, compared to the alternative specification which treat agricultural export as regressand, Specification (2.14) can dodge the empirical challenge of data unavailability. As we mentioned before, the province-level agricultural trade data is inaccessible for us. A feasible way to address this empirical challenge is to calculate its approximation by using the proportion of provincial GDP and its primary output as we will discuss shortly in the next sub-section. Clearly, such an approximation could suffer from some measurement errors. In econometrics there is nothing wrong to put it into the LHS since we could allow such a measurement error to corporate into its error term. But we still suffer from the second whammy–we don't have data on the price elasticity of wage in the RHS. Any estimation or data approximation of the elasticity could create another source of measurement error in the RHS.

By way of comparison, the second alternative approach is statistically feasible. We can put the product of wage bills and elasticity, ηW_{it}, as the regressand. Clearly, the measurement error of the calculated price elasticity would be passed through its error term. One might then worry about the lack of "true" data on agricultural trade. But this can be addressed by focusing on the manufacturing trade data instead as we will explore soon. However, the most severe shortcoming of this approach is that its economic meaning is unclear. It seems difficult to understand that the wage is determined by either agricultural consumption or agricultural trade. Therefore, we also discard this approach and focus on Specification (2.14) instead.

2.4.1 Agricultural Trade

To estimate (2.13), one needs agricultural trade data at province level. Unfortunately, we are unable to access province-level agricultural trade data though the national-level corresponding data are feasible. Also, the agricultural export (A_{it}) is the difference between total export (T_{it}) and manufacturing export (M_{it}): $A_{it} = T_{it} - M_{it}$.[8] Therefore, we can address this problem by constructing a proxy for the "true" province-level manufacturing trade data.

According to Helpman (1987), the gravity equation on trade model predicts that export volume is directly proportional to exporter's GDP, which also holds at disaggregated industry level and province level. Put in another way, province i's export (T_{it}) is directly proportional to its province-level output (Y_{it}). Therefore, we have $T_{it} = \theta_{it} Y_{it}$ where θ_{it} measures share of foreign demand on province i's products (Y_i) at year t.[9] By the same token, the share of foreign demand on province i's manufacturing products is θ_{it}^m. That is, $M_{it} = \theta_{it}^m Y_{it}^m$, where Y_{it}^m is province i's output in manufacturing commodities at year t. Accordingly, we can construct a proxy for manufacturing exports by province i and year t given $M_{it} = s_i^m \left(Y_{it}^m / Y_{it}\right) T_{it}$ where $s_{it}^m \equiv \theta_{it}^m / \theta_{it}$ measures the ratio of demand for manufacturing products relative to that for all commodities. Therefore, the agricultural export is expressed as

$$A_{it} = T_{it} - s_{it}^m \left(Y_{it}^m / Y_{it}\right) T_{it}. \tag{2.15}$$

Note that we have data on Y_{it}^m, Y_{it}, and T_{it}. In contrast, the relative demand ratio, s_{it}^m, is left for estimation.

2.4.2 *Relative Agricultural Price Elasticity of Wage*

Strikingly enough, we find no data on agricultural relative price elasticity of wage which is a key variable in (2.13). To the best of our knowledge, very few studies, if any, provide such elasticities over years. Therefore, the only way left here is to estimate the price elasticity of wage by ourselves. Accordingly, we consider a specification as follows:

$$\ln w_{it} = \alpha + \eta \ln p_{it} + e_{it}, \tag{2.16}$$

where the estimated coefficient, $\hat{\eta}$, is interpreted as the elasticity of the wage with respect to agricultural relative price. Without a doubt, one might suspect that there are some measurement errors for this simple specification. A simple pooled OLS estimation may be good to serve as a benchmark analysis, but this is certainly noisy since we have no idea about the "true" specification for a reduce-form estimation. Put in another way, the endogeneity issue caused by measurement error may be a concern in (2.13). The two-stage least square (TSLS) estimation is a powerful econometric

[8] Note that China's export in service sector is very small in the period 1949–1992 (Naughton 2005).

[9] For example, if $\theta_{it} = 1$, then all province i's products are exported. Conversely, if $\theta_{it} = 0$, then province i's exports no commodities.

method to control the endogeneity issues raised by measurement error.[10] We therefore address the endogeneity issue by adopting appropriate instruments.

Now, we combine (2.12) with (2.17) to derive the new equilibrium condition for estimations:

$$C_{it} = 1/\beta \cdot T_{it} + (\beta - \delta)/\beta \cdot \eta W_{it} - s^m/\beta \cdot \left(Y_{it}^m / Y_{it}\right) T_{it}. \tag{2.17}$$

To the ease of estimations, we presume that relative demand ratio for manufacturing products are identical across provinces and years: $s_{it}^m = s^m$. One might suspect that such a simplification could cause some bias since China's exporting structures before 1978 is much different from that after 1978. Before 1978, China almost only exported agricultural commodities. We therefore consider an indicator I_t (which equals one after 1978 and zero otherwise) into the empirical specification as follows:

$$C_{it} = \gamma_0 + \gamma_1 \cdot T_{it} + \gamma_2 \cdot \hat{\eta} W_{it} + \gamma_3 \cdot \left(Y_{it}^m / Y_{it}\right) T_{it} \cdot I_t + \zeta_i + \phi_t + \mu_{it}, \tag{2.18}$$

where $\hat{\gamma}_1 = 1/\beta$, $\hat{\gamma}_2 = (\beta - \delta)/\beta$, and $\hat{\gamma}_3 = -s^m/\beta$. Put in another way, when we consider cases before 1978, the term $\left(Y_{it}^m / Y_{it}\right) T_{it} \cdot I_t$ disappears given $I_t = 0$. Therefore, the total trade simply equals agricultural trade.

2.5 Data and Empirical Results

In this section, we first describe data sets used in the paper, followed by a presentation of our benchmark empirical results. To control for the endogeneity problem, we then offer a careful scrutiny of the validity of the instruments. Finally, we close the section with a discussion for China's economy in different periods.

To estimate (2.18), we need data on urban agricultural consumption (C_{it}), export (T_{it}), aggregate urban wages (W_{it}), province-level manufacturing output (Y_{it}^m) sand total output (Y_{it}), and price elasticity of wage (η). As mentioned above, data on price elasticity of wage is unavailable but its magnitudes can be estimated instead. China's trade data in our sampel are measured in US dollar price using the *spot* official exchange rates. Data on all variables can be directly accessed from *China Compendium of statistics, 1949–2004*, by the China Bureau of Statistics. Panel B of Table 2.2 presents the basic statical information of each variable.

---

[10] Wooldridge (2002, Chap. 5) provides a careful scrutiny for this topic.

2.5.1 Benchmark Estimates

Table 2.3 presents the estimate of agricultural relative price elasticity of wage. Column (1) reports the whole period of our sample (1949–1992). The rest of Column (1) considers three different perturbations for different time periods: Column (2) is for years 1949–1977, Column (3) is for years 1978–1984, and Column (4) is for years 1985–1992 (Tables 2.1 and 2.2).

Following (2.16), we first run the OLS estimations for different time periods. It turns out that the agricultural relative price elasticity of wage is –2.66 for the

Table 2.1 Main notation of the models

Symbol	Definition
Panel A: Theoretical Framework	
p	Agricultural price relative to industrial price
w	Hourly wage
η	Wage elasticity relative to price
N_a, N_m	Population of the rural and urban sectors, respectively
V_a,	A representative peasant (a)'s indirect utility
V_m	A representative worker (m)'s indirect utility
x_j	Consumer j's agricultural consumption, $\forall j = a, m$
$\overline{x}_m$	Ration of urban worker's agricultural consumption
y_j	Consumer j's manufacturing consumption, $\forall j = a, m$
X	Production of agricultural goods
L_m, L_a	Hours worked by each worker in manufacturing and agricultural sectors, respectively
K	Capital input for manufacturing sector
R	Land input for agricultural sector
S_a	Residual rural surplus: $S_a = X - x_a$
G	Government's surplus
Ω	Government's social objective function
β	Relative weight between peasants and workers
δ	Relative weight between peasants' current consumption and social future investment
ϵ	Agricultural trade markup
Panel B: Empirical Specification	
A_{it}	Value of agricultural export at province i at year t: $A_{it} = pE_{it}$
T_{it}	Value of total export which is the sum of agricultural and manufacturing exports given $T_{it} = A_{it} + M_{it}$
M_{it}	Value of agricultural export which equals $M_{it} = s_{it}^m (Y_{it}^m / Y_{it}) T_{it}$ where $s_{it}^m \equiv \theta_{it}^m / \theta_{it}$
C_{it}	Agricultural consumption from urban workers $C_{it} = pN_m x_m$
W_{it}	Urban wages bill $W_{it} = N_m w L_m$
μ_{it}	Idiosyncratic random variable

Table 2.2 Descriptive statistics of variables

Variable	Mean	Std. dev.	Minimum	Maximum
Export	101136.5	258617.9	1.8	3,345,821
Workers	333.52	217.58	41.7	1045.2
Average wage	1088	667.98	105.2	4,273
Agricultural price index	105.42	7.79	88.20	136.90
Industrial price index	102.82	5.34	89.50	125.90
Urban consumption on agricultural goods	105.30	127.62	1.37	984.16
Urban wage bills	498823.5	504,276	9467.92	3,455,569
Investment in capital construction	30.79	34.19	0.58	338.69
Fixed-asset investment in innovation	15.05	19.52	0.01	128.57

Sources Data is from "China Compendium of Statistics, 1949–2004" by China Statistics Press, 2006

whole period which is highly statistically significant. The economic rationale is straightforward. The lower the agricultural relative price is, the higher the urban wage is. Note that the lower agricultural relative price implies a larger price scissors. When the government imposes a strong price effect against peasants, urban workers' real income will relatively increase since they could access the consumption of necessity goods at a very low cost.

Turning to the rest of Table 2.3, the coefficients of agricultural relative price elasticity of wage are also negative. Most of them are highly statistically significant except the one for period 1949–1977. This is not a surprise for the measurement errors for such estimated magnitude given that we have no idea about the "true" reduced-form specification of the effect of price on wage. But, as mentioned above, we can address this problem by using instrument variable approach.

Our benchmark OLS estimation results of Specification (2.18) are reported in Column (1) of Table 2.4. The coefficient of urban agricultural consumption, $\widehat{\gamma}_1$, is 0.38. Correspondingly, the coefficient of the product of the price elasticity and the urban wage bills, $\widehat{\gamma}_2$, is –1.15.

Both of them are significant at the conventional statistical level, but the coefficient of the manufacturing exports term, $\widehat{\gamma}_3$, is insignificantly negative. We then go further to perform the two-way fixed-effect estimation for Specification (2.18). It turns out that the coefficients of γ_1 and γ_3 changes their signs. Simultaneously, the coefficient

Table 2.3 Estimated agricultural relative price elasticity of wage

Wage elasticity	1949–1992	1949–1978	1978–1984	1985–1992
OLS estimates	– 2.62**	– 2.63	– 0.57**	– 2.09**
	(–6.63)	(–1.14)	(–2.35)	(–7.57)

Notes Numbers in parenthesis are t-value. ** (*) denotes significance at 1 (5)% respectively

Table 2.4 Estimates for structural parameters (1949–1992)

Econometric methods[a] Regressand (urban agricultural consumption)	OLS	Fixed Effect[b]	IV + GMM Estimates	Instruments Included
Total exports (T_{it})	0.38** (2.91)	−0.02 (−0.20)	0.38** (2.96)	0.44** (3.28)
Product of urban wages and elasticity (ηW_{it})	−1.15** (−42.92)	−0.67** (−67.24)	−1.17** (−34.57)	−0.58** (−18.50)
Manufacturing exports $\left(\frac{Y_{it}^m}{Y_{it}} T_{it} I_{it}\right)$	−0.23 (−0.78)	0.63** (2.48)	−0.31 (−1.09)	−0.50* (−1.69)
Investment in capital construction (K_{it})				1666.4 (0.97)
Fixed asset investment in innovation (I_{it})				2107.5 (1.07)
F-statistics	1786.3‡	22.95‡	462.11‡	1288.6‡
First stage F-statistics			1262.1‡	
Anderson likelihood-ratio statistic			845.09‡	
Cragg-Donald F statistic			2421.96‡	
Anderson-rubin χ^2 Statistic			824.37‡	
Shea partial R			0.84	
Sargen over-identification Test			0.09	
P-value of Sargen over-identification Test			0.76	
R^2	0.97	0.93	0.98	0.97
Prob. > F or Prob. > χ^2	0.00	0.00	0.00	0.00

Notes [a] Numbers in parenthesis are t (z)-value. ** (*) denotes significance at 1 (5)% respectively. ‡ indicates p-value of the statistic is less than 0.01
[b]Time-specific and province-specific fixed effects are included here

of γ_1 is now statistically insignificant. We suspect that the endogeneity problem causes such an unexpected result of $\hat{\gamma}_1$ in the fixed-effect estimation.

2.5.2 *Endogeneity and Instruments*

The endogeneity problem of Specification (2.18) could come from the measure error of price elasticity. As we mentioned above, we do not have data on agricultural relative price elasticity of wage. Instead we use the OLS estimated coefficient obtained from the simple Specification (2.16). It is natural to suspect that there is some measurement error between the estimated elasticity coefficient and the "true" inaccessible data.

In order to identify the accurate weights in the government's objective function, one needs to control for the endogeneity problem. Otherwise, the related estimates would be a suspect. A powerful econometric technique of addressing the endogeneity is to perform the two-stage GMM estimations by adopting an appropriate instrument variable. Note that the equilibrium condition (2.17) implies no causal relationship among each variable. Therefore, a GMM estimation would be an ideal approach. Moreover, the GMM requires less assumptions on the error term and has the ability to generate heteroscedasticity-robust standard errors as compared to the general least squares method (Hall 2004).

We then adopt investment in capital construction and fixed-asset investment in innovation as instruments of the price elasticity for following reasons. The lower investment in innovation and capital construction, signals of the insufficient investment for the government, would push the government to depress the agricultural price much more (a lower relative price), which in turn leads to higher real wages. Indeed, such negative relationships between investment in innovation (capital construction) and wage bills are confirmed by the samples of our data. The partial correlation between investment in capital construction and wage bills is –0.93 while the one between investment in innovation and wage bills is –0.94.

Moreover, estimates from the two stages of GMM offer more fruitful and supportive evidence for the instrument's validity. An instrument (i.e., fixed-asset investment in innovation or capital construction) is good if it affects the regressand (i.e., urban agricultural consumption) through and only through the instrumented variable (i.e., price elasticity of wage). To justify this, we perform several useful tests as follows.

First, we perform Anderson's (1984) canonical correlation likelihood-ratio test to check whether or not the excluded instruments (i.e., fixed-asset investment in innovation and investment in capital construction) are correlated with the endogenous regressor. The null hypothesis that the model is under identified is rejected at the 1% level. Second, we also go a step further to see whether or not such instruments are weakly correlated with the price elasticity of wage. If so, then the estimates will perform poorly in this two-step GMM. Luckily enough, the Cragg and Donald (1993) F-statistics provide strong evidence to reject the null hypothesis that the first stage is weakly identified at a highly significant level. Third, the Anderson and Rubin (1949) χ^2 statistic rejects the null hypothesis that the coefficients of the endogenous regressors jointly equal zero. Fourth, the Hanson-Sargen over-identification test also confirms the instruments are valid (p-value $= 0.76$). In a nutshell, all of these statistical tests give us sufficient confidence that the instruments are well performed, and therefore, the specification is indicated well.

Finally, we provide an easy-to-interpret version for the validity of the instrument. We add both the fixed-asset investment in innovation and investment in capital construction as exogenous regressors. If these two variables have a direct effect on the agricultural net export, then we would expect the estimated coefficients to be statistically significant.

However, as shown in last column of Table 2.4, it is statistically insignificant at the 5% level. This again ascertains that these two variables affect the regressand through and only through the channel of its instrumented variable.

2.5.3 Robustness Checks

We have already explored the heterogeneity of price index by different periods in previous sections. Similarly, China's trade structure is changing over years. Before 1978, the year that China began its economic reform, the structure of China's foreign trade is relatively simple. The openness ratio (i.e., the sum of exports and imports relative to the GDP) is only around 5%. Most of China's exportable goods are agricultural products (Naughton 2005). In the late 1970s, China also began to export some oil products since the petroleum products from China's main field at Daqing, Heilongjiang, began to soar. Later, China's foreign trade had expanded steadily in the 1980s. Its openness ratio increased from 0.13 in 1980 to 0.34 in 1992. China's export had also diversified from an initial heavy dependence on primary commodities to a mix of primary goods and manufacturing products. Particularly, the export share of primary goods decreased from 49.7% in year 1980 to 20.0% in year 1992. In contrast, the export share of machinery and transport equipment increased from 4.65% in year 1980 to 15.5% in year 1992.[11]

Given China's economy structures are quite different before and after 1978, we first split our whole sample spread 1949–1992 into two different periods using 1978 as a cut-off year. We perform various econometric methods to estimate Specification (2.18) for years 1949–1977, which results are presented in Table 2.5. Clearly, after controlling the endogeneity issue, the coefficients of γ_1 and γ_2 are relatively higher than those obtained in the OLS. The IV fixed-effect estimations are shown to be close to those obtained in the GMM as well.

We then report the estimation results for different periods in Table 2.6. By way of comparison, empirical evidences from the period 1978–1984, as shown in the middle module of Table 2.6, are relatively weak since coefficients of γ_1 in both GMM and fixed-effect estimates are all insignificant. Turning to the period 1985–1992, estimates for the two key coefficients of γ_1 and γ_2 are significant in the fixed-effect estimation. After controlling for endogeneity, however, these two coefficients turn to be insignificant in the IV-GMM estimate. Therefore, we remind readers to be cautious about the magnitudes of estimates for the two periods after 1978.

[11] Data source is *China Statistical Yearbook (2006)* by National Bureau of Statistics of China.

Table 2.5 Estimates for structural parameters (1949–1977)

Econometric methods[a] Regressand (urban agricultural consumption)	OLS	Fixed Effect[b]	IV + GMM Estimates	Instruments Included
Total exports (T_{it})	0.27** (4.12)	0.30** (4.80)	0.20* (1.73)	0.33** (4.17)
Product of urban wages and elasticity (ηW_{it})	−0.43** (−17.47)	−0.46** (−18.22)	−0.45** (−8.70)	−0.41** (−17.23)
Investment in capital construction (K_{it})				−3133.6 (−1.10)
Fixed asset investment in innovation (I_{it})				1483.6 (1.37)
F-statistics	672.3‡	20.45‡	487.9‡	351.9‡
First stage F-statistics			24.42‡	
Anderson likelihood-ratio statistic			58.96‡	
Cragg-Donald F statistic			35.81‡	
Anderson-Rubin χ^2 statistic			40.76‡	
Shea partial R^2			0.35	
Sargen over-identification test			1.33	
p-value of Sargen over-identification test			0.25	
R^2	0.86	0.82	0.97	0.86
Prob. > F or Prob. > χ^2	0.00	0.00	0.00	0.00

Notes [a] Numbers in parenthesis are t (z)-value. ** (*) denotes significance at 1 (5)% respectively. ‡ indicates p-value of the statistic is less than 0.01
[b] Time-specific and province-specific fixed effects are included here

2.5.4 Identification of the Weights

Based on the estimation results obtained from Tables 2.4, 2.5 and 2.6, it is ready to identify the weights of the objective welfare function for China's government. Recalled that we normalize the weight of agricultural sector as a unity in (2.9). Accordingly, the relative weight of manufacturing sector is β in China's government objective function. Simultaneously, δ measures the relative weight of future investment relative to current consumption. By comparing (2.17) to (2.18), one can precisely identify magnitudes of such weights: $\beta = 1/\widehat{\gamma}_1$ and $\delta = \left(1 - \widehat{\gamma}_2\right)/\widehat{\gamma}_1$. We are therefore able to identify such weights once the estimates of both β and δ are statistically significant.

The results of such weights identification are shown in Table 2.7. We first report weights estimated in the absence of controlling endogeneity problem. As seen from the top module in Table 2.7, the OLS estimates suggest that the relative weight on urban workers is 2.63 while the relative weight on future investment is 5.66. Different from the fixed-effect estimation shown in the second column, the OLS estimated coefficients are significant. Without a doubt, the calculated weights from OLS estimates would have some bias due to the endogeneity problem. Hence, we go a step

Table 2.6 Estimations for different periods

Regressand: exports[a]	OLS	Fixed effects	IV + GMM estimates
Period 1949–1977			
Total exports (T_{it})	0.27** (4.12)	0.30** (4.80)	0.42** (2.81)
Product of urban wages and elasticity (ηW_{it})	– 0.43** (–17.47)	– 0.46** (–18.22)	– 0.65** (–74.94)
Period 1978–1984			
Total exports (T_{it})	0.82** (2.29)	0.13 (0.41)	0.39 (1.28)
Manufacturing exports $\left(\frac{Y_{it}^m}{Y_{it}} T_{it} I_{it}\right)$	– 0.99* (–1.90)	– 0.16 (–0.51)	– 0.65 (–1.58)
Product of urban wages and elasticity (ηW_{it})	– 2.74** (–25.50)	– 3.63** (–22.97)	– 3.05** (–16.53)
Period 1985–1992			
Total exports (T_{it})	0.19 (0.70)	– 0.77* (–1.87)	0.22 (0.78)
Manufacturing exports $\left(\frac{Y_{it}^m}{Y_{it}} T_{it} I_{it}\right)$	0.16 (0.25)	2.17** (2.34)	0.01 (0.01)
Product of urban wages and elasticity (ηW_{it})	– 0.83** (–29.48)	– 0.91** (–29.27)	– 0.85** (–21.00)

Notes [a] Numbers in parenthesis are t (z)-value. ** (*) denotes significance at 1 (5)% respectively. ‡ indicates p-value of the statistic is less than 0.01
[b] Year-specific and province-specific fixed effects are included here

forward to calculate the relative weights in China's government objective function after controlling the endogeneity. The GMM estimates are significant. It suggests that the weight on urban worker is, again, 2.63 while the weight on future investment is 5.71. The implication for such a finding is clear: the welfare of urban workers is much more important than those of peasants in the mind of China's government during 1949–1992. Simultaneously, China's government also cares future investment much more than current consumption.

In addition, for the IV-GMM estimates, the weight on future investment, 5.71, is larger than the weight on urban workers, 2.63. We therefore conclude that China's government paid much more attention to future investment even compared to the welfare of urban workers during 1949–1992. In sum, our estimates clearly confirm that China's government care more on future investment than on current consumption. Moreover, within current consumption, it cares more on urban workers than rural peasants.

One would expect that things should be different before and after year 1978. Before the economic reform, the primary objective of China's government was to develop the heavy industries so that China could catch up with the advanced countries like the U.S. and U.K. as soon as possible (Lin et al. 1994). But, since the reform in

Table 2.7 Identifications of the weights

Econometric methods	OLS	Fixed effects	IV + GMM estimates
Whole period			
Weight on urban workers (β)	2.63‡	– 50.00	2.63‡
Weight on future investment (δ)	5.66‡	– 83.50	5.71‡
Period 1949–1977			
Weight on urban workers (β)	3.70‡	3.33‡	5.00‡
Weight on future investment (δ)	4.30‡	4.86‡	7.25‡
Period 1978–1984			
Weight on urban workers (β)	1.21‡	6.69	2.56
Weight on future investment (δ)	4.56‡	35.62	10.38
Period 1985–1992			
Weight on urban workers (β)	5.26	– 1.30‡	4.55
Weight on future investment (δ)	9.63	– 0.86‡	8.40

Notes Numbers in this table are calculated from Tables 2.4, 2.5, 2.6 respectively. ‡ indicates that the estimates of both $\widehat{\gamma}_1$ and $\widehat{\gamma}_2$ are all significant at 5% level. The weights of 2-step GMM are ignored here since they are the same as their counterparts of 2SLS. The parameters β and δ are calculated from the corresponding estimated coefficients $\widehat{\gamma}_1$ and $\widehat{\gamma}_2$ by $\beta = 1/\widehat{\gamma}_1$ and $\delta = (1-\widehat{\gamma}_2)/\widehat{\gamma}_1$

1978, the government has given more attentions to improve people's living standard. Put another way, the government should care investment less and consumption more since the economic reform started. Our estimation results provide strong evidences to support such a dynamic change. As seen in the second-tier module of Table 2.7, the IV-GMM estimates suggest that, during 1949–1977, the weight on future investment is 5.00 times higher than that on current consumption. Such a weight is higher than that of the whole period 1949–1992, 2.63. Similarly, the weight on future investment before 1978, 7.25, is also much higher than that of the whole period 1949–1992, 5.71. Turning to the period 1978–1984, we see no significance for the coefficients in both fixed-effect and IV-GMM estimates. Therefore we cannot identify a clear government's objective function in this period. But this is exactly consistent with China's reality. At the initial stage of economic reform, the government didn't have a clear direction for their reform. The reform logic is described as "crossing the river by groping the stones" indeed.

After 1985, the direction of economic reform may become clear over years. The statistical significances of the fixed-effect estimates for the period 1985–1992 might practically capture such a change. However, the estimation results are again insignificant in the IV-GMM estimates. This indeed makes a good sense since, as we mentioned above, the prices of all commodities are not fully determined by the government any more during this period.

2.6 Concluding Remarks

Fully guided by a theoretical model initiated by S–S (1984), in the present paper we estimate the structural parameters in China's government objective welfare function, we find that the weight attached to the welfare of urban workers is much higher than that of peasants. Furthermore, the government also pays much more attention on future investment than on current consumption. Overall, our estimates suggest that a revised version of the S–S (1984)'s model fits with China's reality quite well, and it is also very helpful to explain the magnitude of political consideration in the government's mind.

Like other structural parameter estimations, our estimations enjoy several advantages. First, since our estimations closely depend on a theoretical model, we are able to see the connection of each structural variable. Second, the structural parameters estimation is also useful to avoid the arbitrage specifications which are commonly occurred in reduced-form estimation. Last but not least, the economic meaning of each corresponding estimated coefficient is also clear. The magnitudes of each structural variable in our specification are not only statistically but also economically significant.

Turning to the policy implication, our study also has some implication for nowadays' China. Although the phenomenon of price scissors against peasants officially ended in the early 1990s. Today China's government still maintains various price controls over some fields. The manipulated exchange rate policy is an excellent example. It is very true that the price control remained today is different from the price scissors against peasants presented here; but, in essence, the economic meaning behind these policies are, to some extents, similar in terms of government's political concern.

Without a doubt, as in any ambitious attempt to marry a complicated structural parameters model with imperfect data, we have made a variety of compromises. Since we don't have disaggregated data on province-level agricultural export volume, nor do we have data on the agricultural relative price elasticity of wage. We instead use a proxy or estimated value as a substitute. Clearly, it would be better if one could use the "actual" data for such variables to estimate the government's objective function in China, which could be a possible avenue for our future research.

Appendix

From (2.10), we know:

$$\Omega = N_a V_a + \beta N_m V_m + \delta N_m[Y(K/N_m, L_m) - wL_m] + \delta\epsilon E.$$

To determine the optimal terms of trade against peasants, we take the partial derivative of the government's social welfare function Ω with respect to p, and set it zero:

$$\begin{aligned}
\frac{\partial\Omega}{\partial p} &= \frac{\partial\Omega}{\partial p} + \frac{\partial\Omega}{\partial w}\frac{\partial w}{\partial p} \\
&= N_a\frac{\partial V_a}{\partial p} + \beta N_m\frac{\partial V_m}{\partial p} + \beta N_m\frac{\partial V_m}{\partial w}\frac{dw}{dp} - \delta N_m L_m\frac{dw}{dp} \\
&= N_a S_a - \beta N_m x_m + N_m L_m(\beta - \delta)\frac{dw}{dp} \\
&= (N_a S_a - N_m x_m) + N_m x_m - \beta N_m x_m + N_m L_m(\beta - \delta)\frac{w}{p}\left(\frac{dw}{dp}\frac{p}{w}\right) \\
&= E - \beta N_m x_m + (\beta - \delta)\frac{w}{p}N_m L_m \eta + N_m x_m \\
&= 0
\end{aligned}$$

where the second equality is from (2.4) and (2.6). The third equality rearranges the term $\beta N_m x_m$, the fourth equality is from (2.7) and applies the definition of the price elasticity of wage as $\eta \equiv (dw/dp) \cdot p/w$. Finally, we multiple p in both hand sides to obtain Specification (2.12):

$$\beta \cdot pN_m x_m - pE + (\delta - \beta)(N_m w L_m)\eta - pN_m x_m = 0.$$

Chapter 3
Measuring the Impact of Trade Protection on Industrial Production Size

Trade theory has no clear prediction on how import protection affects an importing sector's relative size. In this paper, we estimate the impact of US trade protection on industrial production relative size based on a translog GDP functional system. Using an industrial panel data set and controlling for factor endowments and technology improvement, we find empirical evidence that trade protection does not help much increase a sector's relative size. Such findings are also robust to both the inclusion of the role of political economy and the coverage of various non-tariff measures as proxies of industrial protection.

3.1 Introduction

When a government imposes an instrument of trade policy on its imports, it has a direct impact on both producers and consumers. An import tariff on a small country pushes up its domestic import price which in turn leads to higher domestic production and less consumption on the import. Without a doubt, a very small country bears a deadweight loss owing to both production and consumption distortions. In contrast, a large country might improve its national welfare owing to extra gains from terms of trade. This is because the terms of trade, its world relative price of exports relative to imports, would increase as a result of the change of the relative demand and supply of the import. Regardless of a country's size, an import tariff clearly raises both the import price and the quantity produced; yet the industrial relative size for the import sector does not necessarily increase since the tariff could indirectly change the sizes of other sectors as well.

Therefore, whether strong protection in an industry leads to high output share remains an empirical question. In fact, one can easily find opposing evidence for

This chapter is coauthored with Wei Tian and is originally published in Review of Development Economics, 18(2), 231–253, 2014. 10.1111/rode.12081.

M. Yu, *China's Miracle in Foreign Trade*, Studies in Modern Chinese Economy,
https://doi.org/10.1007/978-981-16-6030-6_3

different industries. For example, in the 1960s, the USA abandoned high trade protection on its footwear industry. As a result, the output in the footwear industry decreased dramatically (Cassing and Hillman 1986). Conversely, the story of the garment industry shows another side of the coin. Traditionally, the garment industry is one of the most highly protected sectors by the US government, yet its output share relative to the gross domestic product (GDP) shows a decreasing trend over the years.

In this paper we therefore estimate the effect of trade protection for an industry on its output share. Our paper contributes to the literature from two important perspectives. First, we extend the seminal work of Harrigan (1997) by considering the role of trade protection in a neoclassical trade specification model which believes that the pattern of international specification and trade is jointly determined by technology difference *a là* the Ricardian model and factor endowment difference *a là* the Heckscher–Ohlin–Vanik model. In contrast to an ideal free-trade setup, our empirical specification is closer to reality by allowing various trade protections such as import tariffs and non-barrier barriers such as import quota or export subsidy. We find strong evidence that trade protection plays a role in determining industrial size for some manufacturing industries.

Second, our empirical findings themselves also enrich the understanding of the effect of trade protection. It is a conventional wisdom that an industry could grow faster under import protection. For more than a century policy makers and even some economists believe the idea of "infant industry protection" as a favorable argument for trade protection. Our empirical findings instead cast doubt on such a theoretical conjecture. After controlling for factor endowments and technology improvement, we find empirical evidence that trade protection does not greatly help increase a sector's relative size, measured by its industrial output share over GDP.

The objective of this paper is to see how an import tariff imposed on an industry can change production sizes of itself and other related industries particularly in the USA. It is important to emphasize that a change in industrial production size could occur for reasons other than the change of an import tariff. First, the change of industrial output share could be due to factor endowment changes caused by a movement of international factors or other reasons. For example, consider a standard Heckscher–Ohlin model, in which labor is migrated from the foreign country to the home country. The home country's labor-intensive sector will expand according to the Rybczynski theorem.

Second, it might be because of the export-biased technology improvement. The advanced technology used in export-biased industries causes the expansion of exportable. Accordingly, resources will shift toward the exporting sectors from the importing sectors, which in turn causes the shrink of the importing sectors. As known as the "Immiserizing growth" initiated by Bhagwati (1958), for a large country, if the exportable-biased growth reduces the output of the importable good, and if the foreign demand for such an importable good is inelastic, then its national welfare would be reduced, in large part, because of the deterioration of its terms of trade.

Third, nontradable sectors grow very fast today. For example, according to the reports from the Bureau of Economic Analysis (BEA), the weight of professional services related to the GDP in the USA reached 20% in 2006. Such a quick move would make tradable sectors shrink relatively, which in turn also leads to a relative decline of import-competing tradable sectors. In addition, other domestic industrial policies such as a production subsidy on import-competing commodities could also make sizes of importing sectors shrink.

Finally, factors from the demand side could affect the industrial output share as well. For instance, an increase in the price of substitutable commodities for an industry could push the industrial demand curve shift right, since consumers will substitute commodities in the industry for their substitutable goods. Accordingly, both the equilibrium price and output increase, given others constant. In other words, an increase in the price of substitutables for an industry could affect its industrial output share.

Therefore, to estimate the effect of trade policy on production size for each industry, we need to control for other factors affecting industrial production size such as factor endowments, technology and price changes from other industries. We adopt a functional form of translog GDP system to handle this task for two reasons.

First, the translog GDP functional form can *systematically* measure effects of tariffs on industrial output shares for many industries. Since a change of one sector's price could affect, though indirectly, other sectors' outputs, it is inappropriate to *separately* estimate each industry. Instead, it is more desirable to jointly estimate a group of equations by allowing error terms for each industry in each equation correlated. The seemingly unrelated regressions (SUR) econometric approach associated with the translog GDP system also make the joint estimations feasible.

Second, the translog GDP functional form is motivated by a theoretical setup. It enjoys a striking advantage to cover neatly tariffs, factor endowments and technological changes into the model. As demonstrated in the next section, the translog GDP function is an ideal way to consider the maximized GDP function with many goods under a perfect competitive market. It hence sheds light on the way in which variables in the system interact with each other.

Possibly owing to such advantages, the translog GDP function is widely adopted by trade economists. Related empirical contributions of estimating a translog GDP function include Burgess (1976), Kohli (1990), Learmer (1984), Harrigan (1997), and Feenstra and Kee (2008), among others. The duality theory suggests that estimating an aggregate cost function is equivalent to estimating a GDP function. Burgess (1976) therefore estimates an aggregate cost function to show that traded goods are capital intensive whereas nontraded goods are labor intensive in the USA.

In contrast, some other works estimate a translog GDP function directly using data on primary inputs—capital and labor. Using this approach, Kohli (1990) suggests that consumption goods are capital intensive, while exports and investments are labor intensive. Harrigan (1997) instead explores how technology differences affect international specification using the translog GDP functional system. Last but not least, Feenstra and Kee (2008) use it to examine the effects of industrial export variety on country productivity.

To summarize, the translog GDP function is a widely accepted approach to explore the relationship among goods' prices, factor endowments, technological changes and industrial output shares. Therefore, we rely on this system to investigate impact of tariffs on production for each industry. Particularly, our data set coverage is the USA and its 14 OECD importing partners for several main industries (i.e. food, garments, paper, chemicals, glass, metals and machinery) over the years 1974–1990. We find empirical support that trade protection does not help much to increase a sector's relative size.

Since the variation in industrial size would reversely affect its protection level, the decline in an industrial output share could force the domestic special interest groups to lobby the government. Accordingly, such special interest groups would push the government to choose high commercial protection in capital-abundant countries such as the USA (Grossman and Helpman 1994). To precisely investigate the impact of tariffs, we also control in the present paper for such endogeneity issues using the instrumental variable (IV) approach.

Our paper joins a growing literature in examining the effects of import tariffs on industry-level and firm-level performance. Previous works such as Trefler (2004) and Bernard et al. (2006) also explore the impact of import tariffs on firm productivity. In particular, Bernard et al. (2006) find that trade liberalization could lead to an intra-industry reallocation toward high-productivity firms. They also find that a decline in trade costs variable would lead to a decrease in domestic market share and domestic revenue for surviving firms. In contrast with their study to explore firm decision on domestic and foreign sales, in this paper we are more interested in the response of trade costs on industrial size. Trefler (2004) examine the effect of the North-American Free Trade Agreement on the performance of Canadian firms. He finds that industries with the deepest tariff cuts in Canadian would have an increase in industrial productivity, mainly by sweeping the less-productive firms out from the market. As opposed to focusing on productivity improvement as in Trefler (2004), this paper focus more on the impact of trade liberalization on industrial size.

3.2 The Empirical Model

Consider an economy with many goods. It has a GDP function as follows:

$$G(P, V, t) = \max \sum_{i=1}^{N} p_i f_{it}(v_i).$$

The country also faces a resource budget constraint:

$$\sum_{i=1}^{M} v_i \leq V,$$

where $P = (p_1, \ldots, p_N)$ is the price vector for N commodities, $V = (v_1, \ldots, v_N)$ is the endowment vector for M factors, and t is the time index which is used to measure the technological improvement. Previous studies like Harrigan (1997) use total factor productivity to measure technological improvement. This is an acceptable approach provided that the technology is Hicks neutral. However, in the present paper we do *not* restrict our scope to a Hicks-neutral technological change since it is mainly a theoretical simplification but earns little empirical support in reality (Basu and Fernald 2002). We instead consider technological change by adopting a more general approach introduced by Mckay et al. (1983). We simply use the time index to control for technology improvement. The idea is that technology shifts over time as a result of technological change so that the representation of technology becomes a function of the time index. However, a caveat also exists. The time trend variable included here may capture various factors other than productivity improvement (e.g. a demand shift for nontraded goods).[1]

We use a conventional translog functional form introduced by Christensen et al. (1973), Diewert (1974), Kohli (1990), Feenstra (1994) and Harrigan (1997), among others. This functional form is flexible in the sense that it provides a second-order approximation of the GDP function. Specifically, it has the following form:

$$\begin{aligned}\ln G(P, V, t) &= \gamma_{00} + \beta t + \sum_{i=1}^{N} \gamma_{0i} \ln p_i + \sum_{k=1}^{M} \delta_{0k} \ln v_k + \frac{1}{2}\phi t^2 \\ &+ \frac{1}{2}\sum_{i=1}^{N}\sum_{j=1}^{N} \gamma_{ij} \ln p_i \ln p_j + \frac{1}{2}\sum_{k=1}^{M}\sum_{l=1}^{M} \delta_{ij} \ln v_k \ln v_l \\ &+ \sum_{i=1}^{N} \phi_{it} (\ln p_i) t + \sum_{k=1}^{M} \delta_{kt} (\ln v_k) t + \sum_{i=1}^{N}\sum_{k=1}^{M} \phi_{ik} \ln p_i \ln v_k.\end{aligned}$$

It is understood that there are three restrictions for the parameters of this translog GDP function. First, technology is assumed to be constant returns to scale following Kohli (1990) and others, which in turn implies the homogeneity of degree one in price. Therefore, we have the following restrictions for related parameters:

$$\sum_{i=1}^{N} \gamma_{0i} = 1, \quad \sum_{i=1}^{N} \gamma_{ij} = 0, \quad \sum_{i=1}^{N} \phi_{ik} = 0, \quad \sum_{i=1}^{N} \phi_{it} = 0.$$

Second, the following restrictions also guarantee that the GDP function is homogeneity of degree one in endowments:

$$\sum_{k=1}^{M} \delta_{0k} = 1, \quad \sum_{k=1}^{M} \delta_{kl} = 0, \quad \sum_{k=1}^{M} \phi_{ik} = 0, \quad \sum_{k=1}^{M} \phi_{it} = 0.$$

[1] We thank a referee for pointing this out.

Third, without loss of generality, we also impose the symmetry constraints on the translog GDP function owing to Young's theorem: $\gamma_{ij} = \gamma_{ji}, \forall i, j$ and $\delta_{kl} = \delta_{lk}, \forall k, l$.

Our main aim is to explore the effect of an import tariff on the industrial output share. Note that we can obtain the output share s_i for industry i from (2).[2] Thus, differentiating the right-hand side of the translog GDP function (2), we obtain the following:

$$s_i = \gamma_{0i} + \sum_{j=1}^{N} \gamma_{ij} \ln p_j + \sum_{k=1}^{M} \phi_{ik} \ln v_k + \phi_{it} t, \quad \forall i = 1, \ldots, N.$$

Clearly, the output share of sector i, which measures sector i's production size, depends on technology, domestic price of importable and factor endowments. With data on these variables, one can estimate the corresponding parameters $\gamma_{0i}, \gamma_{ij}, \phi_{ik}$ and ϕ_{it}.

As we mentioned above, nontradable sectors nowadays account for a significant weight in the USA. To fully explore the effect of tariffs on production size, we control for the effect of nontradable sectors by splitting all commodities into two categories: tradable and nontradable goods. Let tradable prices be represented by p^* and nontradable prices by p^{n*}, then we can write (3) as follows:

$$s_i^* = \gamma_{0i}^* + \sum_{j=1}^{N_T} \gamma_{ij}^* p_j^* + \sum_{k=1}^{M} \phi_{ik}^* \ln v_k^* + \phi_{it}^* t + \sum_{j=N_T+1}^{N} \gamma_{ij}^* \ln p_j^{n*}, \quad \forall i = 1, \ldots, N.$$

where a asterisk-notation (*), N_T and $N - N_T$ denote the USA, and its numbers of tradable sectors and nontradable sectors, respectively.

Similarly, exporting country c's output share function for industry i is:

$$s_{ic} = \gamma_{0ic} + \sum_{j=1}^{N_T} \gamma_{ijc} \ln p_{jc} + \sum_{k=1}^{M} \phi_{ikc} \ln v_{kc} + \phi_{itc} t$$
$$+ \sum_{j=N_T+1}^{N} \gamma_{ijc} \ln p_{jc}^{n}, \quad \forall i = 1, \ldots, N, \forall c.$$

For estimation purposes, we aggregate all commodities into an identical harmonized level (e.g. SIC 2-digit level). Accordingly, we obtain the relative output share for each industry across countries by subtracting (5) from (4):

$$s_i^* - s_{ic} = (\gamma_{0i}^* - \gamma_{0ic}) + (\phi_{it}^* - \phi_{it})t + \sum_{j=1}^{N_T} (\gamma_{ij}^* \ln p_j^* - \gamma_{ijc} \ln p_{jc})$$

[2] This is due to $\partial \ln G / \partial \ln p_i = \partial G / G \cdot p_i / \partial p_i = p_i y_i / G \equiv s_i$ in which the second equality comes from the application of the envelope theorem.

$$+\sum_{k=1}^{M}\left(\phi_{ik}^{*}\ln v_{j}^{*}-\phi_{ikc}\ln v_{kc}\right)+\left(\sum_{j=N_T+1}^{N}\gamma_{ij}^{*}\ln p_{j}^{n*}-\sum_{j=N_T+1}^{N}\gamma_{ijc}\ln p_{jc}^{n}\right).$$

Note that the cross price semielasticity of output share γ_{ij}^{*} measures the impact of sector *j*'s price on sector *i*'s output share since $\gamma_{ij}^{*}=\partial s_{i}^{*}/\partial\ln p_{j}^{*}$. Since an import tariff provides a wedge between the domestic price and the exporter's price for each industry, the cross price semi-elasticity of output share γ_{ij}^{*} is correlated with its exporter *c*'s counterpart γ_{ijc}. To keep our estimations neat, we simply presume that such parameters are identical across trading countries: $\gamma_{ij}^{*}=\gamma_{ijc}$. Accordingly, their difference, if any, is absorbed into the error term. Similarly, we have the identical Rybczynski semi-elasticity ϕ_{ijc} across each country *c*: $\phi_{ij}^{*}=\phi_{ijc}$.

We measure sector *j*'s import tariff for the USA as an *ad-valorem* one (τ) with $1+\tau_{jc}=p_{j}^{*}/p_{jc}$. That is, we ignore other trade-cost factors that affect international price difference (Anderson and Van Wincoop 2004). By choosing a year as a base point, we re-express (6) as follows:

$$s_{i}^{*}-s_{ic}=\left(\phi_{it}^{*}-\phi_{it}\right)t+\sum_{j=1}^{N_T}\gamma_{ijc}\ln\left(1+\tau_{jct}\right)+\sum_{k=1}^{M}\phi_{ikc}\ln\left(v_{k}^{*}/v_{kc}\right)$$

$$+\left[\gamma_{0i}^{*}-\gamma_{0ic}+\sum_{j=N_T+1}^{N}\gamma_{ij}^{*}\ln p_{j}^{n*}-\sum_{j=N_T+1}^{N}\gamma_{ijc}\ln p_{jc}^{n}\right].$$

The last four terms in (7) capture the impacts on the relative own price elasticity of GDP $\left(\gamma_{0i}^{*}-\gamma_{0ic}\right)$ and the relative industrial output share of nontradable sectors' price in both exporter and importer $\left(\sum_{j=N_T+1}^{N}\gamma_{ij}^{*}\ln p_{j}^{n*}-\sum_{j=N_T+1}^{N}\gamma_{ijc}\ln p_{jc}^{n}\right)$. Since price data on nontradable goods are generally unavailable (Harrigan 1997), all of these terms are absorbed into and treated as a random variable ε_{ict}:

$$\varepsilon_{ict}=\left(\gamma_{0i}^{*}-\gamma_{0ic}\right)+\left(\sum_{j=N_T+1}^{N}\gamma_{ij}^{*}\ln p_{j}^{n*}-\sum_{j=N_T+1}^{N}\gamma_{ijc}\ln p_{jc}^{n}\right).$$

We then decompose such a random variable, ε_{ict}, into three components: (1) country fixed-effect, η_{ic}, which captures the unobserved country-specific time-invariant fixed-effects; (2) time-specific fixed effect, μ_{it}; and (3) an idiosyncratic effect e_{ict} with zero expectation and heteroskedastic variance σ_{i}^{2}, which captures all other factors unspecified in this specification such as consumer confidence. Namely, the stochastic process can be characterized using a flexible and simple model:

$$\varepsilon_{ict}=\eta_{ic}+\mu_{it}+e_{ict}.$$

Note that here the role of nontradable sectors is captured by the time-specific fixed effect and country-specific fixed-effect. Thus far, we can write (7) as an empirical specification:

$$s_{it}^* - s_{ict} = \beta_t t + \sum_{j=1}^{N_T} \gamma_{ijc} \ln \tau_{jct} + \sum_{k=1}^{M} \phi_{ikc} \ln\left(v_{kt}^*/v_{kct}\right) + \eta_{ic} + \mu_{it} + e_{ict}.$$

Clearly, in specification (8) sector *i*'s output share in the USA depends on its own *ad-valorem* import tariff, import tariffs for other importing sectors, various relative factor endowments and technology level. Our main interest is the impact of each industrial import tariff on its own output share. To fully explore this effect, we also control for the exporting country's corresponding output share, the industrial fixed effect and the year-specific fixed effect.[3]

3.3 Data and Estimate Results

To estimate specification (8), we distinguish seven main manufacturing industries (i.e. food, garments, chemicals, papers, glass, metals and machinery) which are aggregates from the standard industrial classification (SIC) four-digit level. It is also necessary to drop one equation before the translog GDP functional system is estimated, provided that the sum of industrial output shares is one (Feenstra 2003). However, since the sum of such seven industrial output shares is less than one, we can instead estimate the system directly.

Data

Table 3.1 summarizes the descriptive statistics of our data set. The sources of each variable are listed in Table 3.2. We use two different methods to measure trade protection: (1) *ad-valorem* import tariffs in which we have data for the years from 1974 to 1990; (2) nontariff barriers (NTBs) in which we have 4-year data after 1990 (particularly, 1993, 1994, 1996 and 1999). For each type of trade protection measurement, we include 14 major trading partners of the USA. Our coverage is close to Harrigan (1997): although we do not include West Germany as a result of data unavailability, we instead add several smaller OECD economies such as Australia, Austria, Finland, Ireland, Norway and Portugal. We also include Mexico since it is the third trading partner of the USA today.[4]

---

[3] The SUR system also enjoys an advantage of allowing the error term in an industry correlated with its counterpart in another industry. In other words, the SUR allows for a possible case that different industry-level observations for different exporting countries are relatively dependent observations, owing to the fact that the USA is a member of the GATT/WTO and hence applies the same most favored nation (MFN) tariff rate to all other GATT/WTO members.

[4] According to US Department of Commerce, in 2008 the American top trading partner was Canada whereas the second was China.

Table 3.1 Descriptive statistics of variables

Variables	Mean	Std dev.	Min.	Max.
Log industrial tariffs (1974–1990)				
Food	−2.596	0.739	−4.493	2.869
Garments	−1.919	0.240	−2.576	−1.383
Paper	−3.463	0.566	−5.127	−2.620
Chemicals	−3.075	0.319	−4.794	−2.200
Glass	−2.695	0.739	−4.605	1.445
Metals	−3.519	0.835	−8.148	−2.325
Machinery	−3.057	0.377	−4.543	−2.185
Difference on production relative size (1974–1990)				
Food	−0.176	0.369	−1.461	0.082
Garments	−0.024	0.050	−0.221	0.030
Paper	−0.123	0.284	−1.394	0.065
Chemicals	−0.063	0.204	−0.673	0.129
Glass	−0.028	0.049	−0.181	0.013
Metals	−0.269	0.770	−3.638	0.303
Machinery	−0.095	0.268	−1.264	0.103
Difference on production relative size (after 1990)				
Food	−0.158	0.314	−1.669	0.059
Garments	−0.032	0.099	−0.584	0.020
Chemicals	−0.072	0.193	−0.890	0.079
Metals	−0.326	0.879	−3.787	0.234
Machinery	−0.116	0.341	−1.402	0.082
Log factors difference (1974–1990)				
Durables	2.939	1.174	0.817	4.998
Nonresident construction	2.855	1.150	0.534	5.125
Low educated	−1.492	0.664	−2.598	0.305
Middle educated	0.446	0.400	−0.316	1.661
High educated	1.123	0.588	−0.239	2.379
Agricultural land	3.558	1.280	1.355	5.461
Log factors difference (after 1990)				
Capital	2.831	1.260	−0.272	4.915
Labor	2.653	1.155	0.686	4.545
Land	3.549	1.397	1.182	5.428

Notes The source for each variable is described in Table 3.2. Difference on production relative size for each industry is measured by the US output share minus its counterpart in 14 OECD importers at the average level. The number of observations is 238 given data for 14 countries across 17 years included when the tariff is adopted for estimations. In contrast, the number of observations is 39 for each equation when the NTBs are adapted for estimations since some NTBs data are missing

Table 3.2 Data source

Variables	Definition, Measurement, and Data Sources
	Data before 1990
Tariffs	Data from Feenstra et al. (2001)
Agricultural land	It is the product of arable land and land share. Such data can be accessed from the World Development Indicators (2002)
Non-residential construction capital	Data can be accessed from the Penn World Table 5.6
Production durables capital	Data can be accessed from the Penn World Table 5.6
Highly educated workers	Such education data can be accessed from Barro and Lee (1993) while labor force data is from World Development Indicators (2003)
Medium-educated workers	The same as above
Low-educated workers	The same as above *Data after 1990*
Non-tariff barriers	Data from TRAINS of UNCTAD various years
Capital endowment	It is measured as the product of the fixed capital expenditure and GDP. Data is from the World Development Indicators (2002)
Labor force	It is directly used to measure labor endowments after year 1990. Education measurement is not considered here due to the lack of data for such countries. Data is from the World Development Indicators (2002)

Table 3.1 includes the basic statistics on the differences of output shares between the USA and its trading partners for each of the seven industries. It is interesting to find that of all the seven industries the USA industrial output shares are, on average, relatively lower than their OECD trading partners. This serves as a side evidence to reflect the fact that non-manufacturing sectors in the USA (particularly, services sectors) play a more and more important role in its economy today. According to reports from the BEA, the weight of the service sectors increased rapidly from 6% in 1987 to around 10% in 1999. In contrast, the weight of manufacturing sectors decreased from 28% in 1987 to 23% in 1999.[5]

The SIC two-digit tariffs are aggregated from the SIC four-digit tariffs across industries, which, in turn, are calculated using values of industrial duties divided by their customs value. Overall, as shown in Table 3.3, industries such as food, garments and glass have relatively high import tariffs compared with others like paper, chemicals and metals for each country. These partially demonstrate the fact that the USA historically imposed a relatively high protection for those labor-intensive commodities and senescent industries (Brainard and Verdier 1997). Comparing data from 1974 to 1990, we find that import tariffs decrease over time. This is consistent

[5] One possible reason for this phenomenon is the increasing outsourcing over years. Feenstra (1998) is an excellent survey for the production disintegration. For the data source, see the web pages of the Bureau of Economic Analysis at http://www.bea.gov.

Table 3.3 US import tariffs of seven main industries for 14 countries

Exporter	Year	Food	Garments	Paper	Chemicals	Glass	Metals	Machinery
Australia	1974	0.22	0.16	0.06	0.03	0.12	0.02	0.06
	1990	0.02	0.10	0.02	0.03	0.07	0.02	0.03
Austria	1974	0.08	0.20	0.06	0.05	0.10	0.08	0.07
	1990	0.03	0.14	0.03	0.04	0.05	0.05	0.04
Canada	1974	0.27	0.13	0.01	0.04	0.02	0.02	0.04
	1990	0.07	0.08	0.01	0.03	0.01	0.01	0.02
Denmark	1974	0.08	0.12	0.03	0.06	0.14	0.03	0.07
	1990	0.05	0.11	0.03	0.04	0.05	0.06	0.04
Finland	1974	0.11	0.15	0.04	0.07	0.15	0.03	0.07
	1990	0.06	0.09	0.02	0.04	0.04	0.05	0.04
France	1974	0.09	0.21	0.05	0.05	0.13	0.05	0.08
	1990	0.04	0.13	0.02	0.06	0.07	0.04	0.03
Ireland	1974	0.08	0.21	0.07	0.07	0.06	0.04	0.07
	1990	0.01	0.12	0.04	0.05	0.04	0.05	0.03
Italy	1974	0.17	0.22	0.06	0.05	0.11	0.06	0.08
	1990	0.04	0.14	0.03	0.05	0.10	0.04	0.04
Japan	1974	0.17	0.24	0.06	0.06	0.18	0.05	0.08
	1990	0.09	0.11	0.03	0.06	0.07	0.05	0.04
Mexico	1974	0.12	0.18	0.05	0.06	0.13	0.02	0.08
	1990	0.04	0.10	0.01	0.04	0.04	0.03	0.03
Norway	1974	0.06	0.18	0.05	0.05	0.01	0.02	0.07
	1990	0.04	0.14	0.02	0.03	0.02	0.01	0.03
Portugal	1974	0.11	0.13	0.05	0.06	0.13	0.04	0.12
	1990	0.16	0.12	0.01	0.05	0.07	0.05	0.04
Sweden	1974	0.08	0.18	0.05	0.06	0.13	0.08	0.06
	1990	0.03	0.12	0.02	0.03	0.06	0.05	0.04
U.K	1974	0.10	0.18	0.04	0.05	0.10	0.03	0.07
	1990	0.18	0.12	0.02	0.04	0.06	0.03	0.03

Source Data are from Feenstra et al. (2001)

with the traditional wisdom: trade liberalization over time is an irreversible trend, in a large part owing to the efforts of various rounds of General Agreement on Tariffs and Trade/World Trade Organization (GATT/WTO) negotiations.

To have a rough idea on how a change in import tariff affects an industrial output share relative to GDP, in Fig. 3.1 we plot the industrial output share against tariffs for the seven main industries. Interestingly enough, all of these seven industries demonstrate a trend that high tariffs are associated with low industrial output shares. Though a simple uni-variable ordinary least squares (OLS) estimate is insufficient to

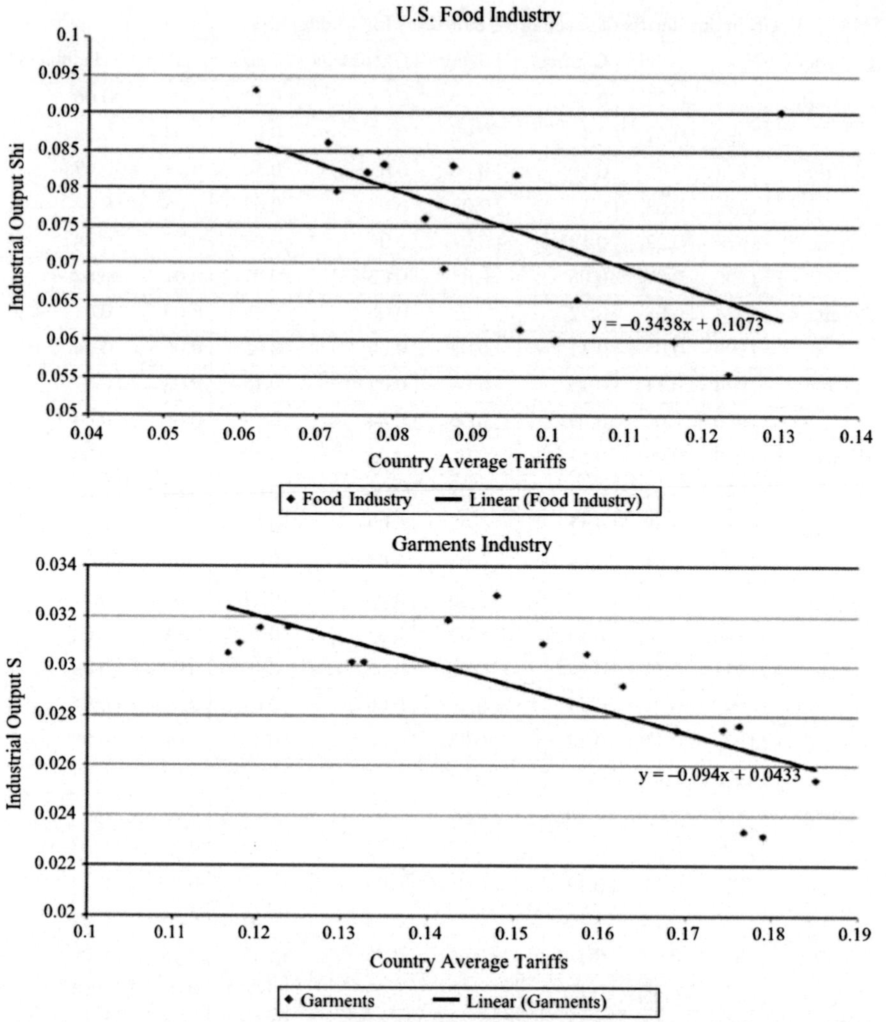

Fig. 3.1 Import tariffs and industrial output shares for the seven industries. *Notes* Graphs for the seven industries are plotted using data mentioned in the text. All of them demonstrate a negative relationship between tariffs and industrial output share

fully capture the complicated impact of trade protection, it still conveys a message that a high import tariff is not necessarily associated with high output share though it indeed increases both the industrial price and quantities produced at home.

Aside from tariffs, various NTBs nowadays play a more important role on trade policy. The Uruguay round of GATT/WTO completed in 1994, in which advanced countries are required to cut down on their tariffs by almost 40%, led to a switch of protection instruments from tariffs to NTBs. We therefore include NTBs as an

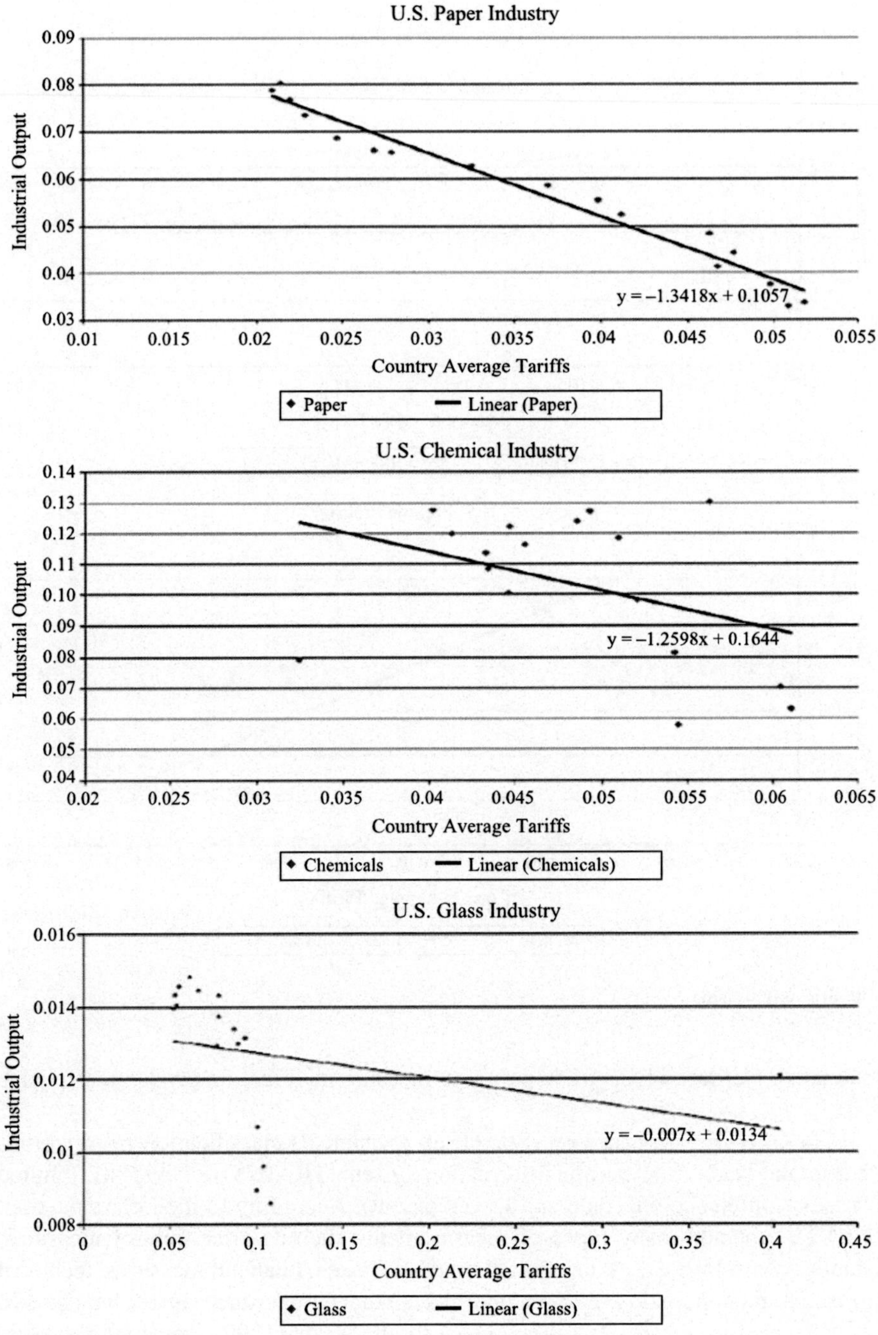

Fig. 3.1 (continued)

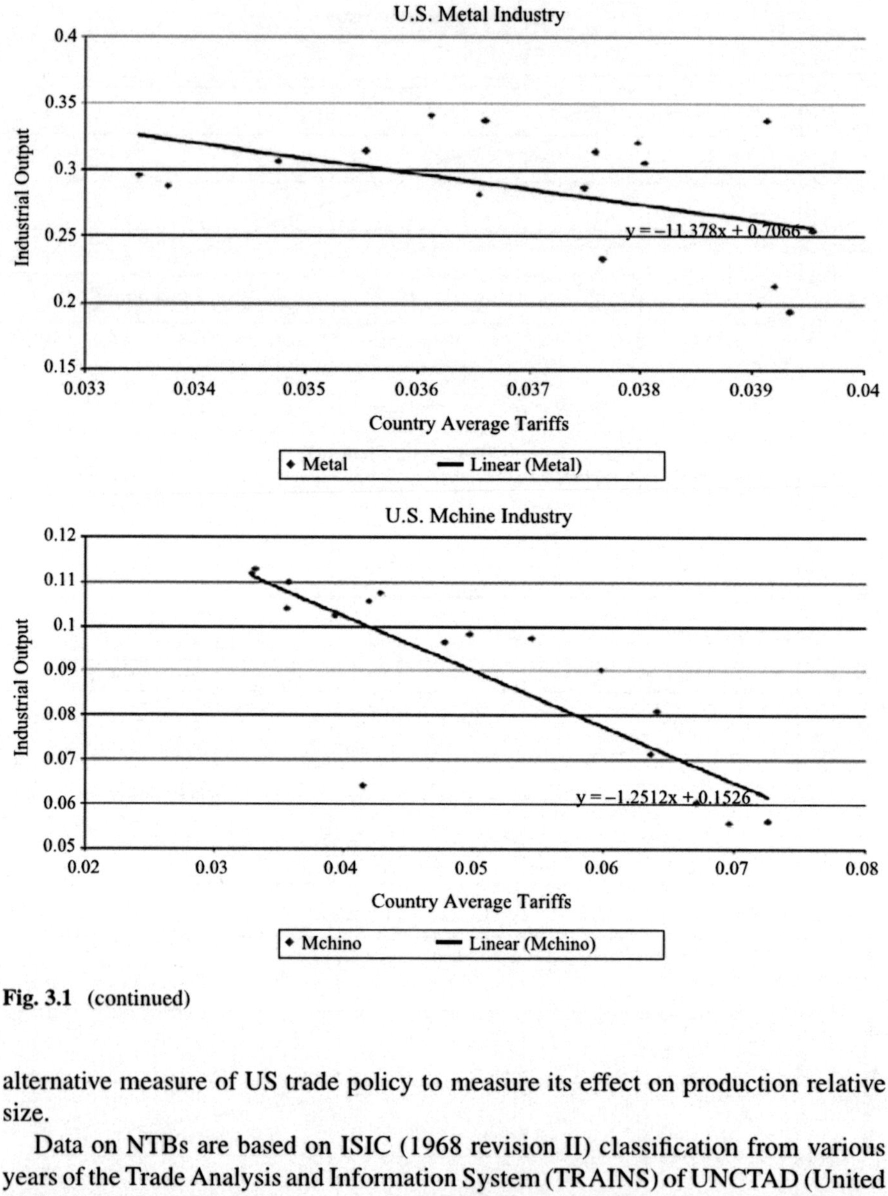

Fig. 3.1 (continued)

alternative measure of US trade policy to measure its effect on production relative size.

Data on NTBs are based on ISIC (1968 revision II) classification from various years of the Trade Analysis and Information System (TRAINS) of UNCTAD (United Nations Conference on Trade and Development). According to their classification, the NTBs include many types of measurements such as price control measures, quantity control measures, customs charges and taxes, financial measures, technical measures, monopolistic measures and miscellaneous measures. Here, we use two ways to measure the NTBs following Laird and Yeats (1990): coverage ratio and frequency ratio. Specifically, the coverage ratio for industry is defined as $\sum_i w_i^l I_i^l$, where w_i^l is the import share of product i relative to total imports in industry l, and I_i^l is the indicator variable that equals one when the product is covered by some measures of NTBs. In contrast, the frequency ratio for industry l is defined as $\sum_i I_i^l / N^l$, where N^l is the total number of commodities in industry l, and I_i^l is the indicator variable that equals one when the product is covered by some measures of NTBs.

Table 3.4 provides the basic statistics about NTB measurements for 14 countries after year 1990 (specifically, the years are 1993, 1994, 1996 and 1999). Of all the seven manufacturing industries, the non-tariff protection in the glass industry is minimal. By contrast, the food industry has the highest level of non-tariff protection regardless of measurement methods. This suggests that US food industry producers have sought protection from tariffs by using NTBs recently. Such an observation fits with reality quite well. For example, an import quota imposed on the US sugar industry was approximately 1.4 million tons in 2002. Accordingly, the domestic price of sugar was more than twice the price in the world sugar market.[6]

Data on factor endowment after year 1990 are the same as Harrigan (1997). We consider three primary factor endowments: capital, labor and agricultural land. Specifically, capital is split into two types of sub-categories: non-residential construction and production durables. We also separate three different labor endowments: (1) highly educated workers (i.e. those who have attained at least a college education); (2) medium-educated workers (i.e. those who have completed or at least attained secondary education), and (3) low-educated workers (those who have not attained any secondary schooling). Finally, agricultural land is measured by the product of arable land and land share.

Estimates

We have seven equations in the system for estimating. In each equation, the dependent variable is US industrial output share, whereas the independent variables include exporting partner's corresponding industrial output share, seven industrial *ad-valorem* tariffs, six types of factor endowments and a time trend that captures the technological improvement. All variables except for time trend are in logarithms, which in turn implies that those estimated coefficients can be interpreted as semi-elasticities.

We perform the iterated seemingly unrelated regression (SUR) of Zellner (1962) with two restrictions. First, the cross-price effect on the output share should be the same between two sectors i and j, $\gamma_{ij} = \gamma_{ji}$, owing to the symmetry setup. Second, all coefficients on the factor endowments should equal zero, $\sum_{k=1}^{M} \phi_{ik} = 0$. Table 3.5 reports the main estimation results using tariff data before 1990. We also include country fixed effects and year-specific fixed effects which are not reported in order to save space, though these are available from the authors upon request.

The tariff semi-elasticities of each industry differ greatly. Of all the seven coefficients, the own tariff semi-elasticities for garments, chemicals and machinery are positive, whereas those for food, paper, glass and metals are negative. The machinery

[6] *Source* U.S. International Trade Commission, *The Economic Effects of Significant U.S. Import Restraints*, Washington, DC (2004).

Table 3.4 US Non-tariff-barriers of seven main industries for 17 countries

Exporter	Type	Food	Garments	Chemicals	Metals	Machinery
Australia	NTM_F	0.52	0.10	0.04	0.11	0.08
	NTM_C	0.65	0.12	0.07	0.04	0.07
Austria	NTM_F	0.52	0.10	0.05	0.10	0.08
	NTM_C	0.45	0.12	0.11	0.10	0.07
Belgium	NTM_F	0.41	0.14	0.04	0.14	0.11
	NTM_C	0.37	0.16	0.09	0.12	0.16
Canada	NTM_F	0.44	0.10	0.05	0.13	0.09
	NTM_C	0.44	0.13	0.07	0.12	0.11
Denmark	NTM_F	0.44	0.11	0.04	0.10	0.08
	NTM_C	0.39	0.13	0.08	0.06	0.07
Finland	NTM_F	0.53	0.10	0.04	0.08	0.08
	NTM_C	0.63	0.08	0.09	0.08	0.10
France	NTM_F	0.44	0.10	0.05	0.13	0.09
	NTM_C	0.46	0.09	0.12	0.12	0.07
Ireland	NTM_F	0.44	0.10	0.04	0.10	0.08
	NTM_C	0.42	0.12	0.09	0.04	0.05
Italy	NTM_F	0.44	0.10	0.06	0.12	0.09
	NTM_C	0.31	0.12	0.13	0.14	0.12
Japan	NTM_F	0.44	0.15	0.08	0.14	0.10
	NTM_C	0.48	0.11	0.07	0.14	0.17
Mexico	NTM_F	0.44	0.11	0.05	0.13	0.08
	NTM_C	0.48	0.12	0.07	0.13	0.11
Netherlands	NTM_F	0.44	0.11	0.04	0.14	0.08
	NTM_C	0.42	0.09	0.08	0.18	0.08
New Zealand	NTM_F	0.45	0.10	0.04	0.08	0.08
	NTM_C	0.58	0.13	0.06	0.10	0.10
Norway	NTM_F	0.44	0.10	0.04	0.08	0.08
	NTM_C	0.32	0.11	0.06	0.00	0.07
Portugal	NTM_F	0.44	0.10	0.04	0.12	0.08
	NTM_C	0.38	0.14	0.06	0.15	0.05
Sweden	NTM_F	0.44	0.10	0.05	0.10	0.09
	NTM_C	0.35	0.08	0.18	0.13	0.10
U.K	NTM_F	0.44	0.10	0.05	0.14	0.09
	NTM_C	0.55	0.10	0.13	0.15	0.08

Source Original Data of NTBs can be accessed from UNCTAD. The data used here cover the years 1993, 1994, 1996 and 1999. NTM_F means non-tariffs frequency ratio measurement (all). NTM_C means non- tariff coverage ratio measurement (all). The difference between these two approaches is introduced in the text in detail. Data on the paper and glass industries are unavailable

Table 3.5 Estimate of the GDP Share Function Using Tariffs Data before 1990

	Food	Garments	Paper	Chemicals	Glass	Metals	Machinery
Tariffs_Food	*−0.02*	−0.01*	−0.02*	−0.00	−0.00	−0.01	−0.04**
	(−1.01)	(−1.83)	(−1.87)	(−0.6)	(−0.5)	−0.4)	(−4.08)
Tariffs_Garment	−0.01*	*0.00*	0.02**	−0.00	−0.01**	−0.01**	0.01
	(−1.83)	*(0.36)*	(3.01)	(−0.45)	(−3.52)	(−4.14)	(0.71)
Tariffs_Paper	−0.02*	0.02**	*−0.00*	−0.00	0.00	−0.00	−0.04**
	(−1.87)	(3.01)	*(−0.45)*	(−0.16)	(1.45)	(−0.18)	(−4.26)
Tariffs_Chemical	−0.00	−0.00	−0.00	*0.02**	0.01**	−0.01	−0.03*
	(−0.6)	(−0.45)	(−0.16)	*(1.77)*	(3.67)	(−0.42)	(−3.13)
Tariffs_Glass	−0.00	−0.01**	0.00	0.01**	*−0.00***	−0.00	−0.01**
	(−0.5)	(−3.52)	(1.45)	(3.67)	*(−2.98)*	(−1.00)	(−3.55)
Tariffs_Metal	−0.01	−0.01**	−0.00	−0.01	−0.00	*−0.03*	−0.05*
	(−0.4)	(−4.14)	(−0.18)	(−0.42)	(−1.00)	*(−0.72)*	(−2.83)
Tariffs_Machinery	−0.04**	0.01	−0.04**	−0.03**	−0.01**	−0.05**	*0.06***
	(−4.08)	(0.71)	(−4.26)	(−3.13)	(−3.55)	(−2.83)	*(3.20)*
Nonresident_Construction	−0.08	−0.01	−0.06	−0.05	−0.02**	−0.09	−0.02
	(−1.35)	(−1.22)	(−1.18)	(−1.5)	(−1.96)	(−0.65)	(−0.36)
Production_Durables	0.02	−0.00	0.05	0.04	0.01	0.09	−0.02
	(0.25)	(−0.24)	(1.01)	(1.26)	(1.15)	(0.62)	(−0.38)
Low_Edu_Workers	0.02	0.01**	−0.01	0.01	0.00	−0.06	−0.01
	(0.62)	(2.10)	(−0.27)	(0.41)	(0.57)	(−0.94)	(−0.44)
Mid_Edu_Workers	−0.20**	−0.02*	−0.15**	−0.12**	−0.02**	−0.34**	−0.13**

(continued)

Table 3.5 (continued)

	Food	Garments	Paper	Chemicals	Glass	Metals	Machinery
	(−3.63)	(−1.84)	(−3.22)	(−3.77)	(−2.98)	(−2.75)	(−3.08)
High_Edu_Workers	0.37**	0.03**	0.27**	0.20**	0.05**	0.70**	0.26**
	(8.03)	(4.50)	(7.27)	(7.70)	(7.15)	(6.78)	(7.29)
Arable land	−0.13**	−0.01**	−0.12**	−0.08**	−0.02**	−0.31**	−0.09**
	(−5.98)	(−3.58)	(−6.80)	(−7.07)	(−6.61)	(−6.43)	(−5.23)
Time trend	−0.02	0.00	−0.01	−0.00	−0.00	−0.04	−0.03**
	(−1.42)	(0.22)	(−1.51)	(−0.55)	(−1.23)	(−1.44)	(−2.66)
Country fixed effects	Yes	Yes	Yes	Yes	Yes	Yes	Yes
Year fixed effects	Yes	Yes	Yes	Yes	Yes	Yes	Yes
R^2	0.43	0.28	0.37	0.42	0.42	0.35	0.35

Notes Estimation results for seven industries are reported in columns. The dependent variable is the percentage output share of the industry. Independent variables are in logarithms except for the term of time trend. Numbers in italic form denote own semi-elasticity. Numbers in parenthesis are t-values. *,**Denote significance at 5% and 1% levels, respectively. Year and country fixed effects are not reported here to save space. There are 238 observations for these restricted seemingly unrelated estimations (SUR) sector has the largest positive effect, followed by the chemicals', garments', paper, glass, food and metals' sectors.

The most interesting findings come from the chemicals, glass and machinery sectors. In particular, the own tariff coefficients of semi-elasticity are significantly positive for the chemical and machinery industries. A positive coefficient means that an increase in US import tariff causes its industry to expand relatively compared with its trading partners. An increase in the import tariff benefits the producers in that industry which, in turn, increases production and thus causes the industry to expand.

An opposite situation happens for the glass industry in which the tariff has a significant negative effect on its output share.

Turning to the cross effects of a tariff on industrial output shares, their signs are a mix of positive and negative. When a cross effect of a tariff has an identical sign with its own effect, the two industries are broadly complemented. By contrast, a different sign between own effect and cross effect of a tariff suggests that the two industries are broadly substitutable. For example, as shown in Table 3.5, a tariff on the glass industry significantly leads to a decline in the glass industry itself, a contraction in the garment industry and an expansion of the chemical industry. This means that the glass sector is broadly a complement of the garment sector but is broadly a substitute for the chemical industry.

Capital endowments are broken into two categories in Table 3.5: production durables and non-residential construction. The production durable is positively related to output share for all manufacturing sectors except the garment and machinery industries. By contrast, non-residential construction is negatively related to output share for all industries. However, the coefficients for production durables are insignificant in all industries and its signs vary across industries. Similarly, the coefficients of non-resident construction are negatively significant only in the glass industry. Both of these suggest that factor endowment does not play an important role on industrial output share for the US economy during the sample period once we control for trade protection.

In addition, highly educated workers are positively associated with the size of the manufacturing sectors, while the medium-educated workers have a reverse connection. This is possible because manufacturing sectors relatively require highly skilled level workers compared with the agricultural sector. The coefficients for low-education workers are mixed. Only the garment industry has a positive significant number (0.09). This is consistent with the fact that the textile industry is relatively a downstream industry and requires less skill. For land endowment, arable land is negatively related to the output share for all manufacturing industries. This also makes good economic sense. An increase in land endowment will shrink the manufacturing sectors unambiguously, according to the prediction of the Rybczynski theorem. Finally, the coefficients of the time trend for all manufacturing industries are all negative, though some are insignificant.

Non-tariff Barriers

To completely explore effects of trade policy on industrial output shares, we also use a data set with non-tariff measurement to serve as robustness checks. The estimation results using this data set are reported in Tables 3.6 and 3.7.

Table 3.6 presents the estimation results for five industries (i.e. food, garments, chemicals, metals and machinery) using the data of non-tariff barriers. The data on the paper industry are completely unavailable, while much of the data on the glass industry are missing. Hence, these two industries are dropped for our estimation. We first use the coverage ratio to measure NTBs, since it has an advantage of considering the weights of each commodity covered by non-tariff protection (Trefler 1993). The own effects of NTBs on their output share vary, as shown by: metals (0.06), food (0.02), chemicals (0.02), machinery (0.01) and garments (0.01). It turns out that the effects of NTBs on output share are all positive. However, only the chemical industry has a significant sign.

Table 3.6 Estimate of the GDP share function using NTBs (coverage) data

	Food	Garments	Chemicals	Metals	Machinery
NTB_Food	*0.02 (0.25)*	−0.02 (−1.36)	0.06 (3.05)	0.07* (1.95)	0.02 (0.92)
NTB_Garment	−0.024 (−1.36)	*0.01 (0.69)*	−0.01 (−1.13)	0.01 (0.8)	−0.00 (−0.1)
NTB_Chemical	0.06** (3.05)	−0.01 (−1.13)	*0.02*** (2.08)*	0.03 (1.28)	0.01 (0.71)
NTB_Metal	0.07* (1.95)	0.01 (0.8)	0.03 (1.28)	*0.06 (0.53)*	0.01 (0.26)
NTB_Machinery	0.02 (0.92)	−0.00 (−0.1)	0.01 (0.71)	0.01 (0.26)	*0.01 (0.34)*
Fixed capital	−0.37** (−5.4)	−0.14** (−6.25)	−0.20** (−4.39)	−0.72** (−3.17)	−0.25** (−2.78)
Labor force	0.42** (4.55)	0.16** (5.41)	0.22** (3.65)	0.77** (2.59)	0.27** (2.31)
Arable land	−0.05 (−1.16)	−0.02** (−1.71)	−0.02 (−0.82)	−0.06 (−0.47)	−0.03 (−0.52)
Time trend	0.03 (0.25)	0.02 (0.64)	−0.01 (−0.2)	−0.16 (−0.49)	−0.05 (−0.37)
Country fixed effects	Yes	Yes	Yes	Yes	Yes
Year fixed effects	Yes	Yes	Yes	Yes	Yes
R^2	0.58	0.53	0.48	0.30	0.25

Notes Non-tariff barriers (NTBs) are measured by its coverage ratios. The glass and paper industries are dropped owing to the lack of data. Estimation results for five industries are reported in columns, with t-statistics in italics. The dependent variable is the percentage output share of the industry. Independent variables are in logarithms. Numbers in italic form denote own semi-elasticity. Numbers in parenthesis are t-values. *,**Denote significance at 5% and 1% levels, respectively. Year and country fixed effects are not reported here to save space. There are 39 observations in each equation

Table 3.7 Estimate of the GDP share function using NTBs (frequency) data

	Food	Garments	Chemicals	Metals	Machinery
NTB_Food	– *0.04* (*–0.18*)	−0.05 (−1.01)	0.01 (0.23)	0.07 (1.00)	0.01 (0.09)
NTB_Garment	−0.05 (−1.01)	– *0.04*** (−2.27)	−0.00 (−0.27)	0.01 (0.30)	0.01 (0.85)
NTB_Chemical	0.01 (0.23)	−0.00 (−0.27)	*0.05*** (*1.91*)	0.03 (0.78)	0.01 (0.22)
NTB_Metal	0.07 (1.00)	0.01 (0.30)	0.03 (0.78)	*0.17* (*0.84*)	0.08 (1.02)
NTB_Machinery	0.01 (0.09)	0.01 (0.85)	0.01 (0.22)	0.08 (1.02)	*0.03* (*0.75*)
Fixed capital	−0.36** (−4.96)	−0.14** (−7.03)	−0.18** (−3.79)	−0.66** (−2.89)	−0.23** (−2.56)
Labor force	0.38** (4.23)	0.15** (6.17)	0.20** (3.30)	0.70** (2.45)	0.26** (2.29)
Arable land	−0.02 (−0.50)	−0.01 (−0.87)	−0.02 (−0.64)	−0.04 (−0.35)	−0.03 (−0.60)
Time trend	0.05 (0.50)	0.03 (1.22)	0.00 (0.02)	−0.14 (−0.44)	−0.05 (−0.42)
Country fixed effects	Yes	Yes	Yes	Yes	Yes
Year fixed effects	Yes	Yes	Yes	Yes	Yes
R^2	0.44	0.59	0.34	0.26	0.23

Notes Non-tariff-barriers (NTBs) are measured by frequency ratios. The glass and paper industries are dropped owing to the lack of data. Estimation results for five industries are reported in columns, with *t*-statistics in italics. The dependent variable is the percentage output share of the industry. Independent variables are in logarithms. Numbers in italic form denote own semi-elasticity. Numbers in parenthesis are *t*-values. *,** Denote significance at 5% and 1% levels, respectively. Year and country fixed effects are not reported here to save space. There are 39 observations in each equation

We then measure the impact of NTBs using the frequency ratio in Table 3.7. Trade protection in the chemical industry again has a positive impact on its output share. In contrast, a significantly negative effect occurs in the garment industry when NTBs are measured by the frequency ratio.

To summarize, estimation results from Tables 3.5, 3.6 and 3.7 demonstrate that trade protection in the chemical industry is significantly positively associated with output share regardless of the protection measurement. Tariffs in the machinery industry have a significant positive effect on output share. By contrast, tariffs in the glass industry are shown to have a negative impact on their output share.

Note that we have already examined the impact on industrial output share of tariffs and non-tariff barriers respectively. For the sake of completeness, it is better to include the two types of trade protection simultaneously in the regressions. As a result of data restrictions, we are not able to conduct such an exercise. In this sense, it is worthwhile to be aware that each separate regression above may suffer from some estimation bias owing to omitted variables.

Political Economy Issues

Previous analysis clearly established a channel that the industrial output share is affected by its trade protection by using a translog GDP system. However, it is reasonable to believe that each industry could inversely seek protection by lobbying the government. Therefore, trade policy is influenced by demands from special interest groups such as unions. Previous studies like Brainard and Verdier (1997) had *theoretically* shown that high protection industries can have declining output shares over time, by considering the cost of lobbying. Similarly, Broda et al. (2006) are also aware that commercial policy could be influenced by domestic political interest groups. In short, to fully explore the impact of trade protection on industrial production size, we need to control the endogeneity problem in our estimations raised by the possibility of reverse causality.

Another potential source of the endogeneity problem is caused by omitted variables. For instance, we ignore the international institutional organization constraint in our previous estimations, in large part, owing to the own limitation of the translog GDP approach. However, it may matter in the US NTB-setting process whether trading partners are members of GATT/WTO or in a preferential trade agreement (PTA) with the USA (see, e.g. Furusawa and Jinji 2007; Zhao and Kondoh 2007). Moreover, the exclusiveness of international organization is partly because of the data unavailability. For example, although it is ideal to consider a trading partner's bar-gaining power (such as retaliatory and bilateral aid) that makes the country more likely suffer from the NTBs imposed by the USA, a scientific index to measure a country's bargaining power, to the best of our knowledge, is unfortunately unavailable.

It is well recognized that the IV approach is a powerful approach to control the endogeneity problem (Wooldridge 2002). However, the challenge of using such an approach is to choose good instruments which, ideally, are exogenous to the instrumented variable and affect the regressand through and only through the instrumented variable. Here, we adopt the percentage of industrial union members and the percentage of unions represented in each industry as instruments for the setting of NTBs for the following reasons.[7]

First, much empirical literature on political economy has recognized that greater industrial labor unions are associated with higher commercial protection. For example, Trefler (1993) provided evidence that various labor characteristics such as labor unions and employment size are positively associated with the NTBs for the USA. However, few works, if any, recognize a *direct* link between the strength of labor union for an industry and its output share, without considering the channel of trade protection. The pre-estimation partial correlations on our data sample also strengthen this idea. For example, for the garment industry, its percentage of industrial union members, one of indexes of labor union strength, is strongly correlated

[7] In addition to the percentage of industrial union members, an alternative index is the percentage of unions represented, which refers to members of a labor union who report no union affiliation but whose jobs are covered by a union or an employee association contract.

with its NTBs (|corr.| = 0.73) but relatively weakly associated with its output share (|corr.| = 0.08).

Second, we concentrate on the endogenous setting of NTB, but not the tariff-setting caused by data unavailability. As shown in Table 3.4, our data samples for estimation of industrial tariffs are the years 1974–1990. The corresponding industrial labor union data are, unfortunately, currently unavailable at the SIC two-digit level.[8] However, we instead consider the role of political economy for the setting of NTBs since union affiliation data for the intermediate industries are available after year 1994. It is reasonable to believe that such a consideration can still capture the US economy well since NTBs played a significant role after the Uruguay round of GATT/WTO in year 1994.

Table 3.8 reports the estimates for the impact of NTBs on output share for each industry by using the two instruments mentioned above. After controlling for the endogeneity, trade protection in garment industry has a significant negative effect on its output share, which is consistent with the findings in Table 3.7. Turning to the chemical industry, the impact of NTBs on output share is insignificant. This implies that the positive coefficients for the chemical industry shown in Tables 3.5, 3.6 and 3.7 are merely correlations but not necessarily causality. In addition, effects of the NTBs for the rest of the industries (i.e. food, metals and machinery) are all insignificant.

We now turn to check the validity of the two instruments used for controlling endogeneity. Technically, various statistical tests suggest that both indexes of the labor union strengths are valid instruments. First, the first-stage F-test for the two instruments are highly significant at the 1% level. Second, to check whether or not instruments are correlated with the endogenous trade platform, Anderson's (1984) canonical correlation likelihood-ratio test is used to verify whether or not our specification is under-identified. The rejections at the 1% level for each specification again show that our specifications are well identified. Third, we take a step forward to see whether or not such instruments are merely weakly correlated with the endogenous trade platform. If so, then the estimates will perform poorly in such estimations. However, the Cragg and Donald's (1993) F-statistic provides strong evidence for rejecting the null hypothesis that the first stage is weakly identified at a highly significant level. Fourth, we include Sargen's over-identification statistic. A rejection at the conventional statistical level would cast doubt on the validity of instruments. As shown in Table 3.8, this test is not rejected at the 10% level for each industry.

Finally, we also provide extra easy-to-interpret evidence for the validity of our instruments. We add the two instruments as exogenous regressors. If the industrial labor union strength has a *direct* effect on its output share, then we would expect the estimated coefficient to be statistically significant. However, as seen in Table 3.9, the coefficients of labor union strength, regardless of its measurements, are statistically

[8] The Bureau of Labor Statistics does have union affiliation data for years 1983–2006 by industry at highly aggregated level. However, data by intermediate industry at SIC 2-digit level are available only for years 1994–2006.

Table 3.8 IV estimates for the garment industry

	Food	Garments	Chemicals	Metals	Machinery
NTB_Food	*0.05 (0.14)*	0.06 (1.22)	0.40* (1.83)	1.29** (2.45)	0.40* (1.83)
NTB_Garment	−0.03 (−1.55)	*−0.02* (−1.89)*	−0.02 (−0.59)	−0.08 (−1.16)	−0.02 (−0.59)
NTB_Chemical	0.14** (1.97)	0.06** (2.58)	*−0.01 (−0.12)*	−0.01 (−0.06)	−0.01 (−0.12)
NTB_Metal	0.00 (0.14)	−0.00 (−0.22)	0.01 (0.65)	*−0.09 (−0.78)*	−0.05 (−0.87)
NTB_Machinery	−0.01 (−0.49)	−0.00 (−0.24)	−0.01 (−0.45)	−0.00 (−0.00)	*0.01 (0.19)*
Fixed capital	−0.35** (−5.01)	−0.12** (−6.00)	−0.19** (−4.01)	−0.63** (−2.95)	−0.26** (−2.88)
Labor force	0.36** (3.87)	0.14** (5.33)	0.18** (3.00)	0.54* (1.92)	0.24** (2.00)
Arable land	−0.03 (−0.67)	−0.01 (−0.94)	0.00 (0.06)	0.07 (0.55)	−0.01 (−0.23)
Time trend	0.09 (1.50)	0.03** (1.96)	−0.01 (−0.19)	−0.06 (−0.35)	0.01 (0.16)
First stage *F*-statistics	4.44[a]	11.59[a]	2.89[a]	16.58[a]	4.49[a]
Anderson (1984) likelihood-ratio statistic	10.57[a]	22.95[a]	7.24[a]	29.60[a]	10.75[a]
Cragg and Donald (1993) test statistic	4.44[a]	32.10[a]	8.02[a]	45.91[a]	12.58[a]
Anderson–Rubin χ^2 statistic	1.41	5.38[a]	0.93	1.22	2.25
Sargan over-identification *P*-value	0.24	0.28	0.64	0.46	0.26
Shea partial R^2	0.25	0.47	0.18	0.56	0.26
R^2	0.60	0.60	0.47	0.43	0.37

Notes Numbers in parenthesis are t-values. *, ** Denote significance at 5% and 1% levels, respectively [a]Indicates p-value of the statistic is less than 0.01. Year and country fixed effects are not reported here to save space. We use percentage of labor union members and percentage of labor union-represented as instruments here. Various statistical tests are used to check their validity

insignificant in all specifications. These again confirm that these two indexes affect output share through and only through the channel of commercial protection.

Table 3.9 Further checks for the validity of instruments

	Food	Garments	Chemicals	Metals	Machinery
NTB_Food	0.36* (1.76)	0.05 (1.09)	0.34** (2.40)	1.70** (2.27)	0.55** (2.26)
NTB_Garment	−0.02 (−0.54)	−0.00 (−0.35)	−0.00 (−0.18)	0.01 (0.14)	−0.02 (−0.37)
Labor union members ratio	−0.47 (−0.77)	0.23 (1.07)	0.01 (0.03)	0.85 (0.74)	−0.81 (−0.38)
Labor union represented ratio	0.47 (0.81)	−0.20 (−1.00)	0.01 (0.09)	−0.75 (−0.70)	0.80 (0.41)
NTB_Chemical	0.17 (1.28)	0.06 (1.28)	0.02 (0.29)	0.02 (0.04)	0.05 (0.24)
NTB_Metal	0.03 (0.90)	0.01 (1.14)	0.01 (0.58)	−0.02 (−0.18)	0.03 (0.66)
NTB_Machinery	0.01 (0.44)	0.00 (0.57)	0.00 (0.00)	−0.07 (−0.98)	0.01 (0.26)
Fixed capital	−0.36** (−2.77)	−0.13** (−2.78)	−0.19** (−2.36)	−0.69* (−1.82)	−0.27* (−1.86)
Labor force	0.38** (2.12)	0.16** (2.51)	0.19* (1.71)	0.61 (1.13)	0.25 (1.38)
Arable land	−0.03 (−0.59)	−0.01 (−1.09)	−0.00 (−0.11)	0.00 (0.01)	−0.02 (−0.42)
Time trend	0.07 (0.60)	0.03 (1.52)	0.01 (0.07)	−0.32 (−0.80)	−0.10 (−1.01)
R^2	0.65	0.68	0.54	0.47	0.45

Notes Numbers in parenthesis are t-values. *,** Denote significance at 5% and 1% levels, respectively

3.4 Concluding Remarks

Trade theory has an ambiguous prediction on how import protection affects industrial production relative size. Based on a model of translog GDP system, in the present paper we are able to fully explore the effects of import protection on the output share for the main manufacturing industries in the USA. After controlling for the endogeneity and various relevant factors, our estimates suggest that trade protection does not seem to help increase the relative size of production for most industries. The impact of trade protection for some industries such as garments may lead to a declining industrial output share once trade protection is particularly measured by non-tariffs barriers.

This paper enriches the literature by introducing trade protection into the traditional neoclassical trade model *à la* a GDP translog system. Previous work assumes a basic free-trade framework to examine the effect of various factor endowments and technology on industrial output share. We instead extend the model by considering a non-free-trade world. Aside from trade policy, effects of other factors such as factor endowments and technology improvement broadly fit well with many previous works such as those of Kohli (1991) and Harrigan (1997).

Several extensions and possible generalizations merit special consideration. One of them is to update data coverage across countries and over time. Owing to data restrictions, this paper only covers the USA and its main OECD trading partners before 2000. Given that international trade has increased dramatically since 2000 and developing countries like China and India are playing a more and more important role in US foreign trade, it would be a great plus to include developing countries by using data after 2000. Another possible extension is to include a full set of intermediate industries within the manufacturing industries. Such enrichment could enjoy more advantages attached to the translog GDP approach (Feenstra 2003). Finally, it would be a plus to integrate the nontradable sectors explicitly into the model. These are the topics which we will pursue in future work once the related data are accessible.

Part III
Export-Led and Firm Productivity

Chapter 4
China's Processing Trade: A Firm-Level Analysis

4.1 Introduction

The processing trade, which has become hugely popular in China, involves domestic firms obtaining raw materials or intermediate inputs from abroad, processing them locally and exporting the value-added goods. Governments usually offer tariff reduction or tariff exemption to encourage the development of processing trade. The current chapter aims to provide a comprehensive review of various trends, characteristics and productivity levels of processing trade as opposed to ordinary trade in China.

We begin with an overview of processing trade, focusing on its size and main types. Thereafter, we analyse why processing trade has developed rapidly in China in the past three decades. China's open-door policy, particularly the establishment of special export zones, has played a significant role in the rapid growth of processing trade. We use transaction- level trade data (2000–06) from China to investigate various factors affecting processing trade. These include origin and destination countries, leading import and export commodities, transport modes, firm ownership, leading ports and their trade volume, and top cities and provinces where producers and consumers are located.

Our transaction-level trade dataset includes firm-level information. Each trade transaction is attributable to a particular firm. We investigate the number of products (that is, scope) imported and exported by firms, as well as their number of trading destinations. More importantly, because firm productivity is key to understanding trade performance (Melitz 2003), we investigate the productivity growth of firms by matching transaction-level trade data with firm-level production data, and using the Olley and Pakes (1996) semi-parametric approach for estimating firm productivity. Furthermore, in carefully scrutinising processing trade in China, the present chapter contributes to the literature by providing a novel and orderly

---

This chapter is co-authored with Wei Tian and and Ligang Song and originally published in Rebalancing and Sustaining Growth in China, Australian National University E-press, 2012, pp. 111–148.

M. Yu, *China's Miracle in Foreign Trade*, Studies in Modern Chinese Economy,
https://doi.org/10.1007/978-981-16-6030-6_4

way of matching two powerful datasets—transaction-level trade data and firm-level production data—given the complexity involved and restrictions in data format.

We find that processing firms mostly come from Korea, Hong Kong of China and Japan. The electrical machinery and transport equipment industry has the largest volume of processing imports. The majority of processing imports are shipped to China by sea and air. Shanghai, Shenzhen and Nanjing are the three busiest customs ports for processing imports, whereas Shenzhen, Pudong and Suzhou are the districts or areas with the highest volume of processing imports. The industry with the highest per-unit value of commodities is the aircraft and spacecraft industry. The top-five countries in terms of quality of goods shipped to China for processing are all in Europe: Norway, France, Finland, Germany and the Netherlands. With regard to importer ownership, foreign-owned enterprises are the major importers of processing goods. Approximately 20% of all processing firms import a single variety, whereas approximately 50% import less than 10 varieties. The number of imported varieties has also declined over the years, suggesting heightened specialisation, greater domestic intermediate input, or both. Moreover, we find that processing firms are considered less productive than ordinary firms.

The rest of the chapter is organised as follows. Section two discusses the policy setting that supports processing trade in China. Section three explores various characteristics of China's processing trade. Section four offers careful scrutiny of correlated data from firm-level production and transaction-level trade, followed by a precise measure of the total factor productivity of firms using a semi-parametric approach. Section five concludes.

4.2 Policy Setting to Promote Processing Trade

China's foreign trade has grown rapidly in the past three decades, alongside overall economic activity. From a low level of openness (the ratio of exports and imports over GDP) in the early 1980s, China increased its openness ratio to about 70% by 2006; the country's exports accounted for 39% of its GDP at this point, whereas imports accounted for 31% of its gross domestic product. Although China's exports declined by 16% in 2009 due to the global financial crisis, it still surpassed Germany in that year to become the world's largest exporter of goods.

Today, China's foreign trade volume (that is, the sum of exports and imports) accounts for more than 10% of the global trade volume (Fig. 4.1).

Processing trade now constitutes a very large proportion—usually one-half—of China's total trade. This trade began in China in the late 1970s. In the early 1980s, processing imports accounted for only a small proportion of total imports; however, China's processing imports dramatically increased in the early 1990s, and began to surpass ordinary imports in 1994 (Table 4.2a). Processing trade peaked at 64% of total trade in 1997 and then consolidated at about 50% for a decade. Processing trade declined to about 37% during the most recent financial crisis (Fig. 4.2).

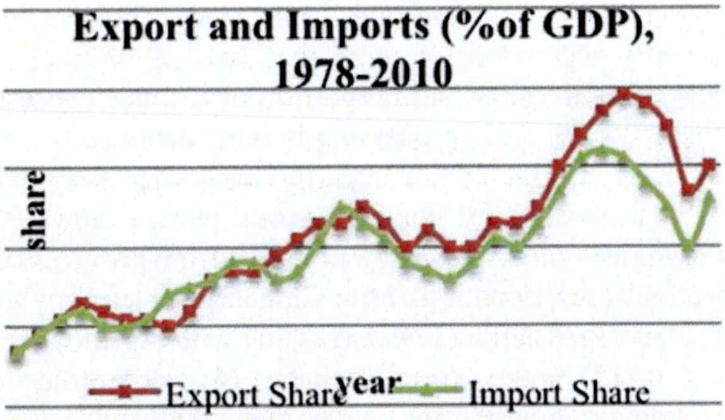

Fig. 4.1 China's exports and imports as a percentage of GDP, 1978–2010. *Source* NBS (2011a)

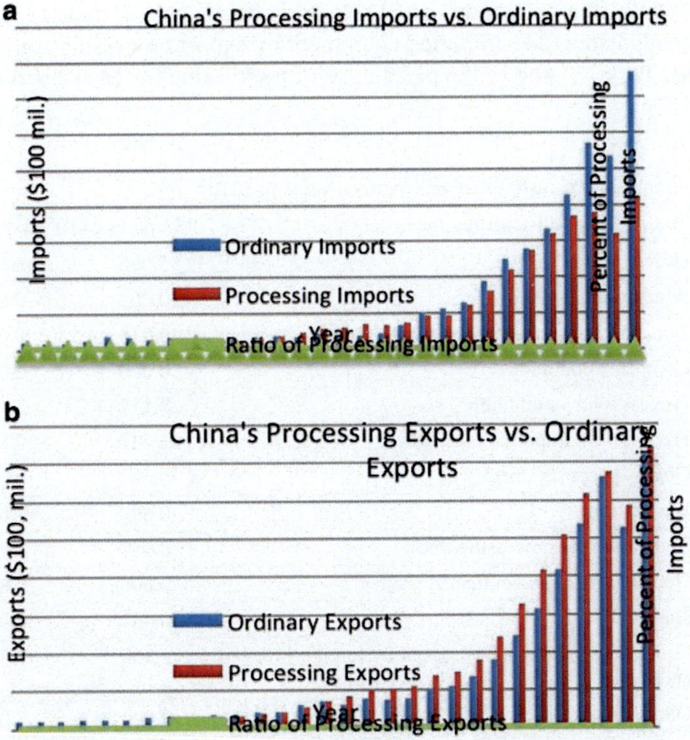

Fig. 4.2 **a** China's processing imports and ordinary imports, 1981–2010. *Source* NBS (2011a). **b** China's processing exports and ordinary exports, 1981–2010. *Source* NBS (2011a)

China's processing exports exhibit a similar evolution. After local assembly and processing, China exports the final value-added goods to the rest of the world. China's processing exports surpassed ordinary exports in 1998, a year after processing imports peaked in volume (Table 4.2b). This suggests that processing and assembly usually take a considerable amount of time in China—on this evidence, more than one year but less than two. In the new century, China's processing exports have steadily accounted for more than half of its total exports. Even with the financial crisis in 2008, the proportion of China's processing exports remained higher than 50%, whereas processing imports declined to about 35%, indicating a gradual increase in value-adding activities associated with processing trade.

Classification by China's customs bureau shows 19 types of trade regimes: ordinary trade (code: 10), aid or donation from government or from international organisations (11), donations from Chinese overseas or Chinese with foreign citizenship (12), compensation (13), processing with assembly (14), processing using imported inputs (15), goods on consignment (16), border trade (19), contracting projects (20), equipment imported for processing and assembly (22), goods on lease (23), equipment investment by foreign-invested enterprises (25), outward processing (27), barter trade (30), duty-free commodities (31), customs warehousing trade (33), entrepot trade by bonded area (34), imported equipment by export processing zone (35), and others (39). Table 4.1 shows the percentage of trade value for each customs regime in 2010.

Table 4.1 Proportion of customs regime by trade value in 2010

Codes	Trade type by customs regime	Imports (%)	Exports (%)
10	Ordinary trade	55.096	45.673
11	International aid	0.002	0.019
12	Donation by overseas Chinese	0.013	0.000
13	Compensation trade	0.000	0.000
14	Process with assembling	7.117	7.118
15	Process with imported materials	22.783	39.802
16	Goods on consignment	0.000	0.000
19	Border trade	0.690	1.040
20	Equipment for processing trade	0.087	0.000
22	Goods for foreign-contracted project	0.000	0.800
23	Goods on lease	0.404	0.009
25	Equipment/materials investment by foreign-invested enterprise	1.168	0.000
27	Outward processing	0.009	0.012
30	Barter trade	0.000	0.000
31	Duty-free commodity	0.001	0.000
33	Warehousing trade	4.377	2.242
34	Entrepot trade by bonded area	7.826	2.313
35	Equipment imported into export processing zone	0.286	0.000
39	Other trade	0.141	0.972

Source NBS (2011b)

Table 4.2 Number of special economic areas in China, up to 2010

Type of special economic area	Number	Proportion of processing imports (%)
Special economic zones (SEZs)	8	3
Export processing zones (EPZs)	55	11.2
Economic and technological development zones (ETDZs)	33	12.8
High-technology industrial development zones (HTIDZs)	49	4
Bonded zones/export-oriented units (EOUs)	5	1

Sources Tian and Yu (forthcoming); and updated using China's customs data (2010)

Table 4.1 shows that processing imports accounted for approximately 45% of total imports, whereas processing exports accounted for approximately 55% of total exports in 2010. Processing imports are supposedly transformed into processing exports after local assembly and processing; however, some firms consider their imported intermediate inputs as 'processing imports' on arrival in the ports but sell their final value-added products in the domestic market.[1] Such behaviour reinforces the idea that the high share of processing exports is due to the addition of value involved in processing trade. Nevertheless, throughout this chapter, we rely on processing *imports* rather than on processing *exports* in measuring processing trade.

Besides ordinary trade, of the 18 other types of trade regime, processing with assembly and processing with intermediate inputs are the most important in China. As shown in Table 4.1, processing imports (exports) with assembly account for roughly 7.12% of China's total imports (exports). In contrast, processing imports with imported materials account for more than 22% of total imports and 39.8% of total exports. Processing with assembly was prevalent in the 1980s, and processing with imported inputs became popular after 1990.

There are two key differences between processing with assembly and processing with intermediate inputs. First, processing with assembly does not require firms to pay for the raw materials. Chinese firms, in fact, import embodied raw materials for free and then send the value-added products to the same firm in the country of origin. Chinese firms do not need to pay for intermediate costs but earn payment for their service (that is, assembly). In contrast, firms engaged in processing with imported materials are required to pay for the imported intermediate inputs. Firms import raw materials or intermediate inputs from abroad and then sell their valued-added products to the rest of the world. Here, the source and destination countries can be different.

Second, processing assembly is 100% duty free. Meanwhile, firms engaged in processing using imported inputs must pay import duties for these inputs first. After exporting their processed or final goods, they may obtain a full duty rebate, indicating that firms engaged in processing using imported inputs face more credit constraints

[1] Such imported intermediate inputs are not eligible for customs duty rebates.

than pure assembly operations because they need to have sufficient cash flow to cover import duties (Feenstra et al. 2011). Table 4.1 clearly shows that processing with imported inputs currently exceeds processing with assembly and other types of processing trade in terms of trade volume. It is worthwhile exploring the rapid growth in China's processing trade over the past three decades.

The prevalence of processing trade in China can be directly attributed to the establishment of various free-trade zones—such as special economic zones (SEZs), economic and technological development zones (ETDZs), high-technology industrial development zones (HTIDZs) and export- processing zones (EPZs)—which underwent three phases. In the first phase, shortly before SEZs were established, several cities were allowed to contract with Hong Kong-based firms for processing with assembly. Small-scale trade was initially established.

In the spring of 1980, four coastal cities in Guangdong and Fujian provinces—namely, Shenzhen, Zhuhai and Shantou in Guangdong and Xiamen in Fujian—were selected as SEZs, mainly for their strong social connections with South-East Asia. People in Shantou and Xiamen, for instance, have enjoyed a long trading tradition and history with the region. Foreign firms found this social network favourable for investment in Mainland China. In SEZs, imports are completely duty free. Foreign investors likewise enjoy additional benefits, such as reduced income taxes. The Chinese Government grants foreign-invested enterprises (FIEs) located in the zones tax exemption in the first two years and tax reduction in the subsequent three years. In addition, firms located in SEZs enjoy greater administrative flexibility and easier access to foreign markets. These policies have proven to be highly effective. Shenzhen, formerly a small and poor village, is now one of two regional financial centres in China, with its own stock exchange.

In 1984, China's government allowed 14 eastern coastal cities to become 'open cities' in the sense that they would have similar privileges as those enjoyed by the four special economic zones. This marked the second phase of trade liberalisation. Shortly thereafter, China established two more SEZs: Pudong SEZ and Hainan Island Special Economic Zone. Furthermore, China designated the Pearl River Delta and the Yangtze River Delta as economic development areas, and opened four northern ports to trade with Mongolia, Russia and North Korea in 1991.

The third phase of China's trade liberalisation occurred in early 1992. China extended its open-door policy from the eastern coast to central and western China. Industrial cities in central and western China established various economic development zones and high-tech development zones. There were at least eight SEZs, 55 EPZs, 33 ETDZs, 49 HTIDZs and five bonded zones or export-oriented units (EOUs) by the end of 2010. Total processing imports in these free-trade zones accounted for more than 22% of China's processing imports.

Perhaps the most direct and relevant policy in promoting processing trade is the establishment of EPZs beginning in the year 2000. Barely a year before China's accession to the World Trade Organisation (WTO), China built EPZs in several eastern coastal cities. Only processing firms were allowed in the zones and were granted various privileges, such as freedom from duties and minimal administrative restrictions. By 2010, China had established 55 export processing zones. Table 4.3

Table 4.3 Ranking of export processing zones by processing import in 2010

Ranking	Name	Percentage	Ranking	Name	Percentage
1	Kunshan, JS	2.6213	29	Jinan, SD	0.0165
2	Songjiang, SH	1.8914	30	Nantong, JS	0.0157
3	Yantai, SD	1.3422	31	Yubei, CQ	0.0146
4	Xuzhou, JS	1.0562	32	Nanchang, JX	0.0144
5	Chengdu, SC	1.0019	33	Jiading, SH	0.0128
6	Wuxi, JS	0.6701	34	Shenyang, LN	0.0113
7	Ningbo, ZJ	0.5542	35	Changshu, JS	0.0109
8	Minhang, SH	0.4190	36	Jiaxing, ZJ	0.0099
9	Xi'an, SX	0.2945	37	Fuzhou, FJ	0.0097
10	Shenzhen, GD	0.1725	38	Zhuhai, GD	0.0081
11	Hanzhou, ZJ	0.1618	39	Zhenjiang, JS	0.0073
12	Fengxian, SH	0.1127	40	Wuhan, HB	0.0065
13	Weihai, SD	0.0971	41	Guangzhou, GD	0.0064
14	Nanjing, JS	0.0834	42	Shijiazhuang, HB	0.0062
15	Changzhou, JS	0.0538	43	Hohhot, IM	0.0057
16	Dalian, JN	0.0531	44	Tanggu, TJ	0.0057
17	Shunli, BJ	0.0437	45	Cixi, ZJ	0.0054
18	Xiamen, FJ	0.0411	46	Binzhou, HN	0.0048
19	Yanzhou, JS	0.0395	47	Lianyungang, JS	0.0040
20	Qingpu, SH	0.0374	48	Kunming, YN	0.0034
21	Beihai, GD	0.0349	49	Hunchun, JL	0.0031
22	Qingdao, SD	0.0339	50	Quanzhou, FJ	0.0028
23	Haiyin, JS	0.0303	51	Weifang, SD	0.0022
24	Zhengzhou, HN	0.0285	52	Mianyan, SC	0.0021
25	Wujiang, JS	0.0227	53	Qinhuangdiao, HB	0.0011
26	Wuhu, AH	0.0198	54	Ganzhou, JX	0.0004
27	Pudong, SH	0.0187	55	Urumqi, XJ	0.0002
28	Jiujiang, JX	0.0169			

Source Authors' own compilation from China's customs data (2010)

ranks these EPZs and their proportion of imports over total country-wide processing imports. In 2010, all processing imports in the EPZs accounted for 11.5% of China's total processing trade. Jiangsu has the largest number of EPZs, with 12 of the 55 export processing zones. Kunshan EPZ in Jiangsu Province is the largest among all EPZs, contributing 2.62% of China's total processing imports.

Note the distribution of EPZs in China. Processing imports are concentrated in three areas: Suzhou in Jiangsu Province and Shanghai and Yantai in Shandong Province. The cities of Xuzhou in Jiangsu Province, Chengdu in Sichuan Province,

Table 4.4 Ranking of special economic zones by processing imports in 2010

Ranking	Name	Percentage	Ranking	Name	Percentage
1	Shenzhen, GD	1.7464	5	Shantou, GD	0.0777
2	Zhuhai, GD	0.6235	6	Yunfu, GD	0.0538
3	Xiamen, FJ	0.5908	7	Other, HN	0.0152
4	Haikou, HN	0.1334	8	Sanya, HN	0.0029

Source Authors' own compilation from China's customs data (2010)

Wuxi in Jiangsu Province and Ningbo in Zhejiang Province yield processing imports that make up more than 1% of country-wide processing imports. Most EPZs are located in eastern coastal cities, as expected. A notable and interesting finding is that all EPZs are located north of the Yangtze River. This suggests, to some degree, the Chinese Government's intention to promote processing trade in northern China.

Aside from EPZs, other free-trade zones have contributed to the surge of processing trade in China. Although China has only eight SEZs, processing imports in these zones make up more than 3% of the country's total processing trade, as illustrated in Table 4.4.

Total processing imports from bonded areas are relatively small. There were five bonded areas in China in 2010: Tanggu, Pudong, Ningbo, Qingdao and Zhanjiagang. Only the bonded area of Tanggu, located in Tianjin Province, yielded a relatively large share of processing imports (0.81%). Contributions from other bonded areas are relatively economically insignificant. By way of comparison, high-technology industrial development zones (HTIDZs) yield approximately 4% of China's total processing imports. As shown in Table 4.5, there are 49 HTIDZs in China today, the largest of which is Suzhou HTIDZ in Jiangsu Province, which accounts for 1.38% of China's total processing imports, as exhibited in Table 4.5.

Economic and technological development zones (ETDZs) are the leading zones for processing imports. As shown in Table 4.6, Suzhou ETDZ in Jiangsu Province accounts for 4.83% of China's total processing imports, which is significantly higher than that accounted for by the largest EPZ, Kunshan EPZ in Jiangsu. Combined processing imports from the 33 ETDZs (12.8%) are higher than those from the 55 EPZs (11.5%). One possible reason is that EPZs were established much later than ETDZs. This implies that the absorption of processing imports takes time to materialise. Jiangsu Province has outperformed other provinces in welcoming processing imports.

In brief, the rapid growth of China's processing trade is largely due to the establishment of various free-trade zones, such as SEZs, ETDZs, HTIDZs and EPZs, in the past three decades. ETDZs and EPZs lead in terms of promoting processing imports.

Table 4.5 Ranking of high-technology industrial development zones by processing imports in 2010

Ranking	Name	Percentage	Ranking	Name	Percentage
1	Suzhou, JS	1.3834	26	Minhang, SH	0.0043
2	Wuxi, JS	1.0092	27	Fengtai, BJ	0.0037
3	Guangzhou, GD	1.0063	28	Xianyang, SX	0.003
4	Huizhou, GD	0.228	29	Mianyang, SC	0.0029
5	Wuhan, HB	0.2104	30	Changping, BJ	0.0028
6	Xuhui, SH	0.1231	31	Jilin, JL	0.0024
7	Shenzhen, GD	0.085	32	Anshan, LN	0.0015
8	Baoding, HB	0.0838	33	Zhongshan, GD	0.0015
9	Xiamen, FJ	0.0819	34	Guilin, GX	0.001
10	Weihai, SD	0.0551	35	Jiulongpo, CQ	0.001
11	Haidion, BJ	0.0534	36	Xiangfan, HB	0.001
12	Nankai, TJ	0.0495	37	Nanjing, JS	0.0009
13	Shenyang, LN	0.0344	38	Chaoyang, BJ	0.0008
14	Chengdu, SC	0.0321	39	Weifang, SD	0.0006
15	Nanchang, JX	0.0311	40	Changsha, HN	0.0003
16	Xi'an, SX	0.0301	41	Zhengzhou, HN	0.0002
17	Dalian, LN	0.021	42	Lanzhou, GS	0.0001
18	Kunming, YN	0.0207	43	Zhuzhou, HN	0.0000
19	Hefei, AH	0.0147	44	Urumqi, XJ	0.0000
20	Changzhou, JS	0.0138	45	Shijiazhuang, HB	0.0000
21	Nanjing, JS	0.012	46	Jinan, SD	0.0000
22	Hangzhou, ZJ	0.0109	47	Nanning, GX	0.0000
23	Zibo, SD	0.0052	48	Guiyang, GZ	0.0000
24	Zhuhai, GD	0.0052	49	Taiyuan, SX	0.0000
25	Changchun, JL	0.0045			

Source Authors' own compilation from China's customs data (2010)

4.2.1 *The Characteristics of Processing Trade*

In this section, we discuss various characteristics of processing trade: the top 10 countries from which China imports processing intermediate inputs, the top 10 industries of processing imports, the percentage distribution of processing imports by transport mode, the percentage distribution of share of imports by ownership of firms, the scope of processing firms, and the quality of processing imports. Processing imports, ordinary imports and total imports are compared. To realise these comparisons, we rely on transaction-level trade data provided by China's customs bureau, which recorded about 3.3 million import transactions in 2010. The dataset includes information on the customs district, the location of the Chinese importer, customs regime, countries

Table 4.6 Ranking of economic and technological development zones by processing imports in 2010

Ranking	Name	Percentage	Ranking	Name	Percentage
1	Suzhou, JS	4.8365	18	Shenyang, LN	0.034
2	Pudong, SH	2.1234	19	Taiyuan, SX	0.0277
3	Tanggu, TJ	1.4245	20	Hefei, AH	0.0277
4	Daxing, BJ	0.8821	21	Nanhui, SH	0.0258
5	Dalian, LN	0.8012	22	Lianyungang, JS	0.0252
6	Guangzhou, GD	0.7714	23	Wuhu, AH	0.0189
7	Yantai, SD	0.3768	24	Zhanjiang, GD	0.0117
8	Ningbo, ZJ	0.296	25	Changchun, JL	0.0047
9	Qingdao, SD	0.2247	26	Harbin, HLJ	0.0042
10	Other, HN	0.1621	27	Wenzhou, ZJ	0.0032
11	Fuzhou, FJ	0.1609	28	Nanan, CQ	0.001
12	Nantong, JS	0.1293	29	Chengdu, SC	0.0008
13	Hangzhou, ZJ	0.123	30	Xining, QH	0.0000
14	Wuhan, HB	0.0766	31	Yinchuan, NX	0.0000
15	Urumqi, XJ	0.0618	32	Shihezi, XJ	0.0000
16	Qinhuangdao, HB	0.0575	33	Changning, SH	0.0000
17	Minhang, SH	0.0469			

Source Authors' own compilation from China's customs data (2010)

of departure/origin, location of Chinese consumers, transport modes, HS eight-digit codes, quantity and monthly values (measured in US dollars). This dataset does not, however, include firm-level information. Considering that firm-level analysis is critical to understanding China's processing trade from the micro-perspective, we resort to using transaction-level trade data (2000–06) from an earlier period, which include firm-level information.

4.2.2 The Origin of Processing Imports

Our initial inquiry rests on the origin of processing imports. We compile customs data for the year 2010 to determine the top 10 countries in terms of total imports, processing imports and ordinary imports. As shown in the last two columns of Table 4.7, China primarily imports from Japan, Korea and Taiwan Province of China. China also imports much from its entrepots, Hong Kong and Macao of China. Although the United States ranks only fifth in terms of total imports, it ranks next to Japan in terms of ordinary imports. In terms of processing imports, Korea ranks first, followed by Hong Kong of China, Japan and Taiwan Province of China. This suggests in part that

Table 4.7 Ranking of imports by region by customs regime in 2010

Ranking	Country and area	Processing imports (%)	Country and area	Ordinary imports (%)	Country and area	Total imports (%)
1	Korea	14.97	Japan	11.77	Japan	12.80
2	China	14.43	United States	8.34	Korea	10.02
3	Japan	14.06	Germany	7.66	Taiwan(China)	8.40
4	Taiwan (China)	13.93	Australia	7.37	China	7.76
5	United States	6.17	Korea	5.95	United States	7.36
6	Malaysia	5.43	Brazil	4.58	Germany	5.40
7	Thailand	3.43	Taiwan(China)	3.87	Australia	4.38
8	Germany	2.65	Saudi Arabia	3.41	Malaysia	3.66
9	Singapore	2.43	Angola	2.78	Brazil	2.77
10	Philippines	1.85	China	2.28	Thailand	2.41
Total		79.34		58.02		64.96

Notes Here proportions denote the ratio of processing (ordinary or both) imports by country over China's total processing (ordinary or both) imports in 2010. 'China' here refers to imports from Hong Kong and Macao special administrative regions
Source Authors' own compilation from China's customs data (2010)

China imports core intermediate inputs from Korea and Japan and then exports final value-added products to the United States and Europe.

In terms of total import volume, the top 10 regions make up two-thirds of China's total imports and 80% of China's processing imports. The remaining 20% of processing imports are produced by 200 trading partners in the rest of the world. The next section discusses the kinds of products that China imports as intermediate inputs.

4.2.3 *Top Products of Processing Imports*

As shown in Table 4.8, the electrical machinery and transport equipment industry yields the largest volume of processing imports, accounting for approximately 40% of China's total. Along with this industry, four other industries—machinery and mechanical appliances, optical and photographic instruments, mineral fuels and oils, and plastic—account for approximately 70% of China's total processing imports. These five industries import a huge volume of intermediate inputs; however, it is still worthwhile investigating whether these industries adopt a large volume of domestic inputs.

Table 4.8 Ranking of imports by industry in 2010

Ranking	HS 2-digit	Proportion of imports	HS 2-digit	Proportion of imports
1	Electrical machinery and equipment	38.97	Electrical machinery and equipment	22.83
2	Machinery and mechanical appliances	13.99	Mineral fuels, mineral oils	13.71
3	Optical, photographic instruments	10.25	Machinery and mechanical appliances	12.51
4	Mineral fuels, mineral oils	5.98	Ores, slag and ash	7.90
5	Plastics and articles thereof	5.44	Optical, photographic instruments	6.54
6	Copper and articles thereof	3.10	Plastics and articles thereof	4.63
7	Organic chemicals	2.35	Vehicles other than railway	3.60
8	Iron and steel	1.74	Organic chemicals	3.50
9	Rubber and articles thereof	1.59	Copper and articles thereof	3.35
10	Aircraft, spacecraft and parts	110	Oil seeds, industrial plants	1.97

Notes Here proportions denote the ratio of processing (or total) imports by HS two-digit industry over China's total processing (total) imports in 2010
Source Authors' own compilation from China's customs data (2010)

We calculate the ratio of *imported* intermediate inputs against total intermediate inputs for several industries. Industrial intermediate inputs combine both imported and domestic intermediate inputs. We utilise data on intermediate inputs maintained by China's customs bureau and China's input–output data for 2005 to calculate the ratio of imported intermediate inputs. As shown in Fig. 4.3, the five aforementioned industries use a large amount of imported intermediate inputs (for example, the ratio for machinery is 30%, whereas the ratio for non-metal minerals is 17%).

4.3 Transportation Modes

There is ample evidence showing electrical machinery and transport equipment commodities are the most dominant among processing imports in China. How these products reach China's ports is another interesting question. Do these imports arrive

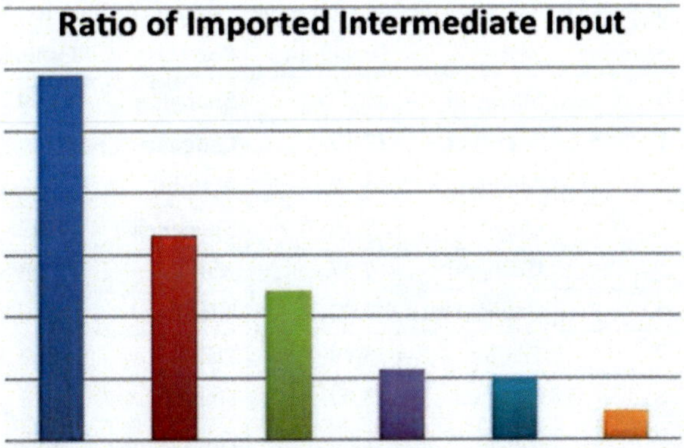

Fig. 4.3 Ratio of Imported Intermediate Inputs, 2006. *Source* Cited in Yu (2011a)

in China by sea, land or air? We classify these imports by transport mode used in 2010. Six types of transport mode are identified in this chapter: sea (or river if applicable), railway, truck, air, post and others. The last column of Table 4.9 shows that 62.52% of processing imports (in terms of value) reached China by sea in 2010, suggesting sea shipment to be the prevailing mode of transportation. This observation is consistent with the fact that most of China's free-trade zones are located along its eastern Pacific coast. The second most common transport mode is air (19.63%) and then by truck (15.72%).

The leading transport modes for all processing imports are the same as above. Sea shipment accounts for 41%, whereas air shipment and truck shipment account for 29.56% and 27.42%, respectively. It is surprising to note that the percentage of air shipment is higher than that of truck shipment because, intuitively, there should be more commodities shipped by truck. The value of imports was used as a measurement, however, not the quantity of goods. The average per-unit price of commodities sent by air shipment is usually higher than that for commodities sent by truck.

Table 4.9 Proportion of imports by transport mode in 2010

Transport mode	Processing	Ordinary	Total
By sea	41.47	79.81	62.52
By railway	1.09	1.58	1.36
By truck	27.42	6.12	15.72
By air	29.56	11.47	19.63
By post	0.01	0.04	0.03
Other	0.45	0.99	0.75

Note Here proportions denote the ratio of processing (ordinary or both) imports by transport mode over China's total processing (ordinary or both) imports in 2010

Source Authors' own compilation from China's customs data (2010)

Table 4.10 The top 10 ports with largest volume of imports, 2010

Ranking	Ports	Processing	Ports	Ordinary	Ports	Total imports
1	Shanghai	22.57	Shanghai	15.99	Shanghai	18.97
2	Shenzhen	17.77	Qingdao	10.46	Shenzhen	12.64
3	Nanjing	15.23	Tianjin	8.57	Nanjing	11.38
4	Qingdao	9.19	Shenzhen	8.42	Qingdao	9.15
5	Huangpu	7.57	Nanjing	8.23	Huangpu	6.46
6	Guangzhou	3.40	Ningbo	6.10	Tianjin	6.14
7	Tianjin	3.19	Dalian	4.62	Ningbo	4.42
8	Gongbei	3.02	Huangpu	4.23	Dalian	3.80
9	Dalian	2.80	Hangzhou	4.05	Guangzhou	3.69
10	Beijing	2.78	Guangzhou	3.92	Beijing	3.38

Source Authors' own compilation from China's customs data (2010)

4.3.1 The Most Important Ports

We switch our interest to customs ports in China with the largest volume of total imports, processing imports and ordinary imports. The top 10 ports in terms of the volume of processing imports in 2010 were Shanghai, Shenzhen, Nanjing, Qingdao, Huangpu in Guangzhou, Guangzhou, Tianjin, Gongbei in Shanghai, Dalian and Beijing (Table 4.10). Except for Beijing, these ports are seaports or river ports (for example, Nanjing) located on the eastern Pacific coast. The port of Shanghai is the largest port not only for processing imports but also for ordinary imports. Moreover, Shanghai's port is the largest port for total imports, followed by Shenzhen—a special economic zone located in Guangdong Province.

The top three ports with the largest share of processing imports are Shanghai, Shenzhen and Nanjing, comprising more than 55% of China's total processing imports. This confirms that most processing imports are located in Shanghai, Guangdong and Jiangsu. In contrast, the top three ports with the most ordinary imports—namely, Shanghai, Qingdao and Tianjin—account for only 35% of China's total ordinary imports. This suggests that China's processing imports are more concentrated than its ordinary imports.

4.3.2 The Most Strongly Demanded Locations

We next examine the destination of processing imports in China. Most processing goods are imported through Shanghai, Shenzhen and Nanjing, so a natural conjecture is that processing importers are concentrated in these areas. Processing firms would choose their closest port to reduce transport costs. To verify this conjecture, we

Table 4.11 The top 10 strongly demanded cities, 2010

Ranking	City	Processing	City	Ordinary	City	Total imports
1	Shenzhen, GD	7.40	Chaoyang, BJ	10.05	Chaoyang, BJ	6.41
2	Pudong, SH	6.11	Xicheng, BJ	5.71	Shenzhen, GD	3.58
3	Suzhou, JS	4.56	Haidian, BJ	3.06	Pudong, SH	3.27
4	Dongguan, GD	3.64	Chaoyang, BJ	2.87	Mentougou, BJ	3.22
5	Shenzhen, GD	2.38	Pudong, SH	1.76	Suzhou, JS	2.38
6	Chaoyang, BJ	1.98	Shenzhen, GD	1.47	Dongguan, GD	1.89
7	Songjiang, SH	1.74	Guangzhou, GD	1.13	Haidian, BJ	1.71
8	Dongguan, GD	1.74	Pudong, SH	1.06	Chanyang, BJ	1.58
9	Kunshan, JS	1.24	Shenzhen, GD	0.95	Pudong, BJ	1.33
10	Dongguan, GD	1.09	Pudong, SH	0.93	Shenzhen, GD	1.08

Note Sometimes a city is displaced more than once since it could contain firms in different zones such as an EPZ, ETDZ or and HTIDZ. Source: Authors' own compilation from China's customs data (2010)

determine the top 10 strongly demanded cities/districts using China's transaction-level trade data for 2010 (Table 4.11).

Shenzhen, Pudong and Suzhou prove to be the top three districts with the most processing imports; however, they account for only 18% of total processing imports. The leading destinations for processing imports are different from the leading destinations for ordinary imports (that is, Chaoyang, Xicheng and Haidian, which are all in Beijing). One possible explanation is that ordinary imports include more final consumption goods, whereas processing imports include mostly intermediate goods. Combining processing imports and ordinary imports, Chaoyang in Beijing replaces Shenzhen and Pudong as the top import destination in 2010, receiving 6.41% of total imports in China.

4.3.3 Quality of Processing Imports

Another interesting issue is the quality of processing imports. China imports raw materials from many trading partners, so which countries ship products of the highest quality? Which goods have the highest quality? Answering these questions requires

Table 4.12 Top 10 industries with highest quality of processing imports, 2010

Code	Descriptions of HS 2-digit codes	Unit value
88	Aircraft, spacecraft, and parts thereof	2 398 441
89	Ships, boats and floating structures	482 843
84	Nuclear reactors, boilers, machinery and mechanical appliances	42 994
90	Optical, photographic, medical or surgical instruments	17 576
87	Vehicles other than railway or tramway rolling stock	13 083
86	Railway or tramway locomotives, rolling stock and parts	3493
85	Electrical machinery and equipment and parts thereof	2890
30	Pharmaceutical products	1064
92	Musical instruments, parts and accessories	878
81	Other base metals, cement, articles thereof	727

Source Authors' own compilation from China's customs data (2010)

coming up with an appropriate measure of the quality of goods, which is a challenging task (Khandelwal 2010). A common gauge is the per-unit value of products (Hallak 2006), which is obtained by dividing a good's value by its quantity.

From the top 10 areas that ship goods with the highest quality to China (data achieved in 2010), we can see that nine of these 10 countries (regimes) are located in Europe. The top five countries are: Norway, France, Finland, Germany and the Netherlands. The United States ranks sixth. Meanwhile, the top five countries (regimes) with the highest quality of *ordinary* imports are Cayman Islands, Finland, Germany, Panama and Austria. Cayman Islands is capable of exporting high-quality products due to its 'tax-haven' privileges. Certain countries can export their products to Cayman Islands, which serves as an entrepot, for eventual shipment to China.

Table 4.12 lists industries that lead in terms of importing high-quality raw materials for processing. Imports for the aircraft and spacecraft industry have the largest per-unit value at approximately $2.39 million, followed by ships and boats, and machinery and mechanical appliances. The table likewise shows very high differences in the per-unit value of products imported by the top three importing industries.

4.3.4 Ownership of Processing Importing Firms

Thus far, we have gained some understanding of China's processing imports from the industrial perspective, specifically the origin countries, main products, transport mode, entry ports, consumption destinations and even quality of commodities. Now, we take a step forward to understand the micro-mechanism. In particular, we explore what types of firms frequently engage in processing trade. In terms of ownership,

Table 4.13 Proportion of imports by ownership of firms in 2010

Firm type	Processing	Ordinary	Total
State-owned enterprise	12.24	41.23	28.16
Sino-foreign contractual joint venture	0.66	0.44	0.54
Sino–foreign equity joint venture	16.53	14.14	15.22
Foreign-invested enterprise	58.76	20.70	37.86
Collective enterprise	1.42	3.45	2.54
Private enterprise	10.17	20.00	15.57
Other, including foreign company's office in China	0.01	0.01	0.01

Note Here proportions denote the ratio of processing (ordinary or both) imports by ownership of firms of China's total processing (ordinary or both) imports in 2010
Source Authors' own compilation from China's customs data (2010)

what types of firms account for the largest proportion of China's processing imports? We use China's customs transaction-level data for 2010 to answer this question.

As shown in Table 4.13, more than half of processing imports are attributable to foreign-invested enterprises. Another 17% of processing imports are attributable to Sino–foreign joint ventures (either contractual or equity joint ventures). State-owned and private enterprises account for only a relatively small proportion (12.2% and 10.2%, respectively). Meanwhile, state-owned enterprises (SOEs) are the most important type of firms involved in ordinary imports (second column of Table 4.12). Combining both processing and ordinary imports (last column of Table 4.10), foreign-invested enterprises are the most important type of importers (37.86%), followed by state-owned enterprises (28.16%).

4.3.5 The Scope of Activity Conducted by Import Processing Firms

How many varieties do processing firms import? Compared with ordinary importing firms, do processing firms import more varieties? Answering these questions requires a dataset containing firm-level information. China's 2010 customs dataset (the most recently released version) does not include such information. As a compromise, we have to rely on an older dataset. We therefore adopt China's transaction-level trade data for 2000–06, which include firm-level information, such as firm name, address, zip code and telephone numbers.

Before investigating the importation scope of processing firms, we need to provide a formal definition of such firms. Yu (2011b) classified firms in China into four types, as shown in Fig. 4.4: (1) non-importing firms that do not use any foreign intermediate inputs; (2) non-processing importing firms that use some foreign intermediate inputs but do not sell their final products abroad; (3) hybrid (or regular) processing firms that engage in both processing and ordinary imports; and (4) pure processing firms that

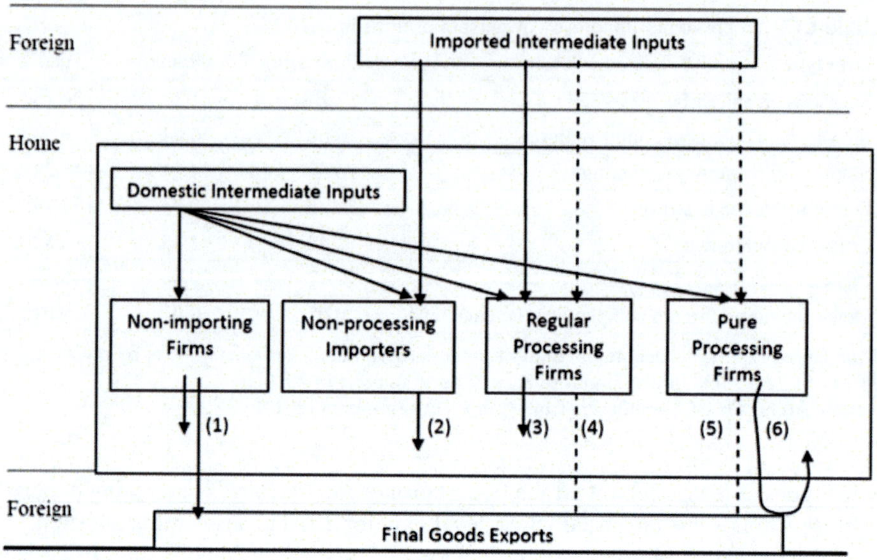

Fig. 4.4 Four types of firms in China. *Note* Dotted lines represent firms' processing imports (exports) whereas solid lines denote firms' non-processing (that is, ordinary) imports (exports). *Sources* Cited from Yu (2011a)

only engage in processing imports and exports, and do not sell their products in the domestic market. In the present chapter, we define both hybrid and pure processing firms as processing importers. In other words, a firm engaging in some processing imports is labelled as a processing firm.

Table 4.14 reports the scope of processing trade by year. In 2000–06, about 20% of firms imported only a single variety, and about 10% imported two varieties. In 2000, about 45% imported less than five varieties, whereas about 50% imported less than 10 varieties. Another 31% imported more than 10 but less than 50 varieties. The other 3.24% imported more than 50 but less than 1000 varieties. Only 0.23% of the firms imported more than 1000 varieties, with 3497 the highest number of varieties imported.

Table 4.14 also shows the dynamic pattern for each cohort. In the same period, the proportion of firms importing less than five varieties increased from 45 to 54%. Similarly, the proportion of firms importing less than 10 varieties increased from 60 to 68%. In contrast, the proportion of firms importing more than 10 varieties but less than 50 varieties declined from 31.2 to 24.5%. The highest number of varieties imported also declined, to 2839 in 2006 (Table 4.15).

Processing and non-processing firms share a similar importation scope pattern; however, more processing firms import a single variety than non- processing firms. In 2006, the proportion of single-variety processing importers (25.4%) was higher than that of single-variety non-processing importers (23.6%). In the same year, the

Table 4.14 The scope of importing firms by year, 2000–06

Scope	2000	2001	2002	2003	2004	2005	2006
1	19.04	18.9	19.76	20.32	21.65	22.66	23.6
2	10.27	10.14	10.55	10.77	11.43	11.97	12.19
3	6.67	7.15	7.23	7.34	7.66	7.93	8.1
4	5.26	5.39	5.42	5.76	5.64	5.78	5.96
5	4.38	4.41	4.5	4.62	4.63	4.65	4.62
6	3.61	3.87	3.9	3.79	3.8	3.69	3.76
7	3.29	3.26	3.34	3.34	3.2	3.17	3.2
8	2.98	2.89	2.89	2.81	2.79	2.7	2.73
9	2.44	2.66	2.54	2.53	2.49	2.38	2.34
10	2.33	2.35	2.36	2.26	2.12	2.13	2.11
11–50	31.21	30.68	28.23	28.24	26.71	25.74	24.51
51–100	5.05	4.23	4.9	4.97	4.78	4.43	4.34
101–1000	3.24	3.1	2.94	2.99	2.86	2.58	2.34
>1000	0.23	0.97	1.34	0.26	0.24	0.19	0.2
Maximum	3497	3404	3321	3211	3070	3023	2839

Source Authors' own calculation from China's customs data (2000–06)

Table 4.15 The scope of processing importing firms by year, 2000–06

Scope	2000	2001	2002	2003	2004	2005	2006
1	20.6	20.34	21.6	22.37	23.41	24.4	25.42
2	10.69	10.56	11.09	11.45	11.71	11.97	12.32
3	6.82	7.21	7.39	7.66	7.7	7.98	8.07
4	5.42	5.7	5.55	5.78	5.77	5.86	6.07
5	4.53	4.57	4.67	4.83	4.72	4.69	4.69
6	3.69	4.06	3.9	3.95	3.87	3.88	3.81
7	3.38	3.32	3.47	3.35	3.46	3.25	3.33
8	2.9	2.95	2.86	2.99	2.98	2.79	2.75
9	2.63	2.72	2.68	2.5	2.54	2.5	2.45
10	2.32	2.44	2.44	2.34	2.29	2.21	2.16
11–50	31.04	30.62	29.37	27.93	26.73	25.96	24.51
51–100	3.96	3.73	3.45	3.36	3.37	3.09	3.1
101–1000	1.83	1.58	1.34	1.3	1.3	1.27	1.18
>1000	0.19	0.2	0.19	0.19	0.15	0.15	0.14
Maximum	3489	3397	3319	3199	3070	3023	2836

Source Authors' own calculation from China's customs data (2000–06)

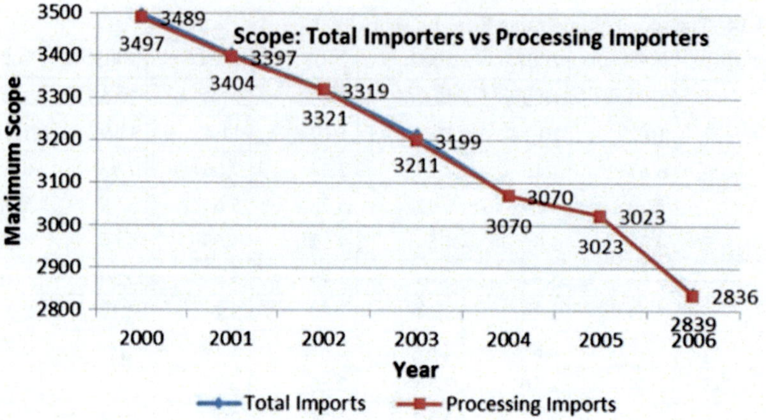

Fig. 4.5 The maximum scope for importing firms and processing importing firms *Source* Authors' own compilation from China's customs data (2000–06)

proportion of processing firms (4.42%) importing more than 50 varieties was lower than that of non-processing firms (6.88%), as shown in Table 4.13a.

Figure 4.5 shows that the number of varieties that firms import has declined over time. Such a pattern is true for both processing and ordinary importers. For most years in the sample, processing firms have imported fewer varieties than ordinary firms. A lower variety of imports could reflect increased specialisation or it could reflect an increased sourcing of domestically produced intermediate goods, or both.

Thus far, we have understood that processing firms mostly come from Korea, Hong Kong (China) and Japan. The industry with the largest processing imports is electrical machinery and transport equipment.

Most of the processing imports are shipped to China by sea and air. The top three busiest customs ports for processing imports are Shanghai, Shenzhen and Nanjing, whereas the three districts/areas that have the most processing imports are Shenzhen, Pudong and Suzhou. The industry with the highest per-unit value of commodities is the aircraft and spacecraft industry. The five countries with the highest quality of goods shipped to China for processing are all located in Europe: Norway, France, Finland, Germany and the Netherlands. In terms of types of importer ownership, foreign-invested enterprises are the top importers of processing goods. About 20% of processing firms import only a single variety, and about 50% import less than 10 varieties. Furthermore, the number of imported varieties declines over time.

An important question, however, is still unanswered: do processing firms have higher (or lower) productivity than non-processing firms? We now seek to answer this question.

4.4 Matching Transaction-Level Trade Data and Firm-Level Production Data

To explore the productivity performance of processing firms, we need data on processing firms' output level and labour input. If productivity is measured as total factor productivity, we also need data on capital and intermediate inputs. Transaction-level trade data offer rich information but do not contain information on production factors, such as output and input factors. Hence, we have to appeal to firm-level production data and use a merged dataset. Below, we begin by describing the two datasets, and we present a detailed technique for their merging. Thereafter, we discuss the performance of the matched dataset. Indeed, the two datasets are widely accepted in the study of China's foreign trade and firm heterogeneity. Yet, as far as we know, beyond our own work there is not yet on offer a detailed and reliable means of matching these two datasets. Thus, our chapter aims to fill a research gap on the heterogeneity of Chinese firms.

4.4.1 Transaction-Level Trade Dataset

Extremely disaggregated transaction-level monthly trade data for 2000–06 are obtained from China's General Administration of Customs. Each transaction is described at the HS eight-digit level. The number of monthly observations increased from about 78 000 in January 2000 to more than 230 000 in December 2006. As shown in column one of Table 4.16, the annual number of observations was more than 10 million in 2000 and 16 million in 2006, ending with a huge number of observations (118 333 831 in total) for seven years. Column two of Table 4.14 shows that 286 819 firms engaged in international trade during this period.

For each transaction, the dataset compiles three types of information: (1) five variables on basic trade information, including value (measured in current US dollars), trade status (export or import), quantity, trade unit and value per unit (value divided by quantity); (2) six variables on trade mode and pattern, including country of destination for exports, country of origin for imports, routing (whether the product is shipped through an intermediate country/regime), customs regime (processing trade or ordinary trade), trade mode (by sea, truck, air or post) and customs port (where the product departs or arrives); and (3) seven variables on firm information associated with each transaction, including firm name, identification number set by customs, Chinese city where the firm is located, telephone number, zip code, name of the manager/CEO and ownership type of firm (foreign affiliate, private or state-owned).

Table 4.16 Matched statistics: number of firms

Year	Trade data		Production data			Matched data		
Number	Transactions	Firms	Raw Firms	Filtered Firms	w/raw Firms	w/filtered Firms	w/raw Firms	w/filtered Firms
	(1)	(2)	(3)	(4)	(5)	(6)	(7)	(8)
2000	10 586 696	80 232	162 883	83 628	18 580	12 842	21 665	15 748
2001	12 667 685	87 404	169 031	100 100	21 583	15 645	25 282	19 091
2002	14 032 675	95 579	181 557	110 530	24 696	18 140	29 144	22 291
2003	18 069 404	113 147	196 222	129 508	28 898	21 837	34 386	26 930
2004	21 402 355	134 895	277 004	199 927	44 338	35 007	50 798	40 711
2005	24 889 639	136 604	271 835	198 302	44 387	34 958	50 426	40 387
2006	16 685 377	197 806	301 960	224 854	53 748	42 833	59 133	47 591
All years	118 333 831	286 819	615 951	438 165	83 679	69 623	90 558	76 823

Notes Column (1) reports the number of observations of HS eight-digit monthly transaction-level trade data from China's General Administration of Customs by year. Column (2) reports the number of firms covered in the transaction-level trade data by year. Column (3) reports the number of firms covered in the firm-level production dataset compiled by China's NBS without any filter or cleaning. In contrast, Column (4) presents the number of firms covered in the firm-level production dataset with careful filtering according to the requirement of GAAP. Accordingly, Column (5) reports the number of matched firms using identical company names in both the trade dataset and the raw production dataset. In contrast, Column (6) reports the number of matched firms using identical company names in both the trade dataset and the filtered production dataset. Finally, Column (7) reports the number of matched firms using identical company names and identical zip code and phone numbers in both the trade dataset and the raw production dataset. In contrast, Column (8) reports the number of matched firms using identical company names and identical zip code and phone numbers in both the trade dataset and the filtered production dataset

4.4.2 Firm-Level Production Dataset

The sample used in this chapter comes from a rich firm-level panel dataset covering about 230 000 manufacturing firms per year for the period 2000–06. The number of firms doubled from 162 885 in 2000 to 301 961 in 2006. The data, including full information on three accounting items—that is, balance, loss and benefit, and cash flow—are collected through an annual survey of manufacturing enterprises and maintained by China's National Bureau of Statistics (NBS). On average, the annual entire value of industrial production covered by this dataset accounts for about 95% of China's total annual industrial production. Aggregated data on the industrial sector in the *China Statistical Yearbook* from the NBS are compiled from this dataset. The dataset includes more than 100 financial variables listed in the balance sheets of all firms covered. Briefly, two types of manufacturing firms are covered: all SOEs and all non-SOEs with annual sales more than RMB5 million. The number of firms increased from more than 160 000 in 2000 to 301 000 in 2006. As shown in column three of Table 4.16, the number of firms included in the dataset at any time in 2000–06 is 615 951 in total.

The raw production dataset is, however, still quite noisy given that many unqualified firms are included, largely due to misreporting by some firms. For example, information on some family-based firms, which usually have no formal accounting system in place, is based on a unit of RMB1, whereas the official requirement is a unit of RMB1000. Following Cai and Liu (2009) and Feenstra et al. (2011), we delete observations according to generally accepted accounting principles if any of the following are true: (1) liquid assets are higher than total assets; (2) total fixed assets are larger than total assets; (3) the net value of fixed assets is larger than total assets; (4) the firm's identification number is missing; or (5) an invalid established time exists (for example, the opening month is later than December or earlier than January). Accordingly, the total number of firms covered in the dataset is reduced to 438 165, and about one-third of firms are dropped from the sample after this filtering process. As shown in column four of Table 4.16, the filter ratio is even higher in the initial years: about one-half of firms in 2000 are dropped.

4.4.3 Matching Method

Although the two available datasets have rich information on production and trade, matching them is challenging. Both datasets contain firm identification numbers; however, the coding systems in these datasets are completely different. For example, the length of firm identifications in the transaction-level dataset is 10 digits, whereas that in the firm-level dataset is only nine digits. China's customs administration has a coding system that is completely different from that adopted by the National Bureau of Statistics.

We go through two stages to match transaction-level trade data with firm-level production data. In the first stage, we match the two datasets by firm name and year. If a firm has the exact same Chinese name in both datasets in a particular year, it should be the same firm. The year variable is necessary as an auxiliary identification variable because some firms could have different names across years and newcomers could possibly take their original names. Using the raw production dataset, we come up with 83 679 matching firms; this number is further reduced to 69 623 with the more accurate filtered production dataset.

In the second stage, we use another matching technique as a supplement. Here, we rely on two other common variables to identify firms: zip code and the last seven digits of a firm's phone number. The rationale is that firms should have different and unique phone numbers within a postal district. Although this method seems straightforward, subtle technical and practical difficulties still exist. For example, the production-level trade dataset includes both area codes and a hyphen in phone numbers, whereas the firm-level production dataset does not. Therefore, we use the last seven digits of the phone number to serve as the proxy for firm identification for two reasons. First, in 2000–06, some large Chinese cities added one more digit at the start of their seven-digit phone numbers. Therefore, sticking to the last seven digits of the number will not confuse firm identification. Second, in the original dataset, phone numbers are defined as a string of characters with the phone zip code; however, it is inappropriate to de-string such characters to numerals because a hyphen is used to connect the zip code and phone number. Using the last seven-digit sub-string neatly solves this problem.

A firm might not include its name information in either the trade or the production dataset. Similarly, a firm could lose its phone and/or zip code information. To be sure that our matched dataset can cover as many common firms as possible, we then include observations in the matched dataset if a firm occurs in *either* the name-adopted matched dataset *or* the phone-and-post-adopted matched dataset. The number of matched firms increases to 90 558 when the raw production dataset is used, as shown in column seven of Table 4.16. Our matching performance is comparable with (or even better than) that of other similar studies. For example, Ge et al. (2011) used the same datasets and similar matching techniques, but ended up with 86 336 matching firms. Meanwhile, if we match the more rigorously filtered production dataset with the firm-level dataset, we end up with 76 823 firms in total, as shown in the last column of Table 4.16.

How does our matched dataset perform? Table 4.17 compares several key firm-level variables between the matched dataset and the full-sample production dataset. The matched sample clearly has higher means for sales, exports, number of employees, log of capital–labour ratio and even the log of labour productivity compared with the full sample, suggesting that the merged sample is skewed towards large firms. By construction, the full-sample firm-level production dataset contains only large firms (that is, with annual sales larger than \$770 000), and our matched dataset contains about 70% of total exports. Thus, our matched dataset is sufficiently representative of large Chinese exporting firms.

Table 4.17 Comparison of the merged dataset and the full-sample production dataset

Variables	Matched data set			Full-sample production data set		
	Mean	Min.	Max.	Mean	Min.	Max.
Sales	156,348	5000	1.57e+08	85,065	5000	1.57e+08
Exports	51,751	0	1.52e+08	16,544	0	1.52e+08
Number of employees	479	10	157,213	274	10	165,878
Log of capital-labor ratio	3.62	−5.71	9.87	3.53	−6.22	11.14
Log of labor productivity	3.86	−7.75	10.78	3.84	−8.96	10.79

Note Variables = matched dataset full-sample production dataset. *Source* Cited from Qiu and Yu (2012)

4.4.4 Productivity for Processing Firms

With a matched trade and firm-level production dataset, we are now ready to explore the productivity of processing firms. Labour productivity is a simple and straightforward measure of productivity; however, labour productivity cannot measure the contribution of input factors other than labour. As such, total factor productivity (TFP) is a better measure because it captures contributions from all input factors.

The TFP literature usually suggests using the Cobb-Douglass production function to introduce technology improvement (Eq. 4.1).

Equation 4.1

$$Y_{it} = \pi_{it} M_{it}^{\beta_m} K_{it}^{\beta_k} L_{it}^{\beta_l}, \tag{4.1}$$

where *Yit*, *Mit*, *Kit*, *Lit* is firm i's output, materials, capital and labour at year t, respectively. To measure a firm's TFP, one needs to estimate Eq. 4.1 by taking a log function first (Eq. 4.2).

Equation 4.2

$$\ln Y_{it} = \beta_0 + \beta_m \ln M_{it} + \beta_k \ln K_{it} + \beta_l \ln L_{it} + \epsilon_{it}, \tag{4.2}$$

Traditionally, TFP is measured by the estimated Solow residual between the true data on output and its fitted value, $\ln \hat{Y}_{it}$. That is Eq. 4.3.

Equation 4.3

$$TFP_{it} = \ln Y_{it} - \ln \hat{Y}_{it}. \tag{4.3}$$

This approach, however, suffers from two problems: simultaneity bias and selection bias. As first suggested by Marschak and Andrews (1944), at least some parts of TFP changes could be observed by firms early enough for them to change their input decisions and maximise profit. Thus, TFP could have reverse endogeneity in its input factors. The lack of such a consideration would make the maximised choice of firms biased. In addition, the dynamic behaviour of firms also introduces selection bias. With international competition, firms with low productivity would die and exit the market, whereas those with high productivity would remain (Melitz 2003). In a panel dataset, the firms observed are those that have already survived. Meanwhile, firms with low productivity, which collapsed and exited the market, are excluded from the dataset. This means that the firms included in the regression are not randomly selected, resulting in estimation bias.

Econometricians have strived to address the empirical challenge of measuring TFP but were unsuccessful until the pioneering work of Olley and Pakes (1996). In the beginning, researchers used two-way (firm-specific and year-specific) fixed-effects estimations to mitigate simultaneity bias. Although the fixed-effect approach controls for several unobserved productivity shocks, it does not offer much help in dealing with reverse endogeneity and thus remains unsatisfactory. Similarly, to mitigate selection bias, one might estimate a balanced panel by dropping observations that have disappeared during the investigation. The problem is that a substantial part of the information contained in the dataset is wasted, and the dynamic behaviour of firms is completely unknown.

Fortunately, the Olley–Pakes methodology contributes significantly in addressing the challenge of TFP measurement. Assuming that the expectation of the future realisation of the unobserved productivity shock, υ_{it}, relies on its contemporaneous value, firm i's investment is modelled as an increasing function of both unobserved productivity and log capital, $k_{it} \equiv \ln K_{it}$. Following previous studies, such as van Biesebroeck (2005) and Amiti and Konings (2007), we revise the Olley–Pakes approach by adding the export decisions of firms as an extra argument in the investment function because most export decisions are determined in the previous period (Tybout 2003) (Eq. 4.4).

Equation 4.4

$$I_{it} = \widetilde{I}(\ln K_{it}, \upsilon_{it}, EF_{it}, IF_{it}), \tag{4.4}$$

In Eq. 4.4, $EF_{it}(IF_{it})$ is a dummy variable measuring whether firm I exports (imports) at year t. Therefore, the inverse function of investment is.

Equation 4.5

$$\upsilon_{it} = \tilde{I}^{-1}(\ln K_{it}, I_{it}, EF_{it}, IF_{it}). \tag{4.5}$$

Unobserved productivity also depends on log capital and firm i's export decisions.[2] Accordingly, estimation specification 1 can now be written as Eq. 4.6.

Equation 4.6

$$\ln Y_{it} = \beta_0 + \beta_m \ln M_{it} + \beta_l \ln L_{it} + g(\ln K_{it}, I_{it}, EF_{it}, IF_{it}) + \varepsilon_{it} \tag{4.6}$$

In Eq. 4.6, $g\left(\ln K_{it},\ \ I_{it},\ \ EF_{it}\right)$ is defined as $\beta_k \ln K_{it} + \tilde{I}^{-1}(\ln K_{it}, I_{it}, EF_{it})$. Following Olley and Pakes (1996) and Amiti and Konings (2007), fourth-order polynomials are used in log-capital, log-investment, export dummy and import dummy to approximate $g(\cdot)$.[3] In addition, our firm dataset covers the period 2000–06, so we include a WTO dummy (that is, one for a year after 2001 and zero for before) to characterise the function $g(\cdot)$ as follows (Eq. 4.7).

Equation 4.7

[2] Olley and Pakes (1996) showed that the investment demand function is monotonically increasing in the productivity shock υ_{ik}, by making some mild assumptions about the production technology of firms.

[3] Using higher-order polynomials to approximate $g(.)$ does not change the estimation results.

$$g(k_{it}, I_{it}, EF_{it}, IF_{it}, WTO_t) = (1 + WTO_t + EF_{it} + IF_{it}) \sum_{h=0}^{4} \sum_{q=0}^{4} \delta_{hq} k_{it}^{h} I_{it}^{q}. \tag{4.7}$$

After finding the estimated coefficients $\hat{\beta}_m$ and $\hat{\beta}_l$, we calculate the residual, R_{it}, which is defined as $R_{it} \equiv \ln Y_{it} - \hat{\beta}_m \ln M_{it} - \hat{\beta}_l \ln L_{it}$.

The next step is to obtain an unbiased estimated coefficient of β_k Amiti and Konings (2007) suggested estimating the probability of a survival indicator on a high-order polynomial in log-capital and log-investment to correct selection bias as mentioned above. We can then accurately estimate the following specification (Eq. 4.8).

Equation 4.8

$$R_{it} = \beta_k \ln K_{it} + \tilde{I}^{-1}\left(g_{i,t-1} - \beta_k \ln K_{i,t-1}, \hat{pr}_{i,t-1}\right) + \varepsilon_{it}, \tag{4.8}$$

In Eq. 4.8, $\hat{pr}_i$ is the fitted value of the probability of firm i's exit in the next year. The specific 'true' functional form of the inverse function $\tilde{I}^{-1}(\cdot)$ is unknown, making it appropriate to use fourth-order polynomials in $g_{i,t-1}$ and $\ln K_{i,t-1}$ as approximation. In addition, Eq. 4.8 requires the estimated coefficients of the log-capital in the first and second terms to be identical. Therefore, nonlinear least squares seem to be the most desirable econometric technique (Arnold 2005; Pavcnik 2002). Finally, the Olley–Pakes type of TFP for each firm i in industry j is obtained once the estimated coefficient $\hat{\beta}_k$ is obtained (Eq. 4.9).

Equation 4.9

$$TFP_{ijt}^{OP} = \ln Y_{it} - \hat{\beta}_m \ln M_{it} - \hat{\beta}_k \ln K_{it} - \hat{\beta}_l \ln L_{it}. \tag{4.9}$$

As discussed above, the revised Olley–Pakes approach assumes that capital responds to an unobserved productivity shock with a Markov process, whereas other input factors do so without any dynamic effects; however, labour could be correlated with unobserved productivity shocks as well (Ackerberg et al. 2006). This consideration might fit with China's case very closely, given that China is a country with abundant labour. When facing unobserved productivity shocks, firms might prefer adjusting their labour rather than their capital to reoptimise their production behaviour. We then use the Blundell and Bond (1998) system GMM approach to capture the dynamic effects of other input factors. Assuming that the unobserved productivity shock depends on firm i's previous period realisations, the system GMM approach models TFP to be affected by all types of firm i's inputs in both current and past realisations.[4] In particular, this model has a dynamic representation as follows (Eq. 4.10).

[4] Note that the first-difference GMM introduced by Arellano and Bond (1991) also allows a firm's output to depend on its past realisation. Such an approach would, however, lose instruments for the factor inputs because the lag of output and factor inputs is correlated with past error shocks and the autoregressive error term. In contrast, by assuming that the first difference of instrumented variables

Equation 4.10

$$\ln y_{it} = \gamma_1 \ln L_{it} + \gamma_2 \ln L_{i,t-1} + \gamma_3 \ln K_{it} + \gamma_4 \ln K_{i,t-1} + \gamma_5 \ln M_{it} + \gamma_6 \ln M_{i,t-1} + \gamma_7 \ln y_{i,t-1} + \varsigma_i + \zeta_t + \omega_{it}. \tag{4.10}$$

In Eq. 4.10, ς_i is firm i's fixed effect and ζ_t is the year-specific fixed effect. The idiosyncratic term ω_{it} is serially uncorrelated if no measurement error exists.[5] We can obtain consistent estimates of the coefficients in (12) using a system GMM approach. The idea is that labour and material inputs are not taken as exogenously given. Instead, they are allowed to change over time as capital grows. Although the system GMM approach still faces a technical challenge to control for selection bias when a firm exits, using this approach to estimate a firm's TFP as a robustness check is still worthwhile.

Table 4.18 summarises the estimates of the Olley–Pakes input elasticity of Chinese firms at the HS two-digit level. We first cluster the 97 HS two- digit industries into 15 categories and calculate their estimated probability and input elasticity. The estimated survival probability of a firm in the next year varies from 0.977 to 0.996, with a mean of 0.994, suggesting that firm exits are less severe in the sample and in the given period.[6]

Table 4.18 presents differences in the estimated coefficients for labour, materials and capital using both the Olley–Pakes methodology and the system GMM approach. The last row of Table 4.18 suggests that, on average, the Olley–Pakes approach yields a higher elasticity of capital $\left(\alpha_k^{OP} = 0.117, \alpha_k^{GMM} = 0.001\right)$, whereas the system GMM approach yields a higher elasticity of labour $\left(\alpha_l^{OP} = 0.052, \alpha_l^{GMM} = 0.240\right)$. Summarising all the estimated elasticity, the implied scale elasticity is 0.989 using the Olley–Pakes approach,[7] which is close to the constant returns-to-scale elasticity.[8] Turning to the comparison between the OLS and the Olley–Pakes approaches, the estimates suggest that the usual OLS approach has a downward bias (TFP^{OLS}= 0.958; TFP^{OP}= 1.188) largely because of the lack of control for simultaneity bias and selection bias.

Finally, for a cross-country comparison of the Olley–Pakes estimates, the estimation results suggest that intermediate inputs are more important for Chinese firms

is uncorrelated with the fixed effects, the system GMM approach can introduce more instruments and thereby dramatically improve efficiency.

5 As discussed by Blundell and Bond (1998), even if there is a transient measurement error in some of the series (that is, $\omega_{it} \sim MA(1)$), the system GMM approach can still reach consistent estimates of the coefficients in Eq. 4.6.

6 Note that here, firm exit means a firm either stops trading and exits the market or has an annual sales figure lower than the 'large-scale' amount (RMB5 million in sales per year) and dropped from the dataset. Owing to dataset restrictions, we cannot distinguish the difference between the two.

7 This is calculated as $0.052 + 0.820 + .0.117 = .0.989$ using the Olley–Pakes approach.

8 Note that here we use the industrial deflator as a proxy of a firm's price. Indeed, it is even possible that Chinese firms exhibit the increasing returns-to-scale property in the new century when the actual prices of firms are used to calculate 'physical' productivity. This is a possible future research topic provided that relevant data are available.

Table 4.18 Estimates of Olley–Pakes input elasticity of chinese firms

HS 2-digit	Labour		Materials		Capital	
	OP	GMM	OP	GMM	OP	GMM
Animal products (01–05)	0.056[b]	0.053	0.888[b]	0.970[b]	0.048[b]	– 0.022
	(3.32)	(0.87)	(55.36)	(17.71)	(1.80)	(–0.43)
Vegetable products (06–15)	0.007	0.031[b]	0.891[b]	0.571[b]	0.052[b]	0.019
	(0.49)	(8.55)	(68.05)	(9.82)	(5.49)	(0.46)
Foodstuffs (16–24)	0.036[b]	– 0.020	0.874[b]	0.595[b]	0.044	0.027
	(2.23)	(–0.25)	(68.48)	(10.73)	(1.07)	(0.46)
Mineral products (25–27)	0.035[a]	0.241[b]	0.872[b]	0.671[b]	0.099[b]	0.089
	(1.70)	(3.78)	(51.00)	(15.51)	(2.69)	(1.57)
Chemicals and allied industries (28–38)	0.014[b]	0.127[b]	0.831[b]	0.488[b]	0.103[b]	0.071
	(1.98)	(1.95)	(121.70)	(10.99)	(7.79)	(1.48)
Plastics/rubber (39–40)	0.064[b]	0.321[b]	0.796[b]	0.298[b]	0.103[b]	– 0.003
	(8.49)	(6.98)	(107.17)	(4.54)	(5.59)	(–0.08)
Raw hides, skins, leather and furs (41–43)	0.102[b]	0.125[a]	0.810[b]	0.738[b]	0.090[b]	0.043
	(7.76)	(1.85)	(65.53)	(11.55)	(3.36)	(0.66)
Wood products (44–49)	0.039[b]	0.041	0.855[b]	0.266[b]	0.012	0.118[b]
	(4.29)	(0.46)	(97.11)	(6.83)	(0.47)	(2.99)
Textiles (50–63)	0.085[b]	0.157[b]	0.810[b]	0.653[b]	0.066[b]	0.043[a]
	(19.50)	(4.81)	(192.59)	(22.96)	(10.38)	(1.95)
Footwear/headgear (64–67)	0.072[b]	0.138	0.864[b]	0.703[b]	0.033[b]	0.108[b]
	(5.93)	(1.62)	(73.17)	(10.77)	(5.43)	(2.38)
Stone/glass (68–71)	0.104[b]	0.233[b]	0.785[b]	0.448[b]	0.103[b]	0.063
	(9.14)	(3.56)	(67.02)	(11.58)	(8.19)	(1.16)
Metals (72–83)	0.045[b]	0.191[b]	0.832[b]	0.400[b]	0.109[b]	0.084[b]
	(6.30)	(4.22)	(131.73)	(11.67)	(16.23)	(2.72)
Machinery/electrical (84–85)	0.065[b]	0.056	0.825[b]	0.548[b]	0.150[b]	0.175[b]
	(13.36)	(1.15)	(206.22)	(13.43)	(10.83)	(4.97)
Transportation (86–89)	0.042[b]	0.147[a]	0.883[b]	0.426[b]	0.043[b]	0.068
	(2.80)	(1.70)	(69.58)	(8.81)	(3.47)	(1.08)
Miscellaneous (90–98)	0.083[b]	0.195[b]	0.796[b]	0.276[b]	0.098[b]	0.007
	(10.32)	(3.58)	(110.01)	(8.15)	(10.70)	(0.22)
All industries	0.052[b]	0.240[b]	0.820[b]	0.486[b]	0.117[b]	0.001
	(30.75)	(17.05)	(493.33)	(44.54)	(27.08)	(0.11)

[a]indicates significance at 5% level
[b]indicates significance at 1% level
Note Numbers in parentheses are robust t-values

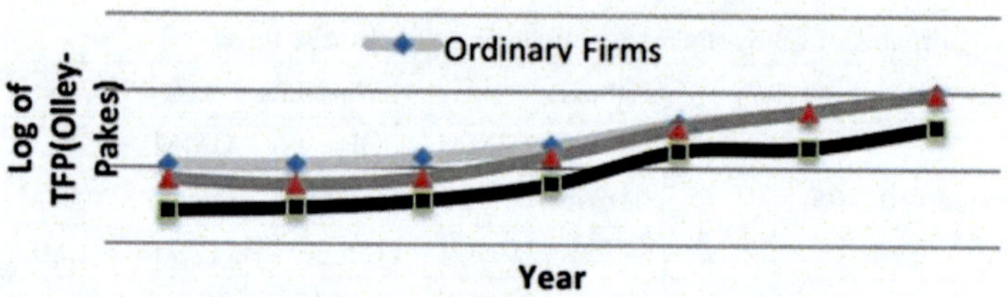

Fig. 4.6 Chinese firms' log of total factor productivity, 2000–06 *Source* Authors' calculation and estimates from China's firm-level production data and transaction-level trade data

than for American firms (Keller and Yeaple 2009) or for Indonesian firms (Amiti and Konings 2007). The elasticity of capital input is, however, less important for Chinese firms than for American or Indonesian firms. This implies that processing trade does play a significant role in China's productivity growth.

Our final interest is in comparing the productivity of processing firms and non-processing firms. As discussed in Fig. 4.5, three types of firms that engage in both processing and non-processing activities are important: non-processing firms (that is, ordinary firms), pure processing firms and hybrid firms. Figure 4.6 shows the dynamic evolution of the productivity of these three firm types. The productivity of all these firms has increased over time in the new century. Processing firms have the lowest productivity and ordinary firms have the highest productivity, with the productivity of hybrid firms in between. This strongly suggests that processing firms, compared with non-processing firms, have lower productivity.

4.5 Conclusions

This chapter aimed to provide an overview of China's processing trade using highly disaggregated data (firm-level data and transaction-level data) from the new century. We started by highlighting that processing trade plays a fundamental role in China's foreign trade, and then explored why processing trade has developed rapidly in the past three decades. China's free-trade policy has dramatically fostered processing trade. Various free-trade zones, such as export processing zones and economic and technological development zones, have served as important instruments boosting processing trade.

With such a background in hand, we then explored various characteristics of processing imports. We investigated China's processing imports from the industrial perspective, including the origin countries, main products, transport mode, entry ports, consumption destinations and even the quality of the commodities. We provided very detailed firm-level evidence for the scope of processing trade.

Similarly, to gain a rich understanding of processing trade, we carefully measured and calculated total factor productivity using the semi-parametric Olley–Pakes and GMM approaches. Our estimates show that the productivity of all firms has increased in the new century; however, processing firms usually have lower productivity levels than non-processing firms.

Last but not least, we also contribute to the literature by providing a careful and very precise method of matching firm-level production data with transaction-level trade data. The match is not perfect due to data format restrictions, but the resulting matched dataset is still sufficiently representative of China's trading firms.

Chapter 5
Estimating Productivity Using Chinese Data: Methods, Challenges and Results

5.1 Introduction

The rise of China as the world's manufacturer has generated considerable interest in the evolution of Chinese productivity, e.g., Yu (2015) and Brandt et al. (2017). Yet how productivity is and should be estimated remains an area of active research. In this paper we review some state-of-the-art methods for estimating productivity, always adopting a practitioner's perspective. We then apply these methods to Chinese manufacturing data over the 2000–2006 period. We estimate dozens of different specifications for 28 industries for a total of 672 production function estimates. We then compare results across specifications and draw conclusions about the strengths and pitfalls of each.

To obtain an estimate of firm-level productivity, the researcher typically estimates some variant of the following model:

$$y_{it} = f(x_{it}) + \omega_{it} \tag{5.1}$$

where y_{it} is log output of firm i, x_{it} is a vector of inputs used by firm i, $f(.)$ is the production function, and ω_{it} is log total factor productivity (TFP).

Generally, the researcher observes y_{it} and x_{it}, while the production function and TFP are unknown. However, if the production function can be estimated, firm-level TFP can be obtained as the estimated *residual* from (1). For example, in the simplest case of Cobb–Douglas production, the researcher estimates the following linear model:

$$y_{it} = \beta_L l_{it} + \beta_K k_{it} + \omega_i \tag{5.2}$$

This chapter is coauthored with Scott Orr at Department of Economics, University of Toronto and Daniel Trefler at Rotman School of Management, University of Toronto, CIFAR, NBER.

M. Yu, *China's Miracle in Foreign Trade*, Studies in Modern Chinese Economy,
https://doi.org/10.1007/978-981-16-6030-6_5

where l_{it} and k_{it} are the logs of the labour and capital inputs, and the parameters β_L and β_K govern the marginal products of labour and capital. TFP is then the portion of firm-level output that is unexplained by input use. To obtain this object, we need estimates of the production function parameters.

Since (5.2) is a simple linear model, one might be tempted to estimate the production function para-meters using OLS. This would likely lead to biased coefficients of the production function parameters and, as a result, misleading estimates of productivity. Since each firm likely knows its own productivity, labour and capital inputs are likely *correlated* with ω_{it}. For example, since high-productivity firms have lower costs of production, they have lower prices and sell more output, requiring that they buy more labour and capital than low-productivity firms. This leads to an *upward* bias in estimated production function coefficients and hence to an upward bias in the estimated returns to scale $\beta_L + \beta_K$. It may even lead to estimates of increasing returns to scale ($\beta_L + \beta_K > 1$) when in fact there are decreasing returns ($\beta_L + \beta_K < 1$). This would be a very misleading picture of the nature of production. Similarly, since by construction OLS chooses production function parameters to minimize the variance of the residual, this approach will tend to *underestimate* productivity dispersion within an industry. This is problematic because accurate measurements of productivity dispersion are central to the literature on macroeconomic misallocation (e.g., Hsieh and Klenow 2009) and the literature on international trade (e.g., Eaton and Kortum 2002; Melitz 2003).

The problems with using OLS to estimate production functions have been recognized at least since Marschak and Andrews (1944). Fortunately, there has been enormous progress since then in developing alternative methods to estimate production functions that alleviate these concerns. See Griliches and Mairesse (1995) and Ackerberg et al. (2007) for a review of some of this literature.

Our paper focuses on one popular approach that has been extensively used in the applied literature over the last 20 years, the so-called “proxy-variable” approach of Olley and Pakes (1996), Levinsohn and Petrin (2003), and Ackerberg et al. (2015). In this approach one uses first-order conditions for inputs (such as capital and labour) to proxy for the direct effect of TFP in (6.1).[1]

In this paper, we estimate the production function using five different versions of the proxy-variable estimation procedure described in Ackerberg et al. (2015) as well as De Loecker and Warzynski (2012). We then compare the production function parameters and productivity estimates obtained across the different methods.

Our main conclusions are as follows. First, gross-output production functions tend to display returns to scale that are centred between 0.9 and 1.1. In contrast, value-added production functions display much greater variation in scale returns (between 0.5 and 1.5). Second, translog gross-output production functions are very stable across proxy-variable methods. The same is not true of the other three production functions (Cobb–Douglas gross-output, Cobb–Douglas value-added, and translog value-added). Third, we examine log TFP dispersion, a topic of great interest for

[1] See also Gandhi et al. (2016) whose first-order-condition approach we do not consider, but only in the interests of space.

thinking about the macro misallocation literature (e.g., Hsieh and Klenow 2009) and the literature on international trade (e.g., Eaton and Kortum 2002; Melitz 2003). We find that the choice of proxy-variable method makes little difference to the estimated dispersion in TFP. However, dispersion is much lower for gross-output production functions than for value-added production functions. Fourth, when examining the TFP premia associated with either capital intensity or size, the premia are present for value-added production functions, but much less so for gross-output production functions. *We conclude from these four observations that gross-output production functions tend to produce more sensible estimates than value-added production functions.*

The outline of the paper is as follows. In Sect. 5.2 we describe the basic model underlying the estimation routine, while in Sect. 5.3 we describe the estimation of productivity in more detail than is typically done. This makes this section more technical than the rest of the paper. Our expectation is that the casual reader will race through it, ignoring the details. However, for those wishing to estimate state-of-the-art productivity, Sect. 5.3 provides a line-by-line guide to all of the details that practitioners need, including some common extensions such as correcting for attrition bias (Olley and Pakes 1996) and the impact of exporting on productivity (De Loecker 2013). Section 5.4 describes the data and implementation. Sections 5.5 and 5.6 present the estimated parameters. Section 5.7 describes the results for TFP dispersion. Section 5.8 describes results for the TFP premia associated with capital intensity, size, and exporting. Section 5.9 concludes.

5.2 Model

Before we outline the actual estimation procedure, it is useful to describe a simple model of firm-level production. This discussion will highlight the basic assumptions we need to obtain consistent estimates of the production function parameters.

Suppose each firm i produces output using the following technology:

$$y_{it} = f(l_{it},\ k_{it},\ m_{it};\ \beta) + \omega_{it} + \epsilon_{it} \tag{5.3}$$

where t indexes years, y_{it}, l_{it}, k_{it}, and m_{it} are the natural logarithms of output, labour input, capital input, and materials input, respectively; β is a vector of production function parameters, ω_{it} is firm-level productivity, and ϵ_{it} is an *ex-post* productivity shock that is not realized until after a firm has made its production decisions.[2] While y_{it}, l_{it}, k_{it}, and m_{it} are observable, ω_{it} and ϵ_{it} are not.[3]

To obtain an estimate of ω_{it}, our primary object of interest, we estimate (5.3) using the two-step proxy-variable estimation procedure described in Ackerberg et al.

---

[2] ϵ_{it} may also be interpreted as measurement error in output.

[3] Ideally, all inputs should be measured in productivity adjusted units; otherwise, differences in input quality show up in ω_{it} or ϵ_{it}.

(2015). For this approach to identify the production function, we need to make some further assumptions. First, we assume that ω_{it} evolves over time according to a fixed Markov process, i.e.,

$$\omega_{it} = g\left(\omega_{i,t-1},\ X_{i,t-1}\right) + \xi_{it} \tag{5.4}$$

where $X_{i,\,t-1}$ is a vector of firm-level characteristics that potentially affect the law of motion for productivity and $g(\omega_{i,\,t-1},\ X_{i,\,t-1}) = [\omega_{it}|\omega_{i,\,t-1},\ X_{i,\,t-1}]$ is expected productivity conditional on past productivity and $X_{i,\,t-1}$. Note that by construction, $[\xi_{it}] = 0$, $Cov(\omega_{i,\,t-1}; \xi_{it}) = 0$ and $Cov(X_{i,\,t-1}; \xi_{it}) = 0$. As in Ackerberg et al. (2015) we assume that (5.4) is known by each firm.

Next we assume that capital requires time to build, with the firm-level capital stock at time t being determined by investment at time $t-1$. Formally, we assume that capital follows a deterministic law of motion given by:

$$k_{it} = \kappa\left(k_{i,t-1},\ i_{i,t-1}\right) \tag{5.5}$$

where $i_{i,\,t-1}$ is investment in capital at time $t-1$.

While (5.5) implies that capital is predetermined at the beginning of each period t, we assume that labour, materials, and investment, are determined by the firm after observing ω_{it}. The particular timing assumptions we make are graphically described in Fig. 5.1. At the beginning of period t, we assume that each firm i inherits a predetermined capital stock k_{it}, and then observes ω_{it}. The firm then chooses $\{l_{it}, m_{it}, i_{it}\}$ to maximize the present discounted value of profits. After making these input decisions, ϵ_{it} is realized. Finally, investment is realized, generating $k_{i,\,t+1}$, which takes us to the start of period $t+1$. Following Ackerberg et al. (2015), we assume that labour may have dynamic implications (e.g., adjustment costs), while materials inputs are "static," in the sense that they have no dynamic implications. This means materials demand will only depend on current state variables of the firm (e.g. current productivity, capital, and labour), while labour demand may depend on a firm's expectations about the future.

Finally, we assume that the conditional demand function for m_{it} only depends on a single unobservable, ω_{it}, and the conditional demand function is strictly increasing in ω_{it}. Let W_{it} denote a vector of firm-level observable characteristics (aside from labour and capital) that may affect materials demand. The final set of assumptions can then be written compactly as:

$$m_{it} = h_t(l_{it},\ k_{it},\ W_{it},\ \omega_{it}),\quad \frac{\partial h_t}{\partial \omega_{it}} > 0. \tag{5.6}$$

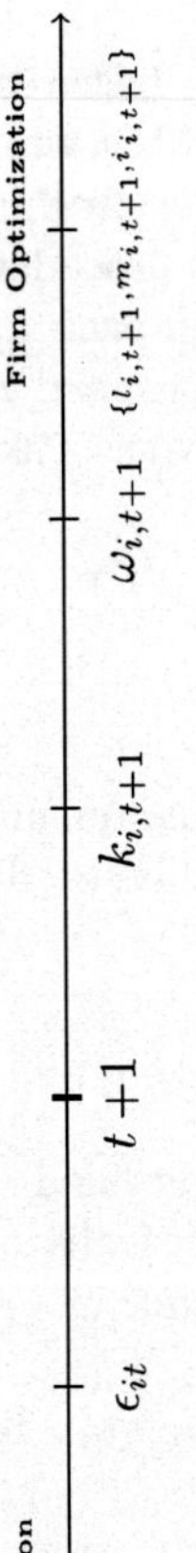

Fig. 5.1 Timeline

5.3 Estimation

The estimation procedure is primarily based on the two-step "proxy-variable" approach described in Ackerberg et al. (2015), while also incorporating some insights from De Loecker and Warzynski (2012). In this section, we describe the details of our empirical implementation of this procedure. Afterwards, we describe some extensions to the general estimation approach that we implement, including estimation with over-identification restrictions, and correcting for attrition bias using a selection-correction approach as in Olley and Pakes (1996).

5.3.1 *First Stage*

To generate the first-stage estimating equation, note that Eq. (5.6) is invertible since we assume conditional materials demand is strictly increasing in ω_{it}. As a result, we can write:

$$\omega_{it} = h_t^{-1}(l_{it},\ k_{it},\ m_{it},\ W_{it}). \tag{5.7}$$

Note that all the variables on the right-hand side of (5.7) are observable. As a result, we should be able to non-parametrically account for the effect of ω_{it} in the production function. In particular, substitute (5.7) into (5.3), yielding:

$$y_{it} = \phi_t(l_{it},\ k_{it},\ m_{it},\ W_{it}) + \epsilon_{it} \tag{5.8}$$

where

$$\phi_t(l_{it},\ k_{it},\ m_{it},\ W_{it}) \equiv f(l_{it},\ k_{it},\ m_{it};\ \beta) + h_t^{-1}(l_{it},\ k_{it},\ m_{it},\ W_{it}).$$

Equation (5.8) is the first-stage estimating equation. Although the production function parameters β cannot be identified from this equation,[4] estimating (5.8) allows us to obtain estimates of ϵ_{it}, the pro-ductivity shocks that the firm observes *after* it has made its input decisions. In practice, we treat ω_{it} as fundamental firm productivity and treat ϵ_{it} as noise that we net out when examining productivity empirically.

There are a variety of ways one could non-parametrically estimate (5.8). The standard approach in the literature, which we also follow, is to approximate φ_t by a cubic polynomial in l_{it}, k_{it}, m_{it} and W_{it}. Since in our particular application, we take W_{it} to only consist of an indicator for whether a firm exports or not, we can write

[4] This is because we cannot separately identify $f\ (l_{it},\ k_{it},\ m_{it};\ \beta)$ from $h_t^{-1}\ (l_{it},\ k_{it},\ m_{it},\ W_{it})$.

the first stage estimating equation as follows[5]:

$$y_{it} = \alpha_0 + V_{it}\alpha_1 + E_{it}V_{it}\alpha_2 + \alpha_t + \epsilon_{it} \tag{5.9}$$

where

$$V_{it} = \Big(l_{it},\ l_{it}^2, l_{it}^3, k_{it}, k_{it}^2, k_{it}^3, m_{it}, m_{it}^2, m_{it}^3, l_{it}k_{it}, l_{it}^2 k_{it}, l_{it}k_{it}^2, l_{it}m_{it}, l_{it}^2 m_{it}, l_{it}m_{it}^2,$$
$$m_{it}k_{it}, m_{it}^2 k_{it}, m_{it}k_{it}^2, l_{it}k_{it}m_{it} \Big)$$

is a vector of input interaction terms, E_{it} is equal to 1 if a firm exports (and is equal to zero otherwise), α_t is a vector of year fixed effects (to control for the variation in φ_t over time), and α_0, α_1, α_2 are parameters to be estimated. We then estimate (5.9) using OLS.

5.3.2 Second Stage

To obtain the second-stage estimating equation we need to take a stance on the particular functional form $f(.)$ takes in (5.3). We consider four different functional forms for the production function; Cobb–Douglas value added (CD VA), translog value added (TL VA), Cobb–Douglas gross output (CD GO) and translog gross output (TL GO). Letting y_{it}^{VA} be the log of value added (sales minus material costs), the two different value-added functional forms are described by:

$$y_{it}^{VA} = \beta_L l_{it} + \beta_K k_{it} + \omega_{it} + \epsilon_{it} \quad \text{(CD VA)}$$

and

$$y_{it}^{VA} = \beta_L l_{it} + \beta_K k_{it} + \beta_{LL}(l_{it})^2 + \beta_{KK}(k_{it})^2 + \beta_{LK} l_{it} k_{it} + \omega_{it} + \epsilon_{it}. \quad \text{(TL VA)}$$

The gross-output functional forms are described by:

$$y_{it} = \beta_L l_{it} + \beta_K k_{it} + \beta_M m_{it} + \omega_{it} + \epsilon_{it} \quad \text{(CD GOS)}$$

and

$$y_{it} = \beta_L l_{it} + \beta_K k_{it} + \beta_M m_{it} + \beta_{LL}(l_{it})^2 + \beta_{KK}(k_{it})^2 + \beta_{MM}(m_{it})^2 + \beta_{LK} l_{it} k_{it}$$

[5] Note that y_{it} in the first stage estimating equation should either be in gross-output or value-added units, depending on the exact specification of the production function one wishes to estimate.

$$+ \beta_{LM} l_{it} m_{it} + \beta_{KM} k_{it} m_{it} + \omega_{it} + {}_{it}. \quad \text{(TLGO)}$$

We begin by discussing the estimator for the simplest case of Cobb–Douglas value added, and then conclude by discussing modifications needed for the more complicated functional forms described by (TL VA), (CD GO), and (TL GO). When the production function is given by (CD VA), the second-stage estimator is based on the following two moment conditions:

$$\mathbb{E}\left[\xi_{it}\begin{pmatrix} l_{i,t-1} \\ k_{it} \end{pmatrix}\right] = \begin{pmatrix} 0 \\ 0 \end{pmatrix}. \tag{5.10}$$

We discuss these in turn. The second moment condition, $[\xi_{it} k_{it}] = 0$, follows from the fact that capital is predetermined (through Eq. 5.5), and as such should not be correlated with the innovation to productivity, ξ_{it}.

Next consider the first moment condition $[\xi_{it} l_{i,t-1}] = 0$. Since ω_{it} (and therefore ξ_{it}) is observed before the firm chooses labour input, $[\xi_{it} l_{it}] \neq 0$. Following Ackerberg et al. (2015), we instrument for labour using it's lagged value, since this choice is made before ξ_{it} is revealed, and hence we should have $[\xi_{it} l_{i,t-1}] = 0$. Relevancy of the instrument is justified by labour adjustment costs (as we assumed in Sect. 5.2) or serial correlation in firm-level wages.

To estimate the model by GMM using the moment conditions (5.10), one must first obtain ξ_{it} as a function of β_L, β_K, and observable parameters. This can be done as follows. First, note that since $\varphi_t\ (l_{it},\ k_{it},\ m_{it},\ W_{it}) = f(l_{it},\ k_{it},\ m_{it};\ \beta) + h_t^{-1}(l_{it},\ k_{it},\ m_{it},\ W_{it})$, we can write $\omega_{it} = \varphi_t(l_{it}, k_{it}, m_{it}, W_{it}) - \beta_L l_{it} - \beta_K k_{it}$ using (5.7) and (CD VA). Since φ_t has been estimated in the first stage, we can obtain an estimate of ω_{it} as a function of β_L, β_K and observable parameters, as follows:

$$\hat{\omega}_{it}\ (\beta_l, \beta_k) = \hat{\phi}_{it} - \beta_L l_{it} - \beta_K k_{it} \tag{5.11}$$

where $\hat{\phi}_{it}$ is the predicted value of each observation from the first-stage regression, i.e., $\hat{\phi}_{it} \equiv \hat{\alpha}_0 + V_{it}\hat{\alpha}_1 + E_{it}V_{it}\hat{\alpha}_2 + \hat{\alpha}_t$.

Next, note that by (5.4), $\xi_{it} = \omega_{it} - g(\omega_{i,\,t-1}, X_{i,\,t-1})$. Hence, if $g(\omega_{i,\,t-1}, X_{i,\,t-1})$ were known, we could recover ξ_{it} using (5.11). In practice, we do this by estimating $g(.)$ non-parametrically for every potential value of (β_L, β_K).[6] In particular, suppose, as in our application, that $X_{i,\,t-1}$ only consists of an indicator variable for whether a firm exports or not (denoted, as before, by $E_{i,\,t-1}$). Approximating $g(.)$ using a cubic polynomial in $\hat{\omega}_{i,\,t-1}$ and $E_{i,\,t-1}$, we then estimate the following model by OLS for every candidate value of (β_L, β_K):

$$\hat{\omega}_{it}(\beta_L,\ \beta_K) = \gamma_0 + \widetilde{V}_{it}(\beta_L,\ \beta_K)\gamma_1 + \left(E_{i,\,t-1}\widetilde{V}_{it}(\beta_L,\ \beta_K)\right)\gamma_2 + \xi_{it} \tag{5.12}$$

[6] This is equivalent to "concentrating out" the parameters governing $g(.)$ in the overall GMM estimation procedure.

where $\tilde{V}_{it}(\beta_L, \beta_K) = \left(\hat{\omega}_{i,t-1}(\beta_L, \beta_K), \hat{\omega}^2_{i,t-1}(\beta_L, \beta_K), \hat{\omega}^3_{i,t-1}(\beta_L, \beta_K)\right)$.

Having estimated (5.12) for a given value of (β_L, β_K), we can now obtain an estimate for ξ_{it} for any trial value of (β_L, β_K), which we denote by:

$$\begin{aligned}\hat{\xi}_{it}(\beta_L, \beta_K) = \widehat{\omega_{it}}(\beta_L, \beta_K) - \hat{\gamma}_0(\beta_L, \beta_K) - \tilde{V}_{it}(\beta_L, \beta_K)\hat{\gamma}_1(\beta_L, \beta_K) \\ - \left(E_{i,t-1}\tilde{V}_{it}(\beta_L, \beta_K)\right)\hat{\gamma}_2 + (\beta_L, \beta_K) \end{aligned} \tag{5.13}$$

where $\widehat{\gamma_i}(\beta_L, \beta_K)$ denotes the OLS estimate of γ_i in (5.12), given (β_L, β_K).

We then use (5.13) to estimate the remaining parameters using standard GMM techniques. In particular, a Nelder-Mead optimization routine is used to choose the value of β that minimizes a quadratic form of the sample equivalent of the moments conditions described by (5.10). Formally, we choose (β_L, β_K) to solve[7]:

$$\min_{\beta} Q(\beta) = \left(Z'\hat{\xi}(\beta)\right)' \left(Z'\hat{\xi}(\beta)\right) \tag{5.14}$$

where, for example, if we observe a balanced panel of n firms for T periods, $\hat{\xi}(\beta)$ is an $n(T-1) \times 1$ vector with typical element given by (5.13) and Z is an $n(T-1) \times 3$ matrix of instruments, with each column corresponding to $l_{i,t-1}$, k_{it}, and a constant, respectively. Note that $\left(Z'\hat{\xi}(\beta)\right)' \left(Z'\hat{\xi}(\beta)\right)$ is just the standard (unweighted) GMM criterion function for the moment conditions described by (5.10).

This completes the estimation algorithm for the Cobb–Douglas value-added case. As discussed by De Loecker and Warzynski (2012), estimation using more complicated functional forms follows the same general procedure. The only modification that needs to be made is the inclusion of extra moment conditions in the GMM criterion function to identify any extra parameters. For example, in the translog value-added case, where the production function is given by (TL VA) above, we define the following moments to estimate the production function:

$$\mathbb{E}\left[\xi_{it}\begin{pmatrix} l_{i,t-1} \\ k_{it} \\ l^2_{i,t-1} \\ k^2_{it} \\ l_{i,t-1}k_{it} \end{pmatrix}\right] = \begin{pmatrix} 0 \\ 0 \\ 0 \\ 0 \\ 0 \end{pmatrix}, \tag{5.15}$$

i.e., we obtain more moments by interacting the instruments in the same manner these variables are being interacted within the production function. In this case, the system is still exactly identified so the form of the criterion function does not change. Note, however, that the matrix of instruments Z will now include the "extra" instruments, $l^2_{i,t-1}$, k^2_{it} and $l_{i,t-1}k_{it}$.

---

[7] Note that β in the GMM criterion function always includes a constant term as well as $(\beta L, \beta K)$.

Estimation of gross-output production functions, as in (CD GO) and (TL GO), proceed analogously, with the extra moment condition for identifying the materials coefficient(s) being given by:

$$\mathbb{E}(\xi_{it} m_{i,t-1}) = 0, \tag{5.16}$$

i.e., we use lagged materials to identify the materials input elasticity, because we would expect current materials to be correlated with the innovation to firm i's current productivity, as in De Loecker and Warzynski (2012) and Brooks et al. (2016).[8]

Having discussed the basic estimation procedure, we now consider some of the extensions to the main approach that we will be using.

5.3.3 Extensions: Over-Identification and Attrition

5.3.3.1 Over-Identification

Note that we can also use $k_{i,\,t-1}$ as an "extra" instrument for k_{it}. In this case, we have more identifying moments than we have parameters to identify and, as a result, we minimize the standard weighted GMM

criterion function to identify β. In particular. We solve:

$$\min_{\beta} Q(\beta) = \left(Z'\hat{\xi}(\beta)\right) \left(Z'Z\right)^{-1} \left(Z'\hat{\xi}(\beta)\right) \tag{5.17}$$

where, in the Cobb–Douglas case, Z is now an $n(T-1) \times 4$ matrix with columns corresponding to a constant, $l_{i,t-1}$, k_{it} and $k_{i,t-1}$, respectively.[9]

5.3.3.2 Attrition

The methods described so far have implicitly been for balanced panels. However, our data involves an unbalanced panel of firms due to firms exiting the market. As a result, our estimates will suffer from attrition bias since firms with high values of ω will tend to stay in our dataset, i.e., high-productivity firms are less likely to exit

[8] Note that Gandhi et al. (2016) have recently pointed out that this sort of identification strategy, which has previously been used in the literature, may run into some identification problems. In particular, they show that proxy-variable approaches that use lagged materials as an instrument for a gross-output production function are non-parametrically non-identified. Put differently, functional form restrictions are not innocuous when one uses this type of estimation strategy, because the production function parameters will only be identified off of these restrictions. This may lead to misleading inference if the functional form restrictions do not hold in practice.

[9] If we are considering the translog case, Z also contains $l_{i,t-1}^2$, k_{it}^2, $l_{i,t-1}$, k_{it}, $k_{i,t-1}$, $k_{i,t-1}^2$ and $l_{i,t-1}k_{i,t-1}$

while low-productivity firms (low ω) are more likely to exit as they are not productive enough to survive in the current market place.

Following Olley and Pakes (1996), we can include an extra selection term in the procedure to correct for attrition bias. In particular, suppose that firm exit is endogenous in the sense that a firm (rationally) decides to exit if it draws a value of ω_{it} that is sufficiently low. Olley and Pakes (1996) point out that if we model entry and exit using the tools developed in Ericson and Pakes (1995), then firm i will exit the market whenever $\omega_{it} < \overline{\omega_{it}} = \overline{\omega_t}(k_{it})$, where $\overline{\omega_t}(k_{it})$ is the cutoff value of ω_{it}, which will depend on k_{it} as well as any other state variables of the firm's dynamic programming problem.

Having put some structure on the firm's exit decision, we can now characterize the probability that a firm in period $t-1$ continues into period t. Let P_{it} denote the probability that we observe firm i at time t, *conditional* on the firm's information set at the end of period $t-1$. Given the optimal cutoff rule, this probability is given by:

$$P_{it} = \Pr\big(\omega_{it} \geq \overline{\omega_{it}} | \overline{\omega_{it}},\ \omega_{i,t-1}\big) = \wp_t\big(\overline{\omega_{it}},\ \omega_{i,t-1}\big) \tag{5.18}$$

where $\wp_t$ is some unknown function. Note that since we are conditioning on the firm's information set at the end of period $t-1$, $\overline{\omega_{i,\,t}} = \overline{\omega_t}(k_{it})$ is *known*, because capital is predetermined.

Notice that we can estimate (5.18) via a probit regression using the information that we have. In particular, note that while a firm's capital stock at time t will not be observed if a firm has exited by time t, we can still infer the level of the capital stock from investment behaviour using (5.5). As a result, k_{it} is going to be some deterministic function of past investment and capital, $\kappa(k_{i,\,t-1},\ i_{i,\,t-1})$. Substituting (5.5) and (5.7) into (5.18) then yields:

$$\begin{aligned} P_{it} &= \wp_t\big(\overline{\omega_{it}}\big(\kappa\big(k_{i,\,t-1},\ i_{i,\,t-1}\big)\big),\ h^{-1}\big(l_{i,\,t-1},\ k_{i,\,t-1},\ m_{i,\,t-1},\ W_{i,\,t-1}\big)\big) \\ &= \wp_t\ \big(k_{i,\,t-1},\ i_{i,\,t-1},\ l_{i,\,t-1},\ m_{i,\,t-1,},\ W_{i,\,t-1}\big). \end{aligned} \tag{5.19}$$

Hence, we can obtain an estimate of the probability of remaining in the dataset at time t by running a non-parametric selection probit on a cubic polynomial in $k_{i,\,t-1}$, $i_{i,\,t-1}$, $l_{i,\,t-1}$, $m_{i,\,t-1}$, and $W_{i,\,t-1}$. Call the predicted values from this regression $\widehat{P}_{it}$.

The final step, following Olley and Pakes (1996), is to note that the bias term that shows up due to non-random exit in the second-stage regression is given by $\mathbb{E}\big[\omega_{i,\,t}|\omega_{i,\,t-1},\ \omega_{i,\,t} \geq \overline{\omega_{i,\,t}}\big] = \overline{g}\big(\omega_{i,\,t-1},\ \overline{\omega_{i,\,t}}\big)$. Hence, to correct for this bias we need to include a non-parametric function of $\overline{\omega_{i,t}}$ and $\omega_{i,\,t-1}$ in the second-stage regression. While we have already discussed in Sects. 5.3.1 and 5.3.2 how to recover estimates of lagged productivity, $\overline{\omega_{i,t}}$ still needs to be estimated.

To estimate $\overline{\omega_{i,t}}$, note that since (5.18) is a conditional survival probability, it *must* be monotonically decreasing in $\overline{\omega_{i,t}}$. As a result, we can invert (5.18), yielding:

$$\overline{\omega_{i,\,t}} = \wp_t^{-1}\big(P_{it},\ \omega_{i,\,t-1}\big). \tag{5.20}$$

Since we already have estimates for the probability of staying in the market, $\widehat{P}_{it}$, and we also have estimates of past productivity, $\widehat{\omega}_{i,\,t-1}$, we actually do not need to estimate $\overline{\omega_{it}}$. Rather, the "bias" term $\overline{g}(\cdot)$ can simple be written as $\overline{g}\left(\omega_{i,t-1}, \wp_t^{-1}\left(P_{it}, \omega_{i,t-1}\right)\right)$, i.e., we can control for endogenous exit by including a cubic in the estimated survival probability $\widehat{P}_{it}$ and lagged productivity $\widehat{\omega}_{i,\,t-1}$ in the regression model (5.12) (i.e., the regression for the law of motion for productivity, where we now include the bias correction terms in this regression). In particular, define the following vector of cubic terms for $\widehat{P}_{it}$ and $\widehat{\omega}_{i,\,t-1}$:

$$\begin{aligned}\overline{V}_{it}(\beta) =& (\hat{\omega}_{i,\,t-1}(\beta),\ \hat{\omega}^2_{i,\,t-1}(\beta),\ \hat{\omega}^3_{i,\,t-1}(\beta),\ \widehat{P}_{it},\ \widehat{P}^2_{it},\ \widehat{P}^3_{it},\ \widehat{P}_{it}\\ &\times \hat{\omega}_{i,\,t-1}(\beta),\ \widehat{P}^2_{it} \times \hat{\omega}_{i,\,t-1}(\beta),\ \widehat{P}_{it} \times \hat{\omega}^2_{i,\,t-1}(\beta)).\end{aligned}$$

Continuing to take lagged export status $E_{i,\,t-1}$ as the only other firm-level variable that affects the law of motion for productivity, we can then estimate the following model by OLS for each candidate value of β:

$$\widehat{\omega}_{it}(\beta) = \theta_0 + \overline{V}_{it}(\beta)\theta_1 + \left(E_{i,t-1}\overline{V}_{it}\right) + \theta_2 + \xi_{it}. \tag{5.21}$$

As before, we then construct an estimate of $\widehat{\xi_{it}}$, for each potential value of β, as follows:

$$\widehat{\xi_{it}}(\beta) = \widehat{\omega_{it}}(\beta) - \widehat{\theta_0}(\beta) - \widehat{V}_{it}(\beta)\widehat{\theta_1}(\beta) - \left(E_{i,t-1}\widetilde{V}_{it}(\beta)\right)\widehat{\theta_2}(\beta) \tag{5.22}$$

which we then use to construct the criterion function (5.14).

5.4 Data and Empirical Implementation

We use firm-level data from the 2000–2006 Chinese Manufacturing Enterprises (CME) dataset. The dataset includes information on all state-owned enterprises (SOEs) as well as non-SOEs with annual sales of more than RMD 5 million. We first clean these data according to the method described in Feenstra et al. (2014) by eliminating observations with (a) incomplete or internally inconsistent financial variables, (b) fewer than 8 employees, (c) missing firm identification, or (d) invalid entries for year. We then drop firms based on four extra criteria that are relevant for productivity analysis. First, the firms must have complete data on sales, employment, material costs, and capital. Second, they cannot have 'holes' over time, i.e., if they appear in years t_0 and t_1 then they must appear in all years between t_0 and t_1. Third, they cannot switch industries or cities over time (city switching is very rare). Industries are defined at the 2-digit Census Industry Classification level (CIC-2). Fourth, we

Table 5.1 Number of firm-years

CIC-2	Industry name	Observations
17	Textiles	74,088
31	Non-metallic minerals	70,632
26	Raw chemicals	65,328
35	General machinery	59,285
18	Apparel	49,456
30	Plastics	43,153
13	Food processing	39,270
37	Transport equipment	32,269
36	Special machinery	31,077
39	Electrical machinery	32,131
34	Metal	30,295
22	Paper	22,733
23	Printing	21,319
32	Smelting, ferrous metals	21,468
19	Leather	20,590
20	Timber	16,724
14	Food manufacturing	16,862
27	Medicines	15,633
40	Communication equipment	16,435
33	Smelting, non-ferrous metals	14,328
42	Art	13,775
24	Toys	11,830
21	Furniture	11,524
15	Beverages	11,103
29	Rubber	10,031
41	Measuring instruments	9,319
25	Petroleum	6,780
28	Chemical fibers	4,676
	Total	772,114

drop Tobacco (CIC-2 = 16) because it has too few firms. This leaves us with 772,788 firm-years and 298,259 firms in 28 industries. See Table 5.1.

To prepare the data for estimation, we deflate each firm's sales using an industry-level price deflator. We deflate materials input expenditures at the industry level using input price deflators that have been filtered through the Chinese input–output tables.[10] We estimate the production function by CIC-2 industry using six different

[10] We measure labour input using employment and thus do not need a labour deflator. However, capital is simply measured in RMB.

methods: OLS and five different variants of the proxy-variable approach outlined in Sect. 5.3. The five proxy-variable estimators are:

1. Case 1 (Vanilla): This specification is exactly as described in Sect. 5.3 except that we do not allow the law of motion for ω_{it} to depend on observables.[11]
2. Case 2 (Exporting): Same as vanilla except we allow the law of motion for firm level productivity to depend on lagged export status. This controls for learning-by-exporting effects as in De Loecker and Warzynski (2012) and De Loecker (2013).
3. Case 3 (Attrition): Same as vanilla, except we include the selection correction terms to correct for attrition bias. See Sect. 5.3.3.2.
4. Case 4 (Over-identification): Same as vanilla, except we include $k_{i,t-1}$ as an extra instrument. We also include $k^2_{i,t-1}$ as an extra instrument in the translog case. See Sect. 5.3.3.1.
5. Case 5 (Full Model): The case 2–4 modifications of case 1 are all introduced simultaneously.

We apply each of these estimation strategies to each of the four functional forms for the production function described in Sect. 5.3.2, i.e.,

1. Cobb–Douglas, Value Added
2. Cobb–Douglas, Gross Output
3. Translog, Value Added
4. Translog, Gross Output

This yields $6 \times 4 = 24$ methods for calculating productivity for each of the 28 industries we observe. Since this results in 672 different production function estimates, to convey a representative picture of the production functions of firms in China we will often present histograms of coefficients *weighted* by the number of observations in Table 5.1. In particular, this approach is ideal for Cobb–Douglas specifications, since many important features of the production function are characterized by production function para-meters that only vary across industries, not firms, e.g., the derivative of the log production function with respect to log labour is β_L. On the other hand, this is no longer the case for translog production functions, as even simple features of the production function, such as derivatives, depend on where the firm is located on the production function. Restated, simple features of the production function vary across firm-year observations, even within an industry. In this case, we will summarize our production function results by showing histograms of various firm-level characteristics, e.g., the derivative of log production function with respect to log labour inputs, at the firm level.

[11] Put differently, X_{it} in (4) is empty. Note, however, that W_{it} is not empty. (Recall that W_{it} is the vector of firm-level variables that affect demand for inputs.) Following De Loecker and Warzynski (2012), W_{it} always includes an export dummy. For the reader interested in the exporting-and-productivity literature, this means that we are *not* allowing exporting to affect the law of motion for productivity in the vanilla case. This is allowed only in cases 2 and 5.

5.5 Results Using Cobb–Douglas

There are a number of possible Cobb–Douglas specifications. We start with *value-added* production functions and consider three cases: OLS, Case 1 (vanilla) and Case 5 (full model). The top panel of Fig. 5.2 reports the labour coefficients β_L. Each curve is a histogram (or, more accurately, smoothed kernel) of the 28 industry-level β_L, but weighted by the number of observations in Table 5.1.[12] The dotted line is OLS histogram, the dashed line is the case 1 (vanilla) histogram, and the solid line is the case 5 (full model) histogram.

Consider the top panel for labour (β_L). The OLS line is left-shifted compared to cases 1 and 5, indicating that the OLS coefficients tend to be smaller. This may be surprising, as we expect OLS to be upward biased. The middle panel is for capital (β_K) and, as expected, OLS tends to generate relatively larger values of β_K than proxy-variable methods. Assuming that our proxy-variable strategy is indeed solving the OLS bias, this may simply indicate that high productivity firms tend to accumulate more capital than labour.

The bottom panel reports the estimated returns to scale, $\beta_L + \beta_K$. OLS estimates almost always display decreasing returns to scale. In contrast, the proxy-variable approaches display much more heterogeneity: There are large masses of firms both above and below unity. While this is surprising, this could also be due to the fact that using a value-added production function does not directly account for the role of materials in production, and therefore we are simply missing the contribution of a very important factor of production.

We can account for this by instead turning to the gross-output production functions in Fig. 5.3. Here we see *much* less variation in the degree of returns to scale. The proxy-variable methods provide estimates of returns to scale in the narrower range of 0.9 to 1.15. These seem much more reasonable than the value-added estimates.[13]

5.6 Results Using Translog

Since translog coefficients are hard to interpret on their own, we instead plot the distribution of the *output elasticities* for each input, e.g., $\partial f/\partial l$ where f is log output and l is log labour. In the Cobb–Douglas case this is just β_L. In the translog case this is:

$$\beta_L + 2\beta_{LL} l_{it} + \beta_{LK} k_{it} + \beta_{LM} m_{it}$$

[12] Point estimates by industry can be found in Appendix 5.1.

[13] Note that for labour and intermediates, all three cases have the same central tendency, but the proxy-variable methods have greater dispersion. In contrast, for capital, the proxy-variable methods yield smaller estimates of β_K.

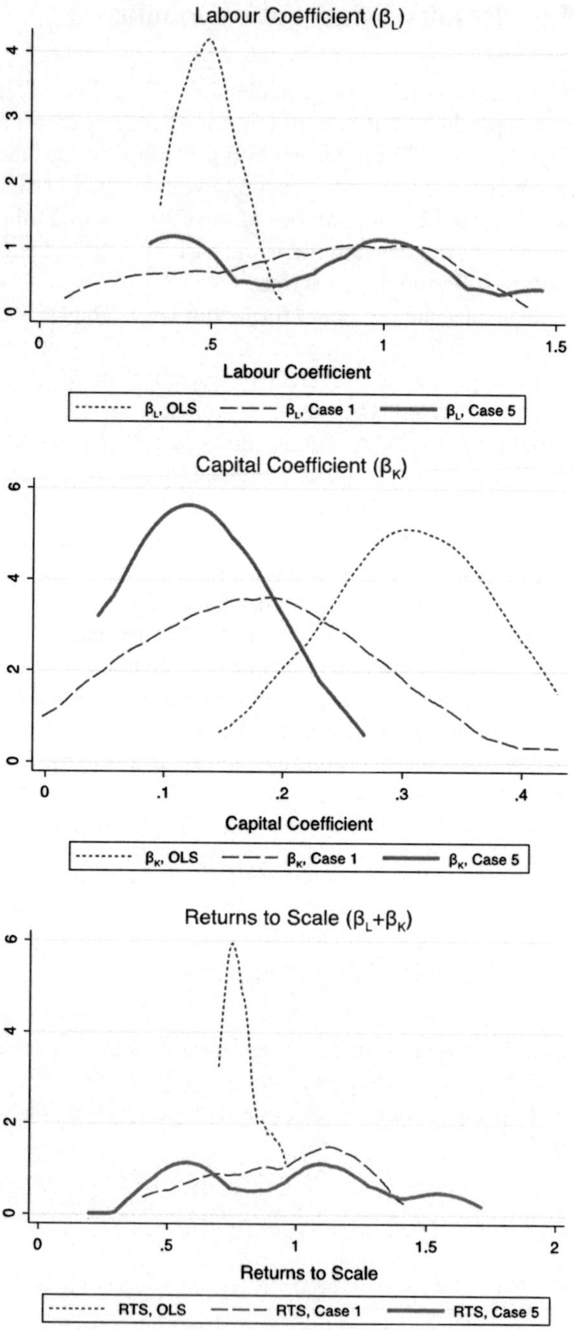

Fig. 5.2 Cobb–Douglas, value-added production functions. *Notes* The top panel reports the labour coefficients β_L. Each curve is a weighted histogram (or more accurately, a smoothed kernel) of the 28 industry-level β_L. The weights are the number of firm-year observations reported in Table 5.1 so that the histograms are representative of the underlying population of firms. The three lines correspond to three different specifications: OLS (dotted line), case 1 or vanilla (dashed line), and case 5 or full model (solid line). The middle panel repeats the exercise for the capital coefficient β_K. The bottom panel repeats the exercise for scale returns $\beta_L + \beta_K$

Fig. 5.3 Cobb–Douglas, gross-output production functions. *Notes* This figure is identical to that in Fig. 5.2, but with three minor differences. First, it is for Cobb–Douglas gross-output production functions (rather than value added). Second, because it is for gross output, there is an additional panel for the materials coefficient β_M. Third, scale returns in the bottom panel is now defined as $\beta_L + \beta_K + \beta_M$. See Fig. 5.2 for additional details

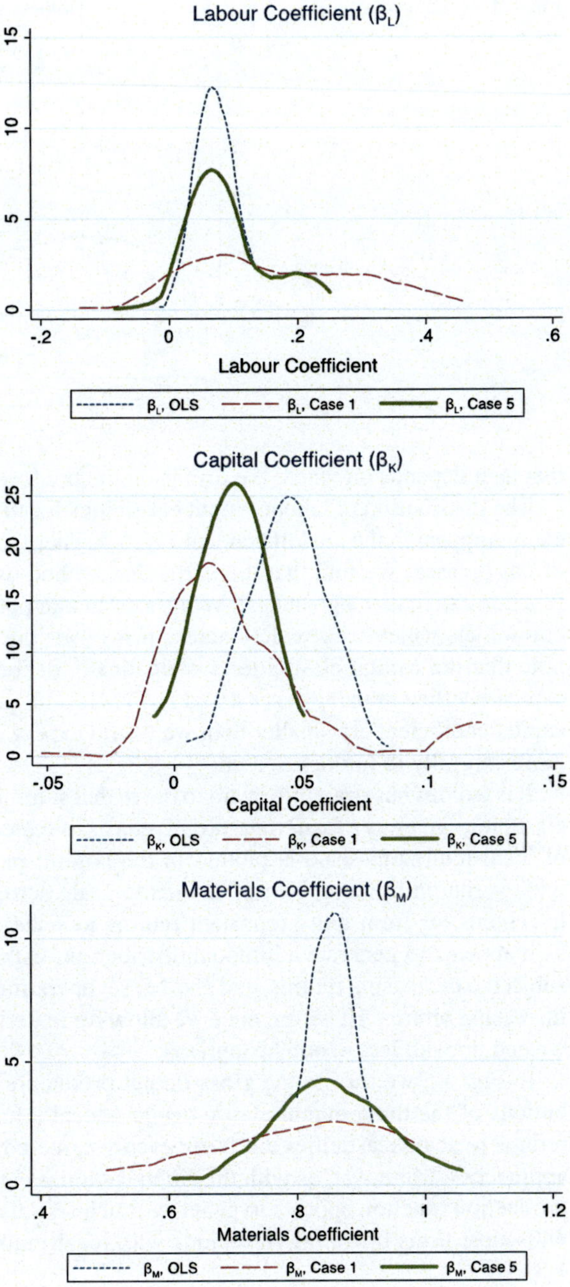

Fig. 5.3 (continued)

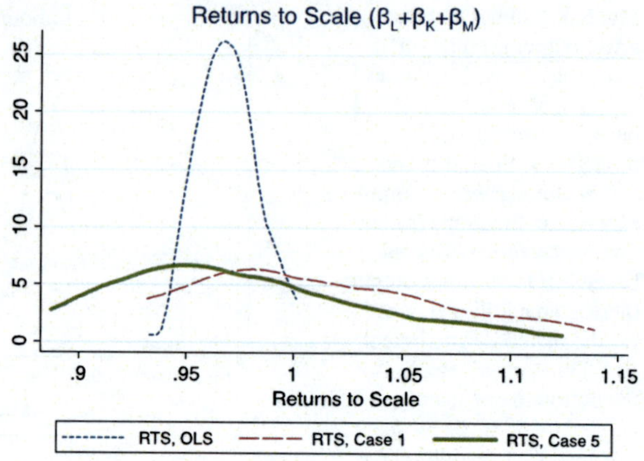

that is, it depends on where the firm is on the production function.

The distribution of labour output elasticities for the translog value-added specifications appear in the top left panel of Fig. 5.4. There are five histograms, one for each of our 5 cases. We find that the particular method used to estimate the production function can matter a great deal. While a particular pattern is hard to see in the labour elasticities, which vary widely across firms over the a priori unlikely range (0, 2), note that the capital elasticities systematically decrease once we over-identify the capital coefficient using cases 4 and 5. This is a bit puzzling, as these values on the capital coefficient are smaller than we would expect. This may be worth examining more carefully in future research.

It is tedious but straightforward to prove that summing the labour and capital input elasticities gives us a *local* measure of returns to scale at the firm level. This measure of local returns to scale is plotted in the bottom panel of Fig. 5.4. We find very wide variation in the degree of returns to scale across firms, with many operating in regions far from unity (constant returns to scale). Case 5 is of particular note, as it appears to generate a bimodal distribution, with a large set of firms operating subject to decreasing returns, and another set operating subject to constant or slightly increasing returns. However, once we allow for materials in the production function, we end up with less exotic histograms.

In Fig. 5.5 we turn to the gross-output production functions and plot the distributions of the three output elasticities and local returns to scale. In particular, the returns to scale elasticities are fairly evenly centered around one for all estimation approaches. Moreover, as with the Cobb–Douglas case, allowing for a gross-output production function appears to generate much less dispersion in the returns to scale, with most firms operating in regions with local returns to scale between 0.75 and 1.3.

One of the most striking features of Fig. 5.5 is how each method appears to provide essentially the same picture of the production technology.

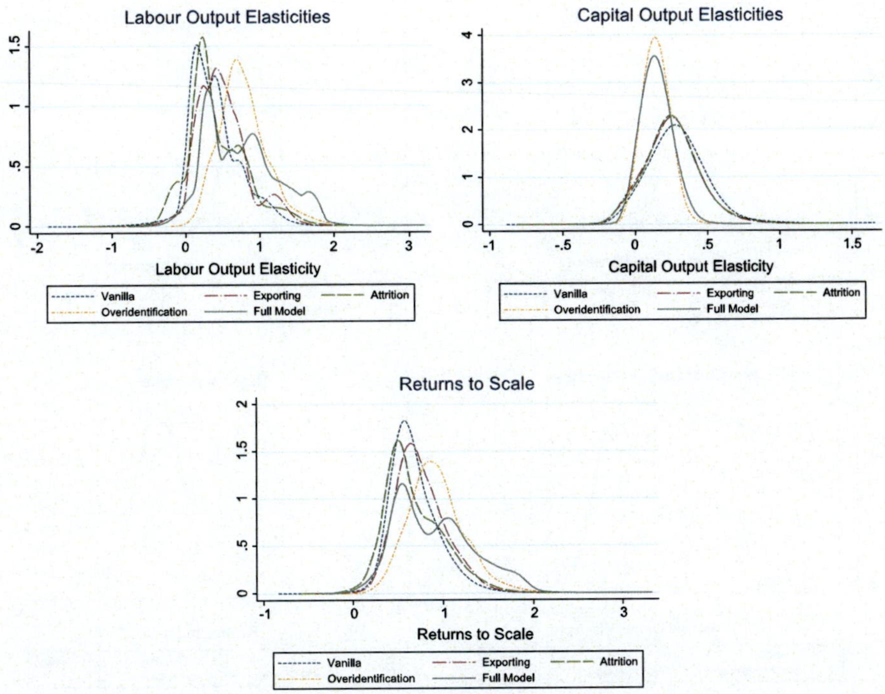

Fig. 5.4 Translog value added: output elasticities and returns to scale. *Notes* Each panel displays 5 histograms and each histogram corresponds to one of the 5 cases described at the start of Sect. 5.4. The panels report labour output elasticities ($\beta_L + 2\beta_{LL}l_{it} + \beta_{LK}k_{it}$), capital output elasticities ($\beta_K + 2\beta_{KK}k_{it} + \beta_{LK}l_{it}$), and returns to scale (the sum of the labour and capital elasticities). Since output elasticities vary across firm-year observations, the histograms are estimated from the 772,788 firm-year observations

It is often the case that estimates of the labour and capital output elasticities (β_L and β_K) are small and even negative for Cobb–Douglas gross-output production functions. Because there is no parameter counterpart to these output elasticities under translog, it is unclear whether this problem persists under translog. Figure 5.5 illustrates that it does. There is a sizeable number of firms operating in regions where increasing labour or capital *decreases output*. In particular, slightly more than 10% of firms have negative labour and capital output elasticities.

This calls for an explanation. One possibility is that there is a problem with the underlying data. According to the Chinese Manufacturing Enterprises dataset, Chinese manufacturers have low labour shares. For the median firm it is 26% in 2000–2006. This is low relative to the aggregate Chinese economy, whose labour share averaged above 40% during 2000–2006 (Karabarbounis and Neiman 2014).[14]

[14] The difference between 26 and 40% might be explained by the fact that services are more labour-intensive than manufacturing. We are skeptical that this is the only reason for the difference.

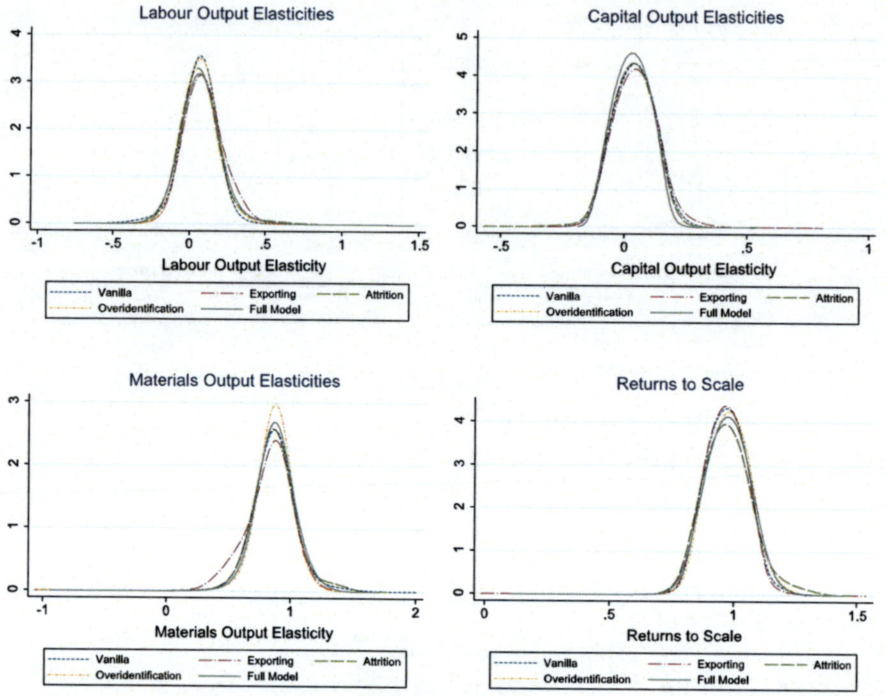

Fig. 5.5 Translog gross output: output elasticities and returns to scale. *Notes* This figure is identical to that in Fig. 5.4, but with three minor differences. First, it is for translog gross-output production functions (rather than value added). Second, because it is for gross output, there is an additional panel for the materials output elasticity ($\beta_M + 2\beta_{MM}\, m_{it} + \beta_{LM}\, m_{it} + \beta_{KM}\, k_{it}$). Third, returns to scale in the bottom panel is now defined as the sum of the labour, capital and materials output elasticities. See Fig. 5.4 for additional details

To investigate the impact of reported labour shares, we re-estimated all of our specifications using the wage bill in place of the number of workers. This did not systematically raise the estimated coefficients associated with labour. Given that small labour and capital coefficients appear in many productivity studies, the explanation is deeper than an appeal to China-specific factors.

It would be useful for future research to determine why these methods generate such small output elasticities for labour and capital and how we are to understand why some firms produce in a region where the increased use of an input decreases output.

5.7 Measures of Within-Industry Productivity Dispersion

In this section, we ask whether the sizeable difference in the production function parameters that we found across many estimation methods in Sects. 5.5 and 5.6 provide different estimates of productivity dispersion. The magnitude of productivity dispersion within an industry is a question of substantive economic interest since industries with greater productivity dispersion have a greater scope for *across-firm* allocative productivity gains. For example, the international trade literature has found that trade liberalization leads to aggregate productivity improvements by reallocating resources away from low productivity firms towards higher productivity firms. See Melitz and Trefler (2012) for a review of this literature. Similarly, a growing literature in macroeconomics and development has argued that various firm-level *wedges* or *distortions* such as taxes and subsidies can generate significant resource misallocation, which can explain a sizeable portion of the large differences in aggregate productivity observed across countries. See Restuccia and Rogerson (2017) for a review of this literature. To quantify the extent to which these mechanisms matter for aggregate productivity and welfare, estimates of industry dispersion in productivity are needed.[15] As a result, it is important to know whether different approaches to estimating productivity will significantly change the degree of dispersion we find in the data.

In Fig. 5.6, we plot the estimated density of log TFP obtained using the five different proxy-variable approaches, for each of the four functional forms of the production function.[16] The most important takeaway from these pictures is how *little* the particular estimation method appears to matter for obtaining an estimate of productivity dispersion, as most of the densities closely align with one another. To see this, note from Fig. 5.6 that in any single panel all 5 curves largely overlap. For the translog value-added production function, which has the largest dispersion, the standard deviations of the 5 estimates range tightly between 0.84 to 0.97. For the Cobb–Douglas gross-output production function, which has the smallest dispersion, the standard deviations of the 5 estimates range tightly between 0.24 and 0.29.

While we obtain similar pictures of TFP dispersion across estimation methods, the assumed functional form of the production function has much larger implications for measuring productivity dispersion. In Fig. 5.7, we plot the dispersion of productivity for our 4 different functional forms using estimation method 5. From the figure, there is *much less* dispersion in productivity when we use a gross-output specification, compared to a value-added specification, with the ratio of standard deviations varying by more than a factor of 3. These are massive differences, likely due to the fact that value-added specifications load the effect of materials on production into the

---

[15] See Melitz and Redding (2015) for a recent discussion on when detailed estimates of micro-level productivity dispersion matter for quantifying the aggregate gains from trade. Similarly, see Hsieh and Klenow (2009) for a detailed discussion on how dispersion in *revenue TFP* can be used to measure the degree of resource misallocation within an industry.

[16] We demean log TFP within an industry in these diagrams, so that we only capture within-industry dispersion in productivity.

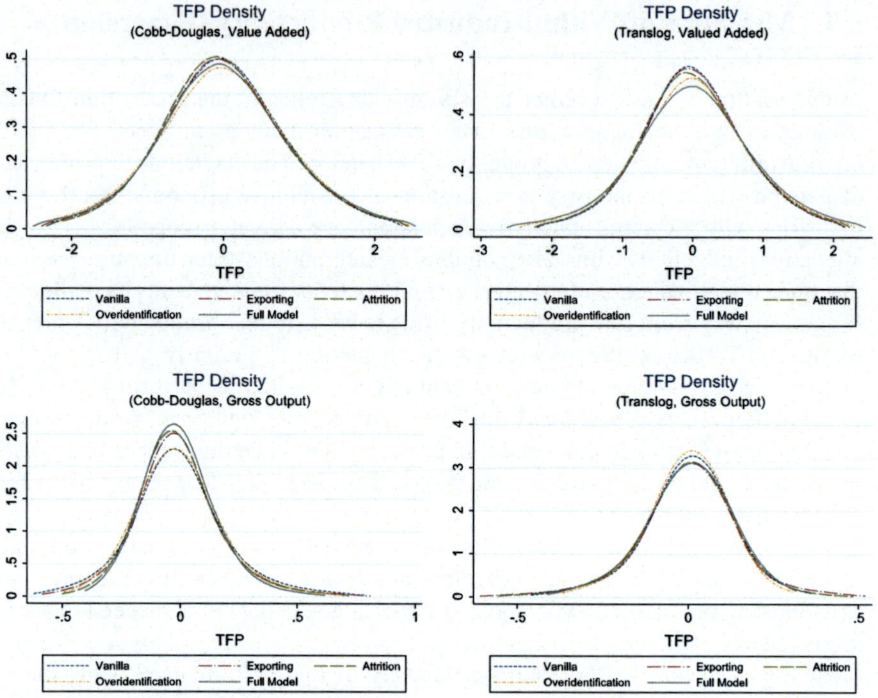

Fig. 5.6 TFP dispersion across estimation methods. *Notes* Each panel plots 5 TFP histograms (kernels), one for each of our 5 cases. TFP has been demeaned at the 2-digit industry level so that the histograms capture within-industry TFP dispersion

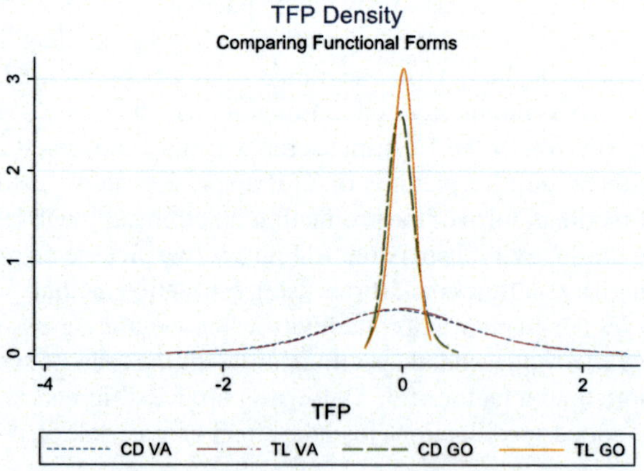

Fig. 5.7 TFP dispersion across functional forms for full model. *Notes* The figure plots 4 TFP histograms (kernels), one for each of our 4 functional forms. CD VA = Cobb–Douglas value added; TL VA = translog value added; CD GO = Cobb–Douglas gross output; TL GO = translog gross output. Only case 5 (Full Model) is used. TFP has been demeaned at the 2-digit industry level so that the histograms capture within-industry TFP dispersion

productivity residual. Since accurately estimating the degree of productivity dispersion matters a great deal for questions related to input reallocations and aggregate efficiency, Fig. 5.7 tells us that thinking carefully about which model more accurately reflects production within the industry is likely of first order importance, as has also been recently argued by Gandhi et al. (2016).

5.8 Assessing Differences in Estimated Productivity—Economic Metrics

We have seen that very different conclusions emerge about productivity dispersion when we compare different methods of estimating TFP. However, with over 700,000 firm-years and 24 different methods of estimating TFP, it is challenging to decide whether these differences carry over to other economic questions of interest. In this section we examine three questions: (1) Are more capital-intensive firms more productive? (2) Are larger firms more productive? (3) Are exporters more productive?

5.8.1 Capital-Intensity and Productivity

Figure 5.8 reports four TFP histogram/kernels for translog specifications. In each panel are two kernels: The solid line is for firms with above-average capital-labour intensities and the dashed line is for firms with below-average capital-labour intensities. On the top left is the kernel associated with a vanilla (case 1) value-added translog production function. It shows that labour-intensive firms are slightly more prominent in the middle of the TFP distribution and capital-intensive firms are slightly more prominent at the top of the TFP distribution. When we move to case 5 (bottom left panel), there is a much clearer separation of the two lines, meaning that there is a much more pronounced 'capital-intensity premium', i.e., capital-intensive firms are more productive.

This is something of a puzzling result given our assumption that, once controlling for capital and labour, we can pool across firms within an industry. The puzzle is resolved by the right-hand panels of Fig. 5.8 which report gross-output translog production functions. In these two pictures, there is very little evidence of a capital-intensity premium. This points to a satisfying feature of gross-output production functions relative to value-added production functions.

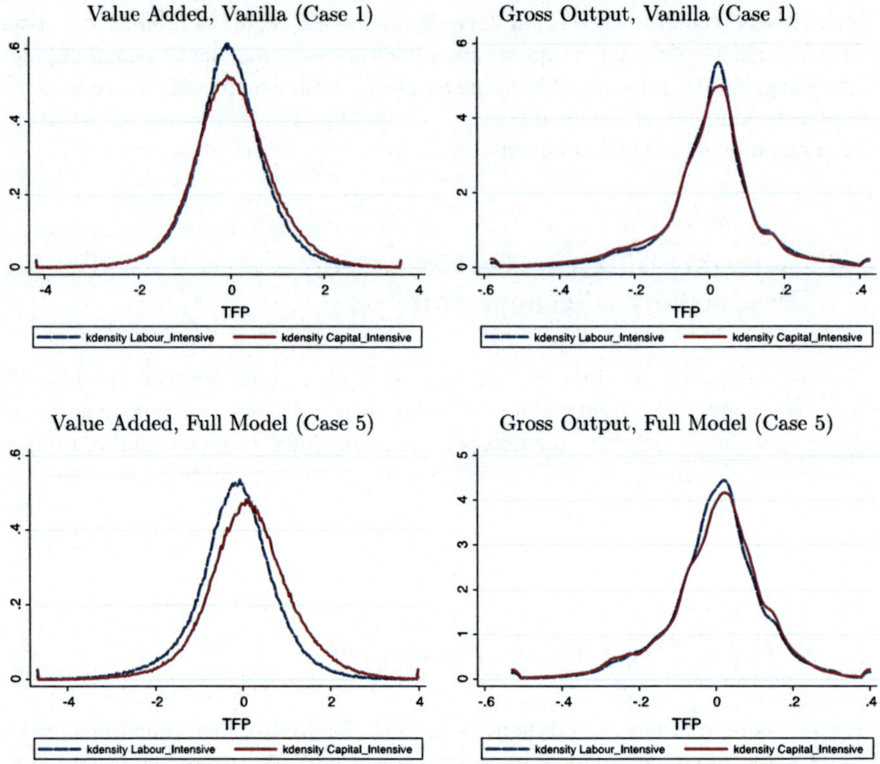

Fig. 5.8 The capital-intensity premium in the translog model. *Notes* This figure plots histograms (kernels) of TFP. TFP has been demeaned at the 2-digit industry level so that the histograms capture within-industry TFP dispersion. There are two histograms per panel. The solid histogram is for capital-intensive firms and the dashed histogram is for labour-intensive firms. A firm is capital-intensive (labour-intensive) if its capital-labour ratio is above (below) the industry's average capital-labour ratio

5.8.2 Sales and Productivity

It is natural to expect that more productive firms will capture a larger share of the market. Without suggesting that we are estimating a causal relationship running from productivity to sales, we can examine the correlation between sales and productivity. To this end, within each industry we divide firms into two groups based on whether the firm has above-average or below-average log sales. We emphasize that this split is done *within* industry.

Each of the four panels in Fig. 5.9 reports two TFP kernels: The solid line is for big firms and the dashed line is for small firms. Consider first the two left panels, which are for value-added production functions. We see that there is a very clear 'size premium,' by which we mean that big firms have higher TFP. The two right panels are for gross-output production functions. They also display a size premium, but it

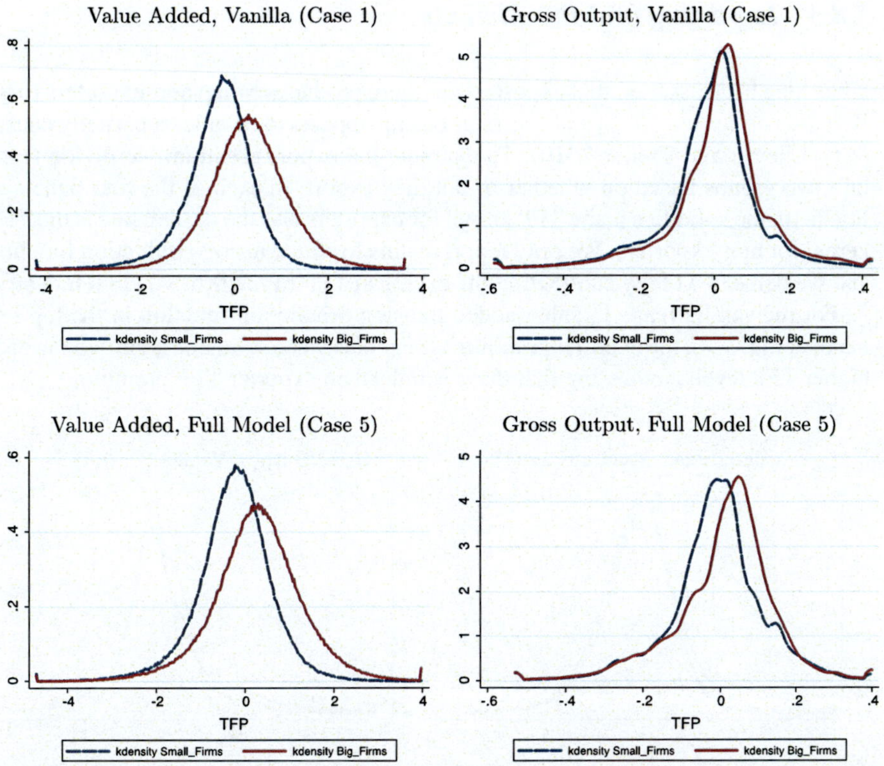

Fig. 5.9 The size premium in the translog model. *Notes* This figure plots histograms (kernels) of TFP. TFP has been demeaned at the 2-digit industry level so that the histograms capture within-industry TFP dispersion. There are two histograms per panel. The solid histogram is for big firms and the dashed histogram is for small firms. A firm is big (small) if its log sales are above (below) its 2-digit industry's average log sales

is less pronounced. This is of interest because translog production functions display non-homotheticities in inputs, i.e., the ratio of inputs to output are allowed to vary with output. Stated more graphically, output expansion paths need not be linear. The difference in size premia between value-added and gross output production functions suggests that much of the non-homotheticities load on capital and labour rather than on materials. This is sensible: a car needs four wheels so the ratio of material inputs (four wheels) to output (cars) is four, independently of the number of cars produced.

5.8.3 Exporting and Productivity

It has long been asserted that exporters are more productive than non-exporters (e.g., Bernard and Jensen 1995) and this relationship appears to be at least partially causal (e.g., Lileeva and Trefler 2010). To examine the export premium we divide firms into two groups based on whether or not they export. In each of the four panels in Fig. 5.10, the solid line is the TFP kernel for exporters and the dashed line is the TFP kernel for non-exporters. We only report results for the translog production function and we demean TFP by subtracting off the mean TFP of the firm's 2-digit industry.

For the vanilla (case 1) value-added translog production function in the top left panel of Fig. 5.10, the exporter premium is very clear. The solid line is shifted towards higher TFP levels, indicating that there is indeed an exporter TFP premium.

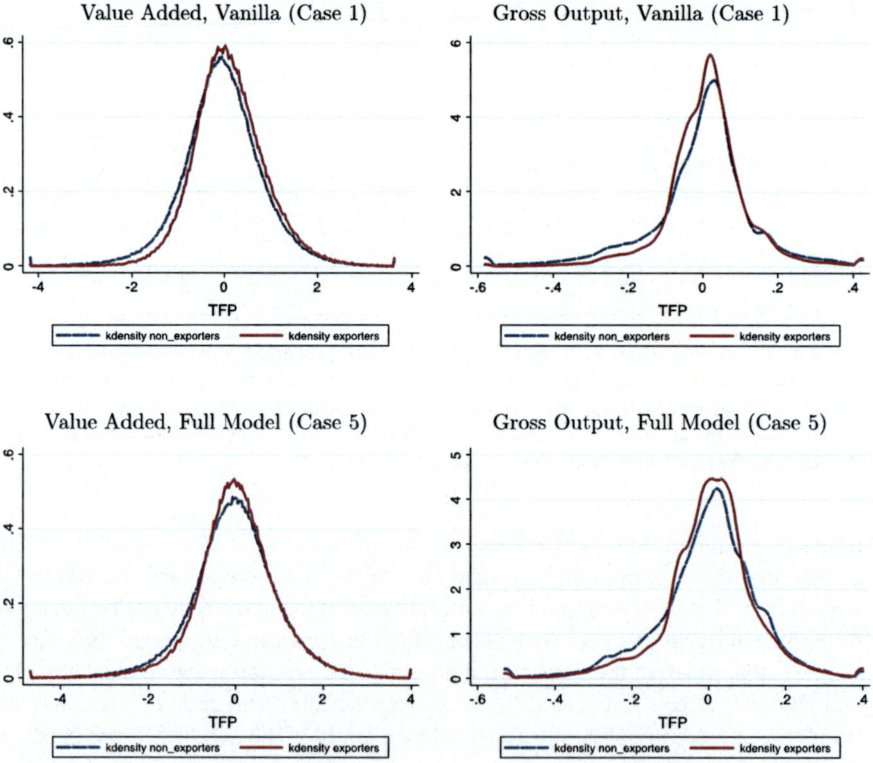

Fig. 5.10 The exporter premium in the translog model. *Notes* This figure plots histograms (kernels) of TFP. TFP has been demeaned at the 2-digit industry level so that the histograms capture within-industry TFP dispersion. There are two histograms per panel. The solid histogram is for firm-years where the firm exports and the dashed histogram is for firm-years where the firm does not export

Recall that in the full model (case 5) we have included a lagged exporter dummy in the equation determining the evolution of productivity (Eq. 5.4).[17] As pointed out by De Loecker (2013), if one theorizes that exporting affects productivity then this is the right thing to do. One then assesses the impact of exporting on productivity by examining the export dummy coefficient in the evolution-of-productivity equation. It is thus of interest that when looking at the value-added translog production function (left panels of Fig. 5.10) and comparing cases 1 with 5, there is a much less pronounced exporter premium. In case 5, where exporting has already been controlled for, there is only a very small exporter premium.

A different conclusion emerges when looking at gross output. See the two right panels of Fig. 5.10. First, the exporter premium in case 1 is confined to firms with productivity below approximately 0.03, which is about 40% of all firms. Second, cases 1 and 5 do not appear to be all that different in terms of inferences about the exporter premium. This may point to the difficulty of including the exporter dummy directly into the evolution-of-productivity equation. Including it solves the problems identified by De Loecker (2013), but the resulting exporter premium may not capture a causal effect because at least some and maybe most of the sample variation in the exporter premium is across firms rather than within firms.[18] In contrast, studies such as Lileeva and Trefler (2010) do not allow for exporting directly in the evolution-of-productivity equation (a drawback), but are able to purely exploit within-firm switching into and out of exporting (an advantage). Tying the two approaches together would be an interesting area for future research.

5.9 Conclusions

We estimated production functions for:

1. 28 industries,
2. OLS plus five proxy-variable methods,
3. gross output and value added, and
4. Cobb–Douglas and translog.

That is, we estimated 672 production functions. While generalizations are somewhat difficult, we find the following empirically.

1. When comparing value-added to gross-output production functions, the former yield very large variations in returns to scale. Looking across specifications, returns to scale ranging to the extremes of 0.5 and 1.5 are not uncommon. In contrast, gross-output production functions display much less variation in returns to scale, which tend to be strongly centred between 0.9 and 1.1. In short, gross-output production functions display more sensible returns to scale.

[17] This dummy is interacted with lagged productivity.

[18] This is what we expect from work on the sunk costs of exporting by Roberts and Tybout (1997).

2. Using the translog gross-output function, estimates of output elasticities and returns to scale are extremely stable across proxy-variable estimation methods. This is not true of Cobb–Douglas or value-added production functions.
3. We examine log TFP dispersion, a topic of great interest for thinking about the macro misallocation literature and the international trade reallocation literature. Conditional on functional form (e.g., Cobb–Douglas value added), the choice of proxy-variable method makes little difference to the estimated dispersion in TFP. However, dispersion is much lower for gross-output production functions than for value-added production functions.
4. When looking at the TFP-premium associated with both capital intensity and size, the premium was present for value-added production functions, but much less so for gross-output production functions.

In collecting these many results, it appears that greater efforts must be made in the literature to demonstrate robustness of results to alternative production function specifications and proxy-variable methods. One theme that appears repeatedly is that we often obtain empirically more sensible results using gross-output production functions rather than value-added production functions.

Appendix 5.1: Cobb–Douglas Point Estimates

		Case 1: value-added		Case 5: value-added		Case 1: cross output			Case 5: cross output		
CIC-2	Industry name	β_L	β_K	β_L	β_K	β_L	β_K	β_M	β_L	β_K	β_M
13	Food processing	0.62	0.20	0.42	0.17	0.33	0.02	0.67	0.11	0.04	0.76
14	Food manufacturing	1.42	0.00	0.90	0.12	0.03	0.05	0.87	0.03	0.02	0.94
15	Beverages	1.21	0.08	1.07	0.12	0.22	0.04	0.78	0.25	0.04	0.72
17	Textiles	0.30	0.26	0.35	0.17	0.17	0.03	0.73	0.09	0.03	0.79
18	Apparel	1.20	0.00	0.79	0.12	0.06	0.01	0.94	0.08	0.00	0.99
19	Leather	0.57	0.21	1.02	0.08	0.04	0.00	0.99	0.24	0.02	0.77
20	Timber	0.19	0.21	0.63	0.10	0.06	0.06	0.91	0.05	0.02	0.92
21	Furniture	1.29	−0.07	0.76	0.09	0.07	0.00	0.90	0.07	0.02	0.86
22	Paper	0.78	0.10	1.12	0.05	0.09	0.03	0.82	0.07	0.01	0.89
23	Printing	0.08	0.43	0.32	0.17	0.08	0.03	0.85	0.06	0.05	0.83
24	Toys	0.70	0.11	0.69	0.10	0.23	0.02	0.70	0.15	0.03	0.76
25	Petroleum	0.79	0.23	1.66	0.06	0.34	−0.05	0.85	0.01	0.02	0.86
26	Raw chemicals	0.45	0.29	0.34	0.18	0.36	0.01	0.73	0.06	0.02	0.86
27	Medicines	0.17	0.38	1.35	0.10	0.12	0.05	0.79	0.09	0.04	0.85
28	Chemical fibers	0.07	0.39	−0.07	0.27	−0.01	0.01	0.97	−0.08	0.03	0.96
29	Rubber	0.93	0.10	0.87	0.10	0.15	0.00	0.89	0.15	0.03	0.79
30	Plastics	0.84	0.13	1.11	0.07	0.04	0.00	0.96	0.07	0.02	0.86
31	Non-metallic minerals	1.00	0.16	1.46	0.04	0.28	0.12	0.53	0.05	0.02	0.89
32	Smelting, ferrous metals	0.71	0.25	0.50	0.16	0.03	0.00	0.97	0.06	0.03	0.84
33	Smelting, non-ferrous metals	0.66	0.19	0.46	0.15	0.14	−0.11	1.44	0.02	0.02	0.91
34	Metal	0.88	0.20	0.49	0.19	0.03	0.01	0.97	0.19	0.03	0.76

(continued)

(continued)

		Case 1: value-added		Case 5: value-added		Case 1: cross output			Case 5: cross output		
CIC-2	Industry name	β_L	β_K	β_L	β_K	β_L	β_K	β_M	β_L	β_K	β_M
35	General machinery	1.03	0.12	1.02	0.12	0.24	0.01	0.84	0.20	0.02	0.83
36	Special machinery	1.11	0.07	0.93	0.13	0.13	0.03	0.85	0.07	−0.01	1.06
37	Transport equipment	1.19	0.10	1.11	0.12	0.02	0.02	0.95	0.04	0.02	0.93
39	Electrical machinery	0.79	0.25	1.56	0.08	0.46	0.05	0.59	0.59	0.02	0.61
40	Communication equipment	1.17	0.07	0.99	0.11	0.16	0.02	0.82	0.20	0.03	0.77
41	Measuring instruments	0.79	0.16	0.34	0.17	0.37	0.09	0.50	−0.01	0.03	0.88
42	Art	0.56	0.18	0.91	0.09	0.10	0.00	0.93	0.06	0.01	0.94

Chapter 6
Place-Based Industrial Policy and Firm Productivity

6.1 Introduction

The last four decades saw spectacular economic growth and a rapid surge of firm productivity in China. A growing body of literature documents evidence that industrial policies improve firm performance and facilitate economic growth (Wei 1995; Wang 2013; Aghion et al. 2015; Alder et al. 2016). Of all industrial policies, the special economic zone (SEZ henceforth), as a typical type of place-based industrial policy, plays a crucial role. Special economic zones like Shenzhen and Pudong in China have boosted the local economic development massively in the past three decades (Alder et al. 2016). The Oriental Industrial Park in Ethiopia has also achieved great success in fostering its employment and exports. Despite the particular importance of such place-based industrial policies in developing countries, empirical studies evaluating these programs are scarce. Wang (2013) and Alder et al. (2016) are two outstanding exceptions, yet they focus on the impact of a SEZ on aggregate economic performance. The investigation into how SEZs affect firm performance is still greatly absent in the current literature. This paper aims to fill this gap by using Chinese Annual Survey of Industrial Firms database in the years 2000–2005.

Distinguishing from previous studies focusing on the relationship between SEZs and aggregate variables, this paper aims to contribute to the evaluation of such policies through the lens of firm productivity. This is important. Advocates of SEZs believe that the SEZ has a positive effect on the treated area. Objections to SEZs argue that these policies may induce a concentration of resources and economic activities within a zone and draw away the resources outside the zone (See reviews by Glaeser and Gottlieb (2008), Kline and Moretti (2014) and Neumark et al. (2015)). Therefore, in a given region, areas within the SEZ may benefit, while the interests of those outside the SEZ may be encroached upon. Mere investigation into the nexus between a SEZ and aggregate performance of the given region covering both the treated and the

---

This chapter is coauthored with Justin Yifu Lin at Peking University and Wei Xiang at Yale University.

M. Yu, *China's Miracle in Foreign Trade*, Studies in Modern Chinese Economy,
https://doi.org/10.1007/978-981-16-6030-6_6

non-treated areas ignores the heterogenous effects of a SEZ; the exploration on the micro agents reveals a more nuanced picture.

I document that a special economic zone has a positive impact on productivity improvement through lower taxation rather than governmental selection or agglomeration for medium and large Chinese firms. On average, the establishment of a SEZ leads to a productivity gain of 19%. Moreover, a firm is affected by the positive spillover generated by the SEZs surrounding it. Generally, the marginal contribution of a nearby SEZ to a productivity increase is 1%. Notably, I find that a SEZ generates a more pronounced effect on non-SEZ firms.

To prepare for the empirical analysis, I assemble Chinese firm-level data from 2000 to 2005 and the geographical information of the state-level special economic zones to identify whether a firm is located in a special economic zone. The reasons why I focus on state-level SEZs are as follows. A special economic zone is an area with convenient access to transportation assigned by state or local government to boost the local economy. Firms in SEZs are entitled to preferential policies including lower taxes. SEZs in China can be classified as state-level or provincial-level. The differences between state-level and provincial-level SEZs are pronounced. First, many provincial-level SEZs fail to carry out enhancing policies and are sparse with firms. Second, universal preferential policies are implemented in state-level SEZs. By contrast, policies in provincial SEZs are uneven. The provincial-level SEZs are thus incomparable. Moreover, Alder et al. (2016) present evidence that the effects of provincial-level SEZs are insignificant on local economic development. Therefore, this paper focuses on state-level special economic zones.

The key measure through which we evaluate the function of the SEZ is firm productivity. To measure a firm's productivity, I follow Yu (2015), who adopts augmented Olley and Pakes (1996) (OP) methodology. This is the standard OP approach with a set of modifications to adapt to the context in China. Although this augmented OP method addresses the selection bias and simultaneity bias incurred in the traditional estimate of "Solow Residuals", it has its own weakness. Its core assumption that capital is more responsive to the productivity is not realistic in the Chinese context, since labor abundance in China makes its labor costs low. Faced with external shock, Chinese firms tend to adjust their labor rather than capital input to optimize their production (Blomström and Kokko 1996). Therefore, I use the system-GMM approach proposed by Blundell and Bond (1998) and the Levinsohn and Petrin (2003) (LP) method to estimate firm productivity. The system-GMM measure not only avoids selection bias and simultaneity bias but also successfully addresses the potential serial correlation of TFP by controlling for the lagged firm productivity (Fernandes 2007). I thus use it as the major indicator and adopt the augmented OP TFP and LP TFP for the robustness check.

The econometric strategy I adopt is essentially a difference-in-difference estimation controlling for time-invariant heterogeneity at firm level. More precisely, I regress the firm productivity measure on the SEZ dummy which equals to one if the firm is in a SEZ and zero otherwise. Special economic zones serve as a type of placed-based industrial policy in China. Consequently, other industrial policies and place-based policies can possibly confound the effects exerted by SEZs on firm performance. To disentangle the effects of SEZs from those of other types of industrial policies and regional policies, I control for time-variant industry and city shocks by including industry-year and city-year fixed effects in my baseline regression model. I find that in general, SEZs do improve firm TFP.

I preclude the possibility that the government chooses an area as a special economic zone in which firms are originally more productive. I follow the methodology adopted by Alder et al. (2016) to examine whether the SEZ firms are more productive before the establishment of the SEZ. After implementing the placebo test by adding pseudo shocks to one period before the establishment of SEZs, we demonstrate that the TFP premium of SEZ firms is not due to the "winner-picking" effect. In other words, the local government does not deliberately select the relatively more productive firms into the SEZ.

The surge of TFP can be attributed to the better policy environment (lower taxes) in the SEZs. I test this proposition in two steps. First, I show that the average tax in a SEZ is lower than that outside. Second, I demonstrate that a decrease in firm taxation significantly improves firm productivity. Neumark et al. (2015) point out that many SEZs are to foster agglomeration. However, I find that the agglomeration effect on the TFP of SEZ firms is rather insignificant both qualitatively and quantitatively. This result is consistent with the finding of Martin et al. (2013). They investigate French firms and conclude that the agglomeration is an automatic result, and the clusters propelled by external force may not generate agglomeration. Furthermore, I provide some evidence to show that SEZs do not generate a "beggar-thy-neighbor" effect. Instead, SEZs generate positive spillover effects on the neighboring firms.

One of the major challenges to identify the impact of special economic zones on economic outcomes is the endogeneity problem caused by the governmental selection of the location of a SEZ. The state-level SEZs began to thrive from the coastal cities whose industrial foundations are relatively better than those in inland cities; the firms in coastal cities generally have higher productivity. The conventional way to deal with this endogeneity problem, though not completely satisfying, is to use a subsample of inland cities, which is arguably less selective, for a robustness check (Wang 2013; Alder et al. 2016). Lu et al. (2015) try to use the strategy of regression discontinuity to solve this problem, yet this approach sacrifices a large number of observations and can merely investigate the boarder effect of a SEZ. This paper proposes a novel instrumental variable to tackle the issue. I carefully control for the endogeneity of the governmental selection of the location of SEZs by using the maximal distance of the SEZs and the non SEZs to their nearest highways as the instrumental variable (IV) for the SEZ dummy. The rationale is that the local government tends to choose to build the SEZ close to the transportation infrastructure to reduce the transportation cost of the SEZ firms. Therefore, the distance to highway is correlated with the establishment of a SEZ. Moreover, the distance measure of the SEZ does not directly affect the productivity of every single firm in it. The instrument thus passes the exogeneity requirement. I use average distance as an alternative IV, and the results are similar.

There are three caveats in my analysis. First, the data set contains a short time period so that it prevents a thorough pre-trend analysis in the placebo test. The strategy this paper takes is to test whether the dummy of one year before the SEZ establishment has positive effect on firm productivity. Hopefully in future, with data having longer time span, I am able to conduct a robust examination by including dummies for more years before SEZ establishment.

Second, highways may be built to favor some cities that later were given the status of SEZ, so the IV I choose in this paper may not be completely exogenous. An alternative can be to find some geography-based measures that determine the location in which a highway should be constructed, rather than the actual locations of highway in the next stage of my analysis.

Third, the difference-in-difference strategy only identifies the partial equilibrium effect of a SEZ on firm productivity. To quantify the general equilibrium (GE) effect, a general equilibrium framework with geographical feature is needed.

This paper contributes to the literature investigating the effect of place-based industrial policies. First, a large body of literature finds positive effects of place-based policies on employment, investment, net entry, wages and so forth (Criscuolo et al. 2012; Busso et al. 2013; Kline and Moretti 2013; Martin et al. 2011). However, the effect of the place-based policy on aggregate level productivity is mixed, because the positive effect on the treated areas may be offset by the beggar-thy-neighbor impact on the non-treated ones. This paper depicts a more nuanced picture about the productivity by examining it at firm level. In addition, many previous studies focus also on the spillovers of the SEZs to the non-treated areas (Criscuolo et al. 2012; Neumark and Kolko 2010; Martin et al. 2011; Kline and Moretti 2013; Greenstone et al. 2010; Briant et al. 2015; Devereux et al. 2007). However, this paper is different from the previous work since we study the spillover effect of the SEZs on firm productivity rather than aggregate performance in a specific region. This paper is also related to the literature on the evaluation of the China's SEZs (Wei 1995; Head and Ries 1996; Cheng and Kwan 2000; Demurger et al. 2002; Jones et al. 2003; Wang 2013; Lu et al. 2015). To the best of our knowledge, this is the first paper that comprehensively investigates the impact of China's SEZs on firm performance.

The rest of the paper is organized as follows. In section two, we describe the data used in this paper. The empirical strategy and the results are presented in section three, while section four concludes.

6.2 Data and Measurement

6.2.1 Data

To explore the effect of the establishment of SEZs on firm productivity, this paper adopts three data sets: firm-level production data, highway data and the geographic data of state-level special economic zones.

Firm-level Data. The firm-level data are the Annual Survey of Industrial Firms (ASIF) data from the years 2000–2005. This data set is compiled by the National Bureau of Statistics and contains rich financial information on firms with annual sales above 500 million RMB (about 71 million USD) across 29 manufacturing industries. The data set includes information on a firm's fixed assets, employment, intermediate inputs, value added and address etc. Though the data set consists of rich information, misreporting exists and leads to misleading samples (Yu 2015). To clean the data, I first exclude observations missing key variables such as total assets, net value of assets and sales following Cai and Liu (2009). Then I follow Brandt et al. (2012) who delete firms with fewer than eight workers. Following Feenstra et al. (2014) and Yu (2015), I drop observations according to the basic rules of the Generally Accepted Accounting Principles (GAAP) if a firm's (1) liquid assets exceed total assets; (2) total fixed assets exceed total assets; (3) net value of fixed assets is greater than total assets; (4) identification number is missing; or (5) establishment time is invalid.

Highway Data. Liu et al. (2017) collect the geographical distance of a firm to its most proximate highway in a given year for samples in ASIF using GIS. To get the instrumental variable for the SEZ dummy, I construct some distance indexes of SEZ and Non-SEZ areas to their nearest highways.

SEZ Data. The SEZ data are derived from *China Development Zone Bulletin 2006* released by National Development and Reform Commission, Bureau of Land Management and Ministry of Construction. This bulletin covers all the state authorized special economic zones with information on their names, types, authorizing offices, time of authorization and total area. It is the official file recording all state-level SEZs and the major data source for related studies such as Wang (2013). To match the SEZ data with the firm-level data, I also collect the SEZs' addresses, zip codes, and the code of the city where they are located.

6.2.2 Measurement

The summary statistics of the key variables are reported in Table 6.1.

Firm TFP. Following the standard approaches to estimate firm TFP, I adopt the augmented OP methodology proposed by Yu (2015), the conventional OP method with a set of modifications to fit the context in China. The traditional way of estimating firm productivity is to calculate the "Solow Residues" using Ordinary Least Square (OLS) method. However, this method will introduce selection bias and simultaneity bias. First, the least productive firms exit the market; the relatively more productive firms tend to survive and continue to operate and produce goods. Sample selection bias is thus incurred; the estimation of firm productivity is consequently not consistent in this case. Second, a firm faced with observable productivity shocks adjusts its production strategies by simultaneously determining its input and output levels, which results in simultaneity bias in the OLS estimation. To address these issues, Olley and Pakes (1996) propose a semi-parametric approach. Many subsequent studies have extended and tailored this approach to estimate firm TFP (Amiti and Konings 2007; De Loecker 2011, 2013; Yu 2015; De Loecker et al. 2016).

Table 6.1 Summary statistics

	Obs	Mean	SE	Obs	Mean	SE	Obs	Mean	SE
	2000			2001			2002		
lnTFP (GMM)	25,159	−0.112	0.282	24,884	−0.104	0.272	32,116	−0.0982	0.268
SEZ	25,159	0.0768	0.266	24,884	0.0795	0.271	32,116	0.0756	0.264
# of firms in a SEZ—1	25,159	1.408	7.057	24,884	1.397	7.314	32,116	1.603	8.726
# if SEZs surrounding a firm	25,159	1.448	1.857	24,884	1.481	1.875	32,116	1.535	1.94
Distance measure	24,172	−2.389	1.441	24,150	−2.486	1.468	31,474	−2.369	1.478
ln(1 + tax)	25,142	2.26	2.38	24,870	2.424	2.33	32,099	2.368	2.3
	2003			2004			2005		
lnTFP (GMM)	65,752	−0.089	0.345	72,503	−0.0579	0.346	128,628	−0.0122	0.34
SEZ	65,752	0.0783	0.269	72,503	0.0845	0.278	128,628	0.0823	0.275
# of firms in a SEZ—1	65,752	3.518	17.86	72,503	4.271	21.36	128,628	5.867	28.83
# if SEZs surrounding a firm	65,752	1.654	2.038	72,503	1.791	2.242	128,628	2.124	2.702
Distance measure	64,122	−2.361	1.501	72,015	−2.237	1.477	127,846	−1.826	1.38
ln(1 + tax)	65,739	2.387	2.279	72,646	2.758	2.171	128,605	2.618	2.216

Notes The data sources are *Annual Survey of Industrial Firms 2000–2005, China Development Zone Audit Bulletin Catalog 2006* and Liu et al. (2017)

I follow Yu (2015) to estimate firm productivity with his proposed type of augmented OP methodology which fits China's context during 2000 to 2005. The technologies adopted by processing and non-processing firms are likely to be different, I differentiate these two types of firms when calculating firm productivity. Second, to exclude the impact of prices on the estimation of firm productivity, I deflate the output level of a firm by its industry-level price index following Brandt et al. (2012). In addition, China's accession to WTO in 2001 is an important shock to a firm, because it serves as a positive demand shock and has spurred Chinese firms to expand their production scales. Since the time span of the data is between 2000 and 2005, I include the WTO dummy into the control function. Moreover, the state-owned enterprises (SOEs) also exert impacts on firm productivity. Hsieh and Klenow (2009) argue that the state intervention makes SOEs not necessarily maximize their profits. I thus add the SOE indicator into the control function. Note that firms in a SEZ and outside a SEZ may be faced with different taxation environments, I also control for firm tax in TFP estimation.

Although the augmented OP method successfully addresses the two types of biases incurred in the traditional OLS estimation, the core assumption it relies on is not consistent with the reality in China. It assumes that the adjustment of capital input is more sensitive than that of labor input. However, China is labor abundant during the sample period, and the firms are more likely to adjust their labor rather than capital input (Yu 2015). To solve this problem, I use system GMM method proposed by Blundell and Bond (1998) as an alternative way to estimate firm TFP. This method avoids the selection and simultaneity biases; moreover, it solves the serial correlation problem when estimating firm TFP. Therefore, I use firm TFP estimated by system GMM as the main measure. I use TFP estimated by augmented OP method and LP method to do robustness checks.

SEZ dummy. I use the zip code of a firm and that of a SEZ to identify whether a firm is located in the SEZ. Some large SEZs may have more than one zip code. As long as a firm has a zip code identical to one of these zip codes of the SEZ, I classify it as a SEZ firm. To be more specific, the SEZ dummy equals 1 as the firm is located in a SEZ and 0 otherwise.

Number of Firms in a SEZ. For each SEZ, I compute the total number of firms. For each firm in a SEZ, the potential agglomeration effect it is exposed to is defined as the total number of firms in the same SEZ minus 1.

Firm Tax. I use firm tax as the proxy for the policy environment that a firm is faced with. The measure is constructed as the logarithm of the sum of firm tax and 1.

Number of SEZs Surrounding a Firm. To explore the spillover effect of the SEZ, I use the number of SEZs surrounding a firm to measure the extent to which the firm is exposed to these spillovers. In practice, I use city id to match SEZs and the city where they are located; the number of SEZs surrounding a firm equals the total number of SEZs in the city in which the firm is located minus the SEZ dummy.

Other Control Variables. Yu (2015) emphasizes that the pure exporters and the pure domestic firms possibly adopt different technologies, while firm size and its ownership also affect a firm's technology adoption. Therefore, I control for pure-exporting-firm dummy, pure-domestic-firm dummy, firm size (measured as a firm's sales) and the SOE indicator.

Instrumental Variables. I follow Liu et al. (2017) to calculate the distance of a firm to its nearest highway. I use the inverse of the logarithm of the distance to measure a firm's proximity to the highways. Furthermore, I classify the regions in a city as SEZ areas or non-SEZ ones and get the minimum of the distance measures in each area as the IV for the SEZ dummy.

6.3 Empirical Strategy and Results

In this section, I first explore the impact of special economic zones on firm productivity. Then I examine the mechanism through which SEZs affect firm performance. Lastly, I test whether SEZs generate spillovers.

6.3.1 Baseline Model

To investigate the relationship between firm productivity and SEZs, I regress the logarithm of firm TFP on the SEZ dummy with a rich set of model specifications. I first run a set of preliminary regressions to show the positive effect of the SEZ on firm productivity and the robustness of this effect after controlling for various fixed effects. The main regressor is the SEZ indicator that switches on as the firm begins to be located in a SEZ. In the more rigorous model specifications, I control for the city-year and industry-year fixed effects to absorb the impacts of other place-based policies and industrial policies. All the standard errors are clustered at the firm level. Formally, the regression model has the form:

$$\ln TFP_{ijct} = \varphi + \beta \times SEZ_{it} + \theta X_{it} + \tau_i + \alpha_t + \gamma_{jt} + \lambda_{ct} + \epsilon_{it},$$

where the dependant variable $\ln TFP_{ijct}$ is the logarithm of TFP of a firm i in industry j, city c, and year t. SEZ_{it} refers to whether firm i in year t is placed in a SEZ. τ_i is a firm fixed effect; α_t is a year fixed effect. γ_{jt} is an industry-year (CIC 4-digit) fixed effect; λ_{ct} is a city-year fixed effect. X_{it} is a set of controls including rich firm-level characteristics such as firm size, firm ownership, exporting status and so forth. φ represents a constant; ϵ_{it} is an error term obeying the standard normal distribution.

The estimation results for the baseline model are reported in Table 6.2. I start from the simplest OLS model regressing the logarithm of firm TFP estimated by system GMM on only the SEZ indicator as shown in column 1 in Table 6.2; the impact of the SEZ on firm TFP is positive and statistically significant. In column (2), I control for city-year and industry-year fixed effects to preclude the impacts of other time-variant place-based policies and industrial policies. Moreover, I control for city-specific and year-specific fixed effects. The estimated coefficient of the SEZ dummy is still positive and statistically significant. In the following settings, I control for more fixed effects. Because the market a firm is faced with reveals its characteristics according to Melitz (2003), the pure exporters generally behave differently from the pure domestic sellers. Therefore in column (3), I further control for the pure-exporting-firm dummy and pure-domestic-firm dummy. The effect of the SEZ on firm productivity is still pronounced. To address the potential bias caused by omitted variables, I need to control for time-invariant firm-level characteristics. Thus, from column (4) to column (6), the specifications are similar to those of column (1) to

Table 6.2 Baseline regression

Regressand: $\ln TFP_{ijct}$	OLS			FE		
	(1)	(2)	(3)	(4)	(5)	(6)
SEZ	0.044***	0.038***	0.040***	0.019*	0.021**	0.021**
	(17.03)	(12.92)	(13.75)	(1.79)	(2.07)	(2.05)
Pure exporting firms	No	No	Yes	No	No	Yes
Pure domestic firms	No	No	Yes	No	No	Yes
Firm-specific fixed effects	No	No	No	Yes	Yes	Yes
Year-specific fixed effects	No	No	No	Yes	Yes	Yes
Industry-specific fixed effects	No	Yes	Yes	No	–	–
City-specific fixed effects	No	Yes	Yes	No	–	–
Industry-year fixed effects	No	Yes	Yes	No	Yes	Yes
City-year fixed effects	No	Yes	Yes	No	Yes	Yes
Observations	349,042	349,042	349,042	349,042	349,042	349,042
R^2	0.001	0.261	0.263	0.000	0.081	0.082

Notes Robust t-statistics in parentheses. Standard errors are clustered at firm level. Significant at *10%, **5% and ***1%. The dependant variable is firm TFP in its natural log form estimated by system GMM. The SEZ indicator equals one if the firm is in a SEZ. The foreign firms indicator equals one if the firm is classified as a foreign firm. The SOE indicator equals one if the firm is state-owned. The variable pure exporting firms is an indicator that equals one if the firm sells only to foreign markets. The variable pure domestic firms is an indicator that equals one if the firm sells only to domestic markets. Column (1)–(3) do not control for firm-specific and year-specific fixed effects, while column (4)–(6) control for both

column (3) except that the firm-specific and year-specific fixed effects are controlled for. The coefficients of the SEZ indicator remain positive and statistically significant.

6.3.2 Robustness Check

To test the robustness of the positive effect of the establishment of a SEZ on firm productivity, I conduct a set of robustness checks by adding more control variables. As a relatively more productive firm tends to have a larger size, if the firms in SEZs are relatively larger, the estimation will be biased. Therefore, I further control for the size of a firm. SOEs are arguably less productive than private firms, as mentioned by Hsieh and Klenow (2009); multinational firms are likely to have higher productivity thanks to fewer credit constraints (Manova et al. 2015). Thus, I construct indicators to identify a firm's type (SOE and foreign firm). The estimation results are presented in Table 6.3.

The firm TFP in each column is estimated by system GMM. In column (1), I control for the firm size (measured by the logarithm of the firm sales). After controlling for the size of the firm, the scale and the significance of the estimated coefficient

Table 6.3 Robustness check

Regressand: $\ln TFP_{ijct}$	(1)	(2)	(3)
SEZ	0.021**	0.021**	0.021**
	(2.06)	(2.06)	(2.07)
ln *Sales*	0.021***	0.021***	0.021***
	(9.47)	(9.47)	(9.47)
Foreign firms		−0.002	−0.002
		(−0.24)	(−0.23)
SOE			0.009
			(1.58)
Pure exporting firms	Yes	Yes	Yes
Pure domestic firms	Yes	Yes	Yes
Firm-specific fixed effects	Yes	Yes	Yes
Year-specific fixed effects	Yes	Yes	Yes
Industry-year fixed effects	Yes	Yes	Yes
City-year fixed effects	Yes	Yes	Yes
Observations	349,005	349,005	349,005
R^2	0.083	0.083	0.083

Notes Robust t-statistics in parentheses. Standard errors are clustered at firm level. Significant at *10%, **5% and ***1%. The dependant variable is firm TFP in its natural log form estimated by system GMM for each column. The SEZ indicator equals one if the firm is in a SEZ. The variable logSales is the natural log of a firm's sales. The foreign firms indicator equals one if the firm is classified as a foreign firm. The SOE indicator equals one if the firm is state-owned. The variable pure exporting firms is an indicator that equals one if the firm sells only to foreign markets. The variable pure domestic firm is an indicator that equals one if the firm sells only to domestic markets

of the SEZ indicator remain unchanged compared with the results in the baseline model. In column (2), I further consider the ownership of the firm as the foreign firms might not have the same credit constraints as the private Chinese firms do. In column (3), I control for the SOE indicator. As shown by these three columns, the impact of the SEZ on firm productivity is still positive and statistically significant.

6.3.3 Placebo Test

The robustness check demonstrates that the state-level SEZ has a significantly positive effect on firm productivity. Yet the direct challenge following the baseline estimation is that the better performance of the SEZ firms may not be caused by the SEZ *per se* but rather due to the deliberate selection of the relatively more productive firms by the local government. I preclude this case by implementing a placebo test. Specifically, I construct a set of year dummies to indicate the years before and after the firm becomes a SEZ firm following Alder et al. (2016). The year dummies can be regarded as the pseudo shocks of the SEZ. The results are reported in Table 6.4. Moreover, I drop firms sitting in a SEZ throughout the whole time span in the data sample.

The indicator of one year before SEZ establishment equals one if the next year the firm begins to sit in a SEZ. If the positive relationship between firm productivity and the SEZ is merely caused by the governmental selection of the relatively more productive firms, one should expect that this indicator should have a positive impact on firm productivity. If the SEZ *per se* contributes to the surge of a firm's productivity, this will be indicated by a positively significant coefficient of the indicator of SEZ (all post years), which equals one if the firm has been in a SEZ. The SEZ can generate

Table 6.4 Placebo test

Regressand: lnTFP_{ijct}	(1)	(2)	(3)	(4)
1 year before SEZ establishment	−0.004	−0.008	−0.008	−0.008
	(−0.17)	(−0.31)	(−0.32)	(−0.32)
Year of SEZ	0.023	0.017	0.016	0.016
	(0.96)	(0.70)	(0.68)	(0.68)
SEZ (all post years)	0.046**	0.039*	0.039*	0.039*
	(2.16)	(1.85)	(1.83)	(1.83)
ln*Sales*		0.029***	0.029***	0.029***
		(14.73)	(14.70)	(14.69)
Foreign firms			0.011	0.011
			(1.51)	(1.51)
SOE				0.003
				(0.43)
Pure exporting firms	−0.003	−0.002	−0.002	−0.002
	(−0.83)	(−0.39)	(−0.40)	(−0.40)
Pure domestic firms	0.012***	0.016***	0.016***	0.016***
	(4.10)	(5.64)	(5.65)	(5.65)
Year-specific fixed effects	Yes	Yes	Yes	Yes
Observations	349,042	349,005	349,005	349,005
R^2	0.001	0.003	0.003	0.003

Notes: Robust t-statistics in parentheses. Standard errors are clustered at firm level. Significant at *10%, **5% and ***1%. The dependant variable is firm TFP in its natural log form estimated by system GMM. The SEZ indicator equals one if the firm is in a SEZ. The variable logSales is the natural log of a firm's sales. The foreign firms indicator equals one if the firm is classified as a foreign firm. The SOE indicator equals one if the firm is state-owned. The variable pure exporting firms is an indicator that equals one if the firm sells only to foreign markets. The variable pure domestic firms is an indicator that equals one if the firm sells only to domestic markets a positive effect on firm performance either instantly or gradually, thus the indicator of the year of the SEZ establishment may or may not have a positive coefficient. In column (1), I control for indicators for pure exporting firms, pure domestic firms and year-specific fixed effects. In the following three columns, I add more control variables including firm size and different types of ownership. As can be seen in Table 6.4, the pseudo shocks have no impact on firm productivity, while the indicator for all post-SEZ-establishment years has a positive and statistically significant effect. The results preclude the challenge that the local government picks the more productive firms into the SEZ.

6.3.4 *Endogeneity*

As mentioned in the beginning, the state-level SEZs started from the cities where the economic conditions are relatively better; the firms in these cities may have higher productivity in the first place. It is also likely that the business environments in these cities improve faster than other areas. Thus the endogeneity problem still exists even though I have carefully precluded the possibility of the governmental selection of more productive firms into a SEZ. The conventional way to deal with this endogeneity problem, though not completely satisfying, is to use a sub-sample of inland cities, which is arguably less selective, for a robustness check (Wang 2013; Alder et al. 2016). In this paper, I use the minimal inverse distance of the treated and the non-treated areas to the highway as the IV for the SEZ indicator. The rationale behind this strategy is that the local government tends to choose the place that is near the highway to establish the special economic zone so as to reduce the transportation costs of the SEZ firms. It is impossible for a place remote to the roads for trucks and cars to carry cargoes to be selected as an area to accommodate hundreds of firms. In addition, the proximity of an area to the highway is likely to be exogenous to the production efficiency of a firm located in that area. The estimation results of the IV regression are presented in Table 6.5.

As shown in all columns, the Kleibergen-Paap Wald χ^2 Statistics and Kleibergen-Paap LM F Statistics exceed 460, which indicates that the IV is relevant. All columns have System GMM TFP as their dependant variables, controlling for firm-specific fixed effects, year-specific fixed effects, pure exporters indicator and pure domestic firms indicator. In column 1, the impact of the SEZ on firm TFP is still statistically significant and positive; the estimated coefficient is larger than those in baseline regressions. In column (2), I control for the size of the firm; in column (4) and (5), I further control for the firm ownership like foreign firms dummy and SOE indicator. The results remain unchanged and show that the SEZ generates a positive effect on firm productivity.

For the robustness check, I use firm TFP estimated by augmented OP and LP methods as the dependant variable. In addition, I use the median and maximal inverse distance of the treated and the non-treated areas to the highway as the IV for the SEZ indicator. Lastly, I use a balance panel for 2000–2005 to conduct the IV regression.

Table 6.5 IV regression

Regressand: $\ln TFP_{ijct}$	(1)	(2)	(3)	(4)
SEZ	0.191**	0.192**	0.192**	0.192**
	(2.17)	(2.19)	(2.18)	(2.18)
ln*Sales*		0.013***	0.013***	0.013***
		(6.36)	(6.35)	(6.35)
Foreign firms			0.004	0.004
			(0.58)	(0.59)
SOE				0.015**
				(2.57)
Pure exporting firms	Yes	Yes	Yes	Yes
Pure domestic firms	Yes	Yes	Yes	Yes
Firm-specific fixed effects	Yes	Yes	Yes	Yes
Year-specific fixed effects2	Yes	Yes	Yes	Yes
Kleibergen-Paap Wald χ statistic	493	493	492.8	492.8
Kleibergen-Paap LM F statistic	465.5	465.5	465.3	465.4
Observations	261,597	261,597	261,597	261,597

Notes Robust t-statistics in parentheses. Standard errors are clustered at firm level. Significant at *10%, **5% and ***1%. The dependant variable is firm TFP in its natural log form estimated by system GMM. The SEZ indicator equals one if the firm is in a SEZ. The variable logSales is the natural log of a firm's sales. The variable foreign firms is an indicator equals one if the firm is classified as a foreign firm. The SOE indicator equals one if the firm is state-owned. Pure exporting firm is an indicator that equals one if the firm sells only to foreign markets. The variable pure domestic firms is an indicator that equals one if the firm sells only to domestic markets

The results are presented in Table 6.6. As shown in all columns, the Kleibergen-Paap Wald χ^2 Statistics and Kleibergen-Paap LM F Statistics exceed 100, which indicates that the IV is relevant. The results robustly show that the effect of the SEZ on firm productivity is significantly positive.

6.3.5 Mechanisms

Thus far, the empirical evidence in the previous sections robustly demonstrates that the SEZ has a positive effect on firm productivity. In this section, I explore the mechanisms through which a SEZ affects a firm's performance. The preferential policies, especially tax deductions, provide exceptional business environments for SEZ firms. On the other hand, the firms in a SEZ may benefit from agglomeration.

Table 6.6 Robustness check for IV regression

Regressand: $\ln TFP_{ijct}$	TFP OP	TFP LP	TFP GMM		
	(1)	(2)	(3)	(4)	(5)
SEZ	0.588***	0.405**	0.256*	0.442*	0.250*
	−6.72	−2.45	−1.74	−1.72	−1.94
ln *Sales*	0.084***	0.868***	0.013***	0.013***	−0.015***
	−47.78	−296	−6.35	−6.37	(−2.98)
Foreign firms	−0.005	0.009	0.004	0.003	−0.002
	(−0.84)	−0.76	−0.56	−0.45	(−0.16)
SOE	−0.022***	−0.006	0.015***	0.015***	0.024***
	(−3.25)	(−0.44)	−2.59	−2.62	−3.03
Pure exporting firms	Yes	Yes	Yes	Yes	Yes
Pure domestic firms	Yes	Yes	Yes	Yes	Yes
Firm-specific fixed effects	Yes	Yes	Yes	Yes	Yes
Year-specific fixed effects	Yes	Yes	Yes	Yes	Yes
Kleibergen-Paap Wald χ^2 statistic	618.1	393	188.7	111.7	127.9
Kleibergen-Paap LM *F* statistic	584.5	375.3	187.3	111.6	117.8
Observations	413,842	320,911	261,600	261,600	39,262

Notes: Robust t-statistics in parentheses. Standard errors are clustered at firm level. Significant at *10%, **5% and ***1%. In column (1), the dependant variable is firm TFP estimated by augmented Olley-Pakes method. In column (2), the dependant variable if firm TFP estimated by Levinsohn and Petrin (2003). The dependant variable is firm TFP in its natural log form estimated by system GMM for column (3)–(5). The median and minimal inverse distance of the treated and the non-treated areas to the highway are used as the IV for the SEZ indicator in column (3) and (4), respectively. Column (5) use the balance panel of 2000–2005. The SEZ indicator equals one if the firm is in a SEZ. The variable logSales is the natural log of a firm's sales. The variable foreign firms is an indicator equals one if the firm is classified as a foreign firm. The SOE indicator equals one if the firm is state-owned. Pure exporting firm is an indicator that equals one if the firm sells only to foreign markets. The variable pure domestic firms is an indicator that equals one if the firm sells only to domestic markets

6.3.5.1 Policy Effect

I show, in two steps, that tax deductions in SEZs are one channel through which SEZs improve firm productivity. First, I demonstrate that the average firm tax in SEZ is lower than that outside. Then I provide empirical evidence that firm productivity is negatively correlated with firm tax.

In Table 6.7, I regress the measure of firm tax on the SEZ indicator with the 2SLS model. In all columns, I control for pure exporters indicator, pure domestic firms indicator, firm-specific fixed effects and year-specific fixed effects. In column (1), the coefficient of the SEZ indicator is negative and statistically significant, which shows that the average firm tax in a SEZ is lower than that outside the SEZ. In column (2)–(4), I further control for more firm-level characteristics; the negative relationship

Table 6.7 Firm tax is relatively lower in SEZs

Regressand: $\ln(1 + tax_{it})$	(1)	(2)	(3)	(4)
SEZ	−1.570***	−1.531***	−1.531***	−1.533***
	(−3.53)	(−3.46)	(−3.46)	(−3.46)
ln*Sales*		0.422***	0.422***	0.422***
		(38.16)	(38.16)	(38.17)
Foreign firms			0.003	0.004
			(0.08)	(0.11)
SOE				0.155***
				(3.58)
Pure exporting firms	Yes	Yes	Yes	Yes
Pure domestic firms	Yes	Yes	Yes	Yes
Firm-specific fixed effects	Yes	Yes	Yes	Yes
Year-specific fixed effects	Yes	Yes	Yes	Yes
Kleibergen-Paap Wald χ^2 statistic	493.7	493	492.7	492.8
Kleibergen-Paap LM F statistic	466.1	465.4	465.2	465.2
Observations	261,978	261,937	261,937	261,937

Notes Robust t-statistics in parentheses. Standard errors are clustered at firm level. Significant at *10%, **5% and ***1%. The dependant variable is the natural log of one plus firm tax. The SEZ indicator equals one if the firm is in a SEZ. The variable logSales is the natural log of a firm's sales. The variable foreign firms is an indicator equals one if the firm is classified as a foreign firm. The SOE indicator equals one if the firm is state-owned. Pure exporting firm is an indicator that equals one if the firm sells only to foreign markets. The variable pure domestic firms is an indicator that equals one if the firm sells only to domestic markets

between firm tax and the SEZ indicator is robust. More precisely, I control for firm size in column (2), further control for foreign firms indicator in column (3) and take into account the SOE indicator in column (4). The empirical results robustly show that SEZ firms enjoy lower level of taxation.

To argue that the state-level SEZs affect firm productivity through preferential tax policies, I need to further prove that firm tax has an impeding impact on firm performance. Therefore, I examine the relationship between firm productivity and firm tax. The regression results are reported in Table 6.8.

In Table 6.8, the dependant variables are the logarithm of the firm TFP estimated by system GMM. In year-specific fixed effects, industry-year fixed effects and city-year fixed effects are controlled. Furthermore, the SEZ indicator serves also as an important control variable in each column. In column (1), the effect of firm tax on firm productivity is negative with statistical significance. In column (2)–(4), more firm-level properties are taken into account. The negative effect is robust. Consistent with the previous findings, the estimated coefficients of the SEZ indicator are significantly positive.

From the results in Tables 6.7 and 6.8, it is clear that the tax reduction in the SEZs is one of the important channels through which SEZs improve firm productivity. To

Table 6.8 The impact of firm tax on firm productivity

Regressand: ln*TFPijct*	(1)	(2)	(3)	(4)
ln(1 + tax)	−0.002***	−0.002***	−0.002***	−0.002***
	(−4.81)	(−6.00)	(−6.00)	(−6.01)
SEZ	0.021**	0.021**	0.021**	0.021**
	(2.03)	(2.04)	(2.04)	(2.04)
ln*Sales*		0.022***	0.022***	0.022***
		(9.83)	(9.83)	(9.83)
Foreign firms			−0.002	−0.002
			(−0.25)	(−0.24)
SOE				0.009
				(1.57)
Pure exporting firms	Yes	Yes	Yes	Yes
Pure domestic firms	Yes	Yes	Yes	Yes
Firm-specific fixed effects	Yes	Yes	Yes	Yes
Year-specific fixed effects	Yes	Yes	Yes	Yes
Industry-year fixed effects	Yes	Yes	Yes	Yes
City-year fixed effects	Yes	Yes	Yes	Yes
Observations	348,955	348,918	348,918	348,918
R^2	0.082	0.083	0.083	0.083

Notes Robust t-statistics in parentheses. Standard errors are clustered at firm level. Significant at *10%, **5% and ***1%. The dependant variable is firm TFP in its natural log form estimated by system GMM. The SEZ indicator equals one if the firm is in a SEZ. The variable log(1 + tax) is the natural log of a firm's tax. The variable logSales is the natural log of a firm's sales. The foreign firms indicator equals one if the firm is classified as a foreign firm. The SOE indicator equals one if the firm is state-owned. The variable pure exporting firms is an indicator that equals one if the firm sells only to foreign markets. The variable pure domestic firms is an indicator that equals one if the firm sells only to domestic markets

further examine this proposition and make comparable the effects of firm tax and firm location on firm productivity, I conduct IV regressions, where firm TFP is the regressand while the SEZ indicator, and firm tax and their interaction term serve as regressors (See Table 6.9).

In all columns, the pure exporting firms indicator, pure domestic firms indicator, firm-specific fixed effects and year-specific fixed effects are controlled. In column (1), the SEZ indicator has a positive effect on firm productivity, which is consistent with our main findings; the coefficient of the interaction term is negative and statistically significant, meaning that for a SEZ firm, the lower the tax the higher its productivity. In column (2)–(4), I further control for firm size, the foreign firms indicator and the SOE indicator on the basis of the previous column, respectively. The results remain the same and show that preferential policies in SEZs is one important mechanism through which SEZs increase firm productivity.

Table 6.9 The heterogeneous impacts of firm tax on firm productivity

Regressand: ln*TFPijct*	(1)	(2)	(3)	(4)
SEZ	0.273***	0.273***	0.273***	0.273***
	(2.76)	(2.76)	(2.75)	(2.76)
ln(1 + tax) × SEZ	−0.035***	−0.035***	−0.035***	−0.035***
	(−3.87)	(−3.91)	(−3.91)	(−3.94)
ln(1 + tax)	0.000	−0.000	−0.000	−0.000
	(0.42)	(−0.08)	(−0.08)	(−0.07)
ln*Sales*		0.015***	0.015***	0.015***
		(6.78)	(6.78)	(6.78)
Foreign firms			0.004	0.004
			(0.54)	(0.55)
SOE				0.017***
				(2.92)
Pure exporting firms	Yes	Yes	Yes	Yes
Pure domestic firms	Yes	Yes	Yes	Yes
Firm-specific fixed effects	Yes	Yes	Yes	Yes
Year-specific fixed effects	Yes	Yes	Yes	Yes
Kleibergen-Paap Wald χ^2 statistic	249.2	248.7	248.6	248.7
Kleibergen-Paap LM F statistic	470	469.2	469	469.1
Observations	261,978	261,937	261,937	261,937

Notes Robust t-statistics in parentheses. Standard errors are clustered at firm level. Significant at *10%, **5% and ***1%. The dependant variable is firm TFP in its natural log form estimated by system GMM. The SEZ indicator equals one if the firm is in a SEZ. The variable log(1 + tax) is the natural log of a firm's tax. The variable logSales is the natural log of a firm's sales. The foreign firm indicator equals one if the firm is classified as a foreign firm. The SOE indicator equals one if the firm is state-owned. The variable pure exporting firms is an indicator that equals one if the firm sells only to foreign markets. The variable pure domestic firm is an indicator that equals one if the firm sells only to domestic markets

6.3.5.2 Agglomeration Effect

Is there any agglomeration in the state-level special economic zones? To answer this question, I focus on all firms in SEZs and investigate the relationship between their productivity and the number of firms in the SEZ. The empirical evidence is presented in Table 6.10.

In Table 6.10, the dependant variable is firm TFP estimated by the system GMM method. The first row reports the estimated coefficients of the number of firms in the SEZ minus one. In all columns, the pure exporting firms indicator, pure domestic firms indicator, firm-specific fixed effects and year-specific fixed effects are controlled. In column (2)–(4), I further control for firm size, the foreign firms indicator and the estimated results in the first row should have sizable magnitudes

Table 6.10 Agglomeration is not obvious

Regressand: $\ln TFP_{ijct}$	(1)	(2)	(3)	(4)
# of firms—1	0.000	0.000	0.000	0.000
	(0.77)	(0.79)	(0.83)	(0.84)
ln*Sales*		0.016	0.016	0.016
		(1.23)	(1.21)	(1.21)
Foreign firms			0.045	0.045
			(1.20)	(1.21)
SOE				0.021
				(0.65)
Pure exporting firms	Yes	Yes	Yes	Yes
Pure domestic firms	Yes	Yes	Yes	Yes
Firm-specific fixed effects	Yes	Yes	Yes	Yes
Year-specific fixed effects	Yes	Yes	Yes	Yes
Industry-year fixed effects	Yes	Yes	Yes	Yes
City-year fixed effects	Yes	Yes	Yes	Yes
Observations	28,206	28,196	28,196	28,196
R^2	0.075	0.075	0.075	0.075

Notes Robust t-statistics in parentheses. Standard errors are clustered at firm level. Significant at * 10%, ** 5% and *** 1%. This table includes samples of only firms in a SEZ. The dependant variable is firm TFP in its natural log form estimated by system GMM. The number of firms in a SEZ is the total number of firms in the SEZ where the firm is located. The variable logSales is the natural log of a firm's sales. The foreign firms indicator equals one if the firm is classified as a foreign firm. The SOE indicator equals one if the firm is state-owned. The variable pure exporting firms is an indicator that equals one if the firm sells only to foreign markets. The variable pure domestic firms is an indicator that equals one if the firm sells only to domestic markets

with statistical significance. However, the coefficients reported in the first row are not statistically significant and close to zero. The results imply that the agglomeration in the state-level SEZs is insignificant, which is consistent with one of the conclusions of Martin et al. (2013): the agglomeration does not necessarily exists in man-made clusters.

6.3.6 Spillovers

This paper also concerns about the spillovers generated by the SEZ. To explore whether the SEZ has spillovers to the surrounding firms, I rely on the following model:

$$\ln TFP_{ijct} = \varphi + \beta_1 \times ZN_{it} + \beta_2 \times ZN_{it} \times SEZ_{it} + \beta_3$$

$$\times SEZ_{it} + \theta X_{it} + \tau_i + \alpha_t + \gamma_{jt} + \lambda_{ct} + {}_{it},$$

where the dependant variable lnTFP_{ijct} is the logarithm of TFP of a firm i in industry j, city c, and year t. ZN_{it} represents the number of SEZs surrounding a firm; SEZ_{it} refers to whether firm i in year t is placed in a SEZ. τ_i is a firm fixed effect; α_t is a year fixed effect. γ_{jt} is an industry-year (CIC 4-digit) fixed effect; λ_{ct} is a city-year fixed effect. X_{it} is a set of controls including many firm-level characteristics such as firm size, firm ownership, exporting status and so forth. φ represents a constant; ϵ_{it} is an error term with standard normal distribution. If there is a positive spillover, we should expect that $\beta_1 + \beta_2 \times \overline{SEZ_{it}}$ is greater than zero, where $\overline{SEZ_{it}}$ is the mean value of the SEZ indicator. The regression results are reported in Table 6.11.

Table 6.11 SEZs have positive spillovers

Regressand: lnTFP_{ijct}	(1)	(2)	(3)	(4)
# of surrounding SEZs	0.024***	0.025***	0.025***	0.025***
	(4.08)	(4.20)	(4.19)	(4.18)
# of surrounding SEZs × SEZ	−0.169***	−0.173***	−0.173***	−0.172***
	(−4.91)	(−5.02)	(−5.03)	(−5.02)
SEZ	0.633***	0.642***	0.642***	0.641***
	(4.01)	(4.07)	(4.07)	(4.06)
ln*Sales*		0.014***	0.014***	0.014***
		(6.41)	(6.40)	(6.41)
Foreign firms			0.005	0.005
			(0.76)	(0.77)
SOE				0.016***
				(2.69)
Pure exporting firms	Yes	Yes	Yes	Yes
Pure domestic firms	Yes	Yes	Yes	Yes
Firm-specific fixed effects	Yes	Yes	Yes	Yes
Year-specific fixed effects	Yes	Yes	Yes	Yes
Kleibergen-Paap Wald χ^2 statistic	202.5	202.8	202.8	202.9
Kleibergen-Paap LM F statistic	393.4	394	394	394.1
Observations	262,056	262,015	262,015	262,015

Notes Robust t-statistics in parentheses. Standard errors are clustered at firm level. Significant at *10%, **5% and ***1%. The dependant variable is firm TFP in its natural log form estimated by system GMM. The SEZ indicator equals one if the firm is in a SEZ. The number of surrounding SEZs is the total number of SEZs in the city where the firm is located minus the SEZ dummy. The variable logSales is the natural log of a firm's sales. The foreign firms indicator equals one if the firm is classified as a foreign firm. The SOE indicator equals one if the firm is state-owned. The variable pure exporting firms is an indicator that equals one if the firm sells only to foreign markets. The variable pure domestic firms is an indicator that equals one if the firm sells only to domestic markets

In Table 6.11, the dependant variable is the logarithm of firm TFP estimated using System GMM. The first row reports the estimated results of the impact of the number of SEZs surrounding a firm. The second row records the coefficients of the interaction term. In column (1), after controlling for the pure exporting firms indicator, pure domestic firms indicator, firm-specific fixed effects and year-specific fixed effects, the coefficients are significantly positive in the first row and are significantly negative in the second row. In column (2)–(4), I further control for firm size, the foreign firms indicator and the SOE indicator on the basis of the previous column, respectively. The results are similar. These results demonstrate that the state-level SEZs generate positive spillovers, and moreover, the spillovers are larger to non-SEZ firms. Because the mean value of the SEZ indicator is lower than 0.1, the term $\beta_1 + \beta_2 \times \overline{SEZ_{it}}$ is positive. Therefore, the state-level special economic zones do have positive spillover effects to the surrounding firms. Although the coefficients of the interaction term is less than zero, the average effect of a SEZ on firm productivity is positive because the average number of SEZs surrounding a firm is greater than 2.

6.4 Concluding Remarks

With Chinese firm-level data from the years 2000–2005 and the geographical information of the state-level special economic zones, this paper comprehensively investigates the impact of the SEZ on firm productivity. SEZs improve productivity and generate positive spillovers. The productivity premium of SEZ firms is not due to governmental selection. The surge of productivity can be attributed to the better policy environment (lower taxes) in the SEZs. The agglomeration effect on the productivity of SEZ firms is insignificant qualitatively and quantitatively. I use a distance measure of the SEZ and the non SEZ to their nearest highway as the instrument for SEZ dummy. On average, the establishment of a SEZ leads to a productivity gain of 19%. The marginal contribution of a nearby SEZ to firm productivity is 1%.

This paper fills the gap in the literature of place-based policies by investigating the impact of the SEZ on firm productivity and thus sheds new light on the understanding of such policies. Despite the comprehensive analysis, there is still room for improvement. This paper mainly focuses on the partial equilibrium effect of a SEZ, while the general equilibrium (GE) effect is absent. A spatial GE model is needed in the future research.

Chapter 7
Managerial Efficiency and Product Decision: Evidence from Chinese Firms

This chapter provides a theoretical and empirical analysis of the effects of market competition and market expansion on firms product line decisions. The theoretical model explicitly incorporates cost of management. Firms are heterogeneous in terms of managerial efficiency. We use import tariff cut as a proxy for increased market competition and export tariff reduction as a proxy for market expansion. The theoretical analysis predicts that the home country is tariff cut reduces all home firm's export product line, whereas in response to the foreign country is tariff cut, firms with high (low) managerial efficiency expand (reduce) export product lines. These predictions are supported by our empirical analysis based on data on Chinese firms from 2000 to 2006.

7.1 Introduction

Firms compete in many dimensions and one for them is product lines. What determine product lines in equilibrium? The literature has emphasized the importance of competition in markets characterized by oligopolistic competition (e.g., Brander and Eaton 1984; Johnson and Myatt 2003; Mendelson and Parlakturk 2008). It is very challenging to empirically test those models and their predictions. In this study, we explore this issue based on monopolistic competition (to avoid strategic interaction) and by making use of tariff changes as proxies for changes in competition (to avoid endogeneity problem).

In response to changes in market conditions, different firms may adjust their product lines (or product scope) differently. In this study, we focus on firm heterogeneity in managerial efficiency because the literature already has extensive studies on firm heterogeneity in production productivity. We also focus on firms' export product scope because our data does not include information of product varieties sold in the domestic market (China). Specifically, we assume (in the theoretical model) that domestic firms are of two types, efficient ones with low management cost and

M. Yu, *China's Miracle in Foreign Trade*, Studies in Modern Chinese Economy,
https://doi.org/10.1007/978-981-16-6030-6_7

inefficient ones with high management cost. All firms produce multiple products and employ the same production structure for their products. Every firm has a core competency and faces increasing marginal costs of production for its other products. Introducing each new product at the firm level incurs a fixed cost. In addition, each product line in each market needs to be managed by a team, and thus incurs a fixed cost, which is product-market specific. A product will be produced if the fixed cost of product introduction is lower than the sum of the profit derived from the domestic market and that derived from the foreign market.

Our model predicts that a drastic domestic tariff cut reduces a firm's export product scope and total product scope (the number of products *produced*). Foreign tariff cuts exert two effects on each product exported by a domestic firm. First, a reduction in foreign tariff lowers the costs of all home country's export products. This phenomenon can be considered an individual shock (positive) because products with different marginal costs of production face different cost reductions in the absolute term. Second, all the home country's export products lower their prices because of cost reduction and thus makes the foreign market competition tougher. This can be considered as a common shock (negative) to all products. Our analysis shows that under certain conditions, the positive individual shock outweighs the negative common shock for the marginal products of efficient firms; however, the opposite is true for the marginal products of inefficient firms. Consequently, efficient firms expand their export product scope in response to foreign tariff cuts, whereas inefficient firms reduce theirs.

To test the hypotheses, we conduct an empirical analysis based on Chinese firms' export product scope data from 2000 to 2006. The key part of the analysis is to construct a measure of managerial efficiency and another measure of productive efficiency. The usual estimated TFP is a mixed of both. We use firm's general and administrative (G&A) expenses *residuals* as a proxy for managerial efficiency, with a higher residual representing lower efficiency. Another key explanatory variable is tariff reduction. To avoid possible bias from using industry-level tariff cuts, we construct and use firm-specific measures of home tariffs and foreign tariffs, following Lileeva and Trefler (2010) and Yu (2015), our main empirical analysis finds strong support for our theoretical prediction: in response to Chinese tariff cuts, all Chinese firms reduce their export product scope; in response to foreign tariff cuts, Chinese firms with high managerial efficiency expand their export product scope, whereas those with low managerial efficiency reduce theirs. The estimation results are robust to different estimation approaches and measurements.

The present study is related to both the management and trade literatures. We introduce managerial efficiency as a source of firm heterogeneity and show that this heterogeneity, rather than heterogeneity in production productivity, differentiates the responses of firms to trade liberalization. The importance of managerial efficiency and its difference from production productivity have been emphasized in management science literature. For example, Gort and Lee (2003) utilize American industrial data and found that managerial efficiency contributes substantially to TFP in American manufacturing sectors. They identify three sources of managerial efficiency, namely, superior initial managerial endowments, the accumulation of managerial knowledge through learning, and the impact of an effective market for managerial resources internal to the firm. These sources of managerial efficiency are different from a firm's production productivity. Bloom and van Reenen (2007) provide a method to measure firm's managerial efficiency. They use international survey data to score firms from one (poor management) to five (best management) based on 18 criteria. They find strong evidence that poor management practices are more likely when family-owned firms choose their Chief Executive Officers (CEO) by *primogeniture* (i.e., the eldest male child in the family). Without such survey data, most studies in the literature use a firm's selling, general and administrative (SG&A) expenses as a proxy for management costs (see, for example, Miller and Vollmann 1985; Cooper and Kaplan 1991; Fisher and Ittner 1999; Lev and Radhakrishnan 2005; Eisfeldt and Papanikolaou 2013). They assume that high management cost implies high organization capital, and thus, represent high managerial efficiency. Different from this approach, inspired by Bloom and van Reenen (2007), we *estimate* a firm's managerial efficiency using general and administrative (G&A) expenses to represent management cost and controlling for firm size, export status and markup. Low G&A expenses residual represents high managerial efficiency.[1]

Although the purpose of the present study is not to investigate the effects of trade liberalization, tariff reductions do provide a good instrument for our empirical analysis of the effects of changing competition on product lines. In the theoretical literature of multiproduct firms in international trade, all studies assume firm heterogeneity in production productivity and most (e.g., Bernard et al. 2009), with the exception of Nocke and Yeaple (2014) and Qiu and Zhou (2013), predict that in response to *bilateral* trade liberalization, all firms (less productive and more productive) reduce their product scope (Arkolakis and Muendler 2011; Baldwin and Gu 2009; Bernard et al. 2011; Dhingra 2013; Eckel and Neary 2010; Feenstra and Ma 2008). Existing theoretical analyses have offered a clear picture and explanation (see Qiu and Zhou 2013). On the one hand, domestic trade liberalization exerts a negative impact (the competition effect) on a firm's profit from each product. On the other hand, a foreign country's trade liberalization provides a positive opportunity (the market expansion effect) to a firm's profit from each product. The net effect is negative (resulting in product scope reduction) for low productivity firms, but may be positive (resulting in product scope expansion) for high productivity firms. However, all studies appear to suggest that the qualitative effects of *unilateral* trade liberalization (i.e., either home tariff cut or foreign tariff cut) on all firms with high or low productivity are similar. However, empirical studies show that firms respond differently. In this paper, we argue that firms differ not only in production productivity, but also in many other

[1] Caliendo and Rossi-Hansberg (2012) point out that a firm has many facets aside from its production technology, and thus, they add organization structure to firms in their model. They assume that firms are heterogeneous with respect to demand for their products to show the importance of the other aspects of firms. In contrast, we assume that firms are heterogenous in terms of their managerial efficiency.

aspects, such as managerial efficiency. Firm heterogeneity in management cost could generate results different from firm heterogeneity in production cost.[2]

Existing empirical studies on multiproduct firms generally find that trade liberalization has significant effects on firms' product scope choice. Despite the fact that most theoretical studies focus on bilateral trade liberalization, many empirical studies highlight *unilateral* trade liberalization.[3] Iacovone and Javorcik (2010) document the phenomenon of product "churning" among Mexican firms as a result of improved access to foreign markets, that is, a substantial number of Mexican firms discontinue several existing products and simultaneously develop new products for export. Goldberg et al. (2010) show that from 1989 to 2003 when intensive trade and other reforms took place in India, Indian firms added more product lines than what they discontinued; the discontinuance was unrelated to tariff reduction. In contrast, Liu (2010) finds that increased import competition results in the US public firms shrinking the product scope through refocusing on the core competence products. In our study, Chinese exporters' data are utilized to examine the effects of tariff cuts in China and foreign countries on export product scope. Our results show that managerial efficiency is important in determining the extent to which firms adjust their export product scope.[4]

The rest of this chapter is organized as follows. In Sect. 7.2, Chinese data are utilized to conduct a preliminary empirical analysis on Chinese firms' response to trade liberalization without differentiating them by managerial efficiency. The theoretical model with firm heterogeneity in managerial efficiency is introduced in Sect. 7.3, and an equilibrium analysis is conducted to derive results related to the effects of trade liberalization on firms' export product scope. Chinese data are employed in Sect. 7.4 to test the main theoretical predictions. Section 7.5 provides the concluding remarks.

7.2 Preliminary Empirical Analysis

7.2.1 Estimation Framework and Measures

A firm's *total product scope* is defined in this study as the total number of products that the firm produces and sells to the markets (either domestic or foreign). *Export product*

---

[2] Nocke and Yeaple (2014) introduced two dimensions of firm heterogeneity: organizational capital and organizational efficiency. These two types of capability result in a trade-off between producing more products with lower productivity and producing less products with higher productivity. Managerial efficiency is very different from organizational capability.

[3] The implications of unilateral trade liberalization can be obtained from the study of Mayer et al. (2014).

[4] Manova and Yu (2017) also employ Chinese data to explore the behavior of multiproduct firms. An important feature of their study is the linkage between multiple products and multiple quality level. Eckel et al.'s (2015) study on Mexican firms also has the same feature.

scope is defined as the total number of products that the firm sells to the foreign markets. A firm's export product scope is mainly determined by the profitability of a firm's products in the foreign market, which in turn is affected by many factors, including GDP, productivity, and trade costs. A firm's domestic market profitability affects its total product scope, but may or may not affect its export product scope.

We focus on two explanatory variables to determine how changes in trade costs affect Chinese firms' export product scope. The first variable is the home country's import tariffs (referred to as home tariff and denoted by HT hereafter), and the second one is the foreign countries' import tariffs (referred to as *foreign tariff* and denoted by FT hereafter). Accordingly, the following empirical equation is established:

$$e_{it} = \beta_0 + \beta_1 TFP_{it} + \beta_2 HT_{it} + \beta_3 FT_{it} + \boldsymbol{\theta}\, \boldsymbol{\Psi}_{it} + \epsilon_{it}, \tag{7.1}$$

where e_{it} is firm i's export product scope, TFP_{it} is firm i' total factor productivity,[5] HT_{it} is the home (Chinese) tariff level faced by firm i, and FT_{it} is the foreign tariff level faced by firm i, all in year t. Ψ_{it} is a vector of control variables, including firm i's export market size (foreign countries' GDP), ownership type (state-owned enterprise, foreign-invested enterprise, or others), and trade mode (processing or ordinary trade).

Although a country has many tariff lines, tariffs that are not relevant to a particular firm may not have an impact on the firm's export product scope. Inspired by Lileeva and Trefler (2010), we thus construct *firm-specific tariff* to better evaluate the effects of tariff changes on firms' export product scope. For home tariffs, suppose that a firm produces a set of products for the domestic market. The firm's profit will be affected directly by all tariff lines in this product set. A tariff line will have a more significant effect if the firm has a larger share of the corresponding product in its total domestic sales. Thus, a firm-specific tariff should be the average of all relevant tariffs weighted by the share of each product's sales. However, data on product-level domestic sales are unavailable. Thus, we adopt a less satisfactory approach by using the share of a firm's export to substitute the share of its domestic sales, as in Yu (2015). Specifically, we introduce the following measure as firm i's home tariff:

$$HT_{it} = \sum_{k \in E_{it}} \left(\frac{X^k_{i,initial\_year}}{\sum_{k \in E_{it}} X^k_{i,initial\_year}} \right) \tau^k_t, \tag{7.2}$$

where E_{it} is the set of firm i's export products in year t, $X^k_{i,initial\_year}$ is firm i's exports of product k in the first year the firm appears in the sample, and τ^k_t is the home country's ad valorem tariff on product k in year t. Inspired by Topalova and Khandelwal (2011), we fix exports for each product at the initial period to avoid possible reverse causality (endogeneity problem) in firm's export scope with respect

[5] Here we assume that firms have a common productivity level and production function across goods given that Chinese product-level production data are unavailable.

to measured home tariffs. However, such a measure still faces some possible caveats which will be discussed later.

The construction of firm-specific foreign tariffs is more complicated than the construction of home tariffs because firms not only export multiple products, but also export them to multiple countries, with different subsets of products for different countries. The following measure of FT_{it} is proposed in this study to capture the relative importance of different tariffs of different foreign countries.

$$FT_{it} = \sum_{k \in E_{it}} \left[\frac{X^{k}_{i,initial\_year}}{\sum_{k \in E_{it}} X^{k}_{i,initial\_year}} \sum_{c \in C_{it}} \left(\frac{X^{kc}_{i,initial\_year}}{X^{k}_{i,initial\_year}} \right) \tau^{kc}_{t} \right], \tag{7.3}$$

where τ^{kc}_{t} is product k's ad valorem tariff imposed by country c in year t, $X^{kc}_{i,initial\_year}$ is the value of firm i's export of product k to country c in the first year the product appears in the sample, $X^{k}_{i,initial\_year} = \sum_{c \in C_{it}} X^{c}_{ik,initial\_year}$, and C_{it} are the sets of countries where firm i has exports in year t. The ratio $\frac{X^{kc}_{i,initial\_year}}{X^{k}_{i,initial\_year}}$ represents the share of firm i's product k exported to country c in the first year the firm appears in the sample; it captures the relative importance of τ^{kc}_{t} in affecting firm i's product k export.

Thus, $\sum_{c \in C_{it}} \left(\frac{X^{kc}_{i,initial\_year}}{X^{k}_{i,initial\_year}} \right) \tau^{kc}_{t}$ is the time-invariant weighted average of foreign tariffs on product k for firm i. Such a time-invariant weight can avoid the aforementioned endogeneity of weighted tariffs.

We next turn to TFP_{it}. Although many methods can be employed to measure a firm's TFP, or productivity, we adopt the Olley-Pakes (1996) approach to estimate each Chinese firm's TFP (referred to as TFP1). We modify the standard Olley-Pakes approach to better reflect the reality in China. First, following Feenstra et al. (2014), we use deflated output and input prices at the firm-product level to measure TFP. Second, we use real capital depreciation to construct a firm's real investment (the perpetual inventory method).[6] Third, we consider the effect of China's WTO accession in 2001 and the processing behavior of firms in TFP realization. A detailed description of the augmented Olley-Pakes TFP measures is provided in Appendix 7.3. We also employ other measures of TFP to verify the robustness of the results.[7]

---

[6] Firm-level data only provide the book value of each firm's capital stock. However, the original value of each firm's capital stock must be obtained for TFP estimation. To solve this problem, we assume $A_t = A_o \Pi^{t}_{s=o}(1 + r_\theta)$, where A_t is the book value of a firm's capital stock in year t, A_o is the original value of the firm's capital stock when it is purchased in year o, and r_s is the estimated province-industry-level growth rate of nominal capital stock in years obtained from Brandt et al. (2012). If A_t and r_s are known for each firm, the firm's original nominal book value can be determined accordingly. Approximately 40% of observations have missing investment data, but this is not a problem because our estimation results do not change qualitatively when other measures of TFP are employed as shown later.

[7] The Levinsohn and Petrin (2003) approach is also a popular method to construct TFP. In this approach, materials (i.e., intermediate inputs) are used as a proxy variable. Yu (2015) argues that this approach is appropriate for firms that do not utilize a large amount of imported intermediate inputs,

7.2.2 Data

Regression of model (7.1) and construction of *HT*, *FT* and *TFP* require extensive information. Thus, we employ three highly disaggregate panel datasets: product-level tariff data of every country, firm-level production data of Chinese firms, and firm and product-level trade data of Chinese firms. A brief description of these datasets is provided below, and detailed discussions are provided in Appendix 7.1.

Tariffs data. Tariff levels of all WTO member countries/regions are provided at HS six-digit level on the WTO official webpage.[8]

Firm production data. China's National Bureau of Statistics maintains a rich database derived from annual surveys of large manufacturing enterprises in China. This database, called the Chinese Manufacturing Enterprises (CME) database, includes all state-owned enterprises (SOEs) and large non-SOEs whose annual sales are more than RMB five million (about US$604,600 at the exchange rate 8.27 yuan/$, prevailing during most of the time in our sample period). Approximately 162,885 firms are included in 2000 and 301,961 in 2006. The CME database contains information of more than 100 financial variables obtained from each firm's accounting statement. The database has obvious omissions and errors. Following Feenstra et al. (2014), we clean the database as follows. We eliminate the observations (i.e., firms) wherein some key financial variables (such as total assets, net value of fixed assets, sales, and gross value of industrial output) are missing, or the number of employees is less than eight.[9] According to the basic rules of the generally accepted accounting principles, we also exclude the observations wherein (i) liquid assets are larger than total assets, (ii) total fixed assets are larger than total assets, (iii) the net value of fixed assets is larger than the total assets, (iv) the firm's identification number is missing, or (v) the firm's establishment time is invalid.

Export data. China's General Administration of Customs maintains a highly disaggregate trade database wherein each international trade transaction is recorded. The database contains a large variety of information about each trading firm, including each product's price, quantity, value, and destination. Product information is available at the HS eight-digit level. We use this database to calculate each Chinese firm's export product scope and construct the weights used in *HT* and *FT* of each firm.

---

and so it is less appropriate for our study because Chinese firms rely substantially on imported intermediate inputs whose prices are significantly different from those of domestic intermediate inputs (Halpern et al. 2015). Nonetheless, our results do not change qualitatively when Levinsohn-Petrin (2003) TFP, System-GMM TFP, or Ackerberg et al. (2006)'s TFP is employed. Estimates that employ such TFP measures are not reported to save space but are available upon request.

[8] Data can be accessed at http://tariffdata.wto.org/ReportersAndProducts.aspx. The data from Trade Analysis and Information System generally have missing values, particularly data on the tariffs imposed by other countries on Chinese exports. The product-destination-year combinations that have missing tariffs are thus dropped out.

[9] The reason for selecting eight workers as the threshold is that firms with less than eight employees fall under a different legal regime, as pointed out by Brandt et al. (2012). We adopt this criterion also because a very small company may not have a good accounting/reporting system. However, our results are not sensitive to this critical level.

Table 7.1A Distribution of firms' export product scope

Export product scope	Number of obs.		Export value	
	Percent	Cumulative	Percent	Cumulative
1	21.06	21.06	8.64	8.64
2	15.66	36.72	8.65	17.29
3	11.54	48.25	7.80	25.10
4	8.91	57.16	7.60	32.70
5	6.90	64.07	5.85	38.54
6–15	25.82	89.89	31.35	69.89
16–25	6.01	95.90	10.99	80.88
26–527	4.10	100.0	19.12	100.0

Some firms export products that belong to more than one industry. Considering that our focus is on within-industry multiproduct analysis, we assign a firm to an industry at HS 2-digit level, in which the firm has the most number of export products.

Our study requires the merging of the Customs database and CME database. Matching the two is challenging because they use completely different firm-identification systems. As in Yu (2015), by using the firms' Chinese names, zip codes, and telephone numbers, we are able to match 76,946 firms, which account for more than 40% of the manufacturing firms reported in the CME database and approximately 53% of the export value reported in the Customs database.[10] This representation is comparable to that of Bernard et al. (2009) for US data and Wang and Yu (2012) for Chinese data.

The summary statistics are reported in Table 7.1 which has three sub-tables. Tables 7.1A and 7.1B show that export product scope has a very large variation: The minimum of export product scope is 1 (i.e., a single product), whereas the maximum is 527, with the mean equal to 6.72. Approximately 79% of the Chinese firms (in our merged dataset) exported more than a single product from 2000 to 2006 and accounted for 91.4% of the total exports. Moreover, approximately two-thirds of the firms exported less than 5 products, 90% exported less than 15 products, and only 5% exported more than 25 products.

As shown in Table 7.1C, China's home tariffs (measured at both industry and firm levels) declined by approximately 50% from 2000 to 2006. Industry-level foreign tariffs (at 2-digit Chinese industrial classification level) also declined around 28% during the same period. By contrast, firm-level foreign tariffs *FT* decreased by only 3%. One possible reason for the slight decline of firm-level foreign tariffs is that most important export destinations for Chinese firms are developed countries which typically had low import tariffs in the beginning year (i.e., in 2000) of our sample [see Yu (2015) for a detailed discussion].

[10] Our merged dataset has higher mean of sales than the full-sample CME database; this finding indicates that large firms are more likely to be matched. The same matching procedure is also used by Yu and Tian (2012).

Table 7.1B Summary statistics

(2000–2006) Variable	Mean	Std. Dev.
Export product scope	6.72	10.19
Firm sales (RMB1,000)	150,053	1,061,312
Number of employees	479	1,687
Home tariffs (firm level)	0.085	0.077
Home tariffs (industry level)	0.117	0.056
Foreign tariffs (firm level)	0.075	0.071
Home input tariffs (firm level)	0.021	0.038
Log China's GDP	28.29	0.265
Log importers' weighted GDP	28.70	2.43
Log G&A expenses	6.83	2.18
Log administrative expenses (after 2004)	4.73	1.46
Log per-capita administrative expenses (after 2004)	1.11	3.16
SOE indicator	0.021	0.141
Foreign indicator	0.589	0.491
Processing indicator	0.286	0.452

Note Value is in Chinese yuan. US$1 was equivalent to approximately 8.20 yuan before July 2005

Table 7.1C Tariff reductions (in percent)

Year	Ind. home tariffs		Firm home tariffs		Ind. foreign tariffs		Firm foreign tariffs	
	Mean (1)	Std. Dev. (2)	Mean (3)	Std. Dev. (4)	Mean (5)	Std. Dev. (6)	Mean (7)	Std. Dev. (8)
2000	20.34	8.44	15.62	4.13	11.22	5.61	7.72	8.77
2006	10.11	4.15	7.69	1.60	8.07	4.17	7.61	8.35
Change (%)	50.29	–	50.77	–	28.07	–	2.43	–

Note Columns (1)–(2) report the mean and standard deviation of 3-digit industry-level home import tariffs whereas columns (3)–(4) report firm-level home import tariffs as described in Eq. (7.2). Columns (5)–(6) report the mean and standard deviation of 2-digit Chinese-industry-classification (CIC) foreign tariffs opposed against Chinese firms. Columns (7)–(8) report the mean and standard deviation of firm-level foreign tariffs as described in Eq. (7.3)

7.2.3 Estimates

The estimation results from model (7.1) could differ both quantitatively and qualitatively depending on our assumption about the distribution of the dependent variable. We first assume a normal distribution. The OLS regression estimates are shown in column (1) of Table 7.2. Both home and foreign tariffs are positively associated with firms' export product scope. This result indicates that firms reduce their export product scope in response to both home and foreign tariff cuts.

Table 7.2 Baseline estimates

Econometric methods	OLS	Poisson	Negative binomial		
Regressand: export product scope	(1)	(2)	(3)	(4)	(5)
Home tariffs (firm-level)	13.438*** (29.77)	1.544*** (21.45)	1.565*** (37.43)	0.660*** (10.91)	0.793*** (10.53)
Foreign tariffs	10.347*** (21.58)	1.322*** (25.27)	1.283*** (27.17)	0.302*** (9.21)	0.263*** (6.73)
Log firm TFP (TFP1)	2.781*** (22.92)	0.273*** (19.85)	0.344*** (40.59)	0.035*** (4.19)	0.051*** (4.77)
Log China's GDP	0.630*** (4.21)	0.093*** (4.25)	0.076*** (5.91)		
Log weighted GDP of importers	1.367*** (60.91)	0.223*** (43.74)	0.155*** (131.14)	0.123*** (54.57)	0.130*** (46.28)
Log capital-labor ratio	0.028 (1.01)	0.007 (1.29)	−0.011*** (−4.69)	−0.001 (−0.28)	0.002 (0.32)
Foreign indicator	0.443*** (5.39)	0.015 (0.77)	0.082*** (12.91)	0.113*** (5.11)	0.113*** (4.25)
SOE indicator	1.062*** (3.28)	0.158*** (2.64)	0.118*** (5.03)	−0.059 (−1.50)	−0.080* (−1.89)
Firm-specific fixed effects	No	No	No	Yes	Yes
Year-specific fixed effects	No	No	No	Yes	Yes
Pure exporting firms dropped	No	No	No	No	Yes
Prob. > χ^2	0.000	0.000	0.000	0.000	0.000
Observations	87,763	87,763	87,763	63,844	43,191

Note T-values in parentheses. * (**,***) indicates significance at the 10% (5%, 1%) level. 23,919 observations are dropped in columns (4) and (5) because of only one observation per group

Our data clearly show that most of the firms export a small number of products, and only a few of them export a very large number of products. This observation suggests that the dependent variable does not follow a normal distribution. Thus, the OLS result could be biased. Because our dependent variable is a non-negative count number, the use of count-data estimates would be more reliable (Cameron and Trivedi 2005). Given that Poisson distribution is the most popular discrete distribution used to capture the characteristics of count data, we also calculate the Poisson estimate (with a clustered robust standard error).[11] The regression results are shown in column (2) of Table 7.2. The result obtained from OLS remain valid qualitatively: Both home and foreign tariffs have positive and significant effects on export product scope.

Although Poisson distribution is the most popular approach for count data, it may not provide the best representation of our sample distribution. Poisson distribution requires that the mean and variance of a firm's export product scope be identical.

[11] Specifically, the dependent variable is assumed to have a probability function $f(e, \mu) = \frac{\exp(-\mu)\mu_e}{e!}$ where, $\mu = \exp(\mathbf{X}\beta)$ and $\mathbf{X}$ denotes the vector of independent variables.

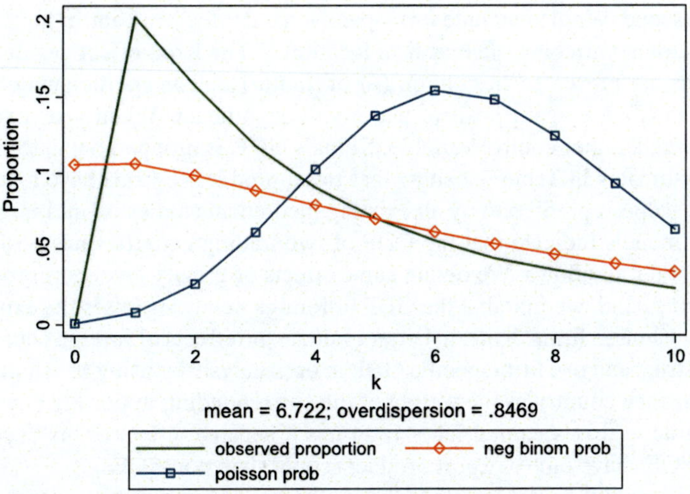

Fig. 7.1 Distribution of Chinese firms' export product scope

However, our data reveal that the variance of the sample ($var(e) = 103.9$) is approximately 15 times larger than its mean ($e = 6.72$), which indicates that Poisson distribution does not provide a good representation of our data. Moreover, our test of the goodness of fit for the Poisson model reports an extremely large χ^2 value (607,445), which again confirms the inappropriateness of Poisson distribution for our dependent variable.

We then resort to negative binomial distribution which allows the sample to exhibit a pattern of over-dispersion.[12] In fact, when drawing a graph based on the proportion of firms with different export product scope (see Fig. 7.1), we notice that the negative binomial distribution approximates the observed distribution much better than the Poisson distribution. Since around 80% of the exporters have export product scope less than 10, we assume 10 as the maximum value of the discrete level.[13] We report the negative binomial regression results in column (3) of Table 7.2. We find that the over-dispersion parameter generated by the likelihood ratio test is significantly different from zero (we obtain $\alpha = 0.847$ from the regression), indicating that negative binomial distribution is a good probabilistic representative of our data.[14] The coefficients of both home and foreign tariffs are positive and statistically significant. We include year-specific fixed effects in the regressions because several other time-variant variables, such as exchange rate, may affect the firms' optimal export

---

[12] The probability density function of negative binomial distribution has the following form $f(e, \mu) = \frac{\Gamma(\alpha^{-1}, \mu+e)}{\Gamma(\alpha-1)\Gamma(e+1)} \frac{-1}{\alpha \quad \mu+\mu} - \left(\frac{{}^{-1}\mu}{\alpha \quad \mu+\mu}\right)^e$ where $\mu = \exp(\boldsymbol{X}\beta)$ and $\Gamma(\cdot)$ is the Gamma function.

[13] Changing the maximum number does not change our estimation results.

[14] We also perform regression based on gamma distribution and obtain results very similar to those from negative binomial distribution. These results are not presented in the table to save space but are available upon request.

product scope. We also include firm-specific fixed effects to control for the effects of firm-invariant variables, such as firm location.[15] The fixed-effect negative binomial estimates are presented in column (4) of Table 7.2. The coefficients of home and foreign tariffs are again positive and highly significant. When year fixed effect is introduced, another control variable, China's GDP, is dropped out automatically.

All estimates in Table 7.2 show that more-productive firms have a larger export product scope, a prediction by all existing theoretical studies on multiproduct firms. Gravity models indicate that the GDP of two trading countries has positive effects on bilateral trade flows. We obtain some effects of gravity on export product scope. On the one hand, we find that the GDP of foreign countries raises the export product scope of Chinese firms. Note, to better evaluate the effects of foreign countries' GDP, we construct and use firm-specific GDP in our analysis by using the share of a firm's export to each country as the weight of the corresponding importing country's GDP. In addition, a firm's capital-labor ratio has a negative effect on its export product scope. SOEs have larger export product scopes than non-SOEs.

Five important caveats relate to the analysis and effects of home tariffs. First, two groups of firms are special. One group includes the pure domestic firms which do not have any exports; thus, their export product scope (zero) is insensitive to changes in home and foreign tariffs. In fact, our estimates do not include any pure domestic firms since, by construction, all firms in our sample are exporting firms. Another group consists of pure exporting firms which have no domestic sales; thus, home tariffs do not have any effect on their export product scope. We also re-run the regression by omitting pure processing firms from the sample. The regression results are shown in column (5) of Table 7.2. All the coefficients are very close to their counterparts in column (4). This result implies that omitting them from the sample does not change our estimation results.

Second, HT_{it} disregards tariffs on intermediate inputs. However, changes in the intermediate inputs' tariffs will affect the final goods' profits, which then affect firms' decisions on export product scopes. Moreover, trade liberalization in final goods is often accompanied by trade liberalization in intermediate goods. Hence, the cost effects associated with tariff changes in intermediate goods must be controlled. Accordingly, we include "home input tariffs" as an additional independent variable. Processing imports are duty-free in China; hence, even firms that import the same set of inputs may face different effective tariffs. This phenomenon makes it more difficult to construct firm-specific "home input tariffs." Given that a firm can engage in both processing and non-processing imports, we adopt the index of firm-specific input tariffs (FIT_{it}) suggested by Yu (2015) as our firm-level "home input tariffs". The index is

$$FIT_{it} = \sum_{k \in O_i} \frac{m^k_{i,initial\_year}}{\sum_{k \in M_i} m^k_{i,initial\_year}} \tau^k_t, \tag{7.4}$$

[15] Firm-specific fixed effects in the negative binomial model apply to the distribution of the dispersion parameter (Hardin and Hilbe 2003).

where $m^k_{i,initial\_year}$ is the value of firm i's imports of intermediate good k in the first year the firm appears in the sample, O_i is the set of firm i's non-processing imports, and M_i is the set of the firm's total imports. The set of processing imports does not appear in (7.4) because processing imports are duty free. FIT_{it} is constructed with time-invariant weights to avoid the afford-mentioned endogeneity of weighted tariffs, measuring the import weight of each product based on data on the firm's first year in the sample. Table 7.3 shows the negative binomial estimates when two new control variables—"home input tariffs" and "processing indicator"—are included. Trade liberalization in intermediate goods imports lowers export product scope. This result is counter-intuitive in the sense that exporters might increase their product scopes with the cost-saving effect from declining input trade costs. However, the result is reversed for firms that are less-integrated to processing trade to be shown later. In addition, firms that engage in processing trade are found to have smaller export product scopes than firms that only engage in non-processing trade.[16] In any case, the inclusion of such a control variable does not alter the effects and significance of the two key variables: home tariffs and foreign tariffs on the final goods.

We now turn to discuss the economic magnitudes of such two key variables. Since our estimates are negative binomial, it is inappropriate to interpret the coefficient as the marginal effect. We hence take a step forward to estimate the semi-elasticity, $dy/d(\ln \mathbf{X})$, where y denotes firm's export product scope and $\mathbf{X}$ denotes all regressors. The results are reported in column (2) of Table 7.3. The marginal effects of home and foreign tariffs are 1.149 and 0.182, respectively, suggesting that a 10 percentage point fall in home (or foreign) tariff leads to a cut of around 11 (or 2) export product varieties. Such effects are indeed sizable.

The third caveat is that input tariff reduction may have an impact on the cost of obtaining capital goods. The effect may be different from the intermediate input cost-saving effects that we have already controlled. To address such a concern, we drop capital goods in our analysis. To do that, we appeal to the classification of Broad Economic Categories (BEC). According to BEC, capital goods are mostly concentrated in Sectors 41 and 521, which broadly concord with products in Chinese Industrial Classification Sectors 36 and 37.[17] We drop these two product categories and re-run the Regression. The results are reported in column (3) of Table 7.3, which are similar as before.

The fourth caveat is that in constructing HT_{it}, we assume that the share of each product a firm sells in the domestic market is the same as that in the foreign markets. This is definitely untrue, but we would not be able to solve the problem directly because of data limitation. As mentioned before, we have tried to eliminate pure exporting firms from the sample to address this problem in part because such firms

---

16 Some firms change their types of ownership and trade mode. Hence, SOE, foreign, and processing indicators are not eliminated from the fixed-effects estimates. The transitional probability matrixes are not reported to save space but are available upon request.

17 Note that Sector 41 in BEC is defined as capital goods (except transport equipment) and parts and accessories thereof, which is broadly consistent with CIC Sector 36—special machinery. Section 521 in BEC is defined as industrial transport equipment and parts which is broadly consistent with CIC Sector 37—transport equipment.

Table 7.3 Negative binomial estimates

Regressand: export product scope	All sample			GSCs integrated		All sample	
				Less	More		
Coefficients reported	b (t) (1)	dy/dlnx (2)	b (t) (3)	b (t) (4)	b (t) (5)	b (t) (6)	b (t) (7)
Home tariffs (firm-level)	1.425*** (27.49)	1.149	1.323*** (28.37)	1.861*** (18.19)	1.289*** (18.59)		2.406*** (8.16)
Home tariffs (industry-level)						0.686*** (13.65)	
Foreign tariffs	0.310*** (9.98)	0.182	0.239*** (8.82)	0.443*** (5.75)	0.386*** (10.24)	0.280*** (12.23)	2.680*** (7.76)
Home input tariffs	0.374*** (4.87)	0.065	0.477*** (6.96)	−0.668*** (−3.47)	0.604*** (6.73)	0.337*** (5.87)	−0.920 (−1.44)
Log firm TFP (TFP1)	0.081*** (11.42)	0.778	0.063*** (10.28)	0.234*** (13.27)	0.069*** (7.74)	0.059*** (11.73)	0.166*** (3.52)
Log weighted GDP of importers	0.119*** (70.51)	28.49	0.116*** (75.93)	0.126*** (33.59)	0.116*** (58.16)	0.105*** (86.23)	0.157*** (13.49)
Log capital-labor ratio	−0.019*** (−5.44)	−0.562	−0.015*** (−4.76)	−0.066*** (−9.84)	0.011** (2.48)	−0.020*** (−7.74)	−0.028* (−1.66)
Foreign indicator	−0.034** (−2.57)	−0.197	−0.029** (−2.22)	0.032 (1.31)	− 0.115*** (−7.14)	−0.008 (−0.74)	− 0.255*** (−3.81)

(continued)

Table 7.3 (continued)

Regressand: export product scope	All sample			GSCs integrated		All sample	
				Less	More		
Coefficients reported	b (t) (1)	dy/dlnx (2)	b (t) (3)	b (t) (4)	b (t) (5)	b (t) (6)	b (t) (7)
SOE indicator	0.032 (1.06)	0.003	0.011 (0.38)	−0.005 (−0.06)	0.080** (2.42)	0.020 (0.82)	0.071 (0.42)
Processing indicator	−0.045*** (−9.76)	−0.154	−0.043*** (−10.85)	−0.048*** (−4.15)	−0.055*** (−9.92)	−0.051*** (−14.33)	−0.120** (−2.11)
Firm-specific fixed effects	Yes		Yes	Yes	Yes	Yes	Yes
Year-specific fixed effects	Yes		Yes	Yes	Yes	Yes	Yes
Pure exporting firms dropped	Yes		Yes	Yes	Yes	No	Yes
Balanced panel considered	No		No	No	No	No	Yes
Prob. > χ^2	0.000		0.000	0.000	0.000	0.000	0.000
Observations	40,925		37,565	14,823	26,102	52,176	1,798

Note T-values corrected for clustering at the firm level in parentheses. * (**) indicates significance at the 10% (5%) level. 19 industries out of 30 are classified as more integrated in global supply chain (GSC) integrated. Columns (1) and (2) are a single estimate. Coefficients in column (1) are in level whereas those in column (2) are the estimated semi-elasticity—dy/d(lnx), where y denotes export product scope. Columns (3)–(7) report the estimated coefficients and t-value (in parentheses). Column (3) drops samples in special machinery and transport equipment violate the aforementioned assumption to the largest degree. We have also performed the following auxiliary regressions to verify the robustness of the main results. China holds an important position in global supply chains (GSCs), and different firms engage in GSCs at different degrees (Yu 2013). As a result, the differences between their sales distribution in the domestic market and that in foreign markets are also different. We classify all two-digit Chinese industries into two groups, namely, less integrated and more integrated, according to their "production depth" of engaging in GSCs, which is measured by the ratio of value-added to gross industrial output (OECD 2010). The division line is the mean of the production depth ratio across industries. We then run the regressions separately for these two groups and obtain the estimates in columns (4) and (5) of Table 7.3. These two groups have different degrees of approximation to the "equal share" assumption; however, we find that for both the less-integrated group and more-integrated group, home tariffs have the same qualitative results (sign and significance) as in the main model and so do the foreign tariffs. Hence, our main findings are not sensitive to the "equal share" assumption.

The fifth caveat is that HT_{it} does not include tariffs on products that firm i does not produce. When there is a change in tariffs on products that a firm does not produce but is competing with, the profits of the firm's existing products and those the firm may potentially produce will be affected. Consequently, the firm's decision on its export product scopes may change. The reason is obvious. Suppose that a firm produces products x and y and product z's tariff experiences a large reduction. Producing z then becomes profitable for the firm. However, if the firm produces z, its profit from existing products may decrease (e.g., drawing resources away from production of existing products). Thus, the total product scope may expand or shrink, depending on how the existing products' profits are affected. We adopt an industry-wide, as opposed to firm-specific, tariff to replace HT_{it} to capture this effect. The regression results are presented in column (6) of Table 7.3. The coefficients of both home and foreign tariffs are positive and significant.

A similar caveat applies to the measure of firm-specific foreign tariffs FT_{it} in which the product-line export compositions of the initial year are used as weights. Although such initial-year export weights can well avoid the endogeneity nexus between tariffs and trade, as discussed before, they are at the expense of ignoring the change in extensive margin of firm exports. They do not account for the fact that a firm's decision to export is also affected by tariffs in goods/countries that the firm does not currently export to. The extensive margin of export is important for China given that Kehoe and Ruhl (2013) found that export's extensive margin contribute to around a quarter of trade growth between the US and China, Chile, and Korea. The missing extensive margin effect is also reflected from the small over-time variation of the index of FT_{it} as discussed in Table 7.1C.[18] To capture such important extensive margin, we adopt an industry-wide, as opposed to firm-specific, tariff to replace FT_{it} as the robustness checks and yield similar results. We will discuss this carefully later.

In addition to the five caveats on home tariff effects, there is another concern, and that is, tariff changes may induce a new entry. The export product scopes of

---

[18] We thank a referee for pointing this out.

new entrants may differ significantly from those of the incumbents. In this case, the estimate may not reflect the actual effects of tariff changes on existing firms' export product scope because it also includes the new entrants' export product scope. We run a balanced panel regression to separate these effects and report the results in the last column of Table 7.3. The sign and significance of the home tariff effects do not change.

7.2.4 *Role of Firm Heterogeneity in Productivity*

The general conclusion from Table 7.3 is that Chinese firms reduce their export product scope in response to home and foreign tariff cuts. As Qiu and Zhou (2013) point out, existing theoretical studies and empirical findings show that heterogeneous firms with different productivity levels may or may not respond to trade liberalization in the same manner with regard to their product scope adjustment. To investigate this issue with Chinese data, we divide all firms into two groups: low productivity and high productivity firms *within* each industry. We then combine all low (high) productivity firms from all industries as the low (high) productivity category. Columns (1) and (2) of Table 7.4 show the negative binomial estimates for the low productivity category and the high productivity category. The coefficients of home and foreign tariffs are again positive and significant. That is, the low productivity and high productivity Chinese firms adjust their export product scope in the same direction in response to tariff cuts. Firm heterogeneity in productivity does not matter in this regard.

7.2.5 *Endogeneity Issues*

Our estimates in Tables 7.2, 7.3 and 7.4 thus far may encounter the endogeneity issue. When firms are forced to reduce their export product scope because of the tough import competition induced by home tariff cuts, they may lobby the government for imposing temporary trade restrictions (Grossman and Helpman 1994; Bown and Crowley 2013). Thus, export product scope could reversely affect home tariffs (HT_{it}).[19] Evidence for such a phenomenon exists in developed countries, such as the U.S. (Goldberg and Maggi 1999). This phenomenon may not occur in China because of China's special policy regime and strong regulations on labor unions. Nevertheless, we check whether our main results are sensitive to this potential problem. We control for such reverse causality by using an IV approach.

Inspired by Trefler (2004) and Amiti and Konings (2007), here we construct a one-year lag of home tariffs as the instrument by replacing τ_t^k in Eq. (7.2) with τ_{t-1}^k.

[19] However, it is not a worry for the reverse causality of foreign tariffs (FT_{it}) since Chinese firm's export product scope would not reversely affect the import tariffs imposed by all trading partners. This is especially true when foreign tariffs are already measured by time-invariant weight.

Table 7.4 Estimates with heterogenous productivity and possible

Endogeneity estimation method	Negative binomial		IV Poisson	
Productivity category	Low Prod	High Prod	2nd stage	1st stage
Regressand: export product scope	(1)	(2)	(3)	(4)
Home tariffs (firm-level)	1.116*** (17.73)	1.280*** (20.23)	0.331** (2.56)	–
Home tariffs w/one lag (firm-level)				0.823*** (269.4)
Foreign tariffs	0.548*** (12.58)	0.676*** (13.90)	0.654*** (4.01)	0.002 (0.73)
Log firm TFP (TFP1)	0.327*** (19.51)	0.080*** (8.40)	0.466*** (12.74)	−0.001 (−0.34)
Log weighted GDP of importers	0.120*** (59.60)	0.168*** (75.74)	0.155*** (37.33)	−0.001 (−0.77)
Foreign indicator	0.155*** (12.92)	0.111*** (9.78)	0.045*** (2.80)	0.001 (0.24)
SOE indicator	0.052 (1.36)	0.091** (2.40)	0.105* (1.78)	0.002 (1.12)
Industry-specific fixed effects	Yes	Yes	Yes	
Year-specific fixed effects	Yes	Yes	Yes	
Pure processing firms dropped	No	No	Yes	
Anderson canon. corr. LM χ^2 statistic			17,320†	
Cragg-Donald Wald F statistic			72,600†	
Observations	30,947	25,311	22,735	

Note T-values in parentheses. * (**,***) indicates significance at the 10% (5%, 1%) level. † indicates p < 0.01. Pure processing firms are dropped in columns (3) and (4). Columns (1) and (2) are negative binomial estimates and include the sample in which firm TFP is lower than its industrial average in column (1) and higher in column (2). Columns (3)–(4) are IV Poisson estimates in which the endogenous variable is home tariff with initial year weight and the instrument is the previous year's home tariffs with initial year weight. Column (3) reports the second-stage estimation results whereas Column (4) reports the first-stage estimation results

The idea is that the government is generally hard to remove the high protection status quo from an industry with high tariffs, perhaps due to the pressure from domestic special interest groups. Thus, compared to other industries, sectors with high tariffs one year ago would still have relatively high tariffs in the current year.

We report the IV Poisson estimates in the rest of Table 7.4 in which column (3) reports the second-stage regression results whereas column (4) exhibits the first-stage estimation results.[20] All variables in columns (3)–(4) are measured at their absolute

[20] The IV Poisson estimates implement a generalized method of moments (GMM) estimator of Poisson regression and allow endogenous variables to be instrumented by excluded instruments. Poisson regression assumes $E(e|x) = \exp(\mathbf{X}b)$ to obtain a consistent estimate of b; thus, is appropriate for a wide variety of models where the dependent variable is non-negative (Mullahy 1997).

levels with "home tariffs" as an endogenous variable whereas a "one-year lag of home tariffs" serves as the instrument. After controlling for such endogeneity, both home tariffs and foreign tariffs are still positive significant. In the first-stage results shown in column (4), the coefficient of one-year lag of home tariffs is found to be highly cytostatically significant, suggesting that our intuition of the high protection persistence is supported by the data. As reported in Table 7.4, the high Anderson canonical correlated LM χ^2 statistic suggests that our IV estimates are not under-estimated. Similarly, the Cragg-Donald F statistics is above the critical values suggested by Stock and Yogo (2005). This result indicates that our IV estimates are not weakly identified.

7.2.6 Summary and Issues

Two important results are obtained in this preliminary empirical analysis and they deserve further investigation and understanding. First, we find that firms adjust their export product scope *similarly* in response to home and foreign tariff cuts. However, these two types of tariff reduction have opposite effects on the firms. As indicated in the literature (e.g., Qiu and Zhou 2013), bilateral trade liberalization poses both a threat and an opportunity to every firm. A home tariff cut intensifies domestic competition; this situation is not good for the home firms. By contrast, a foreign tariff cut makes the domestic firms' export more profitable. This conventional wisdom does not clarify our finding on Chinese firms' export product scope adjustment.

Second, we find that firms with different levels of productivity adjust their export product scope in the same direction in response to tariff cuts. However, recent literature on heterogeneous firms suggests that high productivity firms normally behave differently from low productivity firms.

We explore the two issues mentioned above by first developing a theoretical model (in Sect. 7.3) and then testing the predictions from the model (in Sect. 7.4).

7.3 Theoretical Model and Analysis

Our model consists of a world with two countries: China and Foreign. Each country has two industries, namely, the numeraire goods industry and the differentiated products industry. Differentiated products are produced by a continuum of firms with measure 1, and the numeraire goods is produced by atomic firms.

7.3.1 Technologies

In China, every firm in the differentiated goods industry can produce multiple products. All firms employ the same production technology but have different managerial capabilities.[21] On the production side, we suppose that a firm produces a set of products with measure s. We index the firm's core competency as product 0 and the others in descending productivity in $[0, s]$; this indexing captures the situation wherein products further away from the core competency become less productive. We let the unit cost of producing the ith product be $c_i = c + \theta i$, where $\theta > 0$ captures the decline of productivity. The unit cost of producing the core competency is c. Introducing a product is costly. If a firm introduces s products, a fixed cost equal to ks will exist, where $k > 0$.

On the management side, we assume that each firm in each market incurs a cost of managing *each* product line. This management cost is a fixed cost with regard to the sales value/volume, but is increasing with regard to the number of products.[22] This is justified by the fact that a firm needs to have different sales teams for different product lines which have different features, functions and target consumers. Moreover, we further assume that firms are of two types: *efficient* firms that have lower management cost, denoted by m_l per product line per market, and *inefficient* firms that have higher management cost, denoted by m_h per product line per market, with $m_h > m_l$. Let σ denote the fraction of efficient firms in the economy.

Given that our focus is on Chinese firms, we simplify the situation for foreign firms. We assume that a continuum of identical foreign firms produce the differentiated goods. All of them have the same marginal cost of production, which is assumed to be zero. Each firm produces a single product. Managing sales has no cost, and product introduction has no fixed cost. The measure of foreign firms is also assumed to be 1.

7.3.2 Product Markets

Following Melitz and Ottaviano (2008), we assume that Z identical consumers exist in China, with each having a quasi-linear preference for the numeraire good and all varieties from the differentiated goods industry.

$$U = Q_0 + \alpha \int_{i\in\Omega} q_i di - \frac{1}{2}\beta\left(\int_{i\in\Omega} q_i di\right)^2 - \frac{1}{2}\gamma \int_{i\in\Omega} q_i^2 di,$$

[21] We will examine the case of firm heterogeneity in production productivity in Sect. 7.3.4.

[22] In our earlier version of the paper, we also assume that management cost is increasing in sales. The present assumption is more realistic.

where α, β, and γ are all positive constants; Q_0 is the consumption of the numeraire good; Ω is the set of all varieties sold in the Chinese market; and q_i is the consumption of variety i. A consumer maximizes her utility subject to a budget constraint. As a result, the market demand for variety i by all Z consumers is $p_i = \alpha - \frac{\beta}{Z}\int_{j\in\Omega} q_j dj - \frac{\gamma}{Z} q_i$, from which we obtain the demand function for variety i as

$$p_i = A - bq_i, \text{ where } A = \frac{\alpha\gamma + \beta P}{\beta M + \gamma} \text{ and } b = \frac{\gamma}{Z}. \tag{7.5}$$

In the above demand function, p_i is the price of variety i, M is the measure of Ω, and $P = \int_{i\in\Omega} p_i di$ is the aggregate price of all varieties. Slope b is exogenous, but the intercept A is endogenous, depending on the degree of product substitution (β) and the degree of product market competition (captured by the endogenous P and M).

The set of varieties, Ω, is large; thus, the seller of variety i regards himself as a small monopolist of variety i whose decision has no direct effect on other products.[23] Competition in the market is captured completely by the vertical intercept of the demand function (A).

The foreign country also has Z consumers and the same demand structure as China. In particular, the demand function for variety i is

$$p_i^* = A^* - bq_i^*, \text{ where } A^* = \frac{\alpha\gamma + \beta P^*}{\beta M^* + \gamma}. \tag{7.6}$$

In this demand function, M^* is the measure of the set of varieties sold in the foreign market, which is denoted by Ω_F, and $P^* = \int_{i\in\Omega_F} p_i di$ is the aggregate price of all varieties in the foreign market.

We assume that tariffs take the form of iceberg transport cost. We let t (>1) and t^* (>1) denote China's tariff and the foreign country's tariff. Then, t units of a product must be produced by a foreign firm to sell one unit in the Chinese market, and t^* units of a product must be produced by a Chinese firm to sell one unit in the foreign market. Free trade exists in the numeraire good industry.

7.3.3 Firm's Decision

We first analyze the Chinese firms' decisions. Each firm takes A and A^* as given when making its decisions. Because all Chinese firms have the same production productivity, without loss of generality, we set $c = 0$ to reduce notation. Suppose that firm j ($j = l$ for efficient firm and ($j = h$ for inefficient firm) decides to introduce a

[23] Following most studies in the literature, we do not consider canniberlization, which is about strategic competition among varieties of the same firm. However, it is worthwhile to note that Dhingra (2012) is an outstanding exception to discuss canniberlization.

range of products, $[0, s_j]$, which is called the firm's *total product scope*, and export a range of products $[0, e_j]$, which is called the firm's *export product scope*.[24] With consumer preference and market size (Z) in the two markets being the same, Chinese firms have a disadvantage in the foreign market because they face trade protection in the foreign market. Hence, in equilibrium, a Chinese firm will not introduce a product that is exported to the foreign market but not sold to the domestic market, that is, $e_j \le s_j$. If $e_j < s_j$, then some products ($i \in (e_j, s_j]$) are sold in the domestic market but are not exported; the firm's export products are a subset of its total products. This is the case when the fixed cost of product introduction (k) is not too large. Under this circumstance, the firm's decision in the home market is expressed as

$$\max_{s_j, q_i} \int_0^{s_j} [(A - bq_i)q_i - \theta i q_i]di - m_j s_j - k s_j. \tag{7.7}$$

It is easy to derive the set of first order conditions, from which we first obtain the optimal quantity, price, and profit of each product as

$$q_{ji} = \frac{A - \theta i}{2b}, \; p_{ji} = \frac{A + \theta i}{2}, \text{ and } \pi_{ji} = \frac{1}{4b}(A - \theta i)^2, \text{ for all } i \in [0, s_j]. \tag{7.8}$$

A stronger demand (i.e., a larger A) leads to a larger output, a higher price and a larger profit. We then obtain the optimal total product scope

$$s_j = \frac{A - 2\sqrt{b(m_j + k)}}{\theta}. \tag{7.9}$$

The total product scope is larger with stronger market demand (A), lower management cost (m_j), lower cost of product introduction (k), and slower decline of productivity (θ).

Given $e_j < s_j$, the firm's optimal decision in the foreign market is provided by

$$\max_{e_j, q_i} \int_0^{e_j} \left[(A^* - bq_i)q_i - t^* \theta i q_i\right]di - m_j e_j. \tag{7.10}$$

It is easy to derive the set of first order conditions, from which we obtain the optimal quantity, price and profit of each export product for $i \in [0, e_j]$ as

$$q^*_{ji} = \frac{A^* - \theta i t^*}{2b}, \quad p^*_{ji} = \frac{A^* + \theta i t^*}{2}, \quad \text{and } \pi^*_{ji} = \frac{1}{4b}\left(A^* - \theta i t^*\right)^2, \tag{7.11}$$

[24] If a firm produces product $i \in [0, s]$, it will produce all products $i' < i$ because of the decreasing efficiency in $[0, s]$. If it exports product $i \in [0, e]$, it will export all products $i' < i$.

and the optimal export product scope as

$$e_j = \frac{A^* - 2\sqrt{bm_j}}{\theta t^*}. \tag{7.12}$$

The export product scope is larger with stronger market demand (A^*), lower management cost (m_j), slower decline in productivity (θ), and lower foreign tariff (t^*). A decrease in foreign tariff increases output and profit, but reduces price. Tougher competition (smaller A^*) reduces output, price and profit.

It is easy to obtain

$$\frac{\partial \pi_{ji}^*}{\partial t^*} < 0 \text{ and } \frac{\partial^2 \pi_{ji}^*}{\partial i \partial t^*} < 0. \tag{7.13}$$

That is, every product benefits from foreign country's tariff cut, and due to the iceberg-transportation nature of tariff, products with higher i benefit more from the foreign country's tariff cut.

We now analyze the foreign firms. In the Chinese market, a foreign firm chooses its quantity to maximize its profit $(A - bq_{fc})q_{fc} - tq_{fc}$, where subscript fc stands for a foreign firm in the Chinese market.

Thus, the optimal quantity, price, and profit of a foreign firm in the Chinese market are, respectively,

$$q_{fc} = \frac{A - t}{2b}, p_{fc} = \frac{A + t}{2}, \text{ and } \pi_{fc} = \frac{1}{4b}(A - t)^2. \tag{7.14}$$

In the foreign market, the foreign firm chooses its output to maximize its profit $(A^* - bq_{ff})q_{ff}$, where subscript ff stands for a foreign firm in the foreign market. The optimal quantity, price, and profit of a foreign firm in the foreign market are, respectively,

$$q_{ff} = \frac{A^*}{2b}, p_{ff} = \frac{A^*}{2}, \text{ and } \pi_{ff} = \frac{1}{4b}A^{*2}. \tag{7.15}$$

7.3.4 Market Equilibrium

Lastly, we determine equilibrium A and A^*.

Given that $A = \frac{\alpha\gamma + \beta P}{\beta M + \gamma}$, we first calculate M and P. $M = s_l\sigma + s_h(1 - \sigma) + 1$. From (7.8), we obtain the aggregate price of firm j in the Chinese market as follows:

$$p_j = \int_0^{s_j} p_{ji} di = \frac{1}{2} A s_j + \frac{1}{4} \theta s_j^2.$$

Each foreign firm's price in the Chinese market is given in (7.14). Thus, the aggregate price in the Chinese market is

$$P = \frac{1}{4}\left[2A\sigma s_l + \theta\sigma s_l^2 + 2A(1-\sigma)s_h + \theta(1-\sigma)s_h^2 + 2(A+t)\right].$$

To simplify the notation, we let $\delta = \frac{2\gamma}{\beta}$. Using the results in $A = \frac{\alpha\gamma + \beta P}{\beta M + \gamma}$ yields

$$A = \frac{2\alpha\delta + \theta\left[\sigma s_l^2 + (1-\sigma)s_h^2\right] + 2t}{2[\sigma s_l + (1-\sigma)s_h + 1 + \delta]}. \tag{7.16}$$

In the foreign market, the total number of products sold is $M^* = \sigma e_l + (1-\sigma)e_h + 1$. The aggregate price of Chinese exporter j is

$$p_j^* = \int_0^{e_j} p_{li}^* di = \frac{1}{2} A^* e_l + \frac{1}{4} t^* \theta e_j^2.$$

Each foreign firm's price is provided in (7.15). Thus, the aggregate price in the foreign market is

$$P^* = \frac{1}{4}\left[2A^*\sigma e_l + t^*\theta\sigma e_l^2 + 2A^*(1-\sigma)e_h + t^*\theta(1-\sigma)e_h^2 + 2A^*\right].$$

Using the results in $A^* = \frac{\alpha\gamma + \beta P^*}{\beta M^* + \gamma}$ yields

$$A^* = \frac{2\alpha\delta + \theta t^*\left[\sigma e_l^2 + (1-\sigma)e_h^2\right]}{2[\sigma e_l + (1-\sigma)e_h + 1 + \delta]}. \tag{7.17}$$

Substituting A in (7.9), we obtain two equations jointly determining the optimal total product scopes s_l and s_h, which are functions of t. Substituting A^* in (7.12), we obtain two equations jointly determining the optimal export product scopes e_l and e_h, which are functions of t^*.

7.3.5 Trade Liberalization

We analyze the respective effects of two types of trade liberalization on the export product scope of Chinese firms. The first type of liberalization is tariff reduction in China (t), and the second type is tariff reduction in the foreign country (t^*).

We first examine $\frac{de_l}{dt}$ and $\frac{de_h}{dt}$. Based on the expression of e_j from (7.12) and A^* from (7.17), we immediately know that t does not have any direct effect on e_l and e_h. However, the optimal export product scope given in (7.12) is obtained under the condition that $e_l < s_l$ and $e_h < s_h$. The Chinese tariff cut may eventually result in the violation of this condition. We prove in Appendix 7.2 that $\frac{ds_l}{dt} > 0$ and $\frac{ds_h}{dt} > 0$. Hence, when a tariff cut is implemented in China, Chinese firms reduce their total product scope (s_l and s_h). When tariff cuts are implemented continuously, the total product scope is eventually reduced to the level of the export product scope (e_l and e_h). Once $e_l = s_l$, the optimal export product scope of efficient Chinese firms is no longer given in (7.12), and once $e_h = s_h$, the optimal export product scope of inefficient Chinese firms is no longer given in (7.12). Then, we have $\frac{de_j}{dt} = \frac{ds_j}{dt} > 0$.

We then discuss the effect of foreign tariff cuts on Chinese firms' export product scope. We prove in Appendix 7.2 that

$$\text{(i)} \frac{de_l}{dt^*} < 0, \text{ and (ii)} \frac{de_h}{dt^*} > 0 \text{ iff } m_h \text{ is sufficiently large.} \tag{7.18}$$

The above analysis allows us to establish the following proposition.

Proposition 7.1

(i) *Suppose that there is a drastic cut of import tariffs in China. Then a further tariff cut reduces all Chinese firms' export product scope.*

(ii) *In response to a tariff cut by the foreign country, Chinese firms with high-managerial efficiency expand their export product scope, whereas those with low-managerial efficiency reduce their export product scope if and only if their management cost is sufficiently high (i.e., m_h is sufficiently large).*

The results of the proposition are surprising. On the one hand, one may ask why a domestic tariff cut affects export product scope. On the other hand, one may ask why some exporters are negatively affected by a foreign tariff cut such that they have to reduce their export product scope. The explanation is as follows. With regard to domestic tariff cut, each firm incurs a cost of introducing (or maintaining) every product it produces. By retaining a product, a firm obtains profit from the market; however, discontinuing a product results in saving from the fixed cost of production introduction (k) and the fixed cost of sales (m_j). When the domestic market is very profitable, the profit from the domestic market alone can cover the fixed costs. In that case, $e_l < s_l$ and lowering the Chinese tariff reduces a Chinese firm's domestic market profit, which results in a reduction in total product scope but not in export product scope because the latter is only affected by foreign market profitability. However, when a drastic tariff cut is implemented, the firm reduces its product scope to a large extent that the set of products available for export is likewise reduced. This is how domestic trade liberalization affects exports.

A foreign tariff cut has a direct and an indirect effect on Chinese exporters. Every firm's marginal product earns zero profit from the foreign market. On the one hand, the foreign tariff cut lowers the cost of every exported product and thus increases profits, which induces all firms to expand their export product scope. This phenomenon is the cost effect, which is positive and direct. On the other hand, a low cost causes every firm to reduce the prices of all its products, which increases competition (lowering A^*). This competition effect, which is negative and indirect, reduces the profits of all products (including the marginal products) and tends to reduce every firm's export product scope. The export product scope of a firm is reduced or expanded depending on the net effect on its marginal product. The competition effect is the same for all products as it shifts down the demand intercept (A^*). However, the cost effect is different for the efficient firms and the inefficient firms. An efficient firm's marginal product has a higher marginal cost of production ($e_l\theta$) than that of an inefficient firm ($e_h\theta$) because the former has a larger product scope. As discussed earlier right below (7.13), a reduction in foreign tariff (in the form of iceberg transport cost) reduces all products' cost of production by the same percentage; thus, an efficient firm's marginal product benefits more than an inefficient firm's because the former enjoys a larger cost reduction in the absolute term. This is why under certain conditions, the net effect is positive for efficient firms (the cost effect is larger than the competition effect) but negative for inefficient firms (the competition effect is larger than the cost effect).

7.3.6 Firm Heterogeneity in Production Productivity

The most interesting message from Proposition 7.1 is that when a tariff cut is implemented in the foreign country, Chinese firms with different managerial efficiency levels respond in opposite directions. In this section, we examine whether the heterogeneous response to foreign tariff cuts by firms with different managerial efficiency levels can be reinterpreted as by firms with different production productivity levels, namely, the usual Melitz (2003) type of firm heterogeneity. To this end, we make a few modifications to the main model. First, we assume that Chinese firms are homogeneous in managerial efficiency; for simplicity, we let $m_l = m_h = 0$. Second, Chinese firms differ in production productivity. We assume that the cost of core competency c is uniformly distributed in [0, 1]. Third, we merely focus on equilibrium analysis in the foreign market.

The derivation of optimal export product scope is similar to that in the main model except for one difference: all equilibrium variables are functions of c. Suppose that a firm has the cost of core competence equal to c, called firm c. Then, firm c's optimal export product scope is

$$e(c) = \frac{A^* - ct^*}{\theta t^*} = \frac{A^*}{\theta t^*} - \frac{c}{\theta}. \tag{7.19}$$

We assume that the foreign tariff is not too high or the foreign demand is sufficiently strong such that all Chinese firms export. This condition requires $A^* > t^*$ which we assume to hold below. The export quantity, price, and profit of firm c's ith product are

$$q_i^*(c) = \frac{A^* - (c + \theta i)t^*}{2b}, \quad p_i^*(c) = \frac{A^* + (c + \theta i)t^*}{2}, \quad \text{and}$$
$$\pi_i^*(c) = \frac{1}{4b}\left[A^* - (c + \theta i)t^*\right]^2.$$

Thus, the aggregate price of firm c is given by

$$p^*(c) = \int_0^{e(c)} p_i^*(c)di = \frac{1}{2}\left(A^* + ct^*\right)e(c) + \frac{1}{4}t^*\theta e(c)^2$$
$$= \frac{(A^* - ct^*)}{4\theta t^*}\left(3A^* + ct^*\right).$$

The aggregate price in the foreign market is given by

$$P^* = \int_0^1 p^*(c)dc + \frac{1}{2}A^* = \frac{9A^{*2} - 3A^*t^* + t^*}{12\theta t^*} + \frac{1}{2}A^*.$$

The number of products in the foreign market is given by

$$M^* = \int_0^1 \frac{A^* - ct^*}{\theta t^*}dc + 1 = \frac{2A^* - t^*}{2\theta t^{*2}} + 1.$$

The above expressions of P^* and M^*, together with $A^* = \frac{\alpha\gamma + \beta P^*}{\beta M^* + \gamma}$, allow us to solve for the equilibrium A^* as a function of t^*, expressed as $A^*(t^*)$. Substituting equilibrium A^* into the expression of optimal product scope (7.19), we obtain

$$e\left(t^*, c\right) = \frac{A^*(t^*)}{\theta t^*} - \frac{c}{\theta}.$$

$\frac{de(t^*,c)}{dt^*}$ is independent of c. That is, all firms respond to the foreign tariff cut in the same direction. Our numerical example shows that $\frac{de(t^*,c)}{dt^*} < 0$. That is, in response to the foreign tariff cut, all Chinese firms expand their export product scope.

One may ask why the result is different from Proposition 7.1, which is derived from the model with firm heterogeneity in managerial efficiency. In the main model, the two types of firms have different production productivity levels for their marginal products; thus, foreign tariff reduction affects them differently. However, with homogeneity in managerial efficiency and heterogeneity in production productivity, all firms have the same production productivity for their marginal products. This condition can be seen by substituting (7.19) into the cost of a firm's marginal product: $c + \theta e(c) = \frac{A^*(t^*)}{t^*}$, which is independent of c. Thus, all firms' marginal products will be affected similarly.

7.4 Further Empirical Analysis: The Role of Managerial Efficiency

Guided by our theoretical analysis, we conduct an empirical investigation with emphasis on the responses of heterogenous firms to foreign tariff cuts to examine the role of managerial efficiency. We first construct a measure of managerial efficiency. Particularly, we regress firm's general and administrative expenses (G&A) on firm size, export revenue, and firm markup to obtain the G&A residual. As interpreted below, such G&A residual is used to proxy firm's managerial efficiency. As measured TFP in our previous estimates may include both managerial efficiency and productive efficiency, we construct a new measure of productive efficiency to separate productive efficiency from managerial efficiency. We then conduct the empirical analysis with these two novel measures of efficiency.

7.4.1 Measure of Managerial Efficiency

By definition, if it costs a firm more to achieve the same outcome, then the firm is considered less efficient. Unlike productive efficiency which can be estimated from a production function, managerial efficiency cannot be directly estimated from production side. The mainstream literatures of management science and finance usually take a firm's selling, general and administrative (SG&A) as a proxy for management costs (see, for example, Miller and Vollmann 1985; Cooper and Kaplan 1991; Fisher and Ittner 1999; Eisfeldt and Papanikolaou 2013). We will follow this idea, but with a departure, to construct our managerial efficiency variable.

According to the generally accepted accounting principles (GAAP), SG&A expenses refer to a firm's expenses that occur apart from its actual production function.[25] In line with Lev and Radhakrishnan (2005), Eisfeldt and Papanikolaou (2013) use firm's SG&A expenses to measure organization capital by using the perpetual

[25] Examples include the occupancy expenses for nonmanufacturing facilities (rent, heat, light, property taxes, maintenance, etc.); compensation of nonmanufacturing personnel; expenses for automobiles and trucks used to sell and deliver products, depreciation of nonmanufacturing equipment; etc.

inventory approach. They show that high organization capital firms have higher managerial quality scores, implying that firms with higher SG&A expenses are more managerial efficient. However, Bloom and van Reenen (2007) point out that firms with more SG&A expenses are not necessarily having high managerial efficiency as such firms may also be larger, have higher exporter revenue, or even have higher markups. Their observation suggests that those variables need to be controlled.

In contrast to Eisfeldt and Papanikolaou (2013), we construct our managerial efficiency variable using G&A expenses residuals. First, we exclude selling expenses. Selling expenses refer to advertising, sales commissions, promotional materials distributed, rent of the sales showroom and sales offices, salaries and fringe benefits of sales personnel, utilities and telephone usage in the sales department.[26] These expenses may fit the organizational capital in Eisfeldt and Papanikolaou (2013) as organizational capital could be used as intermediate inputs to boost firm productive efficiency (Nocke and Yeaple 2014). However, it is less relevant to the fixed-cost feature of the managerial efficiency in our model where managerial efficiency is independent of productive efficiency. Second, inspired by Bloom and van Reenen (2007), we control for firm size, export revenue and markup so that our managerial efficiency, the G&A residual, is independent of these factors. Third, given these two features, low G&A expenses residuals will indicate high managerial efficiency, vice versa.

In particular, we consider the following specification:

$$\ln G\&A_{it} = \alpha_1 l_{it} + \alpha_2 \exp_{it} + \alpha_3 markup_{it} + \lambda_i + \eta_t + \varepsilon_{it} \tag{7.20}$$

where ln $G\&A$ is the log value of firm i's G&A expenses; l_{it} is the log value of labor; $\exp_{it}$ is the log value of export; and $markup_{it}$ denotes markup, all in year t. For simplicity, we measure markup as revenue divided by the difference between revenue and profit.[27] Measured managerial efficiency is defined as $\lambda_i + \eta_t + \epsilon_{it}$ since it reflects firm's G&A residuals which cannot be interpreted by firm size (proxied by log labor), firm export value, and firm profitability (proxied by firm markup).[28] Once these firm characteristics are controlled, a firm has low managerial efficiency if it still has a large G&A residual. This managerial efficiency term has three components. The first component λ_i captures the time-invariant factors that lead to higher G&A spending;

[26] In the Chinese firm-level dataset, we are able to breakdown the whole SG&A expenses to two categories: selling expenses and G&A expenses. In Chinese Pinyin, selling expenses refer to "xiao1shou4fei4yong4" whereas G&A expenses refer to "Guan3li3fei4yong4", respectively.

[27] As markup is just a control variable in our estimates, we take a shortcut to measure markup by presuming that marginal costs equal average costs, De Loecker and Warzynski (2012) use a more complicated and ideal way to estimate firm's markup using the product of firm's estimated input elasticity of the production function and the input share. Our estimation results would not change much using this alternative approach. However, it is worthwhile to note that such an alternative approach may be inappropriate to apply to our case given that the estimated input elasticity of the production function does not distinguish the difference between productive efficiency and managerial efficiency.

[28] In principle, this idea is in line with the measured TFP which is measured by the difference between firm's output and the fitted value of output as known with "Solow Residuals".

Table 7.5 Estimates of firm managerial efficiency

Measure of G&A expenses	Total G&A expenses		Administrative expenses	
Regressand: Log G&A expenses	Coefficient (1)	t-value (2)	Coefficient (3)	t-value (4)
Log labor	0.317***	(54.35)	0.249***	(12.89)
Log export	0.101***	(40.19)	0.071***	(9.26)
Firm markup	−0.019***	(−2.37)	−0.005	(−0.26)
Year-specific fixed effects	Yes		Yes	
Firm-specific fixed effects	Yes		Yes	
R-squared	0.41		0.19	
Number of observations	97,776		59,494	
Quantiles for measured managerial efficiency index (in Log)				
10% quantile	−1.290		−1.711	
25% quantile	−0.711		−0.793	
50% quantile	−0.071		0.068	
75% quantile	0.649		0.853	
90% quantile	1.448		1.610	

Note *** indicates significance at the 1% level. There are two regressions in this table. Estimation in columns (1)–(2) regresses firm's log total G&A expenses on its log labor, log export, and firm markup. The residual which includes firm- specific dummies, year-specific dummies, and error term is firm's measured managerial efficiency. The lower module reports each quantile of firm's measured managerial efficiency. The higher the number, the lower the firm's managerial efficiency. The regressand in columns (3)–(4) is firm's administrative expenses

the second component η_t captures the time trend of G&A spending common across all firms; and the third component ϵ_{it} represents the idiosyncratic unspecified factors that affects firm's G&A expenses.

Once a firm's G&A residual is estimated, we construct two indicators of managerial efficiency for each firm in each year: the low managerial efficiency indicator and the high managerial efficiency indicator. Specifically, we rank all firms from the same industry according to their G&A *residuals* (in logarithm) in descending order. If a firm's G&A residual is *higher* than the top 10th quantile of its industry, the firm has *low* managerial efficiency; and its low managerial efficiency indicator takes the value one, and zero otherwise.[29] The managerial efficiency indicator of a firm with G&A residuals between the 10th and 90th quantile take the value zero. We then pool firms from all industries together while maintaining the value of their indicators.

Columns (1) and (2) of Table 7.5 present estimation results of Eq. (7.20). The positive and statistically significant signs of log labor and log exports suggest that firms with more G&A spending usually are larger and have more exports. By contrast,

[29] By the same token, if a firm's G&A residual is *lower* than the top 90th quantile of its industry, the firm has *high* managerial efficiency; and its *high* managerial efficiency indicator takes the value one, and zero otherwise.

firms with smaller markup also have larger G&A expenses. By deducting such effects from the estimates, the bottom module of Table 7.5 reports the quantiles for the measured managerial index (in log). A higher value of the index indicates lower managerial efficiency.

G&A expenses include 27 types of expenses with administrative expenses as the largest and most important one.[30] One may wonder whether it is ideal to use *total* G&A expenses as a measure of managerial efficiency. To check the robustness of our measure, we also use administrative expenses as our measure of managerial efficiency. Accordingly, we regress Eq. (7.20) again by replacing total G&A expenses with administrative expenses. Columns (3)–(4) of Table 7.5 report the estimation results using the new measure. The results are similar to those reported in columns (1) and (2).

7.4.2 Measure of Productive Efficiency

Note that the conventional measure of TFP, including TFP1 in the present study, is a Solow residual that includes both managerial efficiency and productive efficiency. To see this, since product-level production data are unavailable, we presume that firms have a common productivity level and production function across goods following the conventional literature. We consider the standard Cobb-Douglas gross production function.

$$\ln Y_{it} = \alpha_k \ln K_{it} + \alpha_l \ln L_{it} + \alpha_m \ln M_{it} + x_{it} + \varpi_{it} + \varepsilon_{it}, \tag{7.21}$$

where Y_{it}, K_{it}, G_{it}, M_{it}, x_{it} and ϖ_{it} are firm i's sales, capital, labor, intermediate inputs, productive efficiency, and managerial efficiency in year t, respectively. The error term ε_{it} captures measurement error in output and unanticipated idiosyncratic shocks to production (De Loecker 2011). However, the conventional Olley-Pakes (OP) measure of productivity usually ignores the managerial efficiency (ϖ_{it}) and treat the difference between log output and log factor inputs times their estimated coefficients as the productivity:

$$TFP1_{it} = \ln Y_{it} - \hat{\alpha}_k \ln K_{it} - \hat{\alpha}_l \ln L_{it} - \hat{\alpha}_m \ln M_{it}. \tag{7.22}$$

Such a productivity measure (TFP1) is clearly correlated not only with the true productive efficiency (x_{it}) but also with managerial efficiency (ϖ_{it}).

Following Feenstra et al. (2014), we construct a true productive efficiency measure called TFP2 which excludes managerial efficiency from our TFP measure. As in Olley and Pakes (1996), suppose that investment V_{it} in the OP approach depends on

[30] Note that GAAP only specifies the main caption of account and gives much more flexibility to firms to create their detailed caption of account. For example, firms in different countries may have different detailed caption of account under the category of G&A expenses.

productive efficiency x_{it} of the firm and the production innovation ς_{it+1} follows the following process: $\varsigma_{it+1} = x_{it+1} - x_{it}$. Then, we obtain the following function:

$$V_{it} = g_1(x_{it}, \ln K_{it}, HT_{it}, FT_{it}, EX_{it}, PE_{it}, WTO_t, SOE_{it}, FIE_{it}),$$

where EX_{it} (PE_{it}) is the export (processing export) indicator that measures whether firm i exports (has processing exports) in year t, and WTO_t is an indicator that equals one for every year after 2001 and zero before 2001. Inverting this relation, anticipated productivity can be obtained as[31]:

$$\begin{aligned} TFP2_{it} \equiv x_{it} &= g_1^{-1}(V_{it}, \ln K_{it}, HT_{it}, FT_{it}, EX_{it}, PE_{it}, WTO_t, SOE_{it}, FIE_{it}) \\ &= E\big((\ln Y_{it} - \hat{\alpha}_l \ln L_{it} - \hat{\alpha}_m \ln M_{it})|\mathbf{X}_{it}\big) - \hat{\alpha}_k \ln K_{it}. \end{aligned} \tag{7.23}$$

where $\mathbf{X}_{it}$ denotes all right-hand-side regressors used in the third-step OP estimation. The essential difference between the standard gross efficiency (TFP1) and pure productive efficiency (TFP2) is that the regressand of TFP1 uses the actual data on log output whereas that of TFP2 uses the fitted value of log output obtained in the third-step OP estimation. Appendix 7.3 provides a more detailed discussion on our TFP1 and TFP2 construction. Table 7.10 in Appendix provides the industry-level estimates of the firms' TFP1 and TFP2 in each industry, together with the associated coefficients of labor, capital, and materials. Note that different industries have heterogenous variance between TFP1 and TFP2.[32]

A firm's productive efficiency could change when tariff changes. To address such a concern, inspired by De Loecker (2013), we consider that firm's productive efficiency reacts to changes in both home tariff and foreign tariff over time as follows[33]:

$$x_{it+1} = h(x_{it}, HT_{it}, FT_{it}) + \varsigma_{it+1},$$

where the production innovation, ς_{it+1}, is different from the step used to measure $TFP2_{it}$. With this modification, we can have a new measure of true productive efficiency as follows:

[31] Olley and Pakes (1996) show that the investment demand function is monotonically increasing in the productivity shock x_{jt}, by making some mild assumptions about the firm's production technology. The strong correlation between investment and the measured productivity is also confirmed in our sample.

[32] Recent literature (e.g., Ackerberg et al. 2006) points out that, in the first-stage estimation, there may not be any variation left to identify the labor coefficient by considering a nonparametric function of capital and material (or investment). However, De Loecker (2013) highlights that the essential point of the first-stage estimate is to generate an estimate of predicted output as a function of parameters of the production function. Our TFP2 measure thus derives such first-stage estimates in which the coefficient of capital and its interaction terms with home tariff, foreign tariff, export dummy, processing dummy, SOE dummy, foreign dummy, and WTO dummy are all included.

[33] Similar to De Loecker (2013), productive efficiency process adopts the fourth-order polynominal form $h(.) = \sum_{sm} \beta_{sm}(x_{it}^s HT_{it}^m + x_{it}^m \quad FT_{it}^m$ with $E(\varsigma_{it+1} HT_{it}) = 0$ and $E(\varsigma_{it+1} FT_{it}) = 0$.

$$TFP2_{it}^{DL} \equiv x_{it} = q_2(V_{it}, In\,K_{it}, HT_{it}, FT_{it}, EX_{it}, PE_{it}, WTO_t, SOE_{it}, FIE_{it}).$$

The only difference between $g_1^{-1}(.)$ and $g_2^{-1}(.)$ is due to the different realization of production innovation. Note that the simple correlation between $TFP2_{it}^{DL}$ and G&A residuals is only (−0.02), suggesting that the measured pure productive efficiency is not highly correlated with the measured managerial efficiency at all.

7.4.3 Estimates with Heterogeneous Managerial Efficiency

With the above two newly constructed measures of productive efficiency, we consider the following model which includes firm heterogeneity in managerial efficiency:

$$\begin{aligned} e_{it} = \beta_0 + \beta_1 TFP_{it} + \beta_2 HT_{it} + \beta_3 FT_{it} + \beta_4 FT_{it} \\ \times LM_{it} + \beta_5 FT_{it} \times HM_{it} + \boldsymbol{\theta}\Psi_{it} + \varepsilon. \end{aligned} \tag{7.24}$$

In this model, *FT* appears three times: as a separate term, interaction with the low managerial efficiency indicator (LM_{it}), and interaction with the high managerial efficiency indicator (HM_{it}). Our theory predicts that $\beta_3 + \beta_4 > 0$ and $\beta_3 + \beta_5 < 0$ because firms of low (high) managerial efficiency reduce (increase) their export product scope in response to foreign tariff cuts. The regression results are given in Table 7.6. Note that TFP_{it} are measured by $TFP2_{it}$ and $TFP2_{it}$, respectively. For comparison purpose, we also use *TFP*1 in column (1).

In column (2) of Table 7.6, we find that both home and foreign tariffs have positive and statistically significant coefficients. More importantly, the interaction between foreign tariff and the high managerial efficiency dummy is negative and significant, with a larger economic magnitude than the own coefficient of foreign tariff. This result indicates that the effect of foreign tariff on export product scope is negative (i.e., 0.420–0.478 < 0). The difference of such two coefficients is highly statistically significant (as shown by its *p*-value). Thus, a foreign tariff reduction increases the export product scope of high managerial efficiency firms. By contrast, the coefficient of the interaction between foreign tariffs and the low managerial efficiency indicator is positive and significant. Given that 0.420 + 0.146 > 0, a foreign tariff reduction reduces the export product scope of low managerial efficiency firms. Middle managerial efficiency firms also reduce their export product scope (as indicated by the coefficient value 0.419). Note, the value of the TFP coefficient ($\hat{\beta}_1$) in column (2) drops by around 80% from that in column (1) using TFP1. This implies that results based on standard TFP measure overstates productive efficiency's contribution to export product scope.

We next see whether our results are sensitive to our firm-specific measures of tariffs. To this end, we replace firm-level home tariff with industry-level home tariff in column (3), replace firm-specific foreign tariff with industry-level foreign tariff in column (4), and replace both in column (5). All results remain robust. Finally, we

Table 7.6 Managerial efficiency and export product scope using G&A expenses

Cutoffs for G&A residuals indicators	10th						25th	
Measures of TFP	TFP1	TFP2				$TFP2^{DL}$	TFP2	$TFP2^{DL}$
Regressand: export product scope	(1)	(2)	(3)	(4)	(5)	(6)	(7)	(8)
Home tariffs (firm-level: $\hat{\beta}_2$)	0.960*** (22.51)	0.968*** (23.03)		0.983*** (22.72)				
Home tariffs (industry-level: $\hat{\beta}_2$)			0.265*** (3.14)		0.278*** (3.22)	0.486*** (4.94)	0.294*** (3.40)	0.497*** (5.03)
Foreign tariffs (firm-level: $\hat{\beta}_3$)	0.419*** (10.34)	0.420*** (10.65)	0.465*** (6.65)					
Foreign tariffs (industry-level: $\hat{\beta}_3$)				0.245*** (4.84)	0.323*** (3.92)	0.527*** (5.58)	0.345*** (3.96)	0.506*** (5.69)
Foreign tariffs × Low managerial efficiency indicator ($\hat{\beta}_4$)	0.125** (2.17)	0.146*** (2.61)	0.593*** (0.42)	0.358*** (4.45)	1.036*** (8.30)	1.081*** (8.05)	0.786*** (9.15)	0.800*** (8.60)
Foreign tariffs x High managerial efficiency indicator ($\hat{\beta}_5$)	−0.459*** (−6.56)	−0.478*** (−7.01)	−0.727*** (−6.36)	−0.809*** (−11.64)	−1.148*** (−10.80)	−1.226*** (−10.59)	−1.044*** (−13.30)	−1.093*** (−12.73)
Log firm TFP ($\hat{\beta}_1$)	0.126*** (19.97)	0.030*** (3.26)	0.057*** (4.10)	0.035*** (3.71)	0.070*** (4.91)	0.271*** (8.18)	0.078*** (5.47)	0.293*** (8.81)
Log weighted GDP of importers	0.122*** (92.65)	0.122*** (94.91)	0.134*** (72.42)	0.122*** (92.54)	0.134*** (71.48)	0.135*** (67.31)	0.133*** (71.10)	0.134*** (66.90)
Foreign indicator	0.094*** (9.34)	0.099*** (9.93)	0.106*** (9.13)	0.100*** (9.83)	0.104*** (8.88)	0.105*** (8.71)	0.100*** (8.53)	0.101*** (8.36)
SOE indicator	0.034 (1.52)	0.031 (1.42)	0.034 (1.07)	0.030 (1.32)	0.026 (0.80)	0.020 (0.60)	0.022 (0.70)	0.016 (0.48)
P-value of difference between $\hat{\beta}_3$ and $\hat{\beta}_5$	[.000]	[.000]	[.000]	[.000]	[.000]	[.000]	[.000]	[.000]

(continued)

Table 7.6 (continued)

Cutoffs for G&A residuals indicators	10th						25th	
Measures of TFP	TFP1	TFP2				$TFP2^{DL}$	TFP2	$TFP2^{DL}$
Regressand: export product scope	(1)	(2)	(3)	(4)	(5)	(6)	(7)	(8)
Firm-specific fixed effects	Yes	Yes	Yes	Yes	Yes	Yes	Yes	Yes
Year-specific fixed effects	Yes	Yes	Yes	Yes	Yes	Yes	Yes	Yes
Observations	57.385	57.410	53,197	57,416	53,197	49,569	53,197	49,569

Note T-values in parentheses. * (**) indicates significance at the 10% (5%) level. Columns (1)–(6) use top and bottom 10th quantiles of the estimated residuals of firm's G&A expenses within its industry as the cutoffs to define the low and high managerial efficiency indicators whereas columns (7) and (8) use the top and bottom 25th quantiles as the cutoffs. All pure processing firms and pure exporters are dropped in all estimates. Foreign tariffs and their interaction terms with high/low managerial efficiency indicators in columns (1) and (2) are measured at the firm-level whereas those in columns (3)–(8) are measured at the industry-level. Firm productivity in column (1) is measured by the conventional Olley-Pakes TFP (TFP1) whereas those in columns (2)–(5), and (7) are measured by pure productive efficiency (TFP2). By contrast, firm productivity in columns (6) and (8) are measured by the De Loecker-type TFP2 which allows tariffs to react to the realizations of pure productive efficiency check whether the results are sensitive to the 10th and 90th quantile G&A residual thresholds. In column (7) we re-define high managerial efficiency firms as those with G&A residuals lower than the bottom 25th quantile and low managerial efficiency firms as those with G&A residuals higher than the 75th quantile. We find that our results are insensitive to such alternative thresholds.

Thus far, firm productive efficiency is presumed not to change with tariff reduction. We now relax such an assumption and use $TFP2^{DL}$ as the measure of productive efficiency so that it can react to changes in home and foreign tariffs. The estimates are presented in columns (6) and (8) for the 10th/90th thresholds and 25th/75th thresholds, respectively. The results with regard to the key variables, i.e., HT_{it}, FT_{it} and their interaction terms, are qualitatively the same as the previous estimates above. In particular, the coefficient of productive efficiency ($TFP2^{DL}$) is positive an highly significant in both columns (6) and (8).

However, if a firm's managerial efficiency also changes in response to the changes in tariffs, it is possible that a firm is classified as a low managerial efficiency firm this year but switch to a high one next year; and vice versa. To address such a concern, we use two alternative ways to classify managerial efficiency. First, we use a firm's *average* G&A residual during the entire sample period as the time-invariant measure of managerial efficiency. The average G&A residual is the simple average of all years' residuals obtained from Eq. (7.20). A variety of regressions in Table 7.7 with this new managerial efficiency measure show that our main findings stay robust by using different tariff measure (firm-level and industry-level), or by picking different cutoff (10% quantile and 25% quantile), or by adopting different measure of productive efficiency (*TFP*2 and $TFP2^{DL}$), as indicated in the note below the table. Second, inspired by Topalova and Khandelwal (2011), we fix a firm's G&A residual by using the firm's initial-year's G&A residual as a proxy. The results regarding the estimates of the key tariff variables are similar to our previous estimates.[34]

7.4.4 Further Robustness Checks

As managerial efficiency is the key focus of this study, we will explore more alternative measures of this variable. We now propose to use administrative expenses residuals, instead of G&A residuals, to measure managerial efficiency. Since data on administrative expenses are only available for three years, 2004–2006, the size of our sample drops significantly. Despite of this, we run various regressions and report the results in Table 7.8. The negative binomial estimates in columns (1) and (2) have very similar results as those in Tables 7.6 and 7.7. As shown by column

[34] The whole idea of these two alternative measures is to fix the value of a firm's managerial efficiency over the entire period. Such an approach also helps address another concern raised in Bloom et al. (2010) and Bloom et al. (2013): The estimates would be biased if managerial efficiency and productive efficiency affect each other.

Table 7.7 Further estimates of export product scope using G&A expenses

Firm's G&A measure	Average					Initial-year		
Firm's G&A residuals cutoffs	10th			25th		10th		25th
Regressand: export product scope	(1)	(2)	(3)	(4)	(5)	(6)	(7)	(8)
Home tariffs ($\hat{\beta}_2$)	0.953*** (21.71)	0.832*** (12.03)	0.554*** (5.47)	0.218** (2.36)	0.556*** (5.50)	0.191** (2.06)	0.531*** (5.27)	0.234** (2.56)
Foreign tariffs ($\hat{\beta}_3$)	0.408*** (9.95)	0.850*** (12.50)	0.562*** (5.68)	0.333*** (3.31)	0.579*** (5.29)	0.330*** (3.66)	0.555*** (5.67)	0.344*** (3.52)
Foreign tariffs × Low managerial efficiency indicator ($\hat{\beta}_4$)	0.272*** (4.45)	0.512*** (3.94)	1.690*** (10.44)	1 224*** (10.77)	1.195*** (10.02)	1.906*** (11.49)	1.778*** (10.32)	1 274*** −10.7
Foreign tariffs x High managerial efficiency indicator ($\hat{\beta}_5$)	−0.409*** (−4.89)	−1.420*** (−10.32)	−2.026*** (−13.01)	−1.441*** (−12.87)	−1.482*** (−12.60)	−2.068*** (−12.88)	−2.054*** (−12.32)	−1.506*** (−12.97)
Log firm TFP2 ($\hat{\beta}_1$)	0.021** (2.14)	0.031*** (2.63)		0.095*** (6.39)		0.084*** (5.58)		0.093*** (6.25)
Log firm TFP2OLli ($\hat{\beta}_1$)			0.283*** (8.28)		0.307*** (8.98)		0.275*** (8.13)	
Log weighted GDP of importers	0.123*** (93.75)	0.128*** (78.45)	0.136*** (66.40)	0.135*** (70.41)	0.135*** (66.22)	0.136*** (70.37)	0.135*** (66.50)	0.135*** (70.88)
Foreign indicator	0.101*** (9.97)	0.111*** (9.90)	0.102*** (8.38)	0.098*** (8.38)	0.099*** (8.16)	0.102*** (8.68)	0.103*** (8.46)	0.098*** (8.31)
SOE indicator	0.033 (1.45)	0.027 (0.98)	0.005 (0.14)	0.015 (0.47)	0.004 (0.11)	0.015 (0.47)	0.006 (0.18)	0.014 (0.42)
P-value of difference between $\hat{\beta}_3$ and $\hat{\beta}_5$	[.000]	[.000]	[.000]	[.000]	[.000]	[.000]	[.000]	[.000]
Firm-specific fixed effects	Yes	Yes	Yes	Yes	Yes	Yes	Yes	Yes
Year-specific fixed effects	Yes	Yes	Yes	Yes	Yes	Yes	Yes	Yes

(continued)

Table 7.7 (continued)

Firm's G&A measure	Average					Initial-year		
Firm's G&A residuals cutoffs	10th			25th		10th		25th
Regressand: export product scope	(1)	(2)	(3)	(4)	(5)	(6)	(7)	(8)
Observations	57,416	53,197	49,569	53,197	49,569	53,197	49,569	53,197

Note T-values in parentheses. * (**, ***) indicates significance at the 10% (5%, 1%) level. Measure of firm G&A expenses in columns (1)–(5) use firm's average G&A expenses whereas those in columns (6)–(8) use initial-year G&A expenses. Columns (1)–(3), (6) and (7) use top and bottom 10th quantiles of firm's G&A residuals as cutoffs to define the low (high) managerial efficiency indicators whereas columns (4), (5) and (8) use the top and bottom 25th quantiles as cutoffs. Foreign tariffs and their interaction terms with high/low G&A indicators in columns (1) are measured at the firm-level whereas all others are at industry-level. Firm TFP measures in columns (3), (5) and (7) are $TFP2^{DL}$ whereas the rest are TFP2

Table 7.8 Managerial efficiency and export product scope using administrative expense

Measure of log administrative residuals	10th				25th	
Econometric method	Negative binomial				IV Poisson	
Firm's TFP measures	TFP2	TFP	$TFP2^{DL}$	TFP2	TFP2	$TFP2^{DL}$
Regressand: export product scope	(1)	(2)	(3)	(4)	(5)	(6)
Home tariffs (firm-level: $\hat{\beta}_2$)	1.095*** (14.29)	1.215*** (15.12)		0.808*** (5.61)	0.798*** (5.53)	0.949*** (6.24)
Home tariffs (industry-level: $\hat{\beta}_2$)			0.209* (1.64)			
Foreign tariffs (firm-level: $\hat{\beta}_3$)	0.513*** (7.03)	0.390*** (8.45)	0.468*** (8.14)	0.581** (2.57)	0.396** (2.48)	0.374** (2.31)
Foreign tariffs × Low managerial efficiency indicator ($\hat{\beta}_4$)	0.567*** (5.23)	0.514*** (4.68)	0.793*** (6.09)	2 822*** (9.17)	2.087*** (7.70)	2 077*** (7.92)
Foreign tariffs × High managerial efficiency indicator ($\hat{\beta}_5$)	−0.578*** (−4.66)	−0.462*** (−3.62)	−0.622*** (−3.94)	−1.669*** (−6.13)	−1.149*** (−6.22)	−1.035*** (−5.40)
Log firm TFP ($\hat{\beta}_1$)	0.074*** (4.65)	0.365*** (21.35)	0.449*** (24.83)	0.100*** (3.82)	0.095*** (3.56)	0.422*** (18.47)
Log weighted GDP of importers	0.134*** (63.65)	0.132*** (61.21)	0.140*** (57.91)	0.162*** (31.09)	0.163*** (31.58)	0.165*** (32.28)
Foreign indicator	0.143*** (11.48)	0.151*** (11.77)	0.145*** (10.82)	0.089*** (4.79)	0.085*** (4.83)	0.088*** (4.93)
SOE indicator	0.167*** (3.38)	0.166*** (3.34)	0.144*** (2.61)	−0.017 (−0.20)	−0.066 (−0.84)	−0.066 (−0.86)
P-value of difference between $\hat{\beta}_3$ and $\hat{\beta}_5$	[.000]	[.000]	[.000]	[.000]	[.008]	[.008]
Firm-specific fixed effects	Yes	Yes	Yes	Yes	Yes	Yes
Year-specific fixed effects	Yes	Yes	Yes	Yes	Yes	Yes

(continued)

Table 7.8 (continued)

Measure of log administrative residuals	10th				25th	
Econometric method	Negative binomial				IV Poisson	
Firm's TFP measures	TFP2	TFP	TFP2^{DL}	TFP2	TFP2	TFP2^{DL}
Regressand: export product scope	(1)	(2)	(3)	(4)	(5)	(6)
Observations	41,492	38,681	36,081	17,533	17.533	16,842

Note T-values in parentheses. * (**) indicates significance at the 10% (5%) level. Measures of firm managerial efficiency indicator use the estimation residuals of firm annual-average log firm's administrative expenses on firm's characteristics. Columns (1)–(4) use top and bottom 10th quantiles of annual average log firm's administrative expenses within its industry as the cutoffs to define the low and high managerial efficiency indicators whereas columns (5) and (6) use the top and bottom 25th quantiles as the cutoffs. All pure exporters and pure processing firms are dropped in all estimations. Columns (1)–(3) are negative binomial fixed-effect estimates whereas columns (4)–(6) are IV Poisson estimates in which the endogenous variable is home tariff with initial year weight and the instrument is the previous year's home tariffs with initial year weight. TFP measures in Columns (3) and (6) are $TFP2^{DL}$ whereas the rest are TFP2

(3), replacing *TFP2* with $TFP2^{DL}$ generates similar results as their counterparts in columns (1) and (2).

Furthermore, we run the IV Poisson regression by treating home tariff as endogenous. To this end, we use previous year's home tariff (with initial weight) as the instrument. The IV Poisson estimations, in columns (4)–(6), show that the coefficients of home tariff, foreign tariff and the interactions with low high managerial efficiency indicators are significant and have the anticipated signs. More importantly, the magnitude of the coefficient of the interaction term between foreign tariffs and high managerial efficiency indicator is larger than that of the foreign tariff in absolute value.

7.5 Concluding Remarks

In this paper, we conduct theoretical and empirical analyses on the effects of trade liberalization on firms' export product scope. The preliminary empirical analysis based on Chinese data shows that Chinese firms reduce their export product scope in response to a domestic tariff cut and a foreign tariff cut. Low productivity and high productivity firms behave similarly. We then build a theoretical model which explicitly incorporates a new dimension of firm heterogeneity, namely, managerial efficiency. Our model predicts that the home country's tariff cut reduces all home firms' export product scope; however, in response to a foreign country's tariff cut, a home firm's export product scope expands (shrinks) when the firm's managerial efficiency is high (low). We conduct another empirical analysis to test these predictions. In the empirical analysis, we use a firm's total G&A residuals and administrative expenses residuals, respectively, as a proxy for management cost to measure managerial efficiency. We find strong evidence to support our theoretical predictions.

Firm heterogeneity in managerial efficiency is the new element in our theoretical and empirical models. In our theoretical model, we model a firm's management cost as the cost of managing the set of products. It would be interesting to explore other modelling approaches.

Appendix 7.1: Matching Transaction-Level Trade Data and Firm-Level Production Data

Transaction-Level Trade Dataset

The extremely disaggregated transaction-level monthly trade data during 2000–2006 are obtained from China's General Administration of Custom. Each transaction is described at the HS 8-digit level. The number of monthly observations increases from around 78 thousand in January 2000 to more than 230 thousand in December 2006. As shown in column (1) of Table 7.9, the number of observations is more than 10 million in 2000 and 16 million in 2006, with more than 118 million in total for seven years. Column (2) of Table 7.9 exhibits that there are 286,819 firms that ever engaged in international trade during this period.

For each transaction, the dataset consists of three types of information. First, 5 variables about basic trade information. They are value (in current US dollar), trade status (export or import), quantity, trade unit, and value per unit (i.e., value divided by quantity). Second, 6 variables on trade mode and pattern. These include country of destination for exports, country of origin for imports, routing (i.e., whether the product is shipped through an intermediate country/regime), customs regime (e.g., processing trade or ordinary trade), trade mode (i.e., by sea, by truck, by air, or by post), and customs port (i.e., where the product departs or arrives). Third, firms' information associated with each transaction. In particular, it includes 7 variables such as firm's name, identification number set by the customs, city where the firm is located, telephone, zip code, name of the manager/CEO, and ownership type of firm (e.g., foreign affiliate, private, or state-own-enterprises).

Table 7.9 Matched statistics

Year	Trade data		Production data		Matched data			
# of	Transactions	Firms	Raw firms	Filtered firms	w/Raw firms	w/Filtered firms	w/Raw firms	w/Filtered firms
	(1)	(2)	(3)	(4)	(5)	(6)	(7)	(8)
2000	10,586,696	80,232	162,883	83,628	18,580	12,842	21,665	15,748
2001	12,667,685	87,404	169,031	100,100	21,583	15,645	25,282	19,091
2002	14,032,675	95,579	181,557	110,530	24,696	18,140	29,144	22,291
2003	18,069,404	113,147	196,222	129,508	28,898	21,837	34,386	26,930
2004	21,402,355	134,895	277,004	199,927	44,338	35,007	50,798	40,711
2005	24,889,639	136,604	271,835	198,302	44,387	34,958	50,426	40,387
2006	26,685,377	197,806	301,960	224,854	53,748	42,833	59,133	47,591
All year	128,333,831	286,819	615,951	438,165	83,679	69,623	90,558	76,946

Note Column (1) reports the number of observations of HS eight-digit transaction-level trade data from China's General Administration of Customs. Column (2) reports the number of firms covered in the transaction-level trade data. Column (3) reports the number of firms covered in the firm-level production dataset compiled by China's National Bureau of Statistics without any filter and cleaning. By contrast, column (4) presents the number of firms covered in the firm-level production dataset with careful filter according to the requirement of GAAP. Column (5) reports the number of matched firms using exactly identical company's names in both trade dataset and raw production dataset. Column (6) reports the number of matched firms using exactly identical company's names in both trade dataset and filtered production dataset. Column (7) reports the number of matched firms using exactly identical company's name, zip code and phone number in both the trade dataset and the raw production dataset. Column (8) reports the number of matched firms using exactly identical company's name, zip code and phone number in both trade dataset and filtered production dataset

Firm-Level Production Dataset

The firm-level panel dataset covers around an average 230,000 manufacturing firms per year in 2000–2006. The number of firms doubled from 162,885 in 2000 to 301,961 in 2006. The data are collected and maintained by China's National Bureau of Statistics from annual surveys of manufacturing enterprises. It contains all information of three accounting sheets (i.e., Balance Sheet, Loss & Benefit Sheet, and Cash Flow Sheet). On average, the total value of industrial production covered in such a dataset accounts for around 95% of China's total industrial production in each year. In fact, the aggregated data on the industrial sector in China's Statistical Yearbook published by the Natural Bureau of Statistics (NBS) are compiled from this dataset. The dataset includes more than 100 financial variables listed in the main accounting sheets of all these firms. It covers two types of manufacturing firms: (1) all SOEs; (2) non-SOEs whose annual sales are more than five million RMB. The number of firms increases from more than 160 thousand in 2000 to 301 thousand in 2006. As shown in column

(3) of Table 7.9, the total number of firms that ever appear in the dataset during 2000–2006 is 615,951.

The raw production dataset is still quite noisy given that many unqualified firms are included, largely because of mis-reporting by some firms. For example, information on some family-based firms, which usually have no formal accounting system in place, is based on a unit of one RMB, whereas the official requirement is a unit of 1000 RMB. We hence filter the raw production data as introduced in the text. Accordingly, the total number of firms covered in the dataset is reduced to 438,165, around 1/3 of firms are dropped from the sample after such a filter process. As shown in column (4) of Table 7.9, such a filter ratio is even higher in the initial years: around 1/2 of firms are dropped in 2000.

Matching Method

Although these two datasets have rich information on production and trade, it is challenging to match them. Although both datasets contain a variable of each firm's identification number, their coding systems are completely different and share no common characteristics. For example, the lengths of the firm's ID variable in transaction-level dataset are 10 digits whereas those in firm-levels only have 9 digits. China's customs administration just constructs a complete coding system different from the one adopted by the National Bureau of Statistics.

To address this challenge, we take two approaches to match transaction-level trade data and firm-level production data. First, we match the two datasets by firm's name and year. That is, if a firm from one dataset has exactly the same Chinese name as a firm in another dataset in a particular year, they must be the same firm. The year variable is necessary to use for an auxiliary identification variable since some firms could change their name in different years and new comers could possibly take other firms' original

names. As a result, the number of matched firms is 83,679 in total by using the raw production dataset, and reduced to 69,623 in total by using the more accurate filtered production dataset.

Second, we rely on two other common variables to further identify firms, namely, zip code and the last seven digits of a firm's phone number. The rationale is that firms should have different and unique phone numbers within a postal district. Although this method seems straightforward, subtle technical and practical difficulties still remain. For example, the phone numbers in the product-level trade data include both area phone codes and a hyphen, whereas those in the firm-level production data do not. We use the last seven digits of the phone number to serve a proxy for firm identification for two reasons. The first reason is that during 2000–2006, some large Chinese cities changed their phone number digits from seven to eight, which usually added one more digit at the beginning of the number. Therefore, sticking to the last seven digits of the number would not confuse the firm's identification. The second reason is that in the original dataset, phone number is defined as a string of characters with the phone zip code. However, it is inappropriate to de-string such characters to numerals since a hyphen bar is used to connect the zip code and phone number. Using the last seven-digit substring solves this problem neatly.

A firm could miss its name information in either trade or production dataset. Similarly, a firm could lose information on phone and/or zip code. To secure that our matched dataset can cover common firms as many as possible, we include the observations in the matched dataset if a firm appears in either one of the two approaches just described above. As a result, the number of matched firms increases to 90,558 when the raw production dataset is used, as shown in column (7) of Table 7.9. By way of comparison, such a matching performance is in the same magnitude to (or even better than) other similar studies (see Yu (2015) for detailed discussions).

Appendix 7.2: Proof of Proposition 1

Part 1: $e_j < s_j$ for both $j = h$ and l.

(i) Rewrite (7.9) and (7.16) as

$$A - \theta s_l - 2\sqrt{b(m_l + k)} = 0,$$

$$A - \theta s_h - 2\sqrt{b(m_h + k)} = 0,$$

$$2[\sigma s_l + (1-\sigma)s_h + 1 + \delta]A - \theta\left[\sigma s_l^2 + (1-\sigma)s_h^2\right] - 2\alpha\delta - 2t = 0.$$

Differentiating the three equations with respect to t and doing some manipulation yields

$$\frac{ds_l}{dt} = \frac{ds_h}{dt} = \frac{1}{A + 1 + \delta} > 0$$

(ii) We now turn to foreign tariff cuts. Rewrite (7.12) and (7.17) as

$$A^* - \theta t^* e_l - 2\sqrt{bm_l} = 0, \tag{7.25}$$

$$A^* - \theta t^* e_h - 2\sqrt{bm_h} = 0, \tag{7.26}$$

$$2[\sigma e_l + (1-\sigma)e_h + 1 + \delta]A^* - \theta t^*\left[\sigma e_l^2 + (1-\sigma)e_h^2\right] - 2\alpha\delta = 0. \tag{7.27}$$

Differentiating (7.25) and (7.26), respectively, with respect to t^* yields

$$\frac{de_h}{dt^*} = \frac{de_l}{dt^*} + \frac{e_l - e_h}{t^*}. \tag{7.28}$$

Hence, $\frac{de_h}{dt^*} > \frac{de_l}{dt^*}$ because $e_h < e_l$

Differentiating (7.27) with respect to t^* and using (7.28) to substitute $\frac{de_h}{dt^*}$, we obtain

$$\frac{de_l}{dt^*} = \frac{K_l}{2(1+\delta)\theta t^* + 2A^*} < 0,$$

where $K_l = -2\sigma(e_l - e_h)A^*/t^* - 2\theta(1+\delta)e_l - \theta\left[\sigma e_l^2 + (1-\sigma)e_h^2\right] < 0$ Note that $e_l > e_h$; thus $K_l < 0$ and hence the above inequality holds.

Similarly, we can also obtain

$$\frac{de_h}{dt^*} = \frac{K_h}{2(1+\delta)\theta t^* + 2A^*},$$

where $K_h = -2\sigma(e_h - e_l)A^*/t^* - 2\theta(1+\delta)e_h - \theta\left[\sigma e_l^2 + (1-\sigma)e_h^2\right]$. Using (7.26) to substitute A^*, we can simplify

$$K_h = \sigma(e_l - e_h)\left[\frac{4\sqrt{bm_h}}{t^*} - \theta(e_l - e_h)\right] - 2\theta(1+\delta)e_h - \theta e_h^2.$$

From (7.25) and (7.26), we also obtain

$$e_l - e_h = \frac{2\sqrt{b}\left(\sqrt{m_h} - \sqrt{m_l}\right)}{\theta t^*}.$$

Substituting the above in K_h to reduce to

$$K_h = \frac{4\sigma b(m_h - m_l)}{\theta t^{*2}} - 2\theta(1+\delta)e_h - \theta e_h^2.$$

As $\frac{\partial e_h}{\partial m_h} < 0$, it is clear that $K_h > 0$ for sufficiently large m_h, and so under the same condition, $\frac{de_h}{dt^*} > 0$.

Part 2: $e_j = s_j$ for $j = h$ or l.

In this case, the total product scope (which is also the export product scope) will be chosen to maximize the total profits from the two market. Thus, the maximization problem (7.7) should be changed to

$$\max_{s_j, q_i} \int_0^{s_j} \left[(A - bq_i)q_i - \theta i q_i + \left(A^* - bq_i^e\right)q_i^e - t^*\theta i q_i^e\right]di - 2m_j s_j - ks_j.$$

We can derive the set of first order conditions, from which we first obtain the optimal quantity, price, and profit of each product in the home market as given in (7.8), and those in the export market as given in (7.11). With these, we obtain the optimal total product scope

$$s_j = \frac{A + A^*t^* - \sqrt{4b(2m_j + k) - (At^* - A^*)^2}}{\theta(1 + t^{*2})}.$$

With the above expressions, the rest of the analysis mechanically follows that in Part 1. However, it is a bit more complicated in terms of expression. Moreover, we need to consider three cases: (i) $e_h = s_h$ but $e_l < s_l$, (ii) $e_l = s_l$ but $e_h < s_h$, and (ii) $e_h = s_h$ and $e_l = s_l$. Givne the above considerations and to save space, we do not provide the detailed proof here, but it is available upon request.

Appendix 7.3: Measuring Pure Productive Efficiency (TFP2)

In this paper, the Olley-Pakes TFP is measured in three ways:

(i) TFP1 which is used in the benchmark estimates from Tables 7.2 to 7.4, and column (1) of Table 7.5. It includes both productive efficiency and managerial efficiency.
(ii) TFP2 which measures firm's productive efficiency only, which is used in Tables 7.5–7.7.
(iii) TFP2^{DL} which measures firm's productive efficiency only by allowing firm's productive efficiency to react to changes in tariff reductions. It is used in Tables 7.5–7.7.

Inspired by Feenstra et al. (2014), we estimate TFP1 and TFP2 in the following ways. We extend the

Olley–Pakes (1996) approach to fit with China's reality. First, given that the measure of TFP requires real terms of firm's inputs (labor and capital) and output, we adopt different price deflators for inputs and outputs from Brandt et al. (2012) in which the output deflators are constructed using "reference price" information from China's Statistical Yearbooks whereas input deflators are constructed based on output deflators and China's national input-output table (2002).[35]

Second, we take China's WTO accession in 2001 into account since such a positive demand shock would push Chinese firms to expand their economic scales, which in turn can exaggerate the simultaneous bias of their measured TFP. Third, it is essential to construct the real investment variable when using the Olley-Pakes (1996) approach. As usual, we adopt the perpetual inventory method to investigate the law of motion for real capital and real investment. Different from assigning an arbitrary number

[35] A caveat here. The output and input price deflators used in Brandt et al. (2012) and in the present paper are measured at broader Chinese-industrial-classification (CIC) level, thus the thorny problem of omitted firm-level output and input prices are not completed eliminated. De Loecker (2011) provides a possible way to distinguish the difference between physical productivity and revenue productivity by controlling both unobserved productivity shock and unobserved demand shock. This will be one of our future research topic.

for the depreciation ratio, we use firm's real depreciation provided by the Chinese firm-level dataset.

Fourth, we also consider firm's processing behavior in the TFP realization by constructing a processing export indicator (one denotes processing export and zero otherwise). The idea is that processing firms may use different technology than non-processing firms (Feenstra and Hanson 2005).

(i) *TFP1.*

As in Olley and Pakes (1996), suppose that investment V_{it} in the Olley-Pakes approach depends on productive efficiency x_{it} of the firm and the production innovation ς_{it+1} follows the following process: $\varsigma_{it+1} = x_{it+1} - x_{it}$; then, we have the following functional relation:

$$V_{it} = g_1(x_{it}, \ln K_{it}, HT_{it}, FT_{it}, EX_{it}, PE_{it}, WTO_t, SOE_{it}, FIE_{it}),$$

where EX_{it} (PE_{it}) is the export (processing export) indicator to measure whether firm i exports (engages in processing exports) in year t, and WTO_t is an indicator that equals one from 2001 onwards and zero before 2001. Therefore, inverting the investment function with respect to its first argument yields:

$$x_{it} = g_1^{-1}(V_{it}, \ln K_{it}, HT_{it}, FT_{it}, EX_{it}, PE_{it}, WTO_t, SOE_{it}, FIE_{it}).$$

Given the gross production function In $Y_{it} = \alpha_k \ln K_{it} + \alpha_l \ln L_{it} + \alpha_m \ln M_{it} + x_{it} + \varpi_{it} + \varepsilon_{it}$ and letting $h(\cdot) = \alpha_k \ln K_{jt} + g_1^{-1}(V_{it}, \ln K_{it}, HT_{it}, FT_{it}, EX_{it}, PE_{it}, WTO_t, SOE_{it}, FIE_{it})$ the estimation of the labor (materials) coefficients $\alpha_l(\alpha_m)$ are obtained as:

$$\ln Y_{it} = \alpha_l \ln L_{it} + \alpha_m \ln M_{it} + h(V_{it}, \ln K_{it}, HT_{it}, FT_{it}, EX_{it}, PE_{it}, WTO_t, SOE_{it}, FIE_{it}) + \mu_{it},$$

where the error term μ_{it} includes both managerial efficiency (ϖ_{it}) and the idiosyncratic term (ε_{it}). The next step is to obtain an unbiased estimated coefficient of α_k. Olley-Pakes (1996) use the following specification:

$$\ln Y_{it} - \hat{\alpha}_l \ln L_{it} - \hat{\alpha}_m \ln M_{it} = \alpha_k \ln K_{it} + E(x_{it}|x_{it-1}, pr_{it}) + \left[x_{it} - E(x_{it}|x_{it-1}, pr_{it})\right] + \mu_{it}, \quad (7.29)$$

where the estimated values of the labor coefficient and materials coefficient are used on the left. The expectation of productivity appearing in (A5) is modeled as a fourth-order polynomial function of lagged productivity, which can be obtained as $\left(h_{i,t-1} - \alpha_k \ln K_{i,t-1}\right)$, and also the predicted probability of the firm's survival into the year t, pr_{it} based on year $t - 1$ information. The predicted probability is obtained from Probit estimation.[36] The term $[x_{it} - E(x_{it}|x_{it-1}, pr_{it})]$ is the productivity shock for surviving firms. It does not affect the investment or exit choice, and so it is treated as an error.

Once the coefficient of capital $\hat{\alpha}_k$ is estimated in Eq. (7.29), it is ready to obtain the standard gross TFP:

$$TFP1_{it} = \ln Y_{it} - \hat{\alpha}_k \ln K_{it} - \hat{\alpha}_l \ln L_{it} - \hat{\alpha}_m \ln M_{it}.$$

This TFP1 includes both pure productive efficiency (x_{it}) and managerial efficiency (ϖ_{it}).

(ii) *TFP2*.

By contrast, TFP2 which only captures pure productive efficiency (x_{it}) is given by

$$\begin{aligned} TFP2_{it} \equiv x_{it} &= g_1^{-1}(V_{it}, \ln K_{it}, HT_{it}, FT_{it}, EX_{it}, PE_{it}, WTO_t, SOE_{it}, FIE_{it}) \\ &= E\big((\ln Y_{it} - \hat{\alpha}_l \ln L_{it} - \hat{\alpha}_m \ln M_{it})|\mathbf{X}_{it}\big) - \hat{\alpha}_k \ln K_{it} \end{aligned}$$

where $\mathbf{X}_{it}$ denotes all right-hand-side regressors used in the third-step OP estimations. The essential difference between the standard gross efficiency (TFP1) and pure productive efficiency (TFP2) is that the regressand of TFP1 uses the actual data on log output whereas that of TFP2 uses the fitted value of log output obtained in the third-step OP estimations.

(iii) *TFP2^{DL}*.

Our last measure of *firm's productive efficiency TFP2^{DL}* allows firm's productive efficiency to react to changes in both home tariffs (FT_{it}) and foreign tariffs (HT_{it}) over time by using the following functional form:

$$x_{it+1} = \sum_{sm} \beta_{sm}(x_{it}^s HT_{it}^m + x_{it}^s FT_{it}^m) + \varsigma_{it+1}.$$

where $E(\varsigma_{it+1} HT_{it}) = 0$ and $E(\varsigma_{it+1} FT_{it}) = 0$. Thus, a firm's investment function is $g_2(.)$ instead. With this modification, we can have a new measure of true productive efficiency as follows:

$$TFP2_{it}^{DL} \equiv x_{it} = g_2^{-1}(V_{it}, \ln K_{it}, HT_{it}, FT_{it}, EX_{it}, PE_{it}, WTO_t, SOE_{it}, FIE_{it}),$$

where the only difference between $g_1^{-1}(.)$ and $g_2^{-1}(.)$ is the new realization of production innovation. The rest steps are the same as in estimates of TFP1.

[36] Note that here the non-linear least squares approach is adopted to estimate (??) since it requires the estimated coefficients of the log-capital in the first and second term to be identical (Pavcnik 2002).

Table 7.10 Production productivity and G&A

Expenses	CIC	Laor	Capital	Mateirals productivity variance in				G&A (in log)	Administrative expenses (in log)
				ACF	TFP1	TFP2	TFP2DL		
13	0.077	0.060	0.814	0.391	0.322	0.148	0.191	7.018	4.162
14	0.055	0.071	0.857	0.482	0.300	0.172	0.172	7.436	4.550
15	0.094	0.113	0.799	0.505	0.381	0.235	0.235	8.134	4.791
16	0.020	0.270	0.783	0.870	0.631	0.479	0.477	9.929	4.821
17	0.066	0.044	0.868	0.398	0.218	0.103	0.036	7.458	4.490
18	0.110	0.039	0.798	0.475	0.310	0.093	0.199	7.154	4.432
19	0.084	0.041	0.857	0.412	0.276	0.098	0.070	7.195	4.348
20	0.099	0.071	0.841	0.898	0.300	0.167	0.340	6.793	4.071
21	0.103	0.055	0.814	0.647	0.218	0.119	0.067	7.179	4.542
22	0.063	0.053	0.867	0.550	0.234	0.127	0.294	8.159	5.005
23	0.065	0.068	0.815	0.616	0.215	0.210	0.348	7.735	4.795
24	0.091	0.039	0.823	0.509	0.223	0.113	0.117	7.262	4.423
25	0.014	0.069	0.865	0.151	0.324	0.327	0.327	9.101	5.829
26	0.063	0.058	0.820	0.423	0.318	0.175	0.380	8.091	4.955
27	0.062	0.064	0.790	0.634	0.360	0.219	0.202	8.440	5.181
28	0.040	0.060	0.889	0.392	0.313	0.169	0.280	8.239	5.051
29	0.087	0.081	0.769	0.546	0.333	0.186	1.080	7.702	4.947
30	0.069	0.046	0.836	0.677	0.288	0.180	0.227	7.381	4.627
31	0.046	0.059	0.844	0.625	0.287	0.145	0.254	7.439	4.730
32	0.061	0.029	0.891	0.359	0.249	0.116	0.126	8.727	5.344

(continued)

Table 7.10 (continued)

Expenses	CIC	Laor	Capital	Mateirals productivity variance in				G&A (in log)	Administrative expenses (in log)
				ACF	TFP1	TFP2	TFP2DL		
33	0.080	0.079	0.850	0.231	0.278	0.322	0.157	8.198	5.123
34	0.062	0.037	0.841	0.432	0.311	0.093	0.121	7.402	4.811
35	0.061	0.055	0.837	0.448	0.247	0.188	0.150	7.768	4.811
36	0.053	0.049	0.841	0.534	0.326	0.123	0.157	8.082	5.011
37	0.063	0.045	0.835	0.420	0.283	0.160	0.152	8.274	5.178
39	0.077	0.066	0.836	0.314	0.303	0.135	0.170	7.865	4.985
40	0.109	0.075	0.806	0.677	0.358	0.194	0.248	8.136	5.135
41	0.049	0.054	0.806	0.639	0.386	0.208	0.140	8.041	4.914
42	0.091	0.039	0.857	0.500	0.271	0.092	0.092	7.044	4.453

Note The Chinese industries and associated codes are classified as follows: Processing of foods (13), Manufacture of foods (14), Beverages (15), Textile (17), Apparel (18), Leather (19), Timber (20), Furniture (21), Paper (22), Printing(23), Articles for cultures and sports (24), Petroleum (25), Raw Chemicals (26), Medicines (27), Chemical Fibers (28), Rubber (29), Plastics (30), Non-metallic Mineral (31), Smelting of ferrous metals (32), Smelting of non-ferrous metals (33), Metal (34), General machinery (35), Special machinery (36), Transport equipment (37), Electrical machinery (39), Communication equipment (40), Measuring instrument (41), and Manufacture of artwork (42). We do not report standard errors for each coefficient to save space though available upon request. The logarithm of firm productivity for Chinese firms (TFP1, TFP2, TFP2) is estimated by industry using the augmented Olley-Pakes approach introduced in the text. Coefficients of labor, capital, and materials are calculated at the sectorial average. By comparison, ACF productivity is estimated by industry using the Ackerberg et al. (2015)'s approach. The last two columns report log of firm's G&A expenses and log of firm's administrative expenses

Part IV
Trade Liberalization Strategy

Chapter 8
Measured Skill Premia and Input Trade Liberalization: Evidence from Chinese Firms

Using Chinese firm-level production data, this chapter developed a Mincer (1974)-type approach to investigate the impact of input trade liberalization on firms' wage inequality between skilled and unskilled workers (or skill premium). When controlling for product-market tariffs in a firm's industry, we find robust evidence that reduced input tariffs in a firm's industry are associated with a higher skill premium at firms with more skilled workforces. This effect is more pronounced at ordinary (non-processing) firms. We also provide evidence that reduced input tariffs in a firm's industry are associated with higher value added and profits at firms with more skilled workforces.

8.1 Introduction

Tariffs have declined dramatically worldwide as a result of many rounds of trade negotiations under the General Agreement on Tariffs and Trade (GATT)/World Trade Organization (WTO) (Bagwell and Staiger 1999). The labor markets in each country have been impacted by the trade liberalization in final-goods and intermediate-input sectors. The question of how trade liberalization affects wage inequality between skilled and unskilled workers, especially for developing countries, has once again become one of the research focuses in the international trade literature.

Most of the early studies in the literature follow the Heckscher-Ohlin model to test whether trade liberalization benefits the abundant factors. According to the Stopler-Samuelson theorem, trade liberalization would mitigate wage inequality between skilled and unskilled labor in the developing countries. However, this theoretical assertion has received little empirical support because most studies find increased

M. Yu, *China's Miracle in Foreign Trade*, Studies in Modern Chinese Economy,
https://doi.org/10.1007/978-981-16-6030-6_8

skill premium in both developed and developing countries.[1] For example, Feenstra and Hanson (1996, 1999) find that, in the presence of vertical integration and international outsourcing, freer trade could actually increase skill premium in both developed and developing countries.[2]

Recent studies in the literature use firm-level data to investigate the impact of globalization on wage inequality but they mainly focus on the impact of export-side trade liberalization (e.g. Verhoogen 2008; Bustos 2011; Frías et al. 2012, Helpman et al. 2017). For example, using Brazilian data, Helpman et al. (2017) find that much of the overall wage inequality occurs within sector-occupations, which is mainly driven by wage dispersion between, rather than within, firms. However, the impact of input trade liberalization on firm-level wage inequality is equally important and may also have distinct differences in how the employers might share the surplus with various input factors because of their different bargaining power. In particular, imported intermediate inputs have been found to be crucial for boosting firm productivity in both developed and developing countries such as the United States (Hanson et al. 2005), Indonesia (Amiti and Konings 2007), India (Goldberg et al. 2010; Topalova and Khandelwal 2011), and China (Yu 2015).

The purpose of the present paper is to investigate the impact of input trade liberalization on wage inequality in China and intend to make the following two contributions to the literature. First, investigations on the impact of input trade liberalization on wage inequality in developing countries usually rely on industry-level wage data, household survey data, and the Gini coefficient as a proxy for income inequality (e.g., Beyer et al. 1999).[3] For example, using urban industrial survey data, Han et al. (2012) found that widening wage inequality in China was strongly associated with China's accession to the WTO in 2001.[4] In the present paper, we use Chinese firm-level production and customs' trade data to investigate the impact of tariff reductions for imported inputs on firm-level skill premium in China. To our knowledge, this is the first paper to investigate how import trade liberalization affects firm-level skill premium for manufacturing firms in China, the largest developing country in the

[1] Previous works have contributed to an intense discussion on the validity of factor price equalization (FPE) in explaining wage inequality in developed countries. See Johnson and Stafford (1993), Leamer (1993, 1996), and Lawrence and Slaughter (1993), among many others.

[2] Technology is identified as the major factor driving wage inequality; international trade is nevertheless also believed to play an important role. See more details in Feenstra and Hanson (1996, 1999).

[3] An outstanding exception is Akerman et al. (2013), who find that trade liberalization not only enhances the dispersion of revenues across heterogeneous firms, but also widens wage inequality across workers and firms. This paper is also in line with Groizard et al. (2014) who explore the endogenous nexus between trade liberalization and job flow in California and Rodriguez-Lopez and Yu (2017) who examine the relationship between all-around trade liberalization and firm-level employment in China. Furusawa and Konishi (2014) propose a model to interpret why international trade can increase wage inequality between top income earners and others, and thus cause job polarization.

[4] Autor et al. (2013) show that China' s exports to the American market have significantly contributed to the aggregate decline in the U.S. manufacturing employment and caused the sharp increases in U.S. social benefit claims.

world. The study could enrich our understanding of the sources of China's growing income inequality from the wage differentials at the firm levels.[5]

Second, a major challenge to investigate firm-level wage inequality between skilled and unskilled labor in China, as in most developing countries, is lack of data for direct firm-level wages for skilled and unskilled workers. To overcome this major obstacle, the current paper has developed a method of constructing firm-level skill premium from a firm's average wage and share of skilled labor. Together with a Mincer-type regression, we are able to estimate the impact of input trade liberalization on firm-level skill premium in China. This method can be applied to other research facing similar data limitations.

Using firm-level production and transaction-level trade data from China, we find that, when controlling for product-market tariffs in a firm's industry, the reduced input tariffs in a firm's industry are associated with a higher skill premium at firms with more skilled workforces. This effect is more pronounced at ordinary (non-processing) firms. Compared with processing importers, ordinary importers respond more forcefully to input trade liberalization in their wage schedule. Our main finding that input trade liberalization increases firm-level skill premium in China is robust for all three regions (east, central and west) in China, as well as for different measures of wage inequality, different empirical specifications and data spans. By contrast, output trade liberalization, which is measured by product-market tariffs reduction, show opposite signs of the effect of import tariffs on the skill premium at firms with more skill-intensive production. However, the product-market tariff effects are not robustly significant across specifications.

Inspired by the literature on"fair wages" (e.g. Egger and Kreickemeier 2012), we also provide an interpretation for our main finding that input trade liberalization leads to an increase in firm skill premium. If skilled workers have greater bargaining power with their employers than unskilled workers, incomes of the skilled workers shall be more closely linked to firms' economic profits but the incomes of unskilled workers shall be more in line with those of other firms in the same industry. Thus, a fall in input tariffs increases the firm's value-added, which in turn raises the firm's skill premium because the skilled labor commands a larger proportion of the incremental surplus than the unskilled labor. We also provide some evidence for our conjecture.

In addition to the literature discussed earlier, our paper is also closely related to the studies on how import trade liberalization affects skill compositions and factor returns. For example, using data from multinational companies, Biscourp and Kramarz (2007) examine the impact of offshoring on plant-level skill composition in France. Similarly, Becker et al. (2013) investigate the impact of offshoring on firm-level task composition and wages in Germany. Amiti and Davis (2011) is another influential study that investigates the impact of output and input tariff reductions on wages. In particular, they find that a reduction in input tariffs raises wages at import-using firms relative to those using only domestic intermediate inputs. However, these studies do not focus on firm wage inequality, or skill premium.

[5] Khan and Riskin (1998) found that wage inequality contributed to half of the income inequality in China in 1995.

The rest of the paper is organized as follows. Section 8.2 describes the data and introduces the econometric methods to measure firm skill premium and the empirical specifications of Mincer regression. Section 8.3 presents the main empirical evidence, offers robustness checks and discussion on the possible mechanism. Section 8.4 concludes.

8.2 Data, Measures, and Empirics

8.2.1 Data

To investigate the impact of input trade liberalization on firms' skill premium, our analysis uses the following three disaggregated panel data sets: firm-level production data compiled by China's National Bureau of Statistics (NBS), production-level trade data maintained by China's General Administration of Customs, and China's import tariff (ad valorem) data at the HS 6-digit level, maintained by the World Integrated Trade Solution (WITS) database of the World Bank.

China's NBS conducts an annual survey of industrial firms (ASIF) with two types of manufacturing firms: all state-owned enterprises (SOEs) and non-SOEs whose annual sales exceed RMB 5 million (or equivalently $725,000). The sample used in this paper has approximately 230,000 manufacturing firms per year, varying from 162,885 firms in 2000 to 301,961 firms in 2006. On average, the sample accounts for more than 95% of China's total annual output in the manufacturing sectors.[6] The data set covers more than 100 accounting variables and contains all of the information from the main accounting sheets, which includes balance sheets, loss and profit sheets and cash flow statements.

Given its rich information, the firm-level production data set is widely used in research by, among others, Cai and Liu (2009), Brandt et al. (2012), and Feenstra et al. (2014). However, the data set has two limitations for our research purpose. The first one is common: some unqualified firms are wrongly included in the data set, largely because of mis-reporting or false recording. Thus, following Feenstra et al. (2014), we keep the observations in our analysis according to the requirements of the Generally Accepted Accounting Principles (GAAP).[7] Accordingly, the total number of firms covered in the data set was reduced from 615,951 to 438,165, and approximately one-third of the firms were removed from the sample after the rigorous filter was applied. The drop in the percentage of sales is only around 25%. Thus, the drop in sales is smaller, since larger firms meet the GAAP more frequently. This

[6] In 2006, the total value added of all the firms included in the survey was RMB 9,107 billion, which accounted for 99 percent of the value added of all firms in the manufacturing sectors (RMB 9,131 billion), as reported by China' s Statistics Yearbook (2007).

[7] We keep observations if all of the following hold: (1) total assets exceed liquid assets; (2) total assets exceed total fixed assets; (3) the net value of fixed assets is less than that of total assets; (4) the firm's identification number exists and is unique, and (5) the established time is valid.

suggests that larger firms that follow GAAP may generate larger rents per worker, so they have a large surplus to share and the measured effect of reduced input tariffs might be an upper bound.

The second limitation of the data is specific to the present paper. The data set does not separate wages for skilled and unskilled labor. Furthermore, the numbers (i.e. the share) of skilled and unskilled workers are only available for 2004. To overcome this problem, we conduct our baseline test on cross-firm data for 2004. Then we carry out panel data tests that include other years by multiplying the skilled labor shares in 2004 by the change in the skilled labor share (relative to 2004) at the provincial level. To ensure the precision of our estimates, we exclude the pure trade intermediaries (that do not have production activities) from the sample in all the estimates. The trade intermediaries are identified according to the same procedures as in Ahn et al. (2011).

Finally, we use customs' data to match with the firm-level production data so that we are able to identify each firm's importing and processing status. As introduced in Feenstra et al. (2014), the production-level trade data maintained by China's General Administration of Customs include a large variety of information such as each trading firm's importing (or exporting) status and processing (or non-processing) status. Such information is essential for us to conduct our empirical estimations, which will be discussed shortly.

8.2.2 Measures

This subsection starts by introducing the index of input trade liberalization, and then focuses on constructing firm-level measured skill premium because the data sets do not directly provide firm-level wages for skilled and unskilled labor.

8.2.2.1 Measures of Input Tariffs

Inspired by Amiti and Konings (2007) and Topalova and Khandelwal (2011), we construct the industry-level input tariffs, IT_j, as follows:

$$IT_j = \sum\nolimits_n \left(\frac{input_{nj}^{2002}}{\sum\limits_n input_{nj}^{2002}} \right) \tau_n, \tag{8.1}$$

where IT_j denotes the industry-level input tariffs facing firms in industry j in 2004 and τ_n is the tariff on input n in 2004. The weight in parentheses is measured as the production cost share of input n in industry j.

We use China's Input–Output Table of 2002 to construct the weight because NBS reports the Input–Output Table every five years and our data are for 2004. In

Table 8.1 China's industrial input tariffs

Year	2000	2001	2002	2003	2004	2005	2006	Average
Ind. input tariffs	15.73	14.35	10.52	9.21	8.21	7.84	7.71	9.14
Std. dev	3.90	3.10	2.78	2.31	2.08	1.85	1.72	3.22

Notes This table reports the mean and standard deviation of 3-digit industry-level input tariffs

the spirit of Bartik (1991), we use the input–output matrix from 2002 to compute the relevant weighted industry input tariffs since the weight in 2002 reflects the initial conditions prior to China's tariff cuts in 2004.[8] The industrial input tariffs are obtained as follows. First, since there are 71 manufacturing sectors reported in China's Input–Output Table (2002) and only 28 manufacturing sectors reported in the Chinese Industrial Classification (CIC), we start by making a concordance between the Input–Output Table and the CIC sectors. Second, we match the CIC sectors with the International Standard Industrial Classification (ISIC, rev. 3).[9] Third, we make another concordance to link the ISIC and HS 6-digit trade data, where we can find the corresponding tariffs from the WITS database. Fourth, we calculate the industry-level tariffs that are aggregated to the CIC sector level.[10] Since simple-average tariffs cannot take into account the difference of the importance of imports, we consider the following weighted industrial tariffs:

$$\tau_n = \sum_{k \in n} \left(\frac{m_k}{\sum_{k \in n} m_k} \right) \tau_k, \tag{8.2}$$

where m_k is the import values for product k in CIC 2-digit industry n in 2004. Finally, we calculate the industry-level input tariffs using Eq. (8.1). The industry-level *output* tariff for industry n in 2004 is also obtained from Eq. (8.2).

To see how the input tariff reductions affect firms' skill premium, we examine the evolution of China' s trade liberalization throughout the sample period. Table 8.1 reports the mean and standard deviation for this key variable by spreading the sample from 2000 to 2006. As shown in Table 8.1, the average industry input tariffs were cut in half, from 15.73% in 2000 to 7.71% in 2006, and their standard deviation also dropped by about a half over the same period. The industry input tariffs were around half of their initial levels in 2000, before the WTO accession. Finally, the industry input tariffs in 2004 were also lower than the corresponding industry output tariffs, as shown in Table 8.2.

---

[8] By the same token, we use China' s Input–Output Table of 1997 to construct the initial weight of the input tariffs for the sample period of 2000–06 in our robustness checks.

[9] Since Chinese government adjusted its CIC in 2003, we also made similar adjustments in our data.

[10] We do not report the input weight by industry to save space; these data are available upon request.

Table 8.2 Summary statistics of key variables

(2000–06) year coverage	2004 only		2000–06	
Variables	Mean	Std. dev	Mean	Std. dev
Firm average wage	12.807	9.385	13.231	9.843
Firm skilled share	0.449	0.285	0.437	0.272
Industry input tariffs (%)	8.219	2.084	9.147	3.220
Industry output tariffs (%)	10.111	6.591	11.073	8.195
Measured unskilled wage	1.350	1.441	1.382	1.497
Log of firm sales	9.939	1.178	10.161	1.205
Log of firm labor	4.708	1.088	4.903	1.103
Exporter indicator	0.287	0.452	0.292	0.455
Processing indicator	0.32	0.46	–	–
Importer indicator	0.36	0.47	–	–
Log TFP (Olley-Pakes)	1.153	0.354	1.155	0.347
SOEs indicator	0.038	0.191	0.056	0.229
Foreign indicator	0.213	0.409	0.222	0.416
Wage premium	0.453	8.796	0.001	9.235
Year	2004	–	2003	1.739

Notes The import indicator is only available in the customs firm matched data set. The first two columns cover ASIF data for 2004 only, whereas the last two columns cover ASIF data for 2000–06

8.2.2.2 Measures of Skill Premium

The skill premium is defined as $s_{it} \equiv (w_{it}^s - w_{it}^u)/w_{it}^u$ for the skilled wages (w_{it}^s) and unskilled wages (w_{it}^u).[11] Given the share of firm i's skilled workers (θ_{it}), the firm average wage $(\overline{w_{it}})$ can be written as $\overline{w_{it}} = \theta_{it} w_{it}^s + (1 - \theta_{it}) w_{it}^u$ or, relative to the unskilled wages, $\overline{w_{it}}/w_{it}^u = 1 + \theta_{it} s_{it}$. Hence, the log term of the average wage is:

$$\ln(\overline{w_{it}}) = \ln(w_{it}^u) + \ln(1 + \theta_{it} s_{it}). \tag{8.3}$$

When $\theta_{it} s_{it}$ is small, $\ln(1 + \theta_{it} s_{it}) \approx \theta_{it} s_{it}$, after omitting the higher-order terms. Therefore,

we obtain:

$$\ln(\overline{w_{it}}) \approx \ln(w_{it}^u) + \theta_{it} s_{it}. \tag{8.4}$$

The key advantage of Eq. (8.4) is that it gives rise to a plausible Mincer-type regression for our empirical estimation. The trade-off is that, if $\theta_{it} s_{it}$ is not small enough, our

[11] Wage inequality and skilled wage premium are monotonically related although they are two different concepts. Inequality measures are typically statistics that capture dispersion or variance (see e.g. Shorrocks 1980)—that is second-order. In contrast, skill premium reflects a relative difference in first-order moments. We thank a referee for pointing this out.

Mincer-type regressions are not precise enough to interpret the economic magnitudes of the estimated coefficients. Hence, in the rest of the paper, economic interpretation should be focused on the sign, rather than the magnitude, of our estimates.[12]

Table 8.2 reports the summary statistics for the key variables used in our estimations. In the firm data set, information on firms' skilled labor share is available only for 2004, although firms' average wages are available for 2000–06. Since firms' skill share is crucial in Specification (4), we use the cross-section data for 2004 to conduct the main analysis and a panel sample for 2000–06 for robustness checks only. Since the firm-level data set provides employment information on skilled and unskilled labor for 2004, we use a proxy for the skilled labor share for all other years. The proxy $\left(\hat{\theta}_{it}\right)$ is measured by multiplying the skilled labor share in 2004 $\left(\theta_{i,2004}\right)$ by the provincial skilled labor share (η_{rt}) in all years, using 2004 as the base year: $\hat{\theta}_{it} \equiv \eta_{rt}\theta_{i,2004}$. Table 8.2 reports the mean and standard deviation of the key variables for the samples for 2004 and 2000–06.

Three variables in Table 8.2 relate to wage information. The first is firm average wage, which is reported from the data sets directly. The second is the measured wage premium (μ_i), which is defined as firm s's log wage relative to that of the average firm in industry j and region r (to be discussed in details in the next section). The last wage variable is the measured unskilled wage. Since the annual survey of industrial firms does not provide firm-level unskilled wages, we define the measured unskilled wage as the minimum level of firm wages in each (3-digit) industry-province pair based on the following two observations. First, as shown in Table 8.2, firms' average wages are significantly positively correlated with the skill share,[13] but the mean of measured unskilled wages is much lower than that of the firms' average wage (around 15%). Second, according to Anwar and Sun (2012), wages of unskilled workers in China are actually different across industries and provinces, especially after 2004. As a robustness check, however, we also use an alternative measure of the unskilled wages for our estimations. Finally, the firm-level data set for 2004 reports five education levels: graduate (and above), university, college, high school, and below middle school. As in most studies, we define skilled workers as employees with a college degree or.

8.2.3 Mincer Empirical Specification

Let us suppose that firm i's skill premium,s_i, takes a linear form

[12] Higher-order terms under a proper McLaurin expansion, however, would not be estimable given the sample size and measurement error. We appreciate a referee for pointing this out.

[13] A simple regression of firms' average wage on the skilled share, using the sample for 2004 and controlling for 3- digit industry fixed effects and province fixed effects, suggests a positive coefficient of the skilled share that is highly significant at the conventional statistical level (t-value = 77.25).

$$s_{it} = \sum\nolimits_{p=0}^{P} \gamma_{p^x} p_{it} + \epsilon_{it}. \tag{8.5}$$

where x_{it}^{p} denotes a vector of predictors. From Eqs. (8.4) and (8.5), we obtain the following Mincer (1974)-type empirical specification:

$$\begin{aligned} \ln(\overline{w_{it}}) &= \gamma_0 + \gamma_u \ln(w_{it}^{u}) + \gamma_0\hat{\theta}_{it} + \gamma_1\left(\hat{\theta}_{it}IT_{jt}\right) + \gamma_2\left(\hat{\theta}_{it}IT_{jt}\right)IM_{it} + \gamma_3\left(\hat{\theta}_{it}PT_{jt}\right) \\ &+ \gamma_4\left(\hat{\theta}_{it}PT_{jt}\right)FX_{it} + \gamma_5\left(\hat{\theta}_{it}FX_{it}\right) + \gamma_6\left(\hat{\theta}_{it}IM_{it}\right) + \gamma_7 IT_{jt} + \gamma_8 PT_{jt} \\ &+ \gamma_9 IM_{it} + \gamma_{10} FX_{it} + \gamma_{11}\mu_{it} + \gamma_{12}\hat{\theta}_{it}\mu_{it} + \mathbf{sX}_{ijt} + \delta_i + \delta_{jr} + \delta_t + \varepsilon_{it}, \end{aligned} \tag{8.6}$$

where the error term is defined as $\varepsilon_{it} \equiv \hat{\theta}_{it}\epsilon_{it}$. The main regressors in this Mincer regressions includes three sets of variables: we first include unskilled wage $\left(\ln(w_{it}^{u})\right)$, measured skilled labor share $\left(\hat{\theta}_{it}\right)$ and its interaction with input tariffs $\left(IT_{jt}\right)$ and output tariffs $\left(PT_{jt}\right)$.[14] Note that we do not restrict the coefficient of the unskilled wage γ_u to unity given that it is not the observed firm-level low-skilled wage, although our main estimation results won't change even with such a restriction.

We also include import dummy (IM_{it}) (export dummy FX_{it}) and its interaction with tariffs as regressors.

Finally, in addition to firm-specific fixed-effects (δ_i), interacted industry-region fixed-effects $\left(\delta_{jr}\right)$, and year-specific fixed-effects (δ_t), we also include firm wage premium, which is firm *i*'s log relative to the average firm in industry *j* (and province *r*), defined as $\mu_{it} \equiv \ln \overline{w}_{it} - \sum\nolimits_{i \in I(jr)}^{N} (\ln \overline{w}_{it})/|Jr|$ where $|Jr|$ is the cardinality of the set of firms in industry-region pair *jr*, and its interaction with firm's skill share in the regression.

Among the regressors, there are five important points that are worth noting. First and foremost, among the set of predictors, the most important variable of interest is the average intermediate input tariffs in industry $j(IT_j)$ that firm *i* is associated with. If the coefficient γ_1 in Eq. (8.6) is negative and statistically significant, it suggests that input trade liberalization would increase firm skill premium. It is also reasonable to anticipate that the impact of input trade liberalization on skill premium would be stronger for ordinary (i.e., non-processing) importing firms, since processing imports have already enjoyed the special treatment of free duty (Yu 2015) and hence would be less impacted by a further input trade liberalization. Thus, we expect that γ_2, the triple interaction term among skill share, intermediate input tariffs, and the importer indicator, should be negative. By constrast, another triple interaction term among skill share, intermediate input tariffs, and the processing indicator (not shown in the Eq. (8.6)) is expected to be positive.

[14] Note that we do not restrict the coefficient of the unskilled wage γ_u to unity given that it is not the observed firm-level low-skilled wage, although our main estimation results won't change even with such a restriction.

Second, we include the industry average output tariff (PT_j) and its interaction with the firm export indicator as control variables for the reasons as follows. After its accession to the WTO, China cut not only its intermediate input tariffs, but also its final output tariffs (see Yu 2015, for a detailed discussion). It would be expected that the impact of output trade liberalization on wage inequality may be different between exporting firms and non-exporting firms. Thus, the interactions of output tariffs with firm-level exporting indicators are introduced for that purpose (see Biscourp and Kramarz 2007; Verhoogen 2008). Of course, skill premium in exporting (importing) firms may be affected through channels other than trade liberalization. We thus also include firms' own exporting and importing indicators in the regressions.

Third and equally important, the regression Eq. (8.6) requires panel data. Since the proxy of the skilled labor share, $\hat{\theta}_{it}$, is defined as the product between the skilled labor share in 2004 $\left(\theta_{i,2004}\right)$ and the provincial skilled labor share (η_{rt}) in all years by using 2004 as the base year: $\hat{\theta}_{it} \equiv \eta_{rt}\theta_{i,2004}$, the interaction terms with $\hat{\theta}_{it}$ generate within-firm variation mainly from the η_{rt} portion. Still, we can observe firm's skill share θ_i directly in 2004. Thus, we consider the following baseline cross-section regression:

$$\begin{aligned}\ln(\overline{w_i}) = {} & \gamma_c + \gamma_u \ln\left(w_i^u\right) + \gamma_0\theta_i + \gamma_1\left(\theta_i IT_j\right) + \gamma_2\left(\theta_i IT_j\right)IM_i + \gamma_3\left(\theta_i PT_j\right) \\ & + \gamma_4\left(\theta_i PT_j\right)FX_i + \gamma_5(\theta_i FX_i) + \gamma_6(\theta_i IM_i) + \gamma_7 IT_j + \gamma_8 PT_j \\ & + \gamma_9 IM_i + \gamma_{10}FX_i + \gamma_{11}\mu_i + \gamma_{12}\theta_i\mu_i + \gamma\mathbf{X}_i + \delta_{jr} + \varepsilon_i. \qquad (8.7)\end{aligned}$$

Fourth, μ_{it} is firm i's log wage relative to the average firm in industry j and province r. These wage premia (or discounts) can come from different skill composition of firm i's workforce, or the different surplus that firm i generates. It is important to emphasize that this variable plays an important role here. It helps us properly control for between-firm skill premium (e.g. Egger and Kreichemeier 2009; Amiti and Davis 2011; Helpman et al. 2017). In the cross-section regression in Eq. (8.7), with proper region-industry fixed effects, the second component $\left(\sum_{i\in I(jr)}^{N}(\ln\overline{w}_i)/|Jr|\right)$ of the measured between-firm wage premium (μ_{it}) should be fully absorbed industry fixed effects. Thus, the OLS estimator would then exhibit a coefficient of the variable μ_{it} close to unity. The interaction term $\theta_i\mu_i$ is also needed for our Mincer-regression specification.

Finally, our empirical specifications implicitly draw on theory suggested by Helpman et al. (2010). By treating multiple skill groups in the firm-level framework, the regression residuals will depend on (i) the tightness of the local labor market in a province-industry pair, (ii) the locally available skilled workers in an industry and location, (iii) firms' anticipated performance and associated wage offers, and (iv) any firm-specific shocks to the wage bargaining or screening technology (Blaum et al. 2015; Helpman et al. 2017). Thus, we add the following three sets of dummies in the regressions. First, we include province-specific fixed effects to control for province-invariant but unobservable factors (such as export subsidy rates, etc.).

Second, we include 2-digit industry-specific fixed effects, which control for industry-invariant factors such as industrial capital intensity. Third, we allow for a full set of interacted industry-province dummies to absorb local labor market conditions. The remaining identifying assumption is the idiosyncratic effect $\varepsilon_i \sim N(0, \sigma^2)$, which takes into account firms' anticipated performance and firm-specific shocks that do not differentially affect individual skill groups.

Some studies have investigated whether more productive firms use more skill-biased technology (e.g., Verhoogen 2008; Bustos 2011). It is possible that trade liberalization induces the most productive firms to adopt skill-biased technology or upgrade product quality, and hence increases the demand for skilled labor for these firms. If such a multi-collinearity problem is a big concern, our data should exhibit a strong negative correlation between input tariffs and the skill share. However, this is not the case for our sample as the simple correlation in 2004 cross-section data between industrial input tariffs and the skill share is small (–0.11). Moreover, the simple correlation in the whole sample for 2000–06 is even smaller in absolute value (–0.06). The low correlations suggest that the change of firms' skill share is not sensitive to the change of trade liberalization, at least in our current sample.

8.3 Estimation Results

8.3.1 Baseline Mincer Regressions

Table 8.3 presents the baseline results for the cross-section empirical specification (7). Since the firmlevel data set does not report firms' import status, Table 8.3 does not include the importer indicator. Columns (1) and (2) are a single regression in which column (1) reports the own coefficient of each regressor whereas column (2) reports its corresponding coefficient interacted with the skill share. From column (2), the coefficient of industry input tariffs interacted with firm skill share, the key variable of interest, is negative and statistically significant, suggesting that input trade liberalization tends to increase skill premium. Sheng and Yang (2016) provide evidence that foreign firms in China attract more skill-intensive production, which in turn would raise firms' skill premium. Thus, we include the interactions of skill share with the foreign indicator and with the SOE indicator in the regression.[15] The positive sign of the coefficient of the foreign indicator ascertains the finding in Sheng

[15] By the official definition reported in the China City Statistical Yearbook (2006), SOEs include firms such as domestic SOEs (code: 110), state-owned joint venture enterprises (141), and state-owned and collective joint venture enterprises (143), but exclude state-owned limited corporations (151). In contrast, foreign firms include the following firms: foreign-invested joint-stock corporations (code: 310), foreign-invested joint venture enterprises (320), fully foreign-invested firms (330), foreign-invested limited corporations (340), Hong Kong/Macao/Taiwan joint-stock corporations (210), Hong Kong/Macao/Taiwan joint venture enterprises (220), fully Hong Kong/Macao/Taiwan-invested enterprises (230), and Hong Kong/Macao/Taiwan-invested limited corporations (240).

Table 8.3 Baseline mincer regression using data for 2004 firm average wages

	(1)	(2) × skill share	(3)	(4) × skill share
Measured unskilled wages	0.306***		0.309***	
	(13.94)		(12.62)	
Skill share	−0.963**		0.252	
	(−2.55)		(0.39)	
Industry input tariffs	−0.167***	−0.042**	−0.064***	−0.181**
	(−20.13)	(−2.00)	(−6.78)	(−2.37)
Industry input tariffs	–	–	–	0.013*
× log sales				(1.76)
Industry output tariffs	0.005*	−0.012**	0.016***	−0.013***
	(1.88)	(−1.96)	(7.40)	(−2.67)
Industry output tariffs	–	–	–	0.003
× exporter indicator				(0.62)
SOEs	−0.162	0.206	−0.028	−0.194
	(−0.91)	(0.76)	(−0.21)	(−0.94)
Foreign indicator	0.708***	1.175***	0.560***	0.490***
	(18.57)	(14.00)	(18.53)	(7.36)
Log sales	−0.088***	0.133***	−0.128***	−0.017
	(−5.55)	(4.28)	(−10.24)	(−0.28)
TFP (Olley-Pakes)	0.658***	0.453***	0.369***	0.309***
	(10.03)	(3.47)	(8.11)	(3.48)
Exporter indicator	0.080**	0.410***	0.169***	0.004
	(2.52)	(5.42)	(6.47)	(0.05)
Wage premium	0.906***	0.111***	0.955***	0.059***
	(271.6)	(22.81)	(419.9)	(16.80)
Region FE	No		Yes	
Industry FE	No		Yes	
Region × industry FE	No		Yes	
Observations	119,334		119,334	
R-squared	0.90		0.94	

Notes Robust t-values corrected for clustering at the firm level are in parentheses. *, **, and ***indicate significance at the 10, 5, and 1% level, respectively. Columns (1) and (2) are a single OLS regression in which column (2) reports the interaction with skill share for related variables. Similarly, columns (3) and (4) are a single regression with industry-region fixed effects and Yang (2016). We also include firm size (proxied by firms' log sales) and firm total factor productivity (measured by the augmented Olley-Pakes (1996) approach, as suggested by Yu 2015). Exporting firms may have their own channels affecting the skill premium. We thus interact the skill share with the exporting indicator in column (2). Consistent with most of the previous studies, we find that the skill premium is higher for larger firms, more productive firms, and exporting firms.

It is also reasonable to anticipate that firms of different sizes may respond differently to input tariffs. Therefore, we run another regression with results jointly shown in columns (3) and (4). Specifically, we include a triple interaction term among the skill share, input tariffs, and firms' log sales. Importantly, the skill share is an important predictor in itself, beyond size (log sales), and that the skill share prediction is slightly weaker at larger firms. Because the coefficient of the novel triple interaction term among input tariffs, skill share, and log sales has a different (i.e., positive) sign than that of the interaction term between input tariffs and skill share, we take a further step to evaluate their net effect at the sample mean. Overall, the net effect of input tariffs on firm average wages is still negative since $(-0.181 + 0.013 \times 9.94) \times 0.449 < 0$ given that the sample mean of log of firm sales is 9.94 whereas that of firm skilled share is 0.449 as seen from Table 8.2. Thus, the counteracting effect generated by the new triple term with log sales does not overwhelm our previous main finding.

As recognized by Cai (2010), China' s labor force generally migrates from the inland (i.e., western and middle) provinces to the costal (eastern) provinces. It is reasonable to expect that firms have different wage premiums in the different regions. We thus classify all 31 provinces into three regions: east, middle, and west. In the single regression as reported in columns (3) and (4), we also take a step further to control for region-specific fixed effects and industry-specific fixed effects to take into account local market tightness (as discussed earlier). In addition, we also include a full set of interacted industry-region dummies. With such rich sets of fixed effects controlled, the coefficient of input tariffs interacted with skill share—our main interest in the estimation—still remains negative and statistically significant.

Our main empirical specification (6) also permits a regional analysis by grouping the sample for 2004 into three regions: east, central, and west. We first split the entire national sample into 31 provinces and then repeat the Mincer regression, similar to columns (3–4) of Table 8.3, for the east region, central region and west region. Results are reported in columns (1–2), (3–4), and (5–6) of Table 8.4, respectively. In each regression, we control for the interacted province and industry fixed effects.

According to the China Regional Statistical Yearbook, the eastern region includes fifteen provinces, the central includes six provinces, and the western region includes the rest of the provinces.[16] Thus, the regional regression for the eastern region has the largest number of observations, followed by the west region, and then by the central region. In the three regressions shown in Table 8.4, the interaction terms

[16] In particular, the eastern region includes the following 15 provinces: Heilongjiang, Jilin, Liaoning, Beijing, Tianjin, Hebei, Shandong, Jiangsu, Anhui, Zhejiang, Shanghai, Fujian, Guangdong, Guangxi, and Hainan. The middle region includes the following six provinces: Inner Mongolia, Shanxi, Henan, Hubei, Hunan, and Jiangxi. Finally, the western region includes the rest of the provinces.

Table 8.4 Regional mincer regression using data for 2004 firm's regions

Firm average wages	East		Central		West	
	(1)	(2)	(3)	(4)	(5)	(6)
		× skill share		× skill share		× skill share
Measured unskilled wages	0.384***		0.388***		0.304***	
	(21.52)		(17.60)		(24.48)	
Skill share	4.907***		4.694***		9.302***	
	(3.98)		(3.88)		(6.89)	
Industry input tariffs	−0.043***	−0.641***	0.057***	−0.443***	0.064***	−1.079***
	(−7.15)	(−3.85)	(2.61)	(−3.20)	(5.61)	(−6.52)
Industry output tariffs	0.003*	0.003	−0.045***	0.025**	−0.008***	−0.005
	(1.76)	(0.48)	(−6.82)	(2.30)	(−3.67)	(−0.86)
Industry output tariffs		−0.023***		−0.012		−0.015*
× exporter indicator		(−4.42)		(−0.80)		(−1.94)
SOEs	0.250*	−0.052	−0.145	0.572**	0.294**	0.097
	(1.93)	(−0.26)	(−0.90)	(2.27)	(2.05)	(0.42)
Foreign indicator	−0.163***	0.314***	0.105	0.081	−0.076**	0.115
	(−7.81)	(6.81)	(0.75)	(0.37)	(−2.07)	(1.41)
Log sales	0.040***	−0.403***	0.123***	−0.452***	0.094***	−0.827***
	(4.30)	(−3.38)	(4.08)	(−3.91)	(5.56)	(−6.22)
TFP (Olley–Pakes)	0.184***	−0.026	0.405***	−0.223	0.487***	−0.181
	(5.57)	(−0.47)	(3.53)	(−1.39)	(7.64)	(−1.39)
Exporter indicator	−0.185***	0.223***	0.300***	−0.219	−0.146***	0.169*
	(−10.16)	(3.75)	(3.52)	(−1.02)	(−5.28)	(1.84)
Wage premium	0.977***	0.021***	0.959***	0.032***	0.981***	0.017***
	(617.54)	(8.96)	(121.08)	(2.81)	(366.17)	(3.60)
Log sales		0.063***		0.051***		0.106***
× industry input tariffs		(3.82)		(3.93)		(6.57)
Province FE	Yes		Yes		Yes	
Industry FE	Yes		Yes		Yes	
Province × industry FE	Yes		Yes		Yes	
Observations	77,742		7,851		33,741	

(continued)

Table 8.4 (continued)

Firm average wages	East		Central		West	
	(1)	(2)	(3)	(4)	(5)	(6)
		× skill share		× skill share		× skill share
R-squared	0.98		0.97		0.97	

Notes Robust t-values corrected for clustering at the firm level are in parentheses. *, **, and ***indicate significance at the 10, 5, and 1% level, respectively. Columns (1) and (2) are a single OLS regression for firms located in eastern China in which column (2) reports the interaction with skill share for related variables. Similarly, Columns (3) and (4) are a single regression for firms located in central China. Columns (5) and (6) are a single regression for firms located in western China

between industry input tariffs and skill share are all negative and highly statistically significant.[17] Thus, our main finding that reduced input tariffs in a firm' s industry are associated with a higher skill premium at firms with more skilled workforces is robust for all three regions in China.

8.3.2 *Mincer Regressions Using Matched Sample*

Tables 8.3 and 8.4 use the firm-level data set for 2004 to conduct the regressions. The advantage of using only this data set is that it contains all manufacturing firms. Yet, the data set does not contain information on firms' import status. To overcome this data challenge, we match the ASIF data set with the product-level customs data to perform similar Mincer-type regression in Table 8.5.[18]

Columns (1) and (2) in Table 8.5 are a single regression with industry-region fixed-effects in which column (1) reports the own coefficient of each regressor whereas column (2) reports the corresponding variables interacted with skill share. Different from estimates in Table 8.3, we include firms' importing status in estimates of Table 8.5 since this variable can better capture firm' s exposures to globalization. The regression shown in columns (1) and (2) includes the own variable of firms' importing indicator and its interaction with the skill share. The coefficient of industry input tariffs interacted with the skill share is negative and statistically significant, suggesting that reduced input tariffs in a firm's industry are associated with a higher skill premium at firms with more skilled workforces. In addition, the regression includes a triple interaction term among the importer indicator, skill share, and industry input tariffs. The negative, though insignificant, triple interaction term hints that importers might respond more forcefully to input trade liberalization in their wage schedule.

[17] Yet, we also see some regional disparity from Table 8.4. In particular, the own terms of industry input tariffs in each region have different signs and magnitudes.

[18] The detailed matching method and procedure are introduced in Yu (2015).

Table 8.5 Mincer regression using matched data for 2004 firm average wages

	(1)	(2)	(3)	(4)	(5)
		× skill share		× skill share	× skill share × processing indicator
Measured unskilled wages	0.210***		0.209***		
	(8.89)		(8.93)		
Skill share	0.988		1.175*		
	(1.49)		(1.76)		
Industry input tariffs	0.022	−0.069*	0.029	−0.088**	0.137***
	(0.83)	(−1.91)	(1.06)	(−2.34)	(3.77)
Industry input tariffs		−0.013		−0.017	
× Importer indicator		(−0.40)		(−0.53)	
Industry output tariffs	0.029***	−0.012	0.027***	−0.008	0.017
	(5.30)	(−0.68)	(5.05)	(−0.44)	(1.22)
Industry output tariffs		−0.015		−0.018	
× exporter indicator		(−0.91)		(−1.12)	
SOEs	−0.700	1.277	−0.714	1.304	
	(−0.84)	(1.04)	(−0.85)	(1.06)	
Foreign indicator	0.613***	0.122	0.606***	0.162	
	(10.43)	(0.85)	(10.15)	(1.12)	
Log sales	0.079***	−0.172***	0.082***	−0.180***	
	(3.13)	(−3.35)	(3.24)	(−3.49)	
TFP (Olley-Pakes)	0.041	0.673***	0.044	0.667***	
	(0.41)	(2.85)	(0.43)	(2.83)	
Exporter indicator	−0.077	0.500*	−0.083	0.570**	
	(−0.62)	(1.74)	(−0.66)	(1.96)	
Importer indicator	0.138**	0.570*	0.144**	0.596*	
	(2.21)	(1.80)	(2.29)	(1.89)	
Processing indicator			0.044	−1.698***	
			(0.73)	(−4.65)	
Wage premium	0.972***	0.049***	0.972***	0.048***	
	(221.45)	(6.76)	(221.61)	(6.62)	
Region × industry FE		Yes		Yes	

(continued)

Table 8.5 (continued)

	(1)	(2)	(3)	(4)	(5)
		× skill share		× skill share	× skill share × processing indicator
R-squared		0.88		0.93	

Notes Robust t-values corrected for clustering at the firm level are in parentheses. *, **, and ***indicate significance at the 10, 5, and 1% level, respectively. Columns (1) and (2) are a single regression with industry-region fixed effect in which column (2) reports the interaction with skill share for related variables. Similarly, Columns (3)–(5) are a single fixed-effects regression with region-industry fixed effects and additional controls. Numbers of observations in each regression are 18,820

Furthermore, import processing firms may behave differently from ordinary firms, as suggested by Dai et al. (2016). By definition, import processing firms are firms that import raw material or intermediate inputs and then, after local processing or assembly, export the value-added final goods (Feenstra and Hanson, 2005). A processing indicator is defined as one (1) if a firm has any processing imports and zero (0) otherwise. As processing imports have zero import tariffs (Yu 2015), the effect of input trade liberalization on firms' skill premium is expected to be less pronounced for an industry with many import processing firms.

We run another regression which is jointly reported in columns (3)–(5). As before, column (3) reports the own coefficients of regressors whereas column (4) shows the coefficients of their interaction with skill share. Column (5) reports the coefficient of triple interaction among input (output) tariffs, skill share, and processing indicator. Similar to our previous findings, reduced input tariffs in a firm's industry are associated with a higher skill premium at firms with more skilled workforces, because the coefficient between industry input tariffs and skill premium is negative and statistically significant. The novel finding is that the coefficient of the triple interaction term between industry input tariffs, skill share, and processing indicator is positive and statistically significant, suggesting that the effect of input trade liberalization on firms' skill premium is more pronounced for non-processing (i.e., ordinary) firms.

To see this more precisely, we can take one step further to evaluate the net effect of input trade liberalization on firm wages. As shown in the single regression of columns (3)–(5), there are three types of firms in the regression: non-importing firms, ordinary importers, and processing importers. The net effect of input tariffs on firm average wage for non-importing firms is $0.029 - 0.088 \times 0.45 < 0$ given that the sample mean of firm's skill share is 0.45 and the own coefficient of input tariffs is 0.029 whereas that of the interaction between input tariffs and skill share is -0.088. Similarly, the net effect for ordinary importers (i.e., importer indicator equals one) is $0.029 - (0.088 + 0.017) \times 0.45 < 0$ given that the coefficient of the triple interaction term among input tariffs, skill share and import indicator is -0.017. These two results are consistent with our previous main finding that a fall in industry input tariffs is associated with a higher skill premium at firms with more skilled workforce. By contrast, the net effect of input tariffs on firm wages for processing firms is positive since it equals $0.029 + (0.137 - 0.088 - 0.017) \times 0.45 > 0$ given that the coefficient of the triple interaction term among input tariffs, skill share and processing indicator is 0.137. The finding that the sample-mean effect for processing exporters is overturned is also intuitive. Processing imports in China enjoy a special treatment of free duty (see, e.g., Yu 2015). Thus, further import tariff reductions on processing input encourage processing exporters to switch to ordinary exporters over time, as found by Brandt and Morrow (2017), which in turn lower the employment demand for processing exporters. Accordingly, the average wages for processing firms fall, as shown in the regression of Columns (3)–(5) of Table 8.5.

8.3.3 Estimates Using Panel Data

So far, we have used data only for 2004 to estimate the Mincer regressions, because data on firms' skill shares are only available for census year of 2004. The empirical specifications are useful for understanding cross-section firms' skill premium. To gain a better understanding on the variation of within-firm skill premium in response to input trade liberalization, in this section we make an effort to use the panel data for the period of 2000–06.

Since data on the share of skilled labor are available only for year 2004, to compute a proxy for the skilled labor share for all other years from 2000 to 2006, we multiply the skilled labor share in 2004 by the provincial skilled labor share in all the other years using 2004 as the base year. In addition, industry input and output tariffs are now calculated using the Input–Output Table for 1997 to obtain the corresponding weights because the information in the Input–Output Table of 1997 reflects the initial conditions prior to China's trade liberalization in 2001 (Bartik 1991).

As data on the share of skilled labor are unavailable for years other than 2004, we compute a proxy for the skilled labor share (θ_{it}) for all other years from 2000 to 2006 by multiplying the skilled labor share in 2004 with the provincial skilled labor share in all other years using 2004 as the base year. Equally important, industry input and output tariffs are now calculated using the Input–Output Table for 1997 to calculate the corresponding weights, as the weights in 1997 reflect the initial conditions prior to China's trade liberalization in 2001, as suggested by Bartik (1991).

With cross-section data in 2004, Table 8.3 has already demonstrated that the results for empirical specification with both own coefficients and coefficients interacted with skill share for each regressor are very close to those without own coefficients. Since the latter specification follows Mincer regressions more closely, in the panel-data analysis we only report those empirical results of estimation with the coefficients interacted with firms' skill share.

Column (1) of Table 8.6 reports the Mincer regression results by using the 1997 Input–Output Table and controlling year-specific fixed-effects, industry-specific fixed effects, and region-specific fixed effects, respectively. The estimation results are very close to their counterparts in the last two columns of Table 8.3. The coefficient

Table 8.6 Mincer regression using the 1997 IO table (2000–06)

Variable:	Current period		One-lag
Regressand: firm average wages	(1)	(2)	(3)
Measured unskilled wages	0.203***	0.285***	0.255***
	(22.86)	(31.97)	(23.78)
Skill share	0.960*	0.935*	−0.670
	(1.88)	(1.88)	(−1.08)
Skill share × industry input tariffs	−0.454***	−0.244***	−0.153**
	(−8.10)	(−4.43)	(−2.13)
Skill share × industry output tariffs	0.015***	0.012***	0.023***
	(3.82)	(2.94)	(4.54)
Skill share × industry output tariffs	−0.000	0.037***	0.026***
× (One-lag) exporter indicator	(−0.03)	(5.40)	(3.11)
Skill share × SOEs	0.394***	0.433***	0.712***
	(3.79)	(4.48)	(5.85)
Skill share × foreign indicator	2.329***	1.406***	1.293***
	(42.10)	(27.00)	(20.47)
Skill share × log sales	−0.188***	−0.223***	−0.184***
	(−3.79)	(−4.69)	(−3.11)
Skill share × (One-lag) Olley-Pakes TFP	1.876***	1.198***	0.921***
	(27.01)	(18.53)	(11.31)
Skill share × (One-lag) exporter indicator	0.643***	−0.103	0.100
	(6.39)	(−1.09)	(0.89)
Skill share × wage premium	1.288***	1.299***	1.372***
	(574.20)	(623.74)	(552.14)
Skill share × industry input tariffs	0.034***	0.026***	0.020***
× (One-lag) log sales	(6.26)	(4.90)	(2.94)
Year fixed effects	Yes	Yes	Yes
Firm fixed effects	Yes	Yes	Yes
Region fixed effects	Yes	Yes	Yes
Industry fixed effects	Yes	Yes	Yes
Region × industry fixed effects	No	Yes	Yes
Observations	507,084	507,084	345,543
R-squared	0.75	0.78	0.77

Notes Robust t-values corrected for clustering at the firm level are in parentheses. *, **, and ***indicate significance at the 10, 5, and 1% level, respectively. Estimates in column (3) report the results with one-lag variables shown in parentheses of industry input tariffs interacted with firms' skill share is negative and statistically significant, indicating that input trade liberalization increases firm' s skill premium over time. Similar to the estimation results shown in column (6) of Table 8.3, the coefficient of output tariffs interacted with the skill share is positive, for the same reason discussed earlier. Estimates in column (2) take a step further to run a more parsimonious regression by controlling the interacted industry and region fixed effects. All regressors have very similar coefficients to their counterparts in column (1).

Finally, it is possible that firms may take more time to respond to tariff reductions in their wage schedule. In our last enrichment, column (3) of Table 8.6 instead uses firms' past (i.e., one-year lag) export status and past performance (sing log sales or total factor productivity as a proxy). The estimation results for all the variables in column (3), with some variables in one-lag period are close to their counterparts in column (2) when all variables are in the current period. In all cases, the coefficients of industry input tariffs are found to be negative and statistically significant for all the regressions.

8.3.4 Endogeneity Issues

In the previous estimations, input trade liberalization was considered as exogenous. However, tariff formation could be endogenous in the sense that skill premium could have a reverse effect on tariff changes. With widening skill premium, unskilled workers could blame free trade policies and form labor unions to lobby the government for temporary trade protection (Bagwell and Staiger 1990, 1999; Bown and Crowley 2013). Although this happens in developed countries like the United States (Goldberg and Maggi 1999) and in some developing countries like Turkey (Gawande and Bandyopadhyay 2000), it is less likely to happen in China because labor unions in China are symbolic organizations. In addition, if these types of political factors are time invariant, they should have been accounted and statistically controlled for by the fixed-effect panel estimates in Table 8.6 (Goldberg and Pavcnik, 2007). However, if they are time variant, the estimations of the related Mincer regressions in Table 8.6 would be biased.

Moreover, if the residual in Eq. (8.6), ε_{it}^{u}, is related to the firm's measured skill share $\left(\hat{\theta}_{it}\right)$, the estimated coefficients will be biased. As a robustness check, below we use the instrumental variables (IV) approach to address the potential endogeneity issues. If the negative reverse causality is a main source of endogeneity issue, we should expect that the key estimated coefficient for the interaction term between input tariffs and skill share under the two-stage least square (2SLS) approach should be greater than its counterpart under the OLS approach.

It is challenging to find an ideal instrument for tariffs. Inspired by Trefler (2004) and Amiti and Davis (2011), we use the one-year lag of industry input tariffs as the instrument of the first difference in industrial input tariffs. The economic rationale is that lagged input tariffs are less likely to influence the time difference of input tariffs (Trefler, 2004). In particular, we consider the following first-difference Mincer regression:

$$\begin{aligned}\Delta \ln(\overline{w_{it}}) = {} & \gamma_c + \gamma_u \Delta \ln(w_{it}^u) + \gamma_0 \Delta \hat{\theta}_{it} + \gamma_1 \Delta\left(\hat{\theta}_{it} IT_{jt}\right) + \gamma_2 \Delta\left(\hat{\theta}_{it} IT_{jt}\right) IM_{it} \\ & + \gamma_3 \Delta\left(\hat{\theta}_{it} PT_{jt}\right) + \gamma_4 \Delta\left(\hat{\theta}_{it} PT_{jt}\right) FX_{it} + \gamma_5 \Delta\left(\hat{\theta}_{it} FX_{it}\right) \\ & + \gamma_6 \Delta\left(\hat{\theta}_{it} IM_{it}\right) + \gamma_7 \Delta IT_{jt} + \gamma_8 \Delta PT_{jt} + \gamma_9 \Delta IM_{it} + \gamma_{10} \Delta FX_{it} \\ & + \gamma \Delta \mathrm{X}_{it} + \delta_i + \delta_{jr} + \delta_t + \varepsilon_{it} \end{aligned} \tag{8.8}$$

Accordingly, the regressand and all regressors in Table 8.7 are in the first difference. Columns (1) and (2) are a single OLS regression in which IV reports the coefficients of the own one-lag industry input tariffs and its interaction with firm skill share using the first difference in industry input tariffs and its interaction with firm skill share as the regressands. Once again, the interaction term between skill share and industry input tariffs is negative and statistically significant, which is consistent with our previous findings. Finally, to show that our 2SLS estimation results are robust to the inclusion of the own terms of the regressors, we run another single estimation by abstracting away the own coefficients of related regressors, which is jointly reported in columns (3) and (4). Similarly, the regression in columns (3) and (4) use the one-lag industry input tariffs interacted with firm skill share as the instrument whereas the first difference in industry input tariffs interacted with firm skill share is served as the regressand. Again, the coefficient of industry input tariffs, the variable of our key interests, is negative and statistically significant. Thus, the 2SLS estimation results are consistent with our previous OLS estimates.

We now perform related statistical tests to check the validity of the instrument. The bottom module in Table 8.7 provides the first-stage estimates for all specifications. The coefficients of the instruments are negative and highly statistically significant, suggesting that it is more challenging to remove tariff barriers in industries with high initial tariffs. In addition, several tests were performed to verify the quality of the instruments. First, we use the Anderson canon correlated LM χ^2 statistic to check whether the excluded instruments are correlated with the endogenous regressors. As shown in the upper module in Table 8.7, the null hypothesis that the model is under-identified is rejected at the 1% significance level. Second, the Cragg-Donald Wald F-statistic provides strong evidence for rejecting the null hypothesis that the first stage is weakly identified at a high significance level. The tests suggest that the instrument is valid and the specifications are well justified.

Table 8.7 2SLS estimates using panel data (2000–06)

First difference in firm average wages	(1)	(2)	(3)	(4)
First difference in		× skill share		× skill share
Industry input tariffs	0.210***	−0.546***		−0.145***
	(6.71)	(−9.28)		(−2.93)
Measured unskilled wages	0.114***		0.115***	
	(4.28)		(4.34)	
Skill share	−5.251***		−29.285***	
	(−2.66)		(−16.15)	
Industry output tariffs	−0.012***	0.025***		0.004
	(−3.02)	(2.92)		(0.75)
Industry output tariffs		−0.001		−0.001
× Exporter indicator		(−0.13)	(−0.15)	
SOEs	−0.761*	1.430*	0.272	
	(−1.74)	(1.96)	(0.91)	
Foreign indicator	0.744**	−1.322**	−0.148	
	(2.42)	(−2.32)	(−0.49)	
Log sales	1.818***	−0.125	2.856***	
	(29.15)	(−1.04)	(44.71)	
TFP (Olley−Pakes)	0.579***	0.072	0.959***	
	(6.56)	(0.45)	(11.40)	
Exporter indicator	−0.136	0.182	−0.065	
	(−1.50)	(0.91)	(−0.48)	
Anderson canon. corr. LM statistic	43.21†		86.40†	
Cragg-Donald Wald F statistic	1.4e + 05†		2.3e + 05†	
Year fixed effects	Yes		Yes	
Region × industry FE	Yes		Yes	
Observations	326,211		326,211	
First-stage regressions				
IV: one-lag industry input tariffs	−0.577***	−0.112***	–	−0.0128***

(continued)

8.3.5 *On the Possible Mechanism*[19]

The objective of this section is to discuss a possible mechanism to enrich our understanding of the main empirical finding that input trade liberalization leads to an increase in firms' skill premium and provide some evidence for our theoretical conjecture. Inspired by the literature on "fair wages" (e.g. Egger and Kreickemeier 2012),

[19] We thank a referee for providing great comments and suggestions on this sub-section.

Table 8.7 (continued)

First difference in firm average wages	(1)	(2)	(3)	(4)
First difference in		× skill share		× skill share
	(−864.1)	(−472.7)		(−483.8)

Notes Robust t-values corrected for clustering at the firm level are in parentheses. *, **, and ***indicate significance at the 10, 5, and 1% level, respectively. † indicates significance of the p-value at the 1% level

The regressand and all regressors are in the first difference. Columns (1) and (2) are a single OLS regression in which IV reports the coefficients of the own one-lag industry input tariffs and its interaction with firm skill share using the first difference in industry input tariffs and its interaction with firm skill share as the regressands. Similarly, columns (3) and (4) are another single regression in which IV reports the coefficients of the one-lag industry input tariffs interacted with firm skill share using the first difference in industry input tariffs interacted with firm skill share as the regressand

a possible mechanism to interpret our empirical findings is that skilled workers have greater bargaining power with their employers than unskilled workers.[20] As a result, the incomes of skilled workers are more closely linked to firms' profits but the incomes of unskilled workers are more in line with those of other firms in the same industry. Thus, a fall in input tariffs increases the firm's economic profit, which in turn raises firms' skill premium because the skilled labor commands a larger proportion of the incremental surplus than the unskilled labor.[21]

To check whether such a conjecture is supported by the data, we replace the firm's average wage, the regressand in our Mincer-type regressions, with the firm's value-added per worker. Value-added per worker is one possible measure of labor productivity or, more generally, a proxy to the firm's surplus per worker. If input tariff reductions raise the firm's skill premium, we should observe that input trade liberalization also increases the firm's value-added per worker because value-added per worker can be treated as another side of the same coin of firms' skill premium. It is the core of our paper's main hypothesis that intermediate input tariffs move value-added per worker in essentially the same way as they move the average wage (per worker), which is directly testable.

Specifically, we replace log of firm average wage with log of firm value-added per worker in the empirical specification in Eq. (8.7). To ensure that our estimation results are not contaminated by using the time-series proxy of the firm' s skill share, we

[20] We are aware that our findings are also consistent with both the bargaining model of Helpman et al. (2010) and the efficiency wage model of Amiti and Davis (2011). On the broad interpretation of our findings, higher value added means firms generate more surplus to share. The surplus may be skill group specific (see appendix to Helpman et al. 2010) or general. In the former case, workers of different skill might have the same bargaining power but generate more additional surplus. In the latter case, more skilled workers might command stronger bargaining power. Note, all these models do not allow for bargaining power to change with trade liberalization because they have no unions but use individual wage determination instead. This may be quite adequate for China, where labor unions are merely symbolic.

[21] We provide a therotical framework for such a mechanism in our working paper (see Chen et al., 2016).

focus on cross-section data in 2004 and report the estimation results in Table 8.8. The estimates in column (1) of Table 8.8 are obtained by using the ASIF-customs matched data (as used in Table 8.5). After controlling a rich set of interacted region and industry fixed effects, the regression results show that the key coefficient of industry input tariffs interacted with skill share is negative and statistically significant, suggesting that input trade liberalization increases the firm' s value-added per worker.

The advantage of using ASIF-customs matched data is to allow us to govern firms' importing status, but it is at the expense of reducing the number of observations since the matching between the two datasets (i.e., ASIF dataset and customs dataset) is imperfect (see more discussions in Yu 2015). To see whether our findings are robust to different regression samples, column (3) runs the same regression as column (1) but instead uses the ASIF data set only. The key variable of interest, the interaction term between input tariffs and skill share, still exhibits a negative sign and statistically significant, indicating that our findings are robust by using different data sample.

Finally, we also replace the regressand of log average value-added with that of log per-worker profit and run the regressions using ASIF-customs matched data in column (2) and sole ASIF data in column (4), respectively.[22] Our key finding is robust in all specifications: When controlling for product-market tariffs in a firm' s industry, reduced input tariffs in a firm' s industry are associated with higher surplus per worker or overall profits at firms with skill intensive production (skilled workforces).

Although our interpretation is consistent with the evidence, it does not rule out other possible channels or mechanisms. There are other possible interpretations. For instance, an additionally employed skilled worker may generate a larger surplus, all else equal, and yet might receive a smaller share than unskilled workers (after bargaining). The large incremental surplus can be more than proportionally larger than the bargaining share difference to unskilled workers. Thus, skilled workers may seem to capture a larger proportion of the incremental surplus, but really they simply generate more surplus. However, we cannot validate this argument because it requires that the data contain variables that would directly measure the bargaining weight by skill groups, or related quantities.

8.4 Conclusion Remarks

China has experienced dramatic tariff reductions since its accession to the WTO in 2001. On the other hand, wage inequality between skilled and unskilled labor of Chinese manufacturing firms has also increased significantly. To our knowledge, so far there is no study using micro-level evidence to explore the link between the two because there are no firm-level data on wages for skilled and unskilled labor. In this paper, we have developed a Mincer-type econometric approach to estimate firms' skill premium based on imperfect Chinese firm-level data on wage information. As

[22] The number of observations in columns (2) and (4) is smaller than their counterpart in columns (1) and (3), because some firms with negative profits are dropped out.

Table 8.8 Robustness checks with value-added and profit data

Coverage	2004 matched data		2004 data	
Regressand	Value-added per worker	Prot per worker	Value-added per worker	Prot per worker
	(1)	(2)	(3)	(4)
Measured unskilled wages	0.012*	0.070***	−0.010***	0.028***
	(1.72)	(4.86)	(-3.69)	(7.93)
Skill share	−2.561***	−0.422	−5.329***	−4.614***
	(−5.34)	(−1.58)	(−60.12)	(−54.71)
Skill share × industry input tariffs	−0.022**	−0.061***	−0.007*	−0.031***
	(−2.01)	(−4.48)	(−1.94)	(−5.97)
Skill share × industry input tariffs	0.010***	0.030***		
× Importer indicator	(2.81)	(5.99)		
Skill share × industry output tariffs	0.014***	0.009	0.002	0.000
	(3.95)	(1.50)	(1.47)	(0.10)
Skill share × industry output tariffs	−0.015***	−0.017***	−0.001	−0.007***
× Exporter indicator	(−4.85)	(−3.13)	(−0.79)	(−2.89)
Skill share × SOEs	−0.384***	−0.794***	−0.578***	−0.952***
	(−5.21)	(−5.90)	(−21.11)	(−22.87)
Skill share × foreign indicator	0.122***	0.297***	0.179***	0.517***
	(3.94)	(7.00)	(13.09)	(25.09)
Skill share × TFP (Olley-Pakes)	2.688***	1.139***	2.139***	0.777***
	(7.23)	(5.89)	(18.77)	(14.50)
Skill share × wage premium	0.025***	0.035***	0.016***	0.024***
	(12.23)	(16.05)	(24.63)	(27.30)
Region fixed effects	Yes	Yes	Yes	Yes
Industry fixed effects	Yes	Yes	Yes	Yes
Region × industry fixed effects	Yes	Yes	Yes	Yes
Observations	17,709	14,810	111,070	97,772
R-squared	0.40	0.27	0.36	0.22

Notes Robust t-values corrected for clustering at the firm level are in parentheses. *, **, and ***indicate significance at the 10, 5, and 1% level, respectively in other ambitious attempts to investigate important issues with imperfect data, some compromises were made to conduct our estimations. Nevertheless, the finding that a fall in input tariffs is associated with an increase in the skill premium at firms with more skilled workforces is robust under different econometric specifications.

Such a finding is consistent with the idea that firms share the additional surplus generated by input trade liberalization mostly with skilled workers. Potential reasons for the observed increase in relative skill earnings at more skill intensive firms include technological and institutional factors: skills might be complementary with newly accessible foreign inputs on the technological side, or skilled workers might command stronger bargaining power over additional surplus generated under input trade liberalization.

Our findings also have rich policy implications. Trade liberalization can increase skill demand in China by prompting firms to use intermediate inputs that raise firms' surplus. This happens either because less expensive or newly accessible inputs are complementary to skill or because skilled workers have a stronger bargaining power in their negotiation over the newly generated surplus. In any case, input trade liberalization is an appropriate policy instrument to foster firms' surplus.

Appendix 8.1: Estimates Using Alternative Measured Unskilled Wages (Online Only, Not for Publication)

In this subsection we will check whether our main results are robust to an alternative measure of unskilled wages. Specifically, we will check whether the new measure matches the aggregate data reported by the outside data source. If so, we can use the new measure to run empirical specification (6).

From our firm-level data set, we first redefine unskilled wages as the 25th percentile of firms' wage bills by province—reported in column (2) in Table 8.A1. Once we have this unskilled wage variable, we follow the same procedure as in Sect. 8.2.2.2 (i.e.$s_i \equiv \left(w_i^s - w_i^u\right)/w_i^u$) and obtain and skill premium—reported in columns (1) and (3), respectively.

To compare with other publicly available aggregate data sets, we use rural wages from China' s Statistical Yearbook (2004) as a proxy for unskilled wages—reported in column (5) in Table 8.A1. We use the simple average of wages in the computer service, finance, scientific research, and education sectors by province from China' s Statistical Yearbook (2004) as a proxy for skilled wages—reported in column (4), and then calculate the corresponding skill premium—reported in column (6) in Table 8.A1.

Table 8.A1 Wages data comparisons in 2004

Data source	ASIF data in 2004			External data in 2004		
Average wages by skill group	Skilled	Unskilled	Premium	Skilled	Unskilled	Premium
Province	(1)	(2)	(3)	(4)	(5)	(6)
Anhui	17.728	6.323	1.80	16.612	6.758	1.46
Beijing	34.667	10.370	2.34	53.019	14.677	2.61
Chongqing	18.105	7.362	1.46	21.981	9.871	1.23
Fujian	25.190	8.166	2.08	26.482	9.027	1.93
Gansu	14.205	6.000	1.37	15.094	9.310	0.62
Guangdong	25.044	8.509	1.94	36.138	9.952	2.63
Guangxi	16.420	6.132	1.68	19.716	7.661	1.57
Guizhou	18.875	6.538	1.89	16.300	9.665	0.69
Hainan	17.251	6.651	1.59	23.251	6.206	2.75
Hebei	16.121	6.000	1.69	18.233	5.367	2.40
Heilongjiang	14.378	6.120	1.35	21.129	5.872	2.60
Henan	12.364	5.590	1.21	16.228	6.886	1.36
Hubei	14.734	6.295	1.34	16.770	5.600	1.99
Hunan	16.077	7.016	1.29	19.597	6.961	1.82
InnerMongolia	18.282	7.500	1.44	17.316	7.677	1.26
Jiangsu	18.868	8.889	1.12	28.246	8.059	2.50
Jiangxi	13.900	6.032	1.30	16.008	6.291	1.54
Jilin	15.190	6.000	1.53	17.901	5.790	2.09
Liaoning	20.344	6.571	2.10	24.101	5.645	3.27
Ningxia	15.520	6.914	1.24	20.963	8.500	1.47
Qinghai	20.499	7.056	1.91	23.771	12.324	0.93
Shaanxi	14.910	6.298	1.37	20.037	8.783	1.28
Shandong	15.251	6.250	1.44	21.874	9.840	1.22
Shanghai	35.366	11.145	2.17	42.622	22.057	0.93
Shanxi	16.368	6.368	1.57	17.255	8.691	0.99
Sichuan	15.533	6.717	1.31	21.943	9.401	1.33
Tianjin	34.902	8.857	2.94	31.357	15.514	1.02
Tibet	30.107	10.053	1.99	36.299	22.438	0.62
Xinjiang	18.761	8.889	1.11	20.657	9.300	1.22
Yunnan	21.168	7.788	1.72	18.364	10.183	0.80
Zhejiang	23.552	9.575	1.46	38.695	21.149	0.83
Provincial Average	19.667	7.354	1.63	23.805	9.853	1.58

Notes The low-skilled wages in cloumn (1) are defined as the 25% percentile of firm wages by province whereas the high-skilled wages are calculated according to Eq. (8.1). The interpretations on external data see the Appendix

Comparing column (3) with column (6), we find that the measures of skill premium from our firm-level data and the public aggregate data are very close. In particular, the provincial average skill premium is 1.63 from our firm-level data, which is close to 1.58 from the public aggregate data (see the last row of Table 8.A1).

Since the new measure broadly matches the aggregate data reported by the outside data source, we can run empirical specification (6) with the new measured unskilled wages, using the firm-customs matched data for 2004. Since our new measured unskilled wages do not vary by industry, we only control for 2-digit industry fixed effects in all the regressions. As reported in Table 8.A2, the coefficients for all the variables are very close to their counterparts in Table 8.3. In particular, the coefficients of own industry input tariffs and its interaction with the importer indicator are negative and statistically significant, suggesting that.

Table 8.A2 Estimates using matched data and alternative measured unskilled wages (2004)

Firm average wages	(1)	(2)	(3)
Alternative measured unskilled wages	0.008	0.006	0.007
	(0.53)	(0.38)	(0.57)
Skill share industry input tariffs	−0.117***	−0.105***	−0.120***
	(−3.52)	(−3.15)	(−3.50)
Skill share × industry input tariffs	−0.118**	−0.114**	−0.100**
× Importer indicator	(−2.41)	(−2.33)	(−2.05)
Skill share × industry output tariffs	0.032	0.027	0.031**
	(1.35)	(1.15)	(2.20)
Skill share × industry output tariffs	−0.047**	−0.042*	−0.047***
× Exporter indicator	(−1.98)	(−1.74)	(−3.20)
Skill share × SOEs	1.506***	1.498***	1.522***
	(3.56)	(3.55)	(3.81)
Skill share × foreign indicator	1.031***	1.134***	1.003***
	(8.04)	(8.70)	(8.43)
Skill share × log employment	−0.064	−0.075	−0.061**
	(−1.26)	(−1.46)	(−2.39)
Skill share × TFP (Olley-Pakes)	0.969***	0.947***	0.973***
	(4.34)	(4.27)	(3.79)
Skill share × exporter indicator	1.005***	1.052***	1.015***
	(3.37)	(3.53)	(5.03)
Skill share	1.281***	1.279***	1.282***
× Wage premium	(97.77)	(97.30)	(156.18)
Skill share × importer indicator	−0.019	−0.104	−0.186
	(−0.04)	(−0.22)	(−0.42)
Skill share × processing indicator		−0.932***	
		(−5.39)	
Industry fixed effects	Yes	Yes	Yes
Region fixed effects	Yes	Yes	Yes
Province fixed effects	No	No	Yes
Observations	18,820	18,820	18,820
R-squared	0.80	0.80	0.80

Notes Robust t-values corrected for clustering at the firm level in parentheses. *, **(***)indicates significance at the 10,5 and 1% level, respectively. The alternative measured unskilled wages are constructed by the 25 percentile of firm's wage bills by province. Columns (1) and (2) control for region fixed effects. Finally, column (3) controls for province fixed effects. Two-digit industry level fixed effects are included in all specifications

Chapter 9
Input Trade Liberalization and Import Switching: Evidence from Chinese Firms

This paper investigates how input liberalization affects firm import behaviour. By using comprehensive production and trade data of Chinese firms, we show that import sources of Chinese firms switch from developing countries to developed countries as input tariffs fall in China. This is evident for both import value and import scope. The observation still exists after we exclude the possible influence of reducing processing trade. We further demonstrate that the mechanism can be attributed to quality upgrading and innovation led by input cost reductions. We also carefully handle the possible endogeneity problem and the findings are robust and significant to different empirical methodologies and measurement.

9.1 Introduction

China has experienced remarkable trade opening up since it entered WTO early this century. Its simple average tariff dropped from 15.3 to 7.5% in 2018 since China entered WTO during the last two decades. Trade liberalization brought China huge changes in both foreign and domestic markets, one of the most prominent progress is the rising of the quality and value added imbedded in export and import. China's export has been increased rapidly and received rich studies by literature, while import, which takes off later than export, is going to be the next enhancement among China's opening up strategies. China is the second largest importing country, and its import has increased by more than four times by the year 2016 since 2000. Chinese government has launched several policies and activities in further promotion of import, including the first China International Import Exposition and further reducing simple average tariff to 7.5% since late 2018 especially on consumption goods.[1]

[1] According to the executive meeting of the State Council on September 26 chaired by Premier Li Keqiang of the State Council.

M. Yu, *China's Miracle in Foreign Trade*, Studies in Modern Chinese Economy,
https://doi.org/10.1007/978-981-16-6030-6_9

Chinese firms adjust strategies in response to the more liberalized circumstances too. Firms are observed to be more active in both import and export, invest more in R&D, and their import and export decisions are also changing. For example, Tian and Yu (2015) finds that firm increases export intensity (i.e., the ratio of export to domestic sales) as a response of input liberalization.

Among those changes the change of import sources are rarely studied though it may have important impact on the map of world international trade. Firms which used to import large proportion of input from developing countries are now switching to import from developed countries. This happens not only because of the decline of processing trade in China, but also in need of firm innovation and product upgrading. It has been documented by a mass of studies that input tariff reduction encourages import scope and import quality and lowers import prices which further drives innovation and leads to productivity and welfare gain. But the link behind this process is complicated and controversial. We would like to shed some little light on the first step of firm reaction as input tariff reduces, that is, how firm adjusts import sources and import quality.

In this paper, we show the fact of import sources switching and also the importance of second channel. In particular, by using a matched data of a comprehensive transaction level trade data and firm production data, we generate a firm level input tariff index following Yu (2015), and we further distinguish the tariff imposed on developing import sources. We find the reduction of tariff on developing sources, rather than promotes import from developing countries, but enhances the shift of import towards developed countries, suggesting a strong cost saving effect of input trade liberalization. We further investigate the heterogeneous impact on firms with different productivity, and we show that less productive firms are more largely influenced to switch import sources than more productive firms. This impact is also true for firms in high technology industries and engaged in intensive innovation. To figure out the driving force of the switching, we examine the impact for different types of importers, and find that most switching happened to new importers. This suggest that more domestic firms are stimulated to start importing high quality inputs from developed countries to take place with domestic inputs as tariffs reduce.

An important alternative explanation for switching might be the decline of processing trade starting since 2005 in China. As Brandt and Morrow (2016) argued, it can to some extent be attributed to the reduction of input tariff which reduces the opportunity cost of doing ordinary trade. This is unlikely to happen in our paper given our sample ends in 2006 just the starting year of processing decline. We also compare the capital intensive and labour intensive industries, and processing firms and capital goods intensive importers to further exclude it. We also use the difference of tariff as an instrument variable to control for the endogeneity in the first difference regressions following Trefler (2004). The switching does not only happen in intensive margin, but also on import scope. We show the input tariff reduction leads to more import scope from developed countries, which is robust to different measures of import variety and different types of firms.

To verify the mechanism of quality upgrading, we first generate the quality measure following Khandelwal (2010) which well handles the impact on market price of idiosyncratic demand shock. We also take a further step to measure quality function separately for ordinary firms and processing firms. The impact shows that both firm profit and relative import quality from developed origins go up as input tariff reduces, suggesting firms import higher quality goods from developed countries outpacing that from developing countries.

This paper is linked with emerging literatures on imported intermediate input, innovation and trade liberalization. First, it is well documented by the literature that imported intermediate inputs have strong impact on various dimensions of firm performances, including productivity (Amiti and Konings 2007; Topalova and Khandelwal 2011; Yu 2015; Choi and Hahn 2013; Kasahara and Rodrigue 2008), export (Bas and Strauss-Kahn 2014; Kasahara and Lapham 2013; Navas et al. 2013), product scope (Goldberg et al. 2010), quality (Fan et al. 2014), and the affecting the outcome in downstream market, like pricing and exchange rate path- through (Bernini and Tomasi 2014). Among above effects the improvement of productivity is particularly enormous. For example, input trade liberalization is found to be a strongest impellent of productivity growth by a wide range of studies. Amiti and Konings (2007) and Topalova and Khandelwal (2011) show that input trade liberalization contributes two to ten times to productivity growth as output liberalization. Kasahara and Rodrigue (2008) find productivity gain of Chilean firms that import intermediate goods. Yu (2015) confirmed this by using Chinese data after considering the particularity of processing trade. Input liberalization boosts firm productivity from channels including enhancing input quality, augmenting competition, increasing input varieties.

These findings stimulate research on the mechanisms how imported intermediate input boosts productivity. Large research find that the productivity and welfare gain can be explained by the increase of firm innovation, quality upgrading and invention of new product encouraged by increasing imported intermediate imports, especially new imported varieties (Feenstra 1994; Broda and Weinstein 2006; Arkolakis et al. 2008; Klenow and Rodriguez-Clare 1997). Such mechanism may also act dynamically in the long run through further expansion of domestic input scope led by more imported varieties. For example, Halpern et al. (2011) find that increased variety of intermediates genetates productivity gain among Hungarian firms. Goldberg et al. (2009, 2010) find that firms which are exposed to stronger input tariff reduction are more likely to introduce new product and invest in R&D because of the newly available imported input, and 31% of the product expansion by firms could be attributed to the decline of input tariffs.

New imported input may promote innovation and productivity in several ways.

The standard argument is that production technology is loving of variety and the increase of input varieties reduces cost (Kasahara and Lapham 2013; Gopinath and Neiman 2014) Based on this assumption, Feenstra (1994) develops a measure of the welfare gain from more input varieties. Broda and Weinstein (2004, 2006a) show that the raising imported varieties caused by input trade liberalization reduces import prices which in turn generates welfare gain, by using 20 countries data across over 20 years. Other literature highlight the spillover effect of the advanced technology and higher quality embedded in new imported inputs. Coe and Helpman (1995) and Keller

(2002) verify the spillover effect empirically by using country-level data. Murat et al. (2015) illustrates the spillover effect theoretically. Our paper tries to enrich the second channel through showing the resource changes and quality improvement of imported intermediate input. Particularly, we find that import switches from developing countries to developed countries as input tariff reduces and that effect is most pronounced for new importers, suggesting a higher probability of spillover from the increase of high quality imported inputs.

Studies on how input cost reduction affect firm import, though drawing less attention as the research on output and export, show more direct and closer evidence on firm adjustment regarding innovation and productivity. The change of import is also the beginning of the change of all follow-up firm behaviours, and how firm reacts in terms of import is critical to the understand the channel behind. Bas and Strauss-Kahn (2015) finds a robust and significant increase in import and export prices among Chinese firms that experienced input tariff reduction, and the result is specifically significant for firms sourcing import from and also selling output to developed countries. Our paper, from the perspective of how import origin changes, highlights the increasing use of high quality inputs imported from developed countries as a major approach that firms exploit input tariff reduction to upgrade quality. And in the meanwhile, we suggest that trade distribution might be reshaped as a consequence.

Last but not the least, this paper also fits the literature on quality upgrading and firm innovation in China. Liu and Qiu (2016) argues that input trade liberalization hampers firm R&D in China, while Tian and Yu (2015) finds the opposite effect. Lim et al. (2018) examine firm innovation in China and find that, overall, Chinese firms intensify their innovation once they are exposure to stronger competition and face larger market size. Feng et al. (2016) demonstrates that product upgrading in imported inputs helped Chinese firms to increase in export markets. They estimate the benefit of increased use of imported input on firm export, and find that firms benefit most when the intermediate inputs are purchased from the higher-income countries in facilitating exports to the presumably more-demanding developed markets. Different from the above papers, our work studies the resulting changes on China's import structure which is important under China's all around opening-up strategy in the future decade.

The finding of this paper is also important to understand the change of global trade flow associated with liberalization. As the second largest importing country, China's opening up not only affects China's trade, but also the distribution of trade flow across regions among the world. If trade liberalization in China boosts more trade between China and developed countries disproportionally, more unparalleled changes between developed and developing countries in such as labour markets and welfare can be expected to happen as a consequence.

The rest of the paper is organized as follow. Section 9.2 discusses details data and data sources. Section 9.3 presents empirical findings. Section 9.4 concludes.

9.2 Data and Measurement

The data used in the paper is a combination of two disaggregated data sets, the annual survey data of manufacturing firms in China and the customs transaction trade data. The two data sets provide rich information on firm production and trade. We take the year from 2000 to 2006, during which Chinese input tariff drops most significantly. Below we present a brief introduction to the data.

a. *Chinese firm-level production data*

The annual survey data of manufacturing firms is collected and maintained by China's National Bureau of Statistics (NBS), including all state-owned enterprises (SOEs) and non-SOEs whose annual sales exceed RMB5 million ($830,000). The data covers complete information on three major accounting statements (i.e. balance sheet, profit and loss account, and cash flow statement), from which we are acquainted with firm output, profit, R&D, and input on labor, capital and intermediate input and so on.

We start with applying stringent filters to clean the data, especially to exclude the noisy and misleading samples due to misreporting by some firms. We follow the criteria in Feenstra et al. (2014) to omit outliers. First, we drop observations where key financial variables are missed (such as total assets, net value of fixed assets, sales, and gross value of the firm's output productivity). Second, firms with fewer than eight workers are also removed since they fall below the legal regime, as mentioned in Brandt et al. (2012).

We next screen the data according to the basic rules of the Generally Accepted Accounting Principles (GAAP). Observations are excluded if any of the following exists: (1) liquid assets is larger than total assets; (2) total fixed assets is larger than total assets; (3) the net value of fixed assets is larger than total assets; (4) the firm's identification number is missing; or (5) established time is invalid (e.g. the opening month is later than December or earlier than January). The data are reduced by about 50 per cent in each year to guarantee the quality under the strict cleaning.

We exclude trading companies from the sample in all estimations to ensure the preciseness of the estimations. In particular, firms named with any Chinese characters for trading company or importing and exporting company are excluded.

b. *Chinese production-level trade data*

The transaction trade data is at an extremely disaggregated HS eight-digit product-level, obtained from China's General Administration of Customs. It records rich information of each export or import transaction for all trading firm, including trading price, quantity, value, and trade mode telling processing trade from ordinary trade. From this data we know the import value of each product from each original country which we further use to construct the firm average input tariff.

Last we merge manufacturing firm data and customs data. We use the firm name-year, zip code, and the last seven digit of the telephone number to merge the two datasets. Our merged data skew towards large firms as the matched sample has more export, more sales, and more employees. The detail of the approach is introduced in Yu and Tian (2012) and Yu (2015).

c. *Measurement of firm level tariff*

Using the trade data we constructed the measurement of average intermediate input tariff faced by a single firm as Yu (2015). The firm-specific input tariff index is based only on non-processing imports (O) given the processing imports enjoy free duty in China, as follows:

$$FIT_{it} = \sum_{k \in O} \frac{m_{ik,\text{initial\_ year}}}{\sum_{k \in M} m_{ik,\text{initial\_ year}}} \tau_{kt}$$

where $m_{ik,initial\_year}$ is firm i's imports of product k in the first year the firm appears in the sample. M is the set of the firm's total import variety. The import weight for each product in the index is fixed at firm initial year in the sample to avoid endogeneity following Topalova and Khandelwal (2011). Because imports might be reduced to zero by prohibitive tariff, thus using import weight measured in current period in firm tariffs would generate a downward bias.

To precisely capture the impact of input trade liberalisation towards developing origins, we decompose the import from developing countries and construct import tariff based on developing sources using a similar approach. The weight in the following index is the import share of each import from developing countries.

$$FIT_{it}^{\text{poor}} = \sum_{k \in O} \frac{m_{ik,\text{initial\_ year}}^{\text{poor}}}{\sum_{k \in M} m_{ik,\text{initial\_ year}}} \tau_{kt}$$

To better fit with related empirical literature, we also consider two dimensions of trade liberalisation other than input tariff reduction following Goldberg et al. (2010) and Topalova and Khandelwal (2011): (i) home (i.e. China) tariffs cut in final products such as textile and garments, namely output tariff; (ii) tariffs cut in the foreign destination country (i.e. United States [US]), namely external tariff. The first dimension raises competition in home market and the second enlarges markets. Both the output tariff and external tariff are generated at two-digit Chinese industry classification (CIC) industry level. We average the tariff of the HS six-digit within each CIC two-digit industry code according to Amiti and Konings (2007).

We begin with showing some stylized fact on input tariff and the pattern of import. Figure 9.1 shows the correlation between the import share from developing counties and input tariff. A positive correlation implies that input tariff reduction associates with lower import scope share and value share from developing countries, which is consistent to our finding that import is switched to developed countries as input trade liberalization. In Fig. 9.2 we demonstrate the time trend of import from developing countries and developed countries. Both import increases rapidly after Chins enters WTO, however, as trade opens up, import from developed countries is always larger that from developing countries, and the gap is increasing as well.

At last, Table 9.1 shows the summary of statistics of the major variables in our empirical part. It is obvious that firms import 28% of the imported inputs from

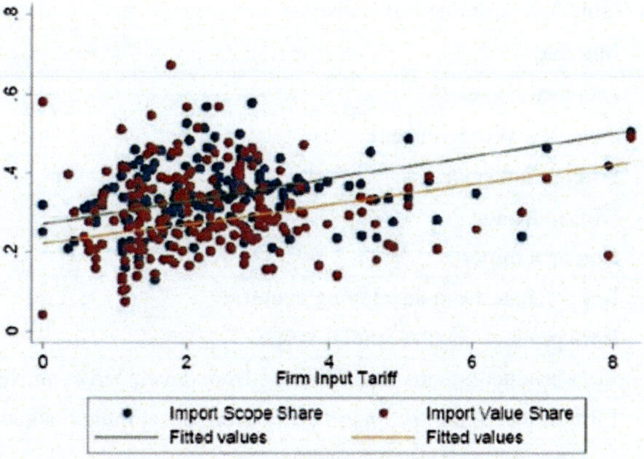

Fig. 9.1 Firm input tariff, import scope and import value

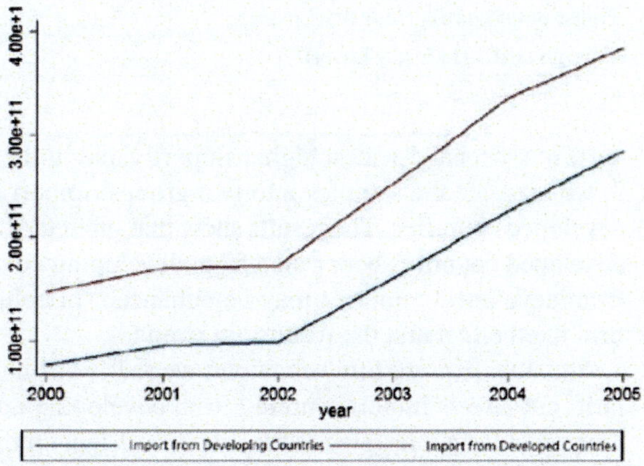

Fig. 9.2 Import from developed and developing countries

developed countries averagely. And firm import more product scope from developed countries than from developing countries.

9.3 Empirical Findings

Before we start the firm level estimation, we first use the transaction level customs trade data to take a preliminary look. In Table 9.2, we regress import value on product level input tariff. We also control for firm total factor productivity (TFP) using Olley and Pakes (1996) approach following Yu (2015), where we take into account firm export status and trade mode in the estimated productivity function. We also use system GMM and its normalization as alternative measurement of TFP in the robustness checks in the later part of the paper. After controlling for industry level output tariff and tariff charged by foreign countries, we show that a lower input

Table 9.1 Summary of statistics

Variable	Mean	Std. dev
Log firm labour	5.456	1.167
Firm TFP (Olley-Pakes)	1.122	0.382
Foreign indicator	0.569	0.495
SOE indicator	0.021	0.142
Log firm import	12.018	2.954
Import share from developing countries	0.281	0.378
Firm product-country import scope	17.664	44.532
Firm product-country import scope from developed countries	15.343	35.507
Firm product-country import scope from developing countries	8.372	21.024
Home input tariff (Firm Level)	3.24	5.922
Home input tariff from developing countries	1.379	3.724
Home output tariffs (Industry Level)	0.117	0.056
Foreign tariffs (Industry Level)	0.096	0.048

tariff is associated with a higher import value in the first column. In column 2 and 3, we separate the samples into two groups: import from developing countries and developed countries. The results show that input tariff reduction favours import from developed countries better than from developing countries, suggesting import share from developed countries may be enhanced. In column 4 and 5, we controlled for firm fixed effect and the results are similar.

To better explore firm behaviour, we seek to firm level data to examine how input tariff cut affects import sourcing from developing and developed countries, and we are particularly interested in the resulting effect on the import share from developed countries. We also separate the tariff on developing sources from the conventional average tariff to compare its impact of boosting import from developed countries and developing countries. The following expresses our benchmark empirical specification, where $impshare_{it}^{rich}$ is the import share from developed countries of firm i in year t, FIT_{it}^{poor} is the average import tariff of firm i in year t for the imports from developing countries constructed before. φ_{it} is the productivity of firm i in year t, X_{jt} is the industry level output tariff and external tariff of firm i in industry j and year t. m$_i$ and y겔 are firm level and year level fixed effect respectively, and μ_i겔 is firm level idiosyncratic shock.

$$\begin{aligned} \text{impshare}_{it}^{rich} &= \beta_0 + \beta_1 FIT_{it}^{poor} + \beta_2 FIT_{it}^{poor} \times \varphi_{it} \\ &+ \beta_3 \varphi_{it} + \theta X_{jt} + \omega_i + \eta_t + \mu_{it} \end{aligned}$$

We report the result of the benchmark regressions in Table 9.3. In column 1, the import share from developed countries increases as the import tariff on developing imports reduces. This suggests a switch of the import from developing countries to developed countries led by input tariff reduction on developing countries. In column

Table 9.2 Preliminary estimation

Regressand	(1)	(2)	(3)	(4)	(5)
Import value (HS6D Level)	All	From Developed Countries	From Developing Countries	From Developed Countries	From Developing Countries
Home input tariff	−0.036***	−0.037***	−0.033***	−0.031***	−0.025***
(Product Level)	(−135.82)	(−119.77)	(−64.31)	(−98.99)	(−47.57)
Home output tariffs	−1.483***	−1.487***	−1.181***	1.274***	0.076
(Industry Level)	(−33.15)	(−27.98)	(−13.87)	(12.60)	(0.4)
Foreign tariffs	0.837***	0.519***	1.554***	−0.135	−0.411**
(Industry Level)	(14.89)	(7.77)	(14.72)	(−1.43)	(−2.46)
Firm TFP (Olley-Pakes)	0.376***	0.369***	0.405***	0.002	0.019
	(85.89)	(74.89)	(42.05)	(0.24)	(0.81)
Foreign indicator	−0.479***	−0.437***	−0.541***	0.051	0.139 **
	(−96.57)	(−70.75)	(−63.98)	(1.58)	(2.10)
SOE indicator	−0.143***	−0.031	−0.276***	−0.145**	−0.067
Log firm labour	(−8.42) 0.187***	(−1.4) 0.201***	(−10.47) 0.147***	(−2.03) 0.248***	(−0.66) 0.066 ***
	(181.64)	(166.48)	(71.41)	(29.33)	(3.4)
Year fixed effects	Yes	Yes	Yes	Yes	Yes
Industry fixed effects	Yes	Yes	Yes	Yes	Yes
Firm fixed effects	No	No	No	Yes	Yes
R-squared	0.0619	0.0603	0.0641	0.0174	0.0136
Observations	3,747,538	2,741,321	1,006,217	2,741,321	1,006,217

Note Numbers in parentheses are robust t-value. * (**, ***) denotes significance at 10% (5%, 1%)

2 and 3 we introduce firm productivity to control for its impact on firm import. In column 2 we use system GMM method to estimate TFP, and column 3 we normalize the TFP to range from 0 to 1 to make it comparable across industries. The impact is still significant and robust. In column 4 we further add the interaction term of input tariff and TFP, and we find the impact of tariff reduction is more pronounced for firms with lower productivity. The reason might be that firms with higher productivity are less financially constrained by high level input tariff before the tariff reduction. In column 5 and 6, we replace TFP measurement with a dummy indicating high TFP firms if their TFP measure is higher than industry mean. We redo the regressions in column 3 and 4, and the results keep the unchanged.

Table 9.3 Benchmark regressions

Regressand: rich import						
Share	(1)	(2)	(3)	(4)	(5)	(6)
TFP measure	System TFP		Relative TFP		High TFP Indicator	
Firm tariffs on poor inputs	−0.013*** (−24.98)	−0.013*** (−24.98)	−0.011*** (−15.19)	−0.018*** (−7.13)	−0.011*** (−15.18)	−0.013*** (−11.87)
Firm tariffs on poor inputs*Firm TFP				0.024*** (2.82)		0.003** (2.23)
Industry output tariff	−0.053 (−0.84)	−0.055 (−0.86)	−0.130 (−1.51)	−0.130 (−1.50)	−0.129 (−1.50)	−0.131 (−1.52)
Industry external tariff	−0.059 (−0.95)	−0.058 (−0.95)	−0.054 (−0.56)	−0.053 (−0.55)	−0.055 (−0.57)	−0.054 (−0.57)
Firm TFP		−0.014* (−1.73)	−0.044 (−0.60)	−0.076 (−1.03)	−0.002 (−0.34)	−0.007 (−1.02)
Observations	37,661	37,534	29,275	29,275	29,379	29,379
R-squared	0.05	0.05	0.05	0.05	0.05	0.05
Number of party_id	23,194	23,132	22,338	22,338	22,405	22,405
Year FE	Yes	Yes	Yes	Yes	Yes	Yes
Firm FE	Yes	Yes	Yes	Yes	Yes	Yes

Note Numbers in parentheses are robust t-value. * (**, ***) denotes significance at 10% (5%, 1%)

In Table 9.4 we try to discuss the mechanism behind the result. First, we would like to see whether the impact exists for firms in all industry due to cost saving or the tariff cut only enables firms in high skill industries to innovate and upgrade production. We examine the impact on skill intensive firms in the first three columns in Table 9.4. In column 2 we use samples with positive R&D, and in column 3 we look at firms with positive patent. The results show that the impact is similar for skill intensive firms to the overall firms shown in column 1, indicating that upgrading exists universally.

Next we regress by firm import status to find the strongest driving party. In column 4 to 6, specifically, we regress for new importers, always imports and imports who exit in the next year. The results show that the impact on new importers is more pronounced than on the other two types of firms. This gives us a hint that input tariff reduction encourages more firms to start importing from developed countries than developing countries. This result is consistent with previous findings that highlight the effect on the extensive margin adjustment under trade liberalization (Bernard et al. 2007).

Table 9.4 More specifications: by firm type

	(1)	(2)	(3)	(4)	(5)	(6)
Regressand: rich Import share	All	Positive R&D	Positive Patent	Type of importers		
				New	Always	Exiters
Firm tariffs on poor inputs	−0.013***	−0.011***	−0.011***	−0.018***	−0.009***	
	(−24.98)	(−5.84)	(−4.87)	(−9.96)	(−12.58)	
Firm tariffs on poor inputs (one lag)						−0.016
						(−1.43)
Industry output tariff	−0.055	−0.097	0.178	0.052	0.015	−1.235
	(−0.86)	(−0.36)	(0.56)	(0.21)	(0.18)	(−0.72)
Industry external tariff	−0.058	−0.071	−0.510*	0.305	−0.195***	−2.385
	(−0.95)	(−0.31)	(−1.66)	(1.00)	(−2.66)	(−1.40)
Firm TFP	−0.014*	0.008	0.058	−0.004	−0.019*	0.128
	(−1.73)	(0.23)	(1.14)	(−0.13)	(−1.78)	(0.59)
Observations	37,534	4,357	2,567	18,935	18,599	1,648
R-squared	0.05	0.06	0.07	0.09	0.03	0.31
Number of party_id	23,132	3,331	1,933	17,499	11,286	1,580
Year FE	Yes	Yes	Yes	Yes	Yes	Yes
Firm FE	Yes	Yes	Yes	Yes	Yes	Yes

Note Numbers in parentheses are robust t-value. * (**, ***) denotes significance at 10% (5%, 1%)

However, the result could also be driven by the decline of processing trade. Brandt and Morrow (2016) argues that China's processing trade declines since 2005 because input tariff reduction reduces the opportunity cost of doing ordinary trade. To nullify this channel, we separate the samples by labour intensive and capital intensive industries, given that processing trade are more concentrated in labour intensive industries. The results in column 1 and 2 of Table 9.5 are both significant and the economic magnitudes are close. Furthermore, we check the effect on processing firms and capital goods importers separately in column 3 and 4, where we still find a consistent and robust result as previous studies. All the works suggest that processing trade is not a challenge to our interpretation.

Next we study the impact of input tariff reduction on firm import from the extensive margin, namely, import scope. Product variety is defined at product- country level, and the estimation results are shown in Table 9.6. In the first two columns we regress respectively the import scope from poor countries on input tariff by using negative binomial estimation to deal with the count data issue. We find that when input tariff decreases, import scope from poor countries are squeezed out in the first two columns. This verifies our argument that input trade liberalization fosters firm to switch import from developing country to developed country from the extensive margin. To show it more directly, we regress the import share from rich countries on input tariff in column 3, and in column 4 we use Tobit method to replace with OLS to correct the

Table 9.5 More specifications by sectors

Regressand: rich import share	(1)	(2)	(3)	(4)
	Intensive sectors by			
	Labor	Capital	Processing	Capital goods
Firm tariffs on poor inputs	−0.011*** (−13.85)	−0.014*** (−20.95)	−0.013*** (−18.49)	−0.013*** (−8.05)
Industry output tariff	−0.145	−0.035	−0.008	−0.171
	(−1.14)	(−0.45)	(−0.09)	(−0.82)
Industry external tariff	−0.162	−0.050	−0.020	−0.302
	(−1.22)	(−0.70)	(−0.23)	(−1.02)
Firm TFP	−0.005	−0.019*	−0.011	−0.083**
	(−0.35)	(−1.80)	(−0.91)	(−2.32)
Observations	11,325	26,209	26,449	3,358
R-squared	0.06	0.05	0.05	0.06
Number of firm	7,002	16,223	18,136	2,155
Year FE	Yes	Yes	Yes	Yes
Firm FE	Yes	Yes	Yes	Yes

Note Numbers in parentheses are robust t-value. * (**, ***) denotes significance at 10% (5%, 1%)

Table 9.6 Esimation on import scope

Regressand: firm import scope (Product-Country)	(1)	(3)	(4)	(6)	(7)
	Poor only	Poor only	Import scope share from rich		Import scope share from East Asian rich to East Asian rich & ASEAN
Method:	OLS	OLS	OLS	Tobit	OLS
Firm tariffs on poor inputs	0.010** (2.26)	0.014*** (4.16)	−0.005*** (−4.87)	−0.003*** (−5.27)	−0.002*** (−2.71)
Industry output tariff	−2.227***	−0.057	0.313***	0.144***	−0.079
	(−5.78)	(−0.19)	(3.26)	(2.77)	(−1.21)
Industry external tariff	−0.010	0.274	−0.034	0.014	−0.049
	(−0.02)	(1.05)	(−0.27)	(0.24)	(−0.85)
Other control	Yes	Yes	Yes	Yes	Yes
Industry FE	Yes	No	Yes	Yes	Yes
Year FE	Yes	Yes	Yes	Yes	Yes
Firm FE	No	Yes	No	No	Yes
Observations	12,902	6,315	11,693	11,693	8,251

Note Numbers in parentheses are robust t-value. * (**, ***) denotes significance at 10% (5%, 1%)

bias from sample truncation, and we also find a robust result. Moreover, most of Chinses import are from Asian countries, and among which ASEAN countries are the most important processing sources. Since ASEAN free trade agreement tariffs have dropped significantly and trade was largely boosted. So in order to exclude the impact through processing declining, we regress the import scope share from rich Asian countries in the summation of that and from ASEAN countries. And similar to our previous finding, we find that poor input tariff reduction promotes firms to import more from rich Asian countries relative to ASEAN countries Table 9.7.

Since the firm average input tariff is constructed by using the import weight of each input variety, the weight might be correlated to the rich import share due to time serial correlation of unobservable shock, though we fix the weight at initial year in all regressions above. To handle the possible endogenous problem, we use one-year lag of tariffs as the instruments of the first difference in tariff following Trefler (2004). The result is shown in Table 9.6. In column 1, we show that the more that input tariff reduces, the more import share from rich countries increases. In column 2 we control for firm TFP as well, where TFP is measured by using system GMM method, and the result does not change. In addition, in column 3 and 4, we use normalized TFP and add an interaction term of poor input tariff and firm TFP in column 4 to test the heterogeneous effect. We find that higher input tariff decrease leads to higher rich import share increase, and the effect is more pronounced for less productive firms. In

Table 9.7 IV estimates with firm heterogeneity

Regressand						
ΔRich import share	(1)	(2)	(3)	(4)	(5)	(6)
TFP measures	System TFP		Relative system TFP		High TFP indicator	
ΔFirm tariffs on poor inputs	−0.012***	−0.012***	−0.013***	−0.021**	−0.012***	−0.013***
	(−10.10)	(−10.10)	(−4.45)	(−2.21)	(−4.41)	(−3.48)
ΔIndustry output tariffs	0.192	0.188	−0.363	−0.350	−0.372	−0.373
	(1.44)	(1.40)	(−1.21)	(−1.17)	(−1.25)	(−1.25)
ΔIndustry external tariffs	−0.078	−0.079	−0.042	−0.034	−0.043	−0.043
	(−1.13)	(−1.15)	(−0.29)	(−0.23)	(−0.30)	(−0.31)
ΔFirm TFP		−0.012	−0.079	−0.123	0.012	0.011
ΔFirm tariffs on poor		(−1.24)	(−0.59)	(−0.88)	(0.99)	(0.80)
Inputs*Firm TFP				0.029		0.001
				(0.96)		(0.14)
Observations	10,520	10,461	2,139	2,139	2,151	2,151
R-squared	0.04	0.04	0.06	0.06	0.06	0.06
Year FE	Yes	Yes	Yes	Yes	Yes	Yes
Firm FE	Yes	Yes	Yes	Yes	Yes	Yes

Note Numbers in parentheses are robust t-value. * (**, ***) denotes significance at 10% (5%, 1%)

the last two columns we replace the TFP measure with high productive firm dummy generated as in Table 9.3, and we redo column 3 and 4 and get a robust result.

In the next part we testify the mechanism of innovation. Import quality from developed countries, compared with that from developing countries, should be disproportionally boosted by lower input tariff, if the scenario is true that firm exploit input tariff reduction to innovate and upgrade quality. To test this, we fist follow Khandelwa (2010) to construct a measure of import quality as below.

$$\log s_{cht} = \lambda_{1,ch} + \lambda_{2,t} + a_1 \log p_{cht} + a_2 \log ns_{cht} + \lambda_{3,cht}$$

$s_{cht} = q_{cht}/market_{it}$ is the import share of product h of industry i from country c at year t. $market_{it} = \sum_{ch \in i} q_{cht}/impen_{it}$ is the market size where $impen_{it}$ refers to industry i's import penetration. $ns_{cht} = \frac{q_{cht}}{\sum_{ch \in h} q_{cht}}$ is the net share of product h from country c in total import of product h. The estimated residual is considered as product-country-year pair import quality, as

$$\widehat{\lambda_{cht}} = \widehat{\lambda_{1,ch}} + \widehat{\lambda_{2,ch}} + \widehat{\lambda_{3,ch}}$$

We estimated import quality by each CIC-2digit industry and separating for processing and ordinary import respectively.

And we next examine the input tariff reduction and import quality in Table 9.8. In column 1 we find that input tariff cut generates more return on assets, implying input tariff reduction saves cost and generates higher profit. We also control for other tariffs including output tariffs and industry level external tariffs charged by other countries. In column 2 and 3, we regress firm input quality on input tariff and poor input tariff respectively and the result shows that import quality is improved as input tariff reduces. we further examine the impact on the quality ratio of import from developed countries over developing countries in column 4, and add ROA and its interaction with tariffs in column 5 to control for the impact of firm productivity and profit. The result shows that poor input tariff reduction boosts the relative import quality from developed countries to developing countries. And we also find that the impact is the same for firms with different ROA, suggesting that there might be other channels to improve import quality other than profit.

9.4 Conclusions

In this paper we examine how input tariff reduction changes firm import behaviour. We find that import sources is switched from developing countries to developed countries as input tariff reduces, using a comprehensive firm level production and trade data of Chinese manufacturing firms. This impact is prevalent to different types of firms including processing firms and ordinary firms, and firms in both labour intensive industries and capital intensive industries. But among different importers,

Table 9.8 Channels of input trade liberalization

Regressand	(1)	(2)	(3)	(4)	(5)
	ROA	Import quality		Developed import quality ratio to developing	
Firm input tariff	−0.048***	−0.835***			
	(−3.42)	(−2.80)			
Firm tariffs on poor inputs			−0.009**	−0.051***	−0.058**
			(−2.06)	(−3.31)	(−1.97)
Firm return on assets (ROA)			−0.451		−2.806
			(−1.28)		(−1.02)
Firm tariffs on poor inputs*Firm ROA			0.051		0.159
			(0.76)		(0.36)
Industy output tariffs	0.036***	−0.558**	−0.631*	0.484	1.315
	(2.82)	(−2.06)	(−1.73)	(0.30)	(0.59)
Industry external tariffs	0.007	1.225***	0.818**	−1.911	−2.599
	(0.59)	(4.66)	(2.23)	(−1.25)	(−1.20)
Firm TFP				−0.182	−0.122
				(−0.78)	(−0.41)
Observations	21,984	36,644	22,551	11,200	6,746
R-squared	0.01	0.06	0.07	0.01	0.01
Number of firm	14,663	22,926	14,843	7,481	4,708
Year FE	Yes	Yes	Yes	Yes	Yes
Firm FE	Yes	Yes	Yes	Yes	Yes

Note Numbers in parentheses are robust t-value. * (**, ***) denotes significance at 10% (5%, 1%)

new importers benefit most from tariff reduction. We also show that the impact exists in terms of both intensive margin and extensive margin, i.e. both import value and scope shift towards developed countries as input tariff reduces. We further explore the mechanism in behind, which, consistent with the scenario of previous literature, can be attributed to the innovation and quality upgrading encouraged by lower input cost. Specifically, we find the import quality from developed countries is large boosted compared with that from developing countries. And after taking careful care of the endogenous problem and a bunch of robustness checks we show the above findings are significant and robust. This paper enriches the study on input liberalization and firm innovation, and provide direct evidence from the change of import pattern. The results of the paper also remind us that the distribution of the world trade flow may be affected by China's open-up as well, in the sense that more trade within developing countries may be replaced with the trade between developing and developed countries.

Part V
All-Round Opening-up Strategy

Chapter 10
Worker Training, Firm Productivity, and Trade Liberalization: Evidence from Chinese Firms

The present paper discuss a novel mechanism–worker training–that output trade liberalization affects firm productivity. With disaggregated Chinese firm-level production data from 2004 to 2006, we find strong evidence that output trade liberalization boost firm productivity. More importantly, after controlling for firm's self-selection to invest on worker training, our extensive empirical search suggests the following findings. First, with fierier import competition, firms experience a decrease in profitability and hence are less likely to invest on firm training. Second, lower productive firms are more likely to train their workers, as otherwise they would collapse and exit from the market. The lower the firm productivity, the more is the firm's worker training expenses. Finally, the effect of output trade liberalization on firm productivity is more pronounced for firms with more training investment. Such results are robust regardless of various empirical specifications and different measures.

This chapter is coauthored with.Qing Liu and Larry Qiu and originally published in Developing Economies, 2017, 55(3), pp. 189–210.

M. Yu, *China's Miracle in Foreign Trade*, Studies in Modern Chinese Economy,
https://doi.org/10.1007/978-981-16-6030-6_10

10.1 Introduction

Research on firm productivity and trade liberalization is an important research topic in international trade and economic development. A growing empirical research using firm-level micro data find evidence that trade liberalization from both input goods and final goods fosters firm productivity. Amiti and Konings (2007) use Indonesian firm-level data to find that firms' gains from reduction of input tariffs are at least twice as much as those from reduction of output tariffs. Similarly, Topalova and Khandelwal (2011) find close evidence for Indian firms. Using Chinese firm-level dataset, Yu (2015) finds that the impact of input tariff reductions on productivity improvement, overall, is weaker than that of output tariff reductions since processing import is already free-duty in China. Both tariff reductions are found to contribute at least 14.5% to economy-wide productivity growth of China.

However, as noted by Bernard and Jensen (2004), a key un-answered important question is "how firms obtain the characteristics that allow them to easily enter the export market". Or equivalently, what mechanisms through which trade policy changes affect welfare gains from trade? Inspired by Melitz (2003), Lileeva and Trefler (2010) and Melitz and Trefler (2012) forcefully argue that foreign market access matters for firm innovation and hence for firm productivity. This paper argues that worker training is another important mechanism, in addition to firm innovation, through which the productivity improvement and hence export growth are realized. With tariff reductions on final goods, Chinese domestic firms face tougher import competition. The competitive effect is stronger for low ex-ante productive firms, which in turn input more on labor training to boost their ex-post productive firms. With realized productivity growth, firms are able to maintain its international competitive advantage and export more. The idea can be illustrated by the following Fig. 10.1.

Different from well-documented mechanism such as firm innovation, Fig. 10.1 introduces a new channel--labor training--that trade liberalization affects firm productivity. Using Chinese firm-level production data from 2004 to 2006, we find strong evidence for such mechanism. Our extensive empirical search supports the following novel findings.

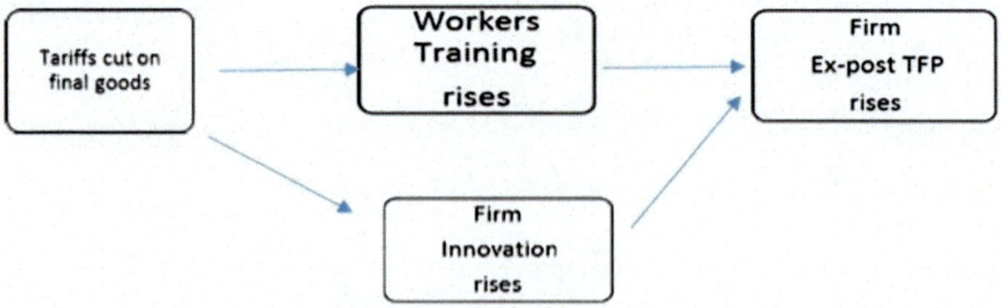

Fig. 10.1 The mechanism

First, we find strong evidence that output trade liberalization fosters firm productivity as before. Second, with fierier import competition, firms experience a decrease in profitability and hence are less likely to invest on firm training. Third, lower productive firms are more likely to train their workers, as otherwise they would collapse and exit from the market. The lower the firm productivity, the more is the firm's worker training expenses. Finally, the effect of output trade liberalization on firm productivity is more pronounced for firms with more training investment.

Note that the first one is already well-documented in the literature. Here we start from this exercise to echo to the well-accepted firm heterogeneity theory and to be in line with previous works. However, the other empirical predictions are novel. To emphasize the role of import competition, in this paper we focus on trade liberalization on final goods. Still, as robustness checks, we include foreign trade liberalization as control variables in our estimates and discuss the case with input tariff cut.

We make the following three contributions to the literature. First, we identify a new mechanism through which trade liberalization affects firm productivity. Trade literature pervasively emphasizes the role of investment on research and development (R&D) for firms exposure to global competition but neglects the role of investment in labor training, with only a few exceptions (e.g., Aw et al., 2011; Helpman et al., 2010). But the importance of worker training is recognized in development economics. For instance, Acemoglou and Pischke (1998) emphasizes that firms invest in general skill of workers when labor market frictions compress the structure of wages. Such a theoretical thought is also warmly endorsed by reality.[1]

Second, we provide evidence on the nexus between trade liberalization, worker training and productivity for China, the second largest economy and the largest trading country in the world. Due to the increasing labor costs in recent years (Cai, 2010), Chinese firms try their very best to boost firm productivity to maintain its international competitiveness. In addition to input more on research and development (R&D), Chinese manufacturing firms invest a lot on their worker trainings, as illustrated in the next section by using Chinese firm-level production data. However, previous firm-level research on China mainly focused on firm productivity and exports but kept silent on the role of firm's training behavior. Our paper also aims to fill in this gap.

Third, we make contributions to the related identification problem. The econometric challenges of this paper come from the following empirical identifications. In particular, we need to empirically distinguish the difference between ex-ante TFP and ex-post TFP. However, typical empirical research use Solow residual to proxy firm TFP, which by definition is an ex-post measure. The recent developed semi-parametric techniques such as Olley-Pakes (1996), Levinsohn-Petrin (2003), and even system GMM cannot solve this challenge. In spired by Feenstra et al. (2014), we first estimate and calculate an ex-ante TFP measure in the estimates.

[1] For example, the UK and Italy governments thought that, one of the key factors behind the loss of competitiveness of their firms in the global economy is the lack of training compared with other countries like Germany and Japan. Thus they initiated large training programs in their countries.

Our paper joins the two strands of the growing literature. The first strand is on the nexus between trade liberalization and labor training. Baldwin (1992) was one of the pioneer works to emphasize the dynamic effect of trade liberalization on human capital accumulation. However, not many empirical works directly investigates the importance of the specific channel--labor training. One outstanding exception is Li (2009) who investigates the effect of the import penetration ratio on firm training using American household-level data from the National Longitudinal Survey of Youth (NLSY). He finds that import competition has a negative impact on training provision. Some recent theoretical papers such as Deardorff (2000) and Long et al. (2007) also look at how trade liberalization affects workers' skill acquisition/accumulation decision and thus affects wage inequality. Lai and Ng (2014) use a subjective measure of market competition and find that increased product market competition is strongly associated with more training provision. Gorlitz and Stiebale (2011) also find no impact of competition on firm training provision.

The second strand of literature is to examine the nexus between labor training and firm productivity but have no conclusive results (see a review by Blundell et al. 1999).

Early works like Blundell et al. (1996) generally uses wage rates to proxy firm productivity to study the effect of training on productivity due to the unavailability of direct productivity measure. Recent studies like Conti (2005) and Dearden et al. (2006) have made efforts to construct industry-level panel data to test the nexus between labor training and firm productivity. Finally, there is a small but growing papers like Black and Lynch (2001) and Almeida and Carneiro (2009) rely on firm-level panel data to investigate the effect of training on firm productivity. However, the results in these papers are constrained by the limited representativeness of the small sample size of the data.

The rest of the paper is organized as follows. Section 2 describes Chinese firm-level data. Section 3 sketches the bone of our empirical specification. Section 4 presents our estimation results. Section 5 briefly discusses policy implications and concludes.

10.2 Data

Our sample is derived from a rich firm-level panel data set that covers between 162,885 firms (in 2000) and 336,768 firms (in 2007). The data are collected and maintained by China's National Bureau of Statistics (NBS) in an annual survey of manufacturing enterprises. Complete information on the three major accounting statements (i.e., balance sheet, profit and loss account, and cash flow statement) is available. In brief, the data set covers two types of manufacturing firms—all state-owned enterprises (SOEs) and non-SOEs whose annual sales exceed RMB 5 million

Table 10.1 TFP, Tariffs and Firm's training expenses

Year	TFP	Training dummy		Log training		Ind. output tariffs	
Mean	Std. Dev	Mean	Std. Dev	Mean	Std. Dev	Mean	Std. Dev
(1)	(2)	(3)	(4)	(5)	(6)	(7)	(8)
2004 1.055	0.317	0.437	0.496	4.244	4.920	8.321	1.863
2005 1.033	0.334	0.408	0.491	4.037	4.960	7.944	1.966
2006 1.046	0.342	0.409	0.492	4.054	4.981	7.582	1.583

Sources Data compiled by the authors

(or equivalently, $770,000, under current exchange rate).[2] The data set includes more than 100 financial variables listed in the main accounting statements of these firms.

Although the data set contains rich information, some samples are still noisy and are therefore misleading, largely because of mis-reporting by some firms.[3] Following Yu (2015), we clean the sample and omit outliers by using the following criteria. First, observations with missing key financial variables (such as total assets, net value of fixed assets, sales, and gross value of the firm's output productivity) are excluded. Second, we drop firms with fewer than eight workers since they fall under a different legal regime, as mentioned in Brandt, Van Biesebroeck, and Zhang (2012). Thirdly, we delete observations according to the basic rules of the Generally Accepted Accounting Principles.[4] After applying such a stringent filter to guarantee the quality of the production data, the filtered firm data are reduced by about 50% in each year. Since the CMS data provides information of worker training after 2004, our panel is shortened to cover the period during 2004–2007. As shown in Table 10.1, firm's worker training expenses are increasing during 2004–2007. Table 10.1 shows that firm's training investment increase over the sample period.[5]

Tariff data can be accessed directly from the WTO and the trade analysis and information system (TRAINS).[6] China's tariff data are available at the Harmonized

[2] Aggregated data on the industrial sector in the annual *China's Statistical Yearbook* by the Natural Bureau of Statistics are compiled from this data set.

[3] For example, information on some family-based firms, which usually have no formal accounting system in place, is based on a unit of one RMB, whereas the official requirement is a unit of 1000 RMB.

[4] For example, observations are dropped if any of the following are true: : (1) liquid assets are greater than total assets; (2) total fixed assets are greater than total assets; (3) the net value of fixed assets is greater than total assets; (4) the firm's identification number is missing; or (5) an invalid established time exists (e.g., the opening month is later than December or earlier than January).

[5] By separating firms into pure exporter (i.e., firms export all of their products), non-pure exporters (i.e., firms at most export some products), and non-exporters (i.e., firms do not export any products), we see that exporters spend more on worker training than non-exporters. Simultaneously, non-pure exporters have larger worker training expenses than pure exporters. Such results are not reported in the text but available upon request.

[6] The data are from WTO webpage http://tariffdata.wto.org/ReportersAndProducts.aspx. Note that TRAINS data generally suffers from missing values problems, particularly regarding the tariffs

Table 10.2 Summary statistics (2004–2006)

Key variables	Mean	Std. Dev
Log of export (RMB)	16.46	1.69
Training dummy	0.412	0.492
Log of training expenses (RMB)	4.11	4.95
Log of training expenses per capita (RMB)	1.99	2.53
Industry-level output tariffs	0.090	3.66
Industry-level input tariffs	0.004	0.808
Firm-level external tariffs	0.009	11.3
SOEs indicator	0.035	0.185
Foreign ownership indicator	0.131	0.338

Notes $1 is equivalent to RMB 8.05 during the period

System (HS) six-digit disaggregated level for 2000–2006. Given that the product-level trade data are at the HS eight-digit level, the product-level trade data is aggregated to the HS six-digit level to correspond with the ad valorem tariff data. Table 10.2 provides the basic statistical information for key variables used in the estimations.

10.3 Empirical Specification

To investigate the effects of input and output tariff reductions on firm productivity, we consider the following empirical framework:

$$\ln TFP_{ijt}^{OP} = \beta_0 + \beta_1 OT_{jt} + \beta_2 TrainDummy_{it} + \theta \mathbf{X}_{it} + \varpi_i + \eta_t + \mu_{it}, \tag{10.1}$$

where ln $Export_{ijt}$ is the logarithm of firm i's export in industry j in year t whereas OT_{it} denotes industry-level output tariffs. $TrainDummy_{it}$ is firm's training indicator which equals one if a firm has any expenses on worker training and zero otherwise. $\mathbf{X}_{it}$ denotes other firm characteristics, such as type of ownership (i.e., state-owned-enterprises or multinational firms). State-owned enterprises (SOEs) are usually low productive and hence export less (Hsieh and Klenow, 2009). By contrast, multinational firms have higher productivity due in part to fewer financial constraints (Feenstra et al, 2014) or more international technology spillover (Keller and Yeaple, 2009) and hence export more. Therefore, we construct two indicators to measure the roles of SOEs and multinational firms. In particular, a firm is classified as a foreign firm if it has any investments from other countries (regimes). A large proportion of the inflow of foreign investment comes from Hong Kong/Macao/Taiwan of China, so

imposed by other countries for Chinese exports. The product-destination-year combinations that have missing tariffs are hence dropped.

these investments are considered in the construction of such an indicator.[7] Similarly, we construct an indicator for SOEs, which is one if a firm has any investment from the government, and zero otherwise.[8] Finally, the error term is divided into three components: (1) firm-specific fixed effects ϖ_t to control for time-invariant but unobservable factors such as managerial ability (Qiu and Yu, 2013); (2) year-specific fixed effects η_t to control for firm-invariant factors such as an appreciation of the *Renminbi*; and (3) an idiosyncratic effect μ_{it} with normal distribution $\mu_{it} \sim N(0, \sigma_i^2)$ to control for other unspecified factors.

However, the training indicator in the specification above is relatively crude. If a firm only spent a very small amount in worker training, it is still identified as a training firm though it is very unlikely that the small amount of worker training can boost firm productivity. Hence, we use firm's actual training expenses to capture firm's training activity with the following specification:

$$\ln TFP_{ijt}^{OP} = \beta_0 + \beta_1 OT_{jt} + \beta_2 \ln Train_{it} + \theta \mathbf{X}_{it} + \varpi_i + \eta_t + \mu_{it} \tag{10.2}$$

10.3.1 Type-2 Tobit Selection Model

Thus far our estimates use firm's log of training expenses as a key variable, but such a variable is endogenous. First, it is possible that low-productivity firms self-select to provide more training since otherwise those firms would collapse and exit from the market. By the same token, tougher import competition raised by lower import tariffs would force firms to raise training to avoiding sweeping out from the market. To control for this, we introduce a type-2 Tobit model, or equivalently, a bivariate sample selection model (Cameron and Trivedi, 2005). The type-2 Tobit specification includes: (i) a training participation equation,

$$Train\ Dummy_{ijt} = \begin{cases} 0 & \left(if\ U_{ijt} < 0 \right) \\ 1 & \left(if\ U_{ijt} \geq 0 \right) \end{cases} \tag{10.3}$$

[7] Specifically, foreign-invested enterprises (FIEs) include the following firms: foreign-invested joint-stock corporations (code: 310), foreign-invested joint venture enterprises (320), fully FIEs (330), foreign-invested limited corporations (340), Hong Kong/Macao/Taiwan of China (henceforth, H/M/T) joint-stock corporations (210), H/M/T joint venture enterprises (220), fully H/M/T-invested enterprises (230), and H/M/T-invested limited corporations (240). Appendix Table 10.5A presents the transitional probability for such foreign firms.

[8] By the official definition reported in the *China City Statistical Yearbook* (2006), SOEs include firms such as domestic SOEs (code: 110), state-owned joint venture enterprises (141), and state-owned and collective joint venture enterprises (143), but exclude state-owned limited corporations (151). Appendix Table 10.5B presents the transitional probability for all SOEs.

where U_{it} denotes a latent variable faced by firm *i* in industry *j*; and (ii) an "outcome" equation whereby the firm's training expenses is modeled as a linear function of other variables.

In particular, we estimate the following selection equation using the Probit model:

$$\Pr(Training_{ijt} = 1) = \Pr(U_{ijt} \geq 0) = \Phi(\alpha_0 + \alpha_1 \ln TFP2_{it-1} + \alpha_2 OT_{jt-1} \\ + \alpha_3 FE_{it-1} + \alpha_3 SOE_{it-1} + \alpha_4 FIE_{it-1} + \alpha_5 \lg L_{it-1} + \alpha_6 Tenure_{it-1} + \lambda_j + \varsigma_t) \tag{10.4}$$

where $\Phi(.)$ is the cumulative density function of the normal distribution. In addition to the logarithm of the firm's productivity, a firm's decision to training investment is also affected by other factors, such as its ownership (whether it is a SOE or a multinational firm) and output tariffs level. Note that the bivariate sample selection estimations require an excluded variable that affects the firm's training decision but does not appear in the level of training expenses (Cameron and Trivedi, 2005). Here the firm's age ($Tenure_{it\text{-}1}$) serves this purpose, since previous studies have found that older firms are more likely to invest on training (OECD, 1993). All regressors in the Type-II Tobit selection model are of a one-period lag since it usually takes times for such factors to affect a firm's training decision. Finally, we include the three-digit CIC industrial dummies λ_j and year and year dummies ς_t to control for other unspecified factors.

In addition, production productivity is also an important factor to determine firm's training decision. We hence shall include it in the regressions in these binary estimates. However, an empirical identification challenge occurs. The conventional TFP measure is a "Solow" residual which is an *ex-post* measure whereas our model suggests that productivity shall be an *ex-ante* measure. Inspired by Feenstra et al. (2014), we construct an *ex-ante* productivity measure (TFP2) which differs from the standard *ex-post* productivity measure (TFP1) but is closer to the framework of Melitz (2003). We hence modify and tailor the standard Olley-Pakes (1996)'s TFP to construct the *ex-ante* TFP2. The detailed discussion and method to construct this measure will be included in the Appendix A. Finally, from the first-step Probit estimates (4), we obtain the estimation results for the type-2 Tobit selection model. Thus, after controlling for the endogenous selection of firm's expenses of worker training, we obtain the fitted value of the expenses of worker training, which shall be used in the related estimates.

10.4 Estimation Results

10.4.1 Baseline Results

We start off the estimations in Table 10.3 by using firm's training dummy. The positive coefficient of training dummy in column (1) as expected: training firms are more productive. Similarly, the coefficient of the industry output tariffs also has an

Table 10.3 Benchmark estimates of worker training

Regressand: Firm TFP	(1)	(2)	(3)	(4)	(5)	(6)
Firm training dummy	0.002					
	(1.01)					
Log firm training			0.001**	0.001		
			(2.24)	(1.50)		
Log firm training per capita					0.004***	0.003**
					(4.08)	(1.99)
Industry output tariffs	0.001	0.002***	0.001	0.000	0.001	0.006*
	(0.66)	(4.67)	(0.65)	(0.24)	(0.14)	(1.80)
Industry output tariffs ×				0.000	0.000***	0.000
Log firm training				(0.87)	(3.04)	(1.28)
Export indicator	0.015***	0.015***	0.015***	0.016***	0.016***	0.011***
	(5.86)	(6.93)	(5.84)	(6.31)	(6.31)	(2.52)
Foreign indicator	0.008	0.007	0.008	0.009	0.009	0.003
	(0.85)	(1.15)	(0.84)	(0.98)	(0.97)	(0.28)
SOE indicator	0.020**	0.009	0.020*	0.022**	0.022**	0.013
	(1.97)	(1.62)	(1.96)	(2.15)	(2.17)	(0.90)
Log firm size				0.023***	0.022***	0.032***
				(12.27)	(11.55)	(10.82)
Industry external tariffs				0.000	0.000	0.001***
				(1.29)	(1.27)	(3.11)
Log R&D expenses						0.002***
						(3.14)
Firm-specific fixed effects	Yes	Yes	Yes	Yes	Yes	Yes
Year-specific fixed effects	Yes	Yes	Yes	Yes	Yes	Yes
Observations	226,513	335,681	226,513	226,513	226,513	147,548
R-squared	0.01	0.01	0.01	0.01	0.01	0.01

Notes Robust t-values clustered at 2-digit Chinese industry level are in parentheses, *, **, (***) indicates significance at or below the 10, 5 and 1% level, respectively. Regressions in columns (1)–(4) use log firm's total training expenses as a proxy of firm training whereas that in columns (5)–(6) uses log firm's per-capita training expenses as a proxy of firm training anticipated negative sign. However, such two variables are insignificant statistically. We suspect this is due the coarse measure of firm training variable as it cannot measure the extent of firm's training expenses.

To overcome such a pitfall, from now on we use firm's log training to capture firm's training activity. The two-way fixed-effects estimates in column (2) abstract away the role of firm's training expenses and still find that industry output tariffs have significant negative impact on firm productivity, indicating that firms overall are more productive when they face tougher import competition due to output tariff reductions. Such findings are consistent with previous findings (Amiti and Konings, 2007; Yu, 2014). We then include log firm training in estimates of column (3). The coefficient of firm training is positive and significant; suggesting that the more the firm's investment on worker training the more productive is the firm. In addition, exporters are more productive.

However, in reality trade liberalization usually happens bilaterally. When China reduces its import tariffs, its trading partners are also likely to reduce their tariffs due to the WTO commitment. We hence include a simple un-weighted industry external tariff in the column (4). The negative, but insignificant, coefficient of external tariffs suggests that the lower foreign trade barrier is helpful to boost firm productivity.

It is interesting to ask whether output trade liberalization boosts firm productivity through the channel of firm training. To check this out, we include an interaction term between output tariffs and firm training in column (5). The coefficient of such a variable has an anticipated negative sign though it is insignificant. We suspect this is possibly due to two reasons. The first one is that we are lack of consider firm size since usually larger firms have more training expenses. To accurately capture the impact of firm training on firm productivity, it is a plus to control for take firm's size into account. We hence replace total log training with log per-capita training and include log firm size as an additional regressor in column (6). Once again, the coefficient of firm's log per-capita training is positive and significant, confirming that the more the firm training expenses, the higher is the firm TFP. Equally importantly, the negative and significant sign of the interaction term between output tariffs and firm training suggests that the effect of trade liberalization on firm productivity is more pronounced for firms with more training investment.

10.4.2 Self-Selection of Training

Table 10.3 uses firm's training expenses to measure training activity and show that training firms are high productive. However, such training variable is endogenous as the low-productive firms may self-select to provide worker training. To control for this, we introduce a bivariate sample selection model, or equivalently, a type-2 Tobit model (Cameron and Trivedi, 2005). As introduced above, the model includes two steps. The first step is to estimate a training participation equation, Eq. (10.3), and the second step is training extent function, Eq. (10.4), which model firm's training expenses as a linear function of other variables conditional on firm's participation on worker training.

Table 10.4 reports our type-2 Tobit estimation results. We first include one-period lag of log TFP in the first-step regression to see whether low-productive firms self-select to provide worker training. To be consistent with the theoretical presumption that firm productivity as exogenous given, we therefore distinguish the difference

Table 10.4 The heckman two-step estimates of bivariate selection model

Heckman two-step	1st step	2nd step
Regressand	Training indicator	Log training expenses
One-period Lag of Log TFP2 ($TFP2_{ijt}^{OP}$)	0.549*** (25.69)	2.157*** (18.57)
One-period Lag of Industry Output Tariffs	0.016*** (3.27)	0.056*** (2.96)
One-period Lag of Export indicator	0.110*** (15.92)	0.388*** (12.50)
One-period Lag of SOEs indicator	0.236*** (13.74)	1.283*** (18.97)
One-period Lag of Foreign Ownership Indicator	0.193*** (25.05)	0.754*** (17.49)
One-period Lag of Log Firm Size	0.203*** (68.49)	1.028*** (29.55)
One-period Lag of Firm Tenure	−0.012*** (11.05)	0.045*** (10.45)
Inverse Mills Ratio		0.991*** (4.12)
Year-specific fixed effects	Yes	Yes
3-digit Industry-specific Fixed Effects	Yes	Yes
	228,288	228,288
Heckman two-step	1st step	2nd Step
Regressand	Training indicator	Log training per-capita
One-period lag of Log TFP2 ($TFP2_{ijt}^{it}$)	0.549*** (25.69)	0.835*** (−14.12)
One-period lag of industry output tariffs	0.016*** (3.27)	0.022*** (2.21)
One-period lag of export indicator	0.110*** (15.92)	0.120*** (7.52)
One-period lag of SOEs indicator	0.236*** (13.74)	0.426*** (12.24)
One-period lag of foreign ownership indicator	0.193***(25.05)	0.285*** (12.87)
One-period lag of log firm size	0.203*** (68.49)	0.135*** (7.68)
One-period lag of firm tenure	0.012***(11.05)	0.017*** (7.64)
Inverse mills ratio		1.253*** (10.14)
Year-specific fixed effects	Yes	Yes
3-digit industry-specific fixed effects	Yes	Yes
Observations	228,288	228,288

Notes Robust t-values corrected for clustering at the 2-digit industry level in parentheses. *, **, (***) indicates significance at or below the 10, 5 and 1% level, respectively. The sample selection model is presented in equations (participation) and (11) in the text. The regressand in the first-step is firm's training dummy whereas that in the second step is firm's log training expenses. The augmented Olley-Pakes TFP2 is adopted as a measure of firm productivity. Firm tenure is used as an exclusion variable that appeared in the first step but not the second step. The three-digit Chinese industry-specific fixed effects and year-specific fixed effects are also included in the estimations between ex-ante measured TFP and standard ex-post measured TFP. The ex-ante measured TFP, *TFP*2, have identical mean but different variance from the standard TFP as introduced above and reported in Appendix A.

As reported in the first-stage estimations, low productive firms are more likely to engage in training behavior. The negative and significant coefficient of output trade liberalization seems striking at first glance. However, such a finding is reasonable. The tougher import competition caused by output trade liberalization results in lower firm profitability, which in turn invests less in firm training. Meanwhile, exporters and SOEs are more likely to invest in firm training. Similarly, large firms are more likely to engage in worker training. By contrast, foreign firms are found to be less likely to invest in training. A possible reason is that multinational firms are more likely to maintain their training investment in their foreign headquarter and have not much training expenses in foreign affiliates. Finally, older firms are found to have less training expenses.

Once the inverse mills ratio obtained in the first-step Probit estimates with three-digit industry-level fixed effects are calculated, we are ready to estimate the second-step of the bivariate selection model by including the inverse mills ratio as an additional regressor. All the coefficients have identical signs as their counterparts in the first stage and highly significant at the conventional statistical level.

10.4.3 Different Measures of TFP

To further check whether our main findings are sensitive to the measure of firm TFP and the empirical specifications, columns (1) and (2) of Table 10.5 use the Levinsohn-Petrin (2003) TFP as the regressand while columns (3) and (4) use the value-added TFP. After controlling for firm's self-selection to training and both firm-specific fixed effects and year-specific fixed effects, estimates in column (1) ascertain that the effect of training on firm productivity is positive and significant. Exporters are found be more productive and SOEs are found to be less productive.

Previous works have recognized that processing firms are less productive (Dai et al., 2016). Since processing firms are usually pure exporters that sell all their products abroad. To make sure that our results are not driven by processing firms, we drop all pure exporters in column (2) and still find all similar results as in column (1).

Thus far, our measured productivity is gross function TFP. It is interesting to see whether our results are robust when measured by value-added TFP. Estimates in the last two columns of Table 10.6 thus pick up this task by using the value-added Olley-Pakes TFP. Precisely, the value-added TFP is measured by using value-added as the output of the production function and estimating the output elasticity with respect to capital and labor, respectively. Estimates in column (3) include pure exporters whereas those in column (4) drop pure exporters from the sample. It turns out that the results are insensitive to the adoption of using value-added TFP as the regressand.

Table 10.5 Further CRC estimates using different TFP measures

Regressand: Firm TFP	TFP (Levinsohn-Petrin)		TFPOP (value-added)	
	(1)	(2)	(3)	(4)
Log firm fitted training	0.028***	0.028***	0.013***	0.015***
	(7.00)	(6.85)	(3.11)	(3.46)
Industry output tariffs	0.002	0.001	0.001	0.001
	(0.57)	(0.52)	(0.19)	(0.25)
Export indicator	0.083***	0.086***	0.050***	0.052***
	(8.02)	(8.23)	(4.49)	(4.64)
Foreign indicator	0.040	0.049	0.011	−0.005
	(1.29)	(1.55)	(0.33)	(0.13)
SOE indicator	0.069***	0.069***	0.098***	0.097***
	(2.72)	(2.70)	(3.44)	(3.41)
Industry external tariffs	0.000	0.000	0.002***	0.002***
	(0.09)	(0.14)	(3.35)	(3.23)
Pure exporters dropped	No	Yes	No	Yes
Firm-specific fixed effects	Yes	Yes	Yes	Yes
Year-specific fixed effects	Yes	Yes	Yes	Yes
Observations	126,757	125,614	151,063	148,894
R-squared	0.05	0.05	0.09	0.09

Notes T-values in parentheses. *, **, (***) indicates significance at or below the 10, 5 and 1% level, respectively. All regressions include firm-level fixed effects and year fixed effects. Pure exporters are dropped in columns (2) and (4)

10.4.4 Further Robustness Checks

It is widely recognized that today China has engaged a great extent in the global supply chain. In previous estimates we abstract away firm's input tariffs from the regressions possibly because imported intermediate inputs for processing trade is already free duty (Yu, 2015). Still, non-processing firms bear some amount of input tariffs. One solution is to adopt the firm-level input tariffs as constructed in Yu (2015). However, such an approach is at the expense of losing large number of observations since the construction of firm-specific input tariffs requires the merged dataset between firm-level production data (which is used to estimate TFP) and production-level trade dataset (which is used to calculate firm-specific input tariffs). As input tariffs reduction is not the key variable in the present paper, we hence abstract it away allow them to be captured in the error term.

Instead, we consider another interesting case. Firm's imported intermediate goods are not necessarily use as intermediate inputs; it is possible for firms to import capital goods which could in turn boost firm productivity from other channels different from

Table 10.6 Further robust estimates

Specifications	No capital-goods	No quota-imposed
Regressand: Firm TFP	TFP ^{OP}TFP ^{OP}	TFP ^{OP}TFP ^{LP}
	(1)(2)	(3)(4)
Log firm fitted training	0.007***0.007***	0.007***0.018***
	(5.41)(5.28)	(5.77)(4.37)
Industry output tariffs	0.008***0.008***	0.007***0.012***
	(8.63)(8.75)	(5.30)(2.84)
Export indicator	0.008**0.008**	0.010***0.065***
	(2.27)(2.36)	(2.99)(6.07)
Foreign indicator	0.0000.002	0.0080.054*
	(0.03)(0.24)	(0.74)(1.65)
SOE indicator	0.0010.001	0.0020.068***
	(0.11)(0.09)	(0.24)(2.58)
Log firm size	0.027***0.027***	0.025***0.204***
	(10.91)(10.97)	(10.30)(26.67)
Industry external tariffs	0.001***0.001***	0.001***0.000
	(3.72)(4.01)	(4.49)(0.15)
Pure exporters dropped	NoYes	YesYes
Firm-specific fixed effects	YesYes	YesYes
Year-specific fixed effects	YesYes	YesYes
Observations	135,377,133,324	135,596,113,132
R-squared	0.020.02	0.010.07

Notes T-values in parentheses. *, **, (***) indicates significance at or below the 10, 5 and 1% level, respectively

firm trainings. To rule out this case, we drop industries which include mostly intermediate inputs. According to description of the Broad Economic Classification (BEC) and its concordance to China's industrial classification, industries like machinery (code 36 and 37) belong to capital goods. We hence drop such two industries in column (1) of Table 10.6. It turns out that higher firm training still leads to higher firm productivity. Column (2) drops pure exporters and yields similar results. Thus, our finding remains robust even dropping capital goods.

Our last exercise is to drop industries that are exposed to various non-tariffs barriers such as import quota, as our main objective is to check whether trade liberalization boosts firm productivity through the channel of firm training. Since exports of textile and garments are restricted by the multi-fiber agreement which last for a decade from 1994 to 2004 (Khandelwal et al., 2013), we hence drop textile and garment from the estimations in columns (3) with the Olley-Pakes TFP as the regressand and (4) with the Levinsohn-Petrin TFP as the regressand. Once again, both estimates suggest that output trade liberalization boosts firm productivity. More importantly, Output trade liberalization affects firm's probability to invest on worker training, which in turn boost firm productivity.

10.5 Concluding Remarks

In this paper we find that trade liberalization increases firms' training investment, which in turn boost firm productivity and increase firm exports. We are thus able to identify a new mechanism through trade liberalization affects firm productivity. Our paper also has strong policy implications as well as academic contributions. The competitiveness of Chinese firms are shrinking due, in large, to the increasing labor costs in recent years. To overcome such challenge, the government in China is working hard to facilitate the macro-environment for firm R&D. Meanwhile, the government helps firms in labor-intensive industries to invest in other lower labor-cost African countries (see Shen, 2013 and Tian and Yu, 2014 for detailed discussions). Our empirical findings in this paper suggest that, in addition to on-the-job training provided by firms themselves, China's government may provide more training by having more technical schools and initiating more training programs to increase worker productivity and hence boost firm productivity.

Appendix A

Measuring Ex-ante TFP (TFP2)

This section draws heavily from Qiu and Yu (2013) to discuss how we construct and measure TFP using two different approaches: *ex-post* TFP (TFP1) and *ex-ante* TFP (TFP2) inspired by Feenstra et al. (2014).

We extend the Olley-Pakes (1996) approach to fit with China's reality in the following ways. Firstly, given that the measure of TFP requires real terms of firm's inputs (labor and capital) and output, we adopt different price deflators for inputs and outputs from Brandt *et al.* (2012) in which the output deflators are constructed using "reference price" information from *China's Statistical Yearbooks* whereas input deflators are constructed based on output deflators and China's national input-output table (2002).

Secondly, we take China's WTO accession in 2001 into account since such a positive demand shock would push Chinese firms to expand their economic scales, which in turn can exaggerate the simultaneous bias of their measured TFP. Thirdly, it is essential to construct the real investment variable when using the Olley-Pakes (1996) approach. As usual, we adopt the perpetual inventory method to investigate the law of motion for real capital and real investment. Different from assigning an arbitrary number for the depreciation ratio, we use the exact firm's real depreciation provided by the Chinese firm-level data set.

Finally, we also consider firm's processing behavior in the TFP realization by constructing a processing export indicator (one denotes processing export and zero otherwise). The idea is that processing firms may use different technology than non-processing firms (Feenstra and Hanson, 2005).

Thus, a firm's investment function is

$$V_{it} = g_1(x_{it}, \ln K_{it}, EX_{it}, PE_{it}, WTO_t)$$

where EX_{it},(PE_{it}) is the export (processing export) indicator to measure whether firm i exports (engages in processing exports) in year t, and WTO_t is an indicator that equals one if the WTO agreement has occurred after 2001 and zero before that. Therefore, inverting the investment function with respect to its first argument we obtain[9]:

$$x_{it} = g_1^{-1}(V_{it}, \ln K_{it}, EX_{it}, PE_{it}, WTO_t)$$

Given the gross production function

$$\ln Y_{it} = \alpha_k \ln K_{it} + \alpha_l \ln L_{it} + \alpha_m \ln M_{it} + x_{it} + \varepsilon_{it}$$

and defining the function $g_2(\cdot)$ as $\alpha_k \ln K_{jt} + g_1^{-1}(V_{it}, \ln K_{it}, EX_{it}, PE_{it}, WTO_t)$, the estimation of the labor (materials) coefficients α_m (α_m) are obtained as:

$$\ln Y_{it} = \alpha_l \ln L_{it} + \alpha_m \ln M_{it} + g_2(V_{it}, \ln K_{it}, EX_{it}, PE_{it}, WTO_t) + \varepsilon_{it}$$

The next step is to obtain an unbiased estimated coefficient of α_k Olley-Pakes (1996) use the following specification:

$$\ln Y_{ir} - \hat{\alpha}_l \ln L_{it} - \hat{\alpha}_m \ln M_{it} = \alpha_k \ln K_{it} + E(x_{it}|x_{it-1}, pr_{it}) + [x_{it} - E(x_{it}|x_{it-1}, pr_{it})] + \varepsilon_{it}$$

where the estimated values of the labor coefficient and materials coefficient are used on the left. The expectation of productivity appearing in (2-step) is modeled as a forth-order polynomial function of lagged productivity, which can be obtained as ($g_{2i,t\text{-}1}$-$\alpha_k$ln $K_{i,t\text{-}1}$), and also the predicted probability of the firm's survival into the year t, pr_{it} , based on year t-1 information. The predicted probability is obtained from Probit estimation.[10] The term [x_{it}-E(x_{it}| $x_{it\text{-}1}$, pr_{it})] is the productivity shock for surviving firms, but does not affect the investment or exit choice so it is treated as an error.

---

[9] Olley and Pakes (1996) show that the investment demand function is monotonically increasing in the productivity shock jt x, by making some mild assumptions about the firm's production technology.

[10] Note that here the non-linear least squares approach is adopted to estimate (2-step) since it requires the estimated coefficients of the log-capital in the first and second term to be identical (Pavcnik, 2002).

Once the coefficient of capital $\hat{\alpha}_k$ is estimated in Eq. (10.2-step), it is ready to obtain the standard ex-post TFP:

$$TFP1_{it} \equiv x_{it} = \ln Y_{it} - \hat{\alpha}_k \ln K_{it} - \hat{\alpha}_l \ln L_{it} - \hat{\alpha}_m \ln M_{it}$$

In this way, TFP1 includes both true production productivity and managerial efficiency. By contrast, the *ex-ante* productivity (TFP2) which only capture true production productivity is given by

$$TFP2_{it} = g_1^{-1}(V_{it}, \ln K_{it}, EX_{it}, PE_{it}, WTO_t)$$

Appendix Table 10.A1 reports the estimated coefficients of labor, capital, materials, TFP1 and TFP2.

Table 10.A1 Total factor productivity of Chinese firms (2000–2007)

CIC	Labor	Capital	Materials	Variance in	
				TFP1	TFP2
13	0.077	0.060	0.814	0.322	0.148
14	0.055	0.071	0.857	0.300	0.172
15	0.094	0.113	0.799	0.381	0.235
16	0.020	0.270	0.783	0.631	0.479
17	0.066	0.044	0.868	0.218	0.103
18	0.110	0.039	0.798	0.310	0.093
19	0.084	0.041	0.857	0.276	0.098
20	0.099	0.071	0.841	0.300	0.167
21	0.103	0.055	0.814	0.218	0.119
22	0.063	0.053	0.867	0.234	0.127
23	0.065	0.068	0.815	0.215	0.210
24	0.091	0.039	0.823	0.223	0.113
25	0.014	0.069	0.865	0.324	0.327
26	0.063	0.058	0.820	0.318	0.175
27	0.062	0.064	0.790	0.360	0.219
28	0.040	0.060	0.889	0.313	0.169
29	0.087	0.081	0.769	0.333	0.186
30	0.069	0.046	0.836	0.288	0.180
31	0.046	0.059	0.844	0.287	0.145
32	0.061	0.029	0.891	0.249	0.116
33	0.080	0.079	0.850	0.278	0.322
34	0.062	0.037	0.841	0.311	0.093
35	0.061	0.055	0.837	0.247	0.188
36	0.053	0.049	0.841	0.326	0.123

(continued)

(continued)

CIC	Labor	Capital	Materials	Variance in	
37	0.063	0.045	0.835	0.283	0.160
39	0.077	0.066	0.836	0.303	0.135
40	0.109	0.075	0.806	0.358	0.194
41	0.049	0.054	0.806	0.386	0.208
42	0.091	0.039	0.857	0.271	0.092

Notes We do not report standard errors for each coefficient to save space though available upon request. The logarithm of firm productivity for Chinese firms (TFP1 and TFP2) is estimated by industry by the augmented Olley-Pakes approach introduced in the text. Coefficients of labor, capital, and materials are calculated at the sectorial average whereas TFP1 and TFP2 is measured at firm-level using firm-level sales, capital, materials, and labor, respectively. The last three columns report the sectorial mean of log TFP1, log TFP2 and log of worker training, respectively.

Chapter 11
China's Free Trade Ports: Effective Action Against the Threat of De-Globalization

With sluggish external demand and increasing trade protectionism by the USA and the European Union, China is facing severe challenges in implementing its deeper, ongoing reforms. To respond actively to such challenges, the Communist Party of China's 19th National Congress proposed to "promote a new pattern of all-round opening up." In particular, the establishment of free trade ports is considered an important means to realize deeper integration with the world economy. This paper discusses the background, the motivation, the possible challenges as well as a feasible path for the successful implementation of free trade ports in China. Based on the international experience, the construction of free trade ports in China requires freer trade in goods, high mobility of talent and free capital flow.

11.1 Introduction

Since the 2008 global financial crisis, there has been a new wave of trade protectionism headed by the USA, casting a shadow on the world economy. The current situation arises from the stagnation of the Doha negotiations, the failure of the Transatlantic Trade and Investment Partnership, negotiations among Western countries, the Brexit negotiations, the Trump regime's abolition of the Trans-Pacific Partnership, renegotiation of the North

American Free Trade Agreement, and the recent threat of a trade friction between the USA and China, which would result in a tremendous shock to world markets. Widespread protectionism could lower global output, making worldwide economic recovery difficult. China is the largest exporter in the world, and, indeed, it has become one of the major beneficiaries of deepening globalization. However, the country faces domestic and external challenges. On the demand side, it is facing

This chapter is coauthored with Wei Tian, Zhuxi Xu andHuihuang Zhu and originally published in China and the World Economy, 2018, 26(4), pp. 62–81.

M. Yu, *China's Miracle in Foreign Trade*, Studies in Modern Chinese Economy,
https://doi.org/10.1007/978-981-16-6030-6_11

weak external demand from its major trading partners. US protectionism against China has worsened the world economic situation, because the USA and China have mutually become the largest trading partners in the world. On the supply side, China's demographic dividend is shrinking. The increasing aging of the population has become a major concern in Chinese society. As other resource constraints, such as land and the environment, have gradually tightened, the overall cost of labor in the manufacturing sector has increased substantially, which, in turn, has weakened China's export competitiveness.

Although the sluggish external demand and intensifying trade protectionism of Western countries has cast a shadow on China's growth momentum, the path for economic reform is clear. First, China should continue to open its domestic markets to increase the volume of trade. Second, China needs to promote industrial transformation to maintain competitiveness in the global economy. An ideal way to kill two birds with one stone would be to establish free trade ports in Chinese mainland.

The notion of free trade ports was first brought up in a report to the 19th National Congress of the Communist Party of China. Chinese President Xi Jinping explicitly pointed out that it is necessary to promote the formation of a new path to full liberalization.[1] Specifically, the country will allow more freedom to reform the pilot free trade zones (PFTZ) and explore the establishment of free trade ports. In the keynote speech at the opening ceremony of the 2018 annual meeting of the Boao Forum for Asia, President Xi emphasized the implementation of trade and investment liberalization and facilitation policies, and the exploration of building free trade ports with Chinese characteristics.[2]

However, a "free trade port" is a relatively new concept in China. It is natural to ask: What is a free trade port? How would it be different from the free trade zones (FTZs) in coastal and inland China? How would a free trade port help the local economy? Finally, what conditions are required for the development of a free trade port? These issues deserve exploration. The current literature on free trade ports mainly focuses on the construction and development experience of free trade ports in developed countries (regions) and is mostly outdated. Research on the motives and applicable path for building free trade ports with Chinese characteristics is limited. Therefore, in this paper, we attempt to answer the above questions. We aim to show that building free trade ports would be an effective action against the threat of de-globalization.

The rest of the paper is organized as follows. Section 2 reviews the emergence of de-globalization in the new era, followed by a discussion of how de-globalization affects trade and economic welfare and a theoretical interpretation of the necessity to establish free trade ports. We suggest that the further economic reform will help increase China's trade volume in the face of an unfavorable world trade environment. Apart from presenting a theoretical justification, we also discuss a path for establishing China's free trade ports. Section 3 compares the development stage and characteristics of China's free trade ports with those of more mature international

[1] See http://cpc.people.com.cn/n1/2017/1028/c64094-29613660.html.

[2] See http://cpc.people.com.cn/n1/2018/0410/c64094-29917187.html.

free trade ports, such as in Singapore port and Shanghai PFTZs. Section 4 offers some policy suggestions for the development of international free trade ports in China.

11.2 Theoretical Framework for the Establishment of Free Trade Ports

11.2.1 New De-Globalization Threat to the World Trade

According to the classical Ricardian trade theory and the neoclassical Heckscher–Ohlin model, exporting and importing countries can benefit from free trade. Empirical evidence shows that globalization, indeed, promotes economic growth, regardless of the different econometric specifications adopted (Dreher, 2006). For China, increased integration with the global economy has contributed to sustained growth in international trade. China has been playing an increasingly important role in regional specialization since its accession to the World Trade Organization (WTO), and its economic development has contributed to its trade partners ' economic growth (Rumbaugh and Blancher, 2004).

However, history tells us that each time the global economy slows down dramatically or a global economic crisis erupts, the prospects for globalization become gloomy. Under the impact of economic crises, developed countries have undergone profound changes. The domestic contradictions in developed economies are intensifying. Problems such as unequal distribution of social wealth, lack of job opportunities and refugee crises become more prominent during an economic downturn and can lead to regime changes. All these changes can trigger a new wave of de-globalization, with unilateralist trade protection policies reemerging (Tong et al., 2017).

Following the financial crisis in 2008, world trade slowed tremendously and theoverall international economic situation has not yet fully recovered. According to theIMF (2017), the growth rates of world GDP in 2015 and 2016 were 3.4 and 3.2%, respectively, and the GDP growth rates of developed economies were only 2.1 and 1.7%, respectively. The growth rates of the world trade volume were 2.6 and 2.3%, respectively, even lower than the world GDP growth rate. Commodity prices continued to below.

Developing countries whose economic growth is highly dependent on export trade are more vulnerable to protectionist policies in the tide of reverse globalization. Therefore, for developing countries to maintain the momentum of economic growth given the unfavorable new world economic situation and safeguard their own interests in international trade will require corresponding adjustments of their domestic economic structure.

Guo et al. (2018) find that a US–China trade friction would generate substantial losses in output and social welfare, measured as real wages. China must consider how to deal with the enhanced trade disputes trigged by USPresident Trump.Inthelong term, to minimize welfare loss, China should continue to open up its domestic markets for its most important trading partners, like countries in the European Union and the 10 ASEAN countries. Specifically, China could import more from the European Union and the Belt and Road countries to reduce its domestic prices and, hence, increase the real income of consumers.

11.2.2 Free Trade Ports: The Next Step in China's Reform and Opening up

Thus far, we have argued that it is necessary for China to push for a new path to all-round opening up. Before its accession to the WTO in 2001, China had already set up many special economic zones, industrial zones and export processing zones. At present, the country's special economic zone with the highest degree of openness is a PFTZ. The Shanghai PFTZ was launched in 2012, and the Guangdong, Tianjin and Fujian FTPZs in 2015. The four PFTZs focus on different areas, such as opening up investment, trade and finance, encouraging entrepreneurship and innovation, as well as carrying out interim and post-establishment administration. The four PFTZs have had some prominent achievements. Building on the successful experience of the first two batches of PFTZ, on 31 March 2017, the State Council officially released the development plan for the third batch of seven new PFTZs,[3] followed by Hainan and Xiongan, forming a "1+3+7+2" "geese" pattern.

Meanwhile, as discussed in Yu (2018), in 2016 the Chinese Government selected 12 cities nationwide to build a new open economy system on a pilot basis. The 12 pilot cities are: coastal and border cities, including Dalian, Fangchenggang, Shanghai and Zhangzhou; provincial capitals, including Jinan, Nanchang and Xi'an; and five Chinese city clusters, including Chongqing, Dongguan, Suzhou, Tangshan and Wuhan.

On 13 April 2018, President Xi Jinping announced the decision to develop the island of Hainan into a PFTZ and gradually explore and promote the establishment of a free trade port with Chinese characteristics. In becoming a PFTZ, Hainan will be granted more autonomy in developing a law-based and international business environment, as well as a fair, open, unified and efficient market environment.

The extensive open practices of the FTZs in various areas has not only contributed to the rapid growth of China's economy, but also has resulted in the accumulation of valuable experience for China in establishing effective market mechanisms. In the new era, the trial FTZs have been given greater autonomy in enacting reform and in the development of free trade ports.

Why does China need free trade ports? Key reasons include that expanding the trade volume requires freer trade in goods, high mobility of talent and free capital

[3] Seven new PFTZs are Liaoning PFTZ, Zhejiang PFTZ, Henan PFTZ, Hubei PFTZ, Chongqing PFTZ, Sichuan PFTZ.

flow. Moreover, development of free trade ports can coincide with the development of the cities where the ports are located and their surrounding areas.

By definition, a free trade port is a port area within the territory of a country or region that is not subject to the usual customs control, with free access to overseas goods and funds. The main feature of a free trade port is that it is outside the control of the customs authority of a country. It has the features of a port and an FTZ, with many trade-related functions, including product processing, logistics and warehousing. Geographically, a free trade port is part of the territory of a country, but from the perspective of administrative supervision, it is outside the customs jurisdiction of the country.

For commodity trade, it is vital to reduce various kinds of costs. Good infrastructure is important for guaranteeing port-clearing efficiency. Limao and Venables (2001) find that poor infrastructure accounts for 40% of predicted transport costs for coastal countries and up to 60% for landlocked countries. Clark et al. (2004) also find that port efficiency is an important determinant of shipping costs. They demonstrate that improving port efficiency from the 25th to the 75th percentile can reduce shipping costs by 12%.

A free trade port must be a cargo hub that can facilitate international trade and logistics information collection and sharing, with resources allocated effectively. Supply and demand information in each link of the supply chain must be matched accurately on the platform provided by the free trade port. Efficient regulatory mechanisms need to be designed to minimize trade costs. Taking the speed of customs clearance as an example, Hu (2014) finds that each 10-percent improvement in import clearance time in an FTZ will lead to a 5.68-percent fall in the volume of agricultural trade within the FTZ. If the cost of trade cannot be reduced effectively, there will be no chance for quick circulation of merchandise trade flow, and the port itself will be at a disadvantage in terms of international competition. The goal of free trade ports is to integrate ports and cities. This is achieved by improving multimodal transport systems, service coverage and functional interaction between ports and cities. Through integrated development, an open and efficient free trade port city can be formed, which, in turn, can promote economic growth in a region.

Human resources are an important factor in economic development. To promote trade, specialized, high-skilled personnel and international talent are particularly valuable. Studies show that increasing the number of undergraduate students will enhance the local economy significantly. Hunt and Gauthier-Loiselle (2010) find that a 1-percentage point increase in the share of immigrant college graduates in the population increases the number of patents per capita by 9 to 18%. Meanwhile, high-technology workers generate large spillover effects. Rosenthal and Strange (2008) find that spatial concentration of employment enhances productivity, and the benefits of spatial concentration are driven by proximity to college-educated workers. Furthermore, the inflow of high-technology talent can dramatically improve the level of technological innovation. Kerr and Lincoln (2010), using US H-1B visa data, find that higher H-1B admissions increases immigrant science and engineering employment and patenting by inventors with Indian and Chinese names in cities and firms dependent upon the program relative to their peers. Most specifications of this study find limited effects for native science and engineering employment or patenting.

Despite the introduction of certain preferential policies, the lack of professionals and international talent has always been a focal point for the development of PFTZs in China. According to the Human Resources Bureau of the Shanghai FTZ, the shortage of professional and technical personnel in the Shanghai FTZ reached 48% in 2014. A free trade port would provide more opportunities and guarantees for the career development of international talent and professionals. Thus, a free trade port would be far more attractive than an FTZ.

Apart from human resources, capital is another crucial factor for economic growth. Xiang and He (2016) find that the establishment of the PFTZ has had a significantly positive impact on capital flows in Shanghai. Latorre et al. (2017) find that the impact of more foreign multinationals in providing services is positive for China. Javorcik (2004) provides strong evidence of positive productivity spillovers from foreign direct investment between foreign affiliates and their local suppliers in upstream sectors. With less restrictions on the financial market, the free trade ports will be the frontier of a new round of financial market liberalization.

A free trade port is a more open platform than an FTZ. From a theoretical perspective, the construction of free trade ports will enhance the institutional environment for China's opening-up reforms, promote the country's economic transition from relying on the demographic dividend to the "system dividend," and enable better response to the profound changes in the global environment. Practically, the experiences of predecessors, such as Singapore and China's Hong Kong Special Administrative Region, may help FTZs advance toward the goal of being a more transparent institutional environment. The world's major free trade centers, such as Dubai and New York, are defining themselves as international free trade ports or global logistics centers, because this practice is an effective way to drive regional growth in the trade, finance and service sectors. Breakthroughs in the areas of trade facilitation measures, ship fuel prices, financial support, customs supervision, inspection and quarantine are necessary for free trade ports. Free trade ports in China could become centers for the exchange of global goods, talent and capital, providing a steady stream of momentum for economic development.

11.2.3 Functional Orientation for the Construction of China's Free Trade Ports

The development of free trade ports serves as an experiment for institutional innovation. China still has a long way to go in many aspects, such as loosening capital control and controlling the movement of people, to promote trade and investment facilitation, and to simplify and unify investment standards. Therefore, the free trade ports need an effective management system and legal framework so that the impacts of external shocks on the onshore market remain controllable. The construction of free trade ports will be important to stimulate institutional innovation. The innovation in the free trade ports will be greater than in Shanghai and other FTZs in Chinese mainland, given that the free trade ports will be larger compared with the FTZs. Therefore, the local governments will have greater rights in regards to policy innovation, which will amplify the effects of new policies.

The free trade ports will also play a significant role in boosting the economic development of Chinese mainland. Trade ports, such as Chinese Hong Kong and Singapore, belong to a separate customs territory. However, the free trade ports to be established in Chinese mainland will be special regulatory areas in the same customs territory. To this end, one of the main aims of the free trade ports is to advance the development of the Chinese mainland economy. At the same time, the development of free trade ports needs to rely on the development of peripheral regions. There aremany places in the world where transportation is convenient but no free trade port has been formed. The main reason is the lack of strong support from the peripheral regions. The peripheral regions can provide goods, talent and capital continuously to the free trade ports, thus bringing about greater demand for re-export, construction and bonded workers.

At the same time, the free trade ports will play a leading role in upgrading high-value links in the global value chain. For example, the development of the complete international service support system that a free trade port requires with intermediaries, such as finance and law companies for all aspects of production and life, can promote a more complete production chain coordinated with the surrounding regions and help the regional economy to develop and upgrade. Most international trade centers have gradually changed from traditional ports of goods trading to international capital and information transition centers, like London, New York, Tokyo, Singapore and Chinese Hong Kong. They have gradually developed into world offshore trade centers and become centers of global trade.

11.3 International Experience and Domestic Exploration

Most of the mature international free trade ports are in developed countries and regions with a long maritime history and sound capital markets. Various countries and regions have developed free trade ports with different characteristics according to their particular conditions and strategic considerations (e.g. the integrated free trade port in Singapore, the free trade ports in Hamburg, Germany and Busan, South Korea, and industrial FTZs such as Rotterdam of the Netherlands). Chinese Hong Kong became a free trade port while it was colonized by Britain. Following more than 100 years of development, it has become a leader in international logistics and trade, and a global financial center. It is also a model for the construction of free trade ports in Chinese mainland.

Over 90% of Chinese mainland's foreign trade is shipped by sea. With the development of the economy and deepening of the opening-up reform, port construction has made

Table 11.1 Top ten world container ports (TEU, millions)

Rank	Port	2011	2012	2013	2014	2015
1	Shanghai, China	31.74	32.53	33.62	35.29	36.54
2	Singapore	29.94	31.65	32.6	33.87	30.92
3	Shenzhen, China	22.57	22.94	23.28	24.03	24.2
4	Ningbo-Zhou Shan, China	14.72	16.83	17.33	19.45	20.63
5	Hong Kong, China	24.38	23.12	22.35	22.23	20.07
6	Busan, South Korea	16.18	17.04	17.69	18.65	19.45
7	Qingdao, China	13.02	14.5	15.52	16.62	17.47
8	Guangzhou harbor, China	14.42	14.74	15.31	16.16	17.22
9	Jebel Ali, Dubai, UAE	13	13.3	13.64	15.25	15.6
10	Tianjin, China	11.59	12.3	13.01	14.05	14.11

Source World Shipping Council, available from: http://www.worldshipping.org/about-the-industry/global-trade/top-50-world-container-ports/. *Notes* TEU, twenty-feet equivalent unit; UAE, United Arab Emirates

great progress in Chinese mainland. China (including Hong Kong) has 7 of the world's 10 largest container ports (Table 11.1). However, many container ships choose to fuel in Singapore due to the oil price gap and other extra services.

To achieve a higher level of openness and acquire a proactive position in foreign trade, the major PFTZs in Chinese mainland are constantly exploring new paths for further reforms. Some bonded port areas are also actively seeking transformation. Although the construction of China's free trade ports has already relied on certain infrastructure and policy support, the specific path for deepening reforms remains unclear. By looking at mature international ports, such as in Singapore and China's most advanced PFTZ in Shanghai, we attempt to identify a path for the successful implementation of free trade ports in China.

11.3.1 Singapore Port

In 1969, Singapore established the first FTZ in the Jurong Pier Industrial Zone. Singapore gradually developed into a highly open free trade port. There are eight FTZs in Singapore currently, which are managed by Singapore Port Group Limited, Jurong Harbor Sdn Bhd and Changi Airport Group.

As a country with zero tariffs, Singapore's free trade ranks second in the world in terms of port trade volume (Table 11.1). Geographically, it is at the center of South-East Asia and has become an important channel for world trade.

Trade in goods depends on an intelligent logistics system, an information-based management approach, and low-cost anchorage, warehousing and transit options. Singapore attaches great importance to infrastructure construction. According to the

World Economic Forum's 2016–2017 Global Competitiveness Index,[4] Singapore ranks second in infrastructure construction. Maintaining the efficiency of logistics was the key for Singapore to become a trade center. To facilitate trade, as early as 1989, the Singapore Government took the world lead in the development of a trade management electronic platform for customs, tax and security, with 35 other government agencies now connected to this network for enterprises to provide a one-stop customs clearance service. With this unified system, companies only need to submit an electronic files to request customs clearance. The declaration and audit procedures related to import and export trade can be completed within the network, and can, in some cases, be completed within 10 s.

Furthermore, Singapore provides special tax relief and financial support for high-technology, high-value-added enterprises, regional headquarters, international shipping companies, export companies, and other special industries and service industries. Singapore has already become the world's main location for logistics companies. Among the world's top 25 logistics companies, 20 have set up regional or global headquarters in Singapore (e.g. DHL, Dexun, Shan Nine Air and Cink Logistics).

Singapore has signed more than 20 free trade agreements with various regions and countries, including China, the USA, ASEAN, New Zealand, India and Japan. Based on these free trade agreements, Singapore-based exporters and investors can enjoy multiple benefits, such as tariff concessions, faster access to markets and access to intellectual property protection. Advanced infrastructure, efficient information management and preferential taxation policies mean that Singapore is unrivaled in facilitating the trade of goods.

From the point of view of talent accumulation, the Singapore Government has set up a "citizen and population group" in the Prime Minister's Office to take charge of overseas immigration projects. The government has passed the following policies: Contact Singapore, the Foreign Talent Settlement Plan, Professional and Technical Talents and the Investment Residency Program. A series of policies to attract entrepreneurs to settle in Singapore and to increase the reserve of technical talent has enabled Singapore to have continuous innovation. The Singapore Government's policy of free entry and exit has greatly facilitated the movement of international personnel and the development of transnational businesses. In the 2017 Passport Index, which ranks global passport freedom, Singapore is positioned first along with Germany.[5]

The development of commerce and trade in a free trade port requires a liberalized financial environment. According to the Global Financial Centres Index (19th) report released by the Z/Yen Group in London in 2016, Singapore surpassed Chinese Hong Kong to become the third largest international financial center, and is the largest financial center in Asia. Singapore also has the third largest international foreign exchange market. Its modern communications equipment is directly connected with the New York Clearing House Interbank Payment System and the European Society for Worldwide Interbank Financial Telecommunications system. Therefore, the currency

[4] See https://cn.weforum.org/reports/2016-2017.

[5] See https://www.passportindex.org/byRank.php.

settlement process is simple. A relaxed currency exchange mechanism and a well-developed leasing system attract foreign investment and there is adequate financial support for trade activities. Singapore's sound financial system has powered the city's economic and trade development, providing an excellent model for the regulation and liberalization of China's financial market.

11.3.2 Shanghai Yangshan Free Trade Port Area

The China Shanghai FTZ bonded area, formally founded in 2013, consists of the Waigaoqiao FTZ, the Waigaoqiao Free Trade Logistics Park, the Yangshan Free Trade Port Area (YSFTPA) and the Pudong Airport FTZ. The customs area of the YSFTPA is 14.16 km2, which accounts for 49.2% of the total area of the Shanghai FTZ. Endowed with an excellent deep-water coastline and shipping lanes, the YSFTPA benefits from the policies of both the PFTZ and the Comprehensive Test Zone for Development of International Shipping, and is one of the most competitive international shipping and off- shore service areas in China. The All-round and In-depth Reform and Opening-up Plan on China Shanghai FTZ, issued by the State Council in March 2017, pointed out that the establishment of free trade port zones in YSFTPA, Pudong Airport FTZ and other areas under special customs supervision marks the reform of YSFTPA entering a new stage.

As the first free trade port area, the YSFTPA has been exploring innovation over 2014–2017 and has made tremendous achievements. For business services, the YSFTPA has advanced infrastructure and core technology and has become the biggest automated container terminal in the world. For logistics, it has developed domestic market channels, connecting the port with Shanghai by a cross-sea bridge. The YSFTPA has formed a business system based on information technology to conduct cross-border e-commerce. Under the guidance of the policy "Two years exemptions and three years 50%- reductions,"[6] the YSFTPA provides tax breaks for logistics enterprises, trade enterprises, and their operation centers. Giving full play to the advantage of "import, export and transit trade," the port area is also committed to exploring the high-end consumer goods market to build a professional and international bulk commodity trade platform.

The Shanghai FTZ has established various programs, such as the "Leading Talents Program" and the "Youth Talents Program" in finance, and the policy of "Permanent Residency for Foreigners" to attract more talent in various industries. In 2015, the Ministry of Public Security issued 12 policies on immigration and visas that would benefit the Shanghai Technology and Innovation Center. At the end of 2016, the

[6] "Two year exemptions and three year 50 percent-reductions" policy means that a foreign-invested company can enjoy business income tax exemptions for the first 2 years and a 50-percent reduction for the next 3 years.

Chinese Government proposed the "new ten" policy,[7] providing a more convenient immigration environment for the exchange of talent.

As the most developed financial center in China, Shanghai FTZ continues to provide financial support for cross-border investment and trade. The FTZ has also made efforts to promote interest rate marketization and to deepen foreign exchange reforms. As a result of these measures, the number of products on the list of exclusions has been reduced from 190 to 122, and approximately 90% of the national industries have implemented pre-establishment national treatment. The China Banking Regulatory Commission has encouraged Chinese and foreign banks to engage in business in the FTZ. The China Securities Regulatory Commission has invited securities and futures institutions to establish subsidiaries in the FTZ, and the China Insurance Regulatory Commission has proposed establishing a pilot professional health insurance institution funded by foreign capital. To strengthen the cross-border financial services to adjust to a more open environment and to prevent financial risks more effectively, the zone has already opened approximately 60,000 free trade accounts that promote the two-way opening up of capital projects and expand the cross-border use of the RMB.

11.3.3 Comparison Between the Shanghai Free Trade Port and International Free Trade Ports

Although there is not a strict common definition of a free trade port, a definition can be found by looking at the most successful international free trade ports and FTZ. Some of their major common characteristics can be identified, which may shed light on the path for the development of China's free trade ports. Table 11.2 highlights the development history and major policies of four international ports.

From Table 11.2, we can identify some common characteristics of the free trade ports. First, greater trade facilitation and an efficient legal system in a free trade port create higher mobility of labor and capital, attracting a large amount of transit shipments, such as value-added services, import and export containers loading and unloading, and multimodal transportation. For example, in Hong Kong, most commodities (except liquor, tobacco, methanol and several other goods) are exempt from tariffs and additional taxes. Most products can pass through customs without submitting paperwork. Customs declarations can be completed through electronic channels within 14 days after the goods are exported or imported, and the cost of goods passing through is only half that in the OECD countries. These factors reduce business costs for enterprises and facilitate small and medium-sized enterprises' participation in international trade activities.

---

[7] The "new ten" policy includes ten different new policies to attract high-technology talent to work and live in Shanghai. For the detail of this policy, see http://www.pudong.gov.cn/shpd/InfoOpen/Detail.aspx?Id=780227.

Table 11.2 Policies and development of four major international free trade ports

	Chinese Hong Kong	Singapore	Colon	Dubai
History and development	Since 1840, from a single re exportportand processing center to a free trade zone with diversified economic and trade structure	Since 1969, including 7 free trade zones (1airport, 6 sea ports), from an international goods and distribution basis to a highly open free trade port, then to a comprehensive technology free trade zone	Since 1948, the world's second largest free trade port; re-exporting dominates	Rashid Port is a traditional container port, built in the 1960s; Jebel Ali Port built in 1985, is a, multi-function zone, including logistics warehousing, importing and exporting, production and processing
Firm registration	3-step online Application Certificate issued within 1 h; no restriction on registration capital;nocapital verification	4 documents and Certificate issued within 3 days; capital required over 0.1 million Singapore dollars	No minimum Investment requirement; 6–7 documents,suchas social contracts or tax records are required; at least 5 Panamanian employees;atleast 60% of imports reexported	Procedure for Investment can be completed within 7 days;customs, banks,postand telecommunications transportation and public security are under unified management
Investment admittance	Equal treatment For all investors in Almost all industries; 100% holdings allowed;conditional admittance for gambling, telecommunications and radio	No admittance limit For most industries; finance,insurance, and securities need to be put onrecord; no foreign capital share limit except retail, newsand publication	No admittance limit inprocessing	100-percent foreign Holdings allowed; no Restriction on domestic employment

(continued)

Second, most international free trade ports have undergone industry and trade upgrading and have good financial, logistical and legal systems, allowing them to develop various types of trade. They are usually offshore financial centers, such as Hong Kong, and have mature capital markets and international clearing services, which enable them to upgrade from low-value-added processing trade and entrepot trade to the rapidly expanding offshore trade in response to increasing labor and capital costs. At the same time, international free trade ports usually have a high level of investment facilitation. For example, in Hong Kong, foreign capital generally

Table 11.2 (continued)

	Chinese Hong Kong	Singapore	Colon	Dubai
Capital and foreign exchange	Any currency allowed for trade settlement; no restrictions on currency tradingor international capital flows;profit sfreely remitted	Any currency allowed fortrade settlement; no restrictions on currency trading and international capital flows;profitsfreely remitted	USdollarasmajor currency for trade; no capital control; profits freely remitted	Allowing profits to beremitted abroad; no limit on currency exchange
Customs supervisio	Declaration complete within 14 days after exportor import	Efficient online customs system for applications, declarations, approvalsand controls	One unified form for imports,exportsand re-exports	Declaration complete within 24 hours
Tax preference	Zerotariff except alcohol,tobacco hydrocarbon and methanol; no value added tax or business tax; no taxon personal investmen income; the main taxes are profit (15–16.5%), salary and property taxes	Unified business income tax f or domestic and foreign firms(17%); partial tax exemption for the first 0.3 million in income zero tariff except; alcoholic beverages, tobacco, petroleum and motor vehicles	Business income tax 2–5%,capital tax 1%	Tariff free or processing intermediates and capital goods; exemption of business income tax for 15 years; no personal income tax

enjoys 100-percent ownership. The procedures for establishing a company are quick; the registration can be completed within 1 hour and there is no minimum capital stock requirement. Fully-opened financial markets allow enterprises to convert foreign exchange and mobilize capital freely inside and outside Hong Kong.

Third, free trade ports are not only logistics and transportation centers, but are also headquarters economies. The agglomeration effect of finance, insurance, design and high-technology industries, and the preferential policies help the free trade ports to encourage the establishment of headquarters of foreign enterprises, foster service trade and offshore trade, and provide a strong motivation for trade and economic growth. For example, the Singapore Government has adopted several measures, including a concessionary international trade plan and rewards for business and multinational headquarters, to encourage foreign enterprises to set up headquarters or regional headquarters in Singapore. Dubai has more than half of the free economic zones of the United Arab Emirates and attracts many multinational enterprises to move their headquarters there. This can be attributed to FTZ policy measures such as that: foreign capital can be wholly owned by enterprises registered in the FTZ;

capital and profit remittances are not restricted; and foreign enterprises can enjoy exemption from business taxes for 50 years, be totally exempt from personal income taxes and pay zero import and export tariffs.

Fourth, the development of free trade ports is based on the industry structure of the surrounding areas. For example, the Dubai Government has attached great importance to the joint development of ports and industry. The Port of Jebel Ali, focuing on the development of trade, logistics, and information and high-technology industry, has established an FTZ. In 2014, there were more than 1225 global multinational corporations and enterprises entering the Jebel Ali FTZ. These enterprises have set up production and logistics centers in the FTZ, which has promoted the growth of Dubai's import and export goods. Beginning in 1995, the "Dubai Internet City" was built in the Jebel Ali FTZ. This is the main project in place by the Dubai Government for developing the network economy. In 1999, it completed the preparatory work for the feasibility study, including planning and formulation of relevant laws and regulations. The construction project included, for instance, an Internet university and a software development center. By the end of 2000, the construction of infrastructure in the city was basically completed. following its completion, the Dubai Internet City contained 30 world famous information technology companies, including Microsoft, Siemens and IBM, with 300 senior managers.

Finally, the administrations of free trade ports are empowered by central governments. The ports of Hamburg, New York, Singapore and Hong Kong were all first legislated before setting up districts to ensure the healthy development of the free trade ports with strict laws and regulations. In addition to the national legislation, the local government formulates corresponding regulations for activities in the free trade ports. Port administrations are authorized by the government to manage their own affairs and to invest in and build necessary infrastructure, and have the right to examine and approve projects. They also promote the economic development of the surrounding cities, especially in relation to finance, insurance, trade and intermediaries.

The New York and Singapore ports have specialized operation companies, which operate in a market-oriented manner, and have powerful government regulators. For example, the Dubai Port Authority was established in 1991, directly under the leadership of the Dubai local government, to manage Dubai ports. At the same time, it is an independent organization and has an independent accounting system. The Jebel Ali FTZ is relatively independent and (i) can acquire and rent land, and operate and manage factories, warehouses and other social infrastructure (e.g. reservoirs, water, communications and transportation); (ii) has jurisdiction over enterprises, can introduce public utilities and services in the FTZ, and can approve the use of facilities, such as land, plants and port facilities; (iii) can impose fees on businesses and public utilities; and (iv) can sign loan contracts with organizations outside the zone and establish other management institutions as needed. Through the comparison of the Shanghai PFTPZ and other international free trade ports, it can be concluded that many ports in Chinese mainland are not merely bonded trade areas or FTZs; their functions are expanding, and they are developing into free trade ports. However, there is still much room for Chinese free trade ports to improve, for instance through improvements in operating systems, establishing support services and the construction of related industries. Table 11.3 shows differences in functions and operating systems between the PFTZs in Chinese mainland and international free trade ports.

Table 11.3 Differences in functions and operating systems between the Pilot Free Trade Zones in Chinese Mainland and International Free Trade Ports

		Chinese Mainland	Chinese Hong Kong	Singapore	Rotterdam
Function	Type	Free trade pilot zone	Free trade port	Free trade port	Free trade port
	Positioning	Experimental field of opening up	Center of international logistics, finance, trade and sightseeing	Center of international logistics, finance, trade and sightseeing	Sustainable, effective, secure and clean port with multi-functions and high technology
	Functions	Transportation, trade, storage, logistics and processing	Trade, international transshipment, fully-opened domestic financial market	Trade, international transshipment, storage, logistics, container distribution, financial services, and sea and air transport	Dealing with dry bulk containers, liquid bulk containers and container cargo; the center of storage, transportation and selling, collection, distribution and reprocessing
Operating System	Infrastructure	Fully automated wharf	Urbanized free trade port with complete support services	Short distance between port and airport	Informatization and integration of the port by establishment of public information platform
	Customs declaration and clearance	"Entry first, clearance then"; "separate inspected collectively"	Documents required and sample inspection	Electronic trade management, clearance as fast as 10 s	Clearance in 24 h (except Sunday); storage before clearance; companies' accounting reports and inventory data required

(continued)

Table 11.3 (continued)

		Chinese Mainland	Chinese Hong Kong	Singapore	Rotterdam
	Law and regulation	Null	The *Basic Law* and *Sales of Goods Ordinance*	Preferential polies on free shipment and trade and the *Special Law*	*Tariff Law of the European Union and the Netherlands*; *Tax Law* and policies on Rotterdam port's development, operation and logistics management by the Netherlands

Through comparison, the capabilities of the ports in Chinese mainland can be comprehensively evaluated in the aspects of attracting talent, investment and trade, which will help to reveal the condition of the ports and guide their future development

International free trade ports should have complete infrastructure, advanced logistics and information management systems, user-friendly declaration and clearance processes, preferential tax policies, and low costs for calling, storage and transshipment. After more than 20 years of development, the ports in Chinese mainland are becoming increasingly competitive. On 13 February and 1 March 2017, the world's largest 450,000-ton supertanker, TI Europe, called at Daxie Port in Ningbo and Dalian Port. On 27 March, the world's biggest container ship, Mitsui Osk Achievement (MOL Triumph), was put into service and it was decided that it would follow the Dalian–Europe lane. It would call at ports in Tianjin, Yangshan, Ningbo, Zhoushan and Yantian, indicating that the infrastructure and operational efficiency of the ports have gained the recognition of the international community.

However, there are also some problems that need to be solved, such as the imbalance between the development of the ports in coastal developed areas and those in developing areas infrastructure and logistics, and the weak connection between ports. In the World Bank's 2014 Business Environment Report, Singapore's cross-border trade facilitation level ranks first among the world's 189 economies. Specifically, Singapore has a free system of trade settlement, the least restrictions on investors and investment capital, and a comprehensive shipping service system. For the ports in Chinese mainland, there are no automated and electronic customs declaration and clearance services available, reflected in the low efficiency of customs. Although the ports in Chinese mainland have many preferential tax policies (e.g. tax reductions), which have already attracted increased foreign capital, compared with the Singapore and Busan ports, which are well-known for their tax exemptions and low call fees, Chinese ports still have a long way to go.

With the deepening of globalization, increasing numbers of talented workers are choosing to come to China. There are many preferential policies in place to attract talented workers to the free trade ports. However, the number of scientific, professional and versatile workers still does not meet that required with the fast development of the ports. The proportion of foreign high-technology professional talent is still low among employees. The development of supporting infrastructure and services has been unbalanced among different regions in China. Moreover, because of historical and diplomatic factors, Chinese mainland passports are not used as widely as Chinese Hong Kong, Singaporean and South Korean passports. Although the Chinese mainland passport has scored higher in the Passport Index recently, it still ranks behind those countries and regions, and ranked 64th on the Passport Index for 2017. The low fluidity of immigration hinders international trade. For example, the duration of visas available for immigrant workers to Chinese mainland is relatively short.[8] To solve all these problems, China's central and local governments are seeking to improve immigration management in bonded areas and FTZs, to create a more open and effective environment for those with the skills needed in free trade ports.

Finally, international free trade ports require fewer formalities, better exchange mechanisms, and more complete and flexible rental systems. For example, Hong Kong is the only integrated city for offshore and local businesses in Asia in terms of having a unified free exchange system for both business types. With the most open currency market in the world, Hong Kong offers freedom to invest and free flow of funds across the border. However, because of its short history and low level of openness of the Chinese mainland financial market, with the exception of the Shanghai port, the coastal ports in China lack well-established financial systems. Thus, it is difficult to promote the development of trade and business in the port areas. China is still a developing country and although it has signed bilateral reciprocal swap agreements with several countries, and the RMB has joined the Special Drawing Right basket, the Chinese Government maintains a relatively prudent attitude toward finance, especially capital account liberalization. It is experimenting in the Shanghai FTZ to promote the reform of the financial system, focusing on convenience, free exchange, cross-border use of the RMB, and free rein of interest rates and foreign exchange.

11.4 Path for the Construction of Free Trade Ports in China

Even though economies are becoming increasingly interdependent, trade protectionism still exists. The trend of de-globalization may not be an obstacle to trade and business development in China; conversely, de-globalization presents an opportunity for China to deepen reforms. China is actively seeking solutions to the challenges faced and putting forward new opening-up strategies. The Chinese Government is deepening the FTZ reform and improving the functionality of free trade ports to push the opening-up reform to a new stage.

[8] For example, the duration of a visa for a Vietnamese worker is only 1 month. See http://www.gxswt.gov.cn/htmlcontent/zwgkdetail/429aa457-f1df-4e61-9654-b80995113146.

Although China has a way to go in relation to economic openness and liberalization, the economy is developing and foreign trade is expanding. Now is the best time for China to develop free trade ports. China has a vast domestic market and is enjoying policy dividends from the Belt and Road Initiative, for example. China has gained much practical experience from developing comprehensive bonded areas and PFTZs. However, compared with international free trade ports, there is still much room for improvement, including in attacting trade, talent and finance. Therefore, the Chinese Government should focus on policies in these three areas to promote the development of free trade ports.

First, it is necessary to improve the convenience for businesses engaging in trade in the ports. "Fast trade" requires a simple approval process. "Convenient trade" requires a complete logistics system and informationized, comprehensive management. Improvements in these areas will help create a low-cost environment for manufacturing and delivery, to ensure that all products flow into the world market in an effective way. The Chinese Government should provide preferential policies for goods trade. China should build an integrated, international, standardized transportation network that combines river ports, sea ports, highways, railways and aviation. It should build a large-scale, intelligent and multi-functional information network, and a secure and effective electronic customs clearance system to speed up the integration of customs and to simplify its procedures. The ports in underdeveloped areas should ensure the implementation of the policy of "inside the territory while outside customs" and "free entry into China's territory while strict inspection before entering the domestic market, free entry and exit in the FTZ while separate management of people and goods."[9] For the ports in developed areas, a more competitive offshore taxation system should be explored.

[9] See http://www.customs.gov.cn/publish/portal0/tab46391/info343506.htm.

Chapter 12
Forty Years of Opening Up Has Greatly Benefited China's Foreign Trade

It has been four decades since China embarked on the great course of reform and opening up in 1978. Over the past four decades, the Chinese economy has maintained an average annual growth of 8%, which was unprecedented in human economic history. Meanwhile, China has grown from a closed and underdeveloped agrarian country to the world's second largest economy, the largest trader and exporter of goods, the second largest importer of goods, and the second largest trader of services. As a major country with its doors wide open, China also boasts the second largest amount of outward foreign direct investment. China has transformed itself from a least- developed country to a middle- and high-income developing country. In the coming years, per capita income is expected to reach USD12,000, making China a developed country. It is beyond all doubt that, within only four decades, China has greatly improved its status in foreign trade by reform and opening up, and integrated into the world economy.

12.1 The Remarkable Achievements of Chinese Foreign Trade

Four decades ago, China started from zero. By now, it has made significant headway in foreign trade, two-way direct investment, trade in good sand services, and other international economic cooperation projects. More specifically, from the early days of reform and opening up to 2017, Chinese foreign trade in goods grew 196-fold from USD21 billion to USD4.1 trillion, accounting for 11.5% of global foreign trade and ranking the first in the world. In more detail, goods worth USD2.26 trillion were exported, accounting for 12.8% of global exports and ranking the first in the world; and imports of goods reached USD1.84 trillion, accounting for 10.2% of the world total and ranking the second in the world. China's dependence degree on

---

This chapter is originally published in China Economic Transition, 2019, 2(3), pp. 67–72.

M. Yu, *China's Miracle in Foreign Trade*, Studies in Modern Chinese Economy,
https://doi.org/10.1007/978-981-16-6030-6_12

foreign trade in goods was 33.6%. In the meantime, China's foreign trade in services grew approximately 172-fold from USD4 billion to USD690.5 billion, accounting for 6.7% of the world's total foreign trade and ranking the second in the world.

Four decades of reform and opening up produced remarkable achievements in foreign trade, which was demonstrated by the development of China's international cooperation. First, in 2017, the lump sum of foreign capital utilization reached USD136.3 billion, accounting for 9.5% of the world total, ranking the second in the world and registering a 40-fold increase over the 40 years. Additionally, China's outward foreign direct investment stood at USD158.2 billion, accounting for 9.9% of the world's total amount of foreign investment utilization, ranking the second in the world, up 55 times since the beginning of reform and opening up. Furthermore, Chinese foreign contracted projects generated an USD168.5 billion turnover, and the number of dispatched workers engaging in foreign labor service cooperation reached 522,000. Clearly, four decades of reform and opening up have made China a well-deserved "world factory."

12.2 From a Wider and Deeper to an All-Around Opening Up Over Four Decades

The 40 years of China's reform and opening up can be divided into three phases: opening up wider, opening up deeper, and opening up all-around. From 1978 through 2001, China was committed to opening up wider, mainly by setting up special economic zones, economic development zones, industrial parks, high-tech zones, and export processing zones. This phase featured extensive opening up that focused on quantity and advanced from coastal to inland areas through the creation of industrial parks. The foreign trade policies were transformed from the import substitution strategy prior to reform and opening up to export-oriented development.

The second phase, which featured a deeper opening up, spanned the period from the end of 2001, when China joined the WTO, to 2017, before the convening of the 19th National Congress of the Communist Party of China (CPC). On the one hand, China's entry into the WTO has earned it larger markets and more opportunities for its exports. On the other hand, the previous export-oriented model characterized by labor-intensive products was challenged by rising labor costs, diminishing demographic dividends, and weak external demand as a result of the 2008 global financial crisis. During this period, China expedited economic growth by setting up 11 pilot free-trade zones to experiment on new economic reforms, improving the quality of products, especially exports, while continuing to reduce tariffs and promoting trade liberalization. During this period, the country focused on quality and intensive opening up. The foreign trade policies shifted from the previous export-oriented development to trade liberalization.

The third phase began after the 19th National Congress of the CPC in 2017 as the country ushered in a new era of all-around opening up. Presently, economic and trade globalization are confronted with a reversing trend and undermined by some countries' trade hegemony and protectionist trade policies. To facilitate global trade liberalization and economic development, and pursue win-win outcomes through mutually beneficial global economic cooperation, the 19th National Congress of the CPC underscored the importance of "making new ground in pursuing opening up on all fronts," which was a priority in China's economic development. As of now, all-around opening up has manifested itself in three ways: expanding imports, building free-trade ports, and building the Guangdong–Hong Kong–Macao Greater Bay Area. This trio is of great significance to trade globalization.

12.3 Key Practices of Reform and Opening Up During the Past Four Decades

In addition to the aforementioned three phases, the reform and opening up can be analyzed from other perspectives. The dominant strategy prior to reform and opening up was the import substitution strategy, which was then replaced by an export-oriented model in the early 1980s. Further on, as China gradually integrated into the world economy, its trade liberalization policies and accession into the WTO began to make a difference. Then, the global financial crisis broke out, stressing the need to open up deeper. Finally, understanding the influence of all-around opening up in the new era is of practical significance.

12.3.1 From the Import Substitution Strategy to an Export-Oriented Strategy

Since 1978, China has made significant headway in economic restructuring and industrial upgrading and has turned to development strategies in alignment with its comparative advantages. China adopted the "dual track" reform to provide temporary shelter to outdated capital-intensive industries. Such incremental reforms approached Pareto Optimality and were easy to implement. The government has proactively contributed to industry assessing and economic upgrading. The successful economic restructuring and upgrading of manufacturing have also created more jobs for urban and rural workers. As a result, the poor population has sharply decreased. During this phase, which spanned a period of 30 years, China has grown from a under-developed country to a middle- and high-income country.

From 1992, when China announced the establishment of the socialist market economic system, to 2008, when the global financial crisis hit, China's economic development should be mostly attributed to its export-oriented strategy. In this context, what is the relationship between international trade and an export-oriented strategy? Further, how did the export-oriented strategy supercharge China's economic development? The export-oriented strategy was necessary in light of the country's demographic features and low urbanization rate. A low dependency ratio and urbanization rate resulted in an excessive amount of labor supply and a slow growth of income, which consequently helped accumulate capital rapidly and fueled the manufacturing development.

However, they also meant that the domestic market was inevitably small, which rendered exports the only solution for market clearing. The analysis of China's processing trade based on highly detailed transaction data from 2010 showed that free-trade zones were important for facilitating the development of processing trade. According to the customs data from 2000 to 2005, the abundance of processing enterprises in China led to a comparatively lower productivity in export enterprises.

Therefore, distinguishing processing trade from non-processing trade was crucial for correctly understanding the performance of Chinese export enterprises.

12.3.2 Trade Liberalization and WTO's Influence

To expedite WTO accession, China, first as an "observer" in 1994, sharply slashed import tariffs from 35% to 17% within only three years, securing its membership by the end of 2001 as the 143rd member state. Subsequently, China has been adhering to a trade liberalization strategy. More specifically, based on highly detailed trade and production data from 2000 to 2006, it can be investigated how the tariff cuts and exemptions for imported intermediate goods and final products influenced the productivity of major Chinese enterprises engaged in international trade. The results show that the cuts and exemptions had a positive impact on productivity, and the impact decreased as the share of imports increased in the processing trade.

In general, tariff cuts for imported intermediate goods had a greater positive impact on productivity compared to tariff exemptions, whereas the opposite was true for enterprises not involved in processing trade. In addition, the reduction of tariffs on intermediate goods would enhance enterprise R&D.

12.3.3 Opening Up Deeper Amid the Global Financial Crisis

The 2008 global financial crisis has plagued the world economy, especially developed economies which suffered from weak external demand.

In China, the previous export-driven development model was no longer viable. Due to the financial crisis, Chinese businesses were facing overwhelming credit constraints. In July 2005, China adopted a managed floating exchange rate mechanism, and the Chinese yuan appreciated against the U.S. dollar. China's export model has shifted from simply relying on cost advantage (low wages) to quality improvement of exports. China has also transformed its strategy from opening up wider to opening up deeper. Moreover, exchange rate fluctuations might affect enterprise decision-making through other, previously unknown channels, and competition is the decisive factor in quality improvement.

12.4 Policy Suggestions for the All-Around Opening Up Strategy

Facing the new international economic landscape with weak external demand, and rising protectionism in Western countries, China is also stepping into a complicated situation in its opening up. As mentioned above, at the 19th National Congress of the CPC in 2017, the Central Party Committee proposed to "make new ground in pursuing opening up on all fronts." Profound changes have taken place since the beginning of the new century. To achieve sustainable industrial upgrading and continuous productivity improvement, reform and opening up policies should be refined to adapt to the needs of the new era. Therefore, "internal reform and external opening up" was changed to "external reform and internal opening up." External reform means identifying new trading partners to disperse systemic risks of over-reliance on a few developed countries. Furthermore, free-trade areas among neighboring countries should be quickly established and the model of processing trade should be adjusted. Internal opening up aims to break down regional trade barriers, liberalize factor markets, and open up product markets further. Industrial upgrading will gain ceaseless momentum from external reform and internal opening up.

Over the past 40 years, China has adopted a series of measures to facilitate trade and investment, such as reducing import tariffs, building interregional free-trade areas, signing bilateral investment agreements, opening up pilot free-trade zones, streamlining administration and delegating powers, providing favorable policy in land and tax, and aiding infrastructure construction. These measures have boosted productivity, improved consumers' benefits, and drove economic development. China still has a large room for improvement in interregional free-trade zones, pilot free-trade areas, and infrastructure construction.

To address the challenges of anti-globalization and stay active in international economic and trade relations, China is ready to build free-trade ports that are more open and liberalized by drawing upon the experiences of existing bonded free-trade ports and free-trade zones. The free-trade ports serve as a global hub for goods, professionals, and capital.

China should stay aligned with advanced international experiences and blaze a new trail for building free-trade ports. Hopefully, the country will achieve new breakthroughs in facilitation of trade in goods, flow of people, and financial openness.

References

Acemoglu, Daron, and Jörn-Steffen. Pischke. 1998. The structure of wages and investment in general training. *Journal of Political Economy* 107 (3): 539–572.

Ackerberg, D., Caves, K., and Frazer, G. 2006. *Structural identification of production functions.* Los Angeles: Mimeo, University of California.

Ackerberg, Daniel A, Kevin Caves, and Garth Frazer. 2015. Identification properties of recent production function estimators. *Econometrica* 83 (6): 2411–2451.

Ackerberg, Daniel, Benkard Lanier, Steven Berry, and Ariel Pakes. 2007. Econometric tools for analyzing market outcomes. In *Handbook of econometrics*, vol 6, eds. J. J. Heckman and E.E. Leamer, Elsevier.

Ackerberg, Daniel, Kevin Caves, and Garth Fraser. 2015. Identification properties of recent production function estimators. *Econometrica* 83 (6): 2411–2451.

Aghion, Philippe, Jing Cai, Mathias Dewatripont, Luosha Du, Ann Harrison, and Patrick Legros. 2015. Industrial policy and competition. *American Economic Journal: Macroeconomics* 7 (4): 1–32.

Ahn, JaeBin, Amit Khandelwal, and Shang-jin Wei. 2011. The role of intermediaries in facilitating trade. *Journal of International Economics* 84 (1): 73–85.

Akerman, Anders, Elhanan Helpman, Oleg Itskhoki, Marc-Andreas. Muendler, and Stephen Redding. 2013. Sources of wage inequality. *American Economic Review: Papers & Proceedings* 103 (3): 214–219.

Alder, Simon, Lin Shao, and Fabrizio Zilibotti. 2016. Economic reforms and industrial policy in a panel of Chinese cities. *Journal of Economic Growth* 21 (4): 305–349.

Almeida, Rita, and Pedro Carneiro. 2009. The return to firm investments in human capital. *Labour Economics* 16 (1): 97–106.

Amiti, M., and J. Konings. 2007. Trade liberalization, intermediate inputs, and productivity: Evidence from Indonesia. *American Economic Review* 93: 1611–1638.

Amiti, Mary, and Jozef Konings. 2007. Trade liberalization, intermediate inputs, and productivity: Evidence from Indonesia. *American Economic Review* 97 (5): 1611–1638.

Amiti, Mary, and Donald Davis. 2011. Trade, firms, and wages: Theory and evidence. *Review of Economic Studies* 79: 1Œ36.

Anderson, James E., Eric van Wincoop. 2004. Trade costs. *Journal of Economic Literature* 42: 691–751.

Anderson, T. W. 1984. *Introduction to multivariate statistical analysis*, 2nd edn, New York: John Wiley.

Bernard, Andrew B., J. Bradford Jensen, Stephen J. Redding, and Peter K. Schott. 2007. Firms in international trade. *The Journal of Economic Perspectives* 21 (3): 105–130.

Anwar, Sajid, and Sizhong Sun. 2012. Trade liberalization, market competition, and wages gap in China™s manufacturing sectors. *Economic Modelling* 29: 1268–1277.

M. Yu, *China's Miracle in Foreign Trade*, Studies in Modern Chinese Economy,
https://doi.org/10.1007/978-981-16-6030-6

Applied Economics 38 (10): 1091–110.
Arellano, M., and S. Bond. 1991. Some tests of specification for panel data: Monte Carlo evidence and an application to employment equations. *Review of Economic Studies* 58: 277–297.
Arkolakis, C., S. Demidova, P. Klenow, and A. Rodriguez-Clare. 2008. Endogenous variety and the gains from trade. *American Economic Review Papers and Proceedings* 98: 444–450.
Arkolakis, Costas. Marc-Andreas Muendler. 2011. The extensive margin of exporting products: A firm-level analysis. In *NBER working paper, no.* 17991.
Arnold, J. M. 2005. *Productivity estimation at the plant level: A practical guide.*. Milan: Mimeo, Bocconi University.
Autor, David, David Dorn, and Gordon Hanson. 2013. The China syndrome: Local labor market effects of import competition in the United States. *American Economic Review* 103 (6): 2121–2168.
Aw, Bee Yan, Mark J. Roberts. and Daniel Yi Xu. 2011. R&D investment, exporting, and productivity dynamics. *American Economic Review* 101 (4): 1312–1344.
Bagwell, Kyle, and Robert W. Staiger. 1990. A theory of managed trade. *American Economic Review* 80 (4): 779–795.
Bagwell, Kyle, and Robert W. Staiger. 1999. An economic theory of GATT. *American Economic Review* 89 (1): 215–248.
Baldwin, Richard E. 1992. Measurable dynamic gains from trade. *Journal of Political Economy* 100 (1): 162–174.
Baldwin, John, and Wulong Gu. 2009. The impact of trade on plant scale, production-run length and diversification. In *Producer dynamics: New evidence from micro data*, eds. T. Dunne, J. B. Jensen and M. J. Roberts. University of Chicago Press.
Barro, Robert J., and Jong-Wha, Lee. 1993. International comparisons of educational attainment. *Journal of Monetary Economics* 32: 363–394.
Bartik, Timothy J. 1991. *Who benefits from state and local economic development policies?* Kalamazoo, Mich: W. E. Upjohn Institute for Employment Research.
Bas, M., and V. Strauss-Kahn. 2014. Does importing more inputs raise exports? Firm level evidence from France. *Review of World Economics* 150 (2): 241–475.
Bas, Maria, and Vanessa Strauss-Kahn. 2015. Input-trade liberalization, export prices and quality upgrading. *Journal of International Economics* 95 (2015): 250–262.
Basu, Susanto, and John Fernald. 2002. Aggregate productivity and aggregate technology. *European Economic Review* 46: 963–991.
Becker, Sascha, Karolina Ekholm, and Marc-Andreas. Muendler. 2013. Offshoring and the onshore composition of tasks and skills. *Journal of International Economics* 90 (1): 91–106.
Bernard, Andrew, and Brad Jensen. 2004. Why some firms export. *Review of Economics and Statistics* 86 (2): 561–569.
Bernard, Andrew B., and J. Bradford Jensen. 1995. Exporters, jobs, and wages in U.S. manufacturing: 1976–1987. In *Brookings papers on economic activity*, 67–112. Microeconomics.
Bernard, Andrew B., J. Bradford Jensen. Peter K. Schott. 2006. Trade costs, firms and productivity. *Journal of Monetary Economy* 53: 917–37.
Bernard, Andrew, Bradford Jensen, and Peter Scott. 2009. Importers, exporters, and multinationals: A portrait of firms in the U.S. that trade goods. In *Producer dynamics: New evidence from micro data*, eds. Timothy Dunne, Bradford Jensen, and Mark Roberts. University of Chicago Press.
Bernard, Andrew, Stephen J. Redding, and Peter K. Schott. 2011. Multiple-product firms and trade liberalization. *Quarterly Journal of Economics* 126 (1): 70–97.
Bernini, M., and C. Tomasi. 2015. Exchange rate pass-through and product heterogeneity: Does quality matter on the import side? *European Economic Review* 77: 117–138.
Berthou, Antoine, and Lionei Fontagne. 2013. How do multi-product exporters react to a change in trade costs? *Scandinavian Journal of Economics* 115 (2): 326–353.
Beyer, Harald, Patricio Rojas, and Rodrigo Vergara. 1999. Trade liberalization and wage inequality. *Journal of International Economics* 59 (1): 103–123.

Bhagwati, Jagdish N. 1958. Immiserizing growth: A geometrical note. *Review of Economic Studies* 25: 201–205.

Biscourp, Pierre, and Francis Kramarz. 2007. Employment, skill structure and international trade: Firm-level evidence for France. *Journal of International Economics* 72 (1): 22–51.

Black, Sandra, and Lisa Lynch. 2001. How to compete: The impact of workplace practices and information technology on productivity. *Review of Economics and Statistics* 83 (3): 434–445.

Blaum, Joaquin, Claire Lelarge, and Michael Peters. 2015. *The gains from input trade in firm-based models of importing*. Yale University (unpublished manuscript).

Blomqvist, Ave. 1986. The economics of price scissors: Comment. *American Economic Review* 76: 1188–1191.

Blomström, Magnus, and Ari Kokko. 1996. The impact of foreign investment on host countries: a review of the empirical evidence. In *Policy research working paper*, 1745.

Bloom, Nicholas, and John van Reenen. 2007. Measuring and explaining management practices across firms and countries. *Quarterly Journal of Economics* 122: 1351–1408.

Bloom, Nicholas, Benn Eifert, David McKenzie, Aprajit Mahajan, and John Roberts. 2013. Does management matter: Evidence from India. *Quarterly Journal of Economics* 128: 1–51.

Bloom,Nicholas, Christos Genakos, Ralf Martin, and Raffaella Sadun. 2010. Modern management: Good for the environment or just hot air? *Economic Journal*, 120 (May): 551–572.

Blundell, R., and S. Bond. 1998. Initial conditions and moment restrictions in dynamic panel data models. *Journal of Econometrics* 87: 11–143.

Blundell, Richard, and Stephen Bond. 1998. Initial conditions and moment restrictions in dynamic panel data models. *Journal of Econometrics* 87 (1): 115–143.

Blundell, Richard, Dearden Lorraine, Costas Meghir, and Barbara Sianesi. 1999. Human capital investment: The returns from education and training to the individual, the firm and the economy. *Fiscal Studies* 20 (1): 1–23.

Blundell, Richard, Lorraine Dearden, and Costas Meghir. 1996. *The determinants of work-related training in Britain*. London: Institute for Fiscal Studies.

Bown, Chad, and Meredith Crowley. 2013. Self-enforcing trade agreements: Evidence from time-varying trade policy. *American Economic Review* 103 (2): 1071–90.

Lael, Brainard S., and Thierry Verdier. 1997. The political economy of declining industries: Senescent industry collapse revisited. *Journal of International Economics* 42: 221–237.

Brander, James, and Jonathan Eaton. 1984. Product line rivalry. *American Economic Review* 74 (3): 323–334.

Brandt, L., and P. M. Morrow. 2016. Tariffs and the organization of trade in china. *Journal of International Economics*, 104.

Brandt, Loren, and Peter Morrow. 2017. Tariffs and the organization of trade in China. *Journal of International Economics* 104 (1): 85–103.

Brandt, Loren, Johannes van Biesebroeck, and Yifan Zhang. 2012. Creative accounting or creative destruction? Firm-level productivity growth in Chinese manufacturing. *Journal of Development Economics* 97 (2): 339–351.

Brandt, Loren, Johannes Van Biesebroeck, Luhang Wang, and Yifan Zhang. 2017. WTO accession and performance of Chinese manufacturing firms. *American Economic Review* 107 (9): 2784–2820.

Briant, Anthony, Miren Lafourcade, and Benoît Schmutz. 2015. Can tax breaks beat geography? Lessons from the French enterprise zone experience. *American Economic Journal: Economic Policy* 7 (2): 88–124.

Broda, C., and D. Weinstein. 2004. Variety growth and world welfare. *American Economic Review: Papers and Proceedings* 94: 139–144.

Broda, C., and D. Weinstein. 2006a. Globalization and the gains from variety. *Quarterly Journal of Economics* 121: 541–585.

Broda, C., and D. Weinstein. 2006b. From groundnuts to globalization: a structural estimate of trade and growth. In *National Bureau of Economic research working paper, no. 12512*. Cambridge, MA: National Bureau of Economic Research.

Broda, Christan, Nuno Limão, and David E. Weinstein. 2006. Optimal tariffs: The evidence. In *NBER working paper 12033.*

Brooks, Wyatt J, Joseph P Kaboski, and Yao Amber Li. 2016. Growth policy, agglomeration, and (the Lack of) competition. In *Working paper, National Bureau of Economic Research.*

Brunello Giorgio, Pietro Garibaldi, and Etiennne Wasmer. 2007. *Education and training in Europe.* Oxford University Press.

Burgess, David F. 1976. Tariffs and income distribution: Some empirical evidence for the United States. *Journal of Political Economy* 84 (1): 17–45.

Busso, Matias, Jesse Gregory, and Patrick Kline. 2013. Assessing the incidence and efficiency of a prominent place based policy. *The American Economic Review* 103 (2): 897–947.

Bustos, Paula. 2011. Trade liberalization, exports, and technology upgrading: Evidence on the impact of MERCOSUR on argentinian firms. *American Economic Review* 101 (1): 304–340.

Cai, Fan. 2010. Demographic transition, demographic dividend, and lewis turning point in China. *China Economic Journal* 3 (2): 107–119.

Cai, H., and Q. Liu. 2009. Does competition encourage unethical behavior? The case of corporate profit hiding in China. *Economic Journal* 119: 764–795.

Caliendo Lorenzo, and Esteban Rossi-Hansberg. 2012. The impact of trade on organization and productivity. *Quarterly Journal of Economics* 27 (3): 1393–1464.

Cameron, Colin, and Pravin Trivedi. 2005. *Microeconometrics: Methods and applications.* Cambridge University Press.

Carter, Michael. 1986. The economics of price scissors: comment. *American Economic Review* 76: 1192–1194.

Cassing, James H., and Arye L. Hillman. 1986. Shifting comparative advantage and senescent industry collapse. *American Economic Review* 76: 516–523.

Chen, Bo, Miaojie Yu, and Zhihao Yu. 2016. Measured wage inequality and input trade liberalization: Evidence from Chinese firms. In *CCER working paper series no. E2016006.* China Center for Economic Research, Peking University.

Cheng, Leonard K., and Yum K Kwan. 2000. What are the determinants of the location of foreign direct investment? The Chinese experience. *Journal of International Economics* 51 (2): 379–400.

China Bureau of Statistics. 2005. *China compendium of statistics, 1949–2004.* China Statistics Press.

Choi, and Hahn. 2013. Effects of imported intermediate varieties on plant total factor productivity and product switching: Evidence from Korean manufacturing. *Asian Economic Journal*, 27 (2): 125–143.

Christensen, L. R., D. W. Jorgenson, and L. J. Lawrence. 1973. Transcendental logarithmic production frontiers. *Review of Economics and Statistics* 55: 28–45.

Clark, X., D. Dollar, and A. Micco. 2004. Port efficiency, maritime transport costs, and bilateral trade. *Journal of Development Economics* 75 (2): 417–450.

Coe, D., and E. Helpman. 1995. International R&D spillovers. *European Economic Review* 39: 859–887.

Conti, Gabriella. 2005. Training, productivity and wages in Italy. *Labour Economics* 12 (4): 557–576.

Cooper, Robin, and Robert Kaplan. 1992. Activity-based systems: Measuring the cost of resource usage. *Accounting Horizons* 6 (3): 1–13.

Cragg, J.G., and S.G. Donald. 1993. Testing Identfiability and specification in instrumental variables models. *Econometric Theory* 9: 222–240.

Criscuolo, Chiara, Ralf Martin, Henry Overman, and John Van Reenen. 2012. The causal effects of an industrial policy. In *Technical report, National Bureau of Economic Research.*

Dai, Mi, and Miaojie Yu. 2013. Firm R&D, absorptive capacity, and learning by exporting: firm-level evidence from China. *The World Economy* 1131–1145.

Dai, Mi, Madura Maitra, and Miaojie Yu. 2016. Unexceptional exporter performance in China? Role of processing trade. *Journal of Development Economics* 121: 177–189.

De Loecker. 2013. Detecting learning by exporting. *American Economic Journal: Microeconomics* 5 (3): 1–21; Frederic Warzynski. 2012. Markups and firm-level export status. *American Economic Review* 102 (6): 2437–2471.

De Loecker. 2011. Product differentiation, multiproduct firms, and estimating the impact of trade liberalization on productivity. *Econometrica* 79 (5): 1407–1451. Detecting learning by exporting. 2013. *American Economic Journal: Microeconomics* 5 (3): 1–21; Pinelopi K Goldberg, Amit K Khandelwal, and Nina Pavcnik. 2016. Prices, markups, and trade reform. *Econometrica* 84 (2): 445–510.

Dearden, L., H. Reed, and J. Van Reenen. 2006. The impact of training on productivity and wages: Evidence from British panel data. *Oxford Bulletin of Economics and Statistics* 68 (4): 397–421.

Deardorff, Alan. 2000. Policy implications of trade and wage debates. *Review of International Economics* 8: 478–496.

DeLoecker, Jan. 2011. Product differentiation, multiproduct firms, and estimating the impact of trade liberalization on productivity. *Econometrica* 79 (5): 1407–1451.

DeLoecker, Jan. 2013. Detecting learning by exporting. *American Economic Journal: Microeconomics* 5 (3): 1–21.

DeLoecker, Jan, and Frederic Warzynski. 2012. Markups and firm-level export status. *American Economic Review* 102 (6): 2437–2471.

Demurger, Sylvie, Jeffrey D SACHS, Wing Thye Woo, BAO Shuming, and Gene Chang. 2002. The relative contributions of location and preferential policies in China's regional development: Being in the right place and having the right incentives. *China Economic Review* 13 (4): 444–465.

Devereux, Michael P, Rachel Griffith, and Helen Simpson. 2007. Firm location decisions, regional grants and agglomeration externalities. *Journal of Public Economics* 91 (3): 413–435.

Dhingra, Swati. 2013. Trading away wide brands for cheap brands. *American Economic Review* 103 (6): 2554–2584.

Diewert, W. Erwin. 1974. Functional forms for revenue and factor requirements functions. *International Economic Review* 15: 119–30.

Dreher, A. 2006. *Does globalization affect growth? Evidence from a new index of globalization.*

Eaton, Jonathan, and Samuel Kortum. 2002. Technology, geography, and trade. *Econometrica* 75 (5): 1741–1779.

Eaton Jonathan, Samuel Kortum, and Francis Kramarz. 2011. An anatomy of international trade: Evidence from french firms. *Econometrica* 1453–1498.

Eckel, Carsten, and J. Peter Neary. 2010. Multi-product firms and flexible manufacturing in the global economy. *Review of Economic Studies* 77: 188–217.

Eckel,Carsten, Leonardo Iacovone, Beata Javorcik, and J. Peter Neary. 2015. Multi-product firms at home and away: Cost-versus quality-based competence. *Journal of International Economics* (forthcoming).

Egger, Hartmut, and Udo Kreickemeier. 2009. Firm heterogeneity and the labor market effects of trade liberalization. *International Economic Review* 50 (1): 187–216.

Egger, Hartmut, and Udo Kreickemeier. 2012. Fairness, trade, and inequality. *Journal of International Economics* 86 (2): 184–196.

Eisfeldt, L. Andrea, and Dimitris Papanikolaou. 2013. Organization capital and the cross-section of expected return. *Journal of Finance* 1365–1406.

Ericson, Richard, and Ariel Pakes. 1995. Markov-perfect industry dynamic: A framework for empirical Work. *Review of Economic Studies* 62 (1): 53–82.

Fan, Haichao, Yao Amber Li, Stephen R Yeaple, Trade. 2014. Liberalization, quality, and export prices. *Review of Economics and Statistics* (forthcoming).

Feenstra, R.C., and G.H. Hanson. 2005. Ownership and control in outsourcing to China: Estimating the property-rights theory of the firm. *Quarterly Journal of Economics* 120 (2): 729–761.

Feenstra, R. 1994. New product varieties and the measurement of international prices. *American Economic Review* 84: 157–177.

Feenstra, R., D. Madani, T.-H. Yang, and C.-Y. Liang. 1999. Testing endogenous growth in South Korea and Taiwan. *Journal of Development Economics* 60: 317–341.

Feenstra, R., Z. Li, and M. Yu. 2010. *Export and credit constraints under private information: Theory and empirical investigation from China*. Mimeo, University of California, Davis.

Feenstra, Robert, and Gordon Hanson. 2005. Ownership and control in outsourcing to China: Estimating the property-rights theory of the firm. *Quarterly Journal of Economics* 120 (2): 729–762.

Feenstra, Robert C., and Hiau Looi Kee. 2008. Export variety and country productivity: Estimating the monopolistic competition model, with endogenous productivity. *Journal of International Economics* 74: 500–518.

Feenstra, Robert C. 1994. New product varieties and the measurement of international prices. *American Economic Review* 84: 157–177; Feenstra, Robert C. 1998. Integration and disintegration in the global economy. *Journal of Economic Perspective* 12: 31–50; Feenstra, Robert C. 2003. *Advanced International Trade: Theory and Evidence*, Princeton, NJ: Princeton University Press (2003).

Feenstra, Robert C., John Romalis, and Peter K. Schott. 2001. U.S. imports, exports, and tariff data, 1989–2001. In *NBER working paper 9387*.

Feenstra, Robert, and Gordon Hanson. 1996. Foreign investment, outsourcing and relative wages. In *The political economy of trade policy: Papers in honor of Jagdish Bhagwati*, eds. Robert Feenstra, Gene Grossman and Douglas Irwin, 89–127. MIT Press.

Feenstra, Robert, and Gordon Hanson. 1999. The impact of outsourcing and high-technology capital on wages: Estimates for the U.S., 1979–1990. *Quarterly Journal of Economics* 114 (3): 907–940.

Feenstra, Robert, Zhiyuan Li, and Miaojie Yu. 2014. Exports and credit constraints under incomplete information: Theory and applications to China. *Review of Economics and Statistics* 96 (4): 729–744.

Feenstra, Robert, and Hong Ma. 2008. Optimal choice of product scope for multiproduct firms. In *The organization of firms in a global economy*, eds. E. Helpman, D. Marin and T. Verdier. Harvard University Press.

Fernandes, Ana M. 2007. Trade policy, trade volumes and plant-level productivity in Colombian manufacturing industries. *Journal of International Economics* 71 (1): 52–71.

Fisher Marshall, and Christopher Ittner. 1999. Impact of product variety on automobile assembly operations. *Management Science* 45 (6): 771–786.

Frías, Judith, Eric Verhoogen, and David Kaplan. 2012. Exports and within-plant wage distributions: Evidence from Mexico. *American Economic Review Papers & Proceedings* 102 (3): 435–440.

Furusawa, Taiji, and Naoto Jinji. 2007. Tariff revenue competition in a free trade area: The case of asymmetric countries. *Review of Development Economics* 11: 300–312.

Furusawa, Taiji, and Hideo Konishi. 2014. *International trade and income inequality*. Mimeo, Hitotsubashi University.

Gandhi, Amit, Salvador Navarro, and David Rivers. 2016. On the identification of production functions: How heterogeneous is productivity? In *Working paper*.

Ge, Y., Lai, H., and Zhu, S. 2011. *Intermediates import and gains from trade liberalization.*. China: Mimeo, University of International Business and Economics.

Glaeser, Edward L., and Joshua D Gottlieb. 2008. The economics of place-making policies. In *Brookings papers on economic activity*, 155–239.

Goldberg, P.K., A.K. Khandelwal, N. Pavcnik, and P. Topalova. 2009. Trade liberalization and new imported inputs. *American Economic Review* 99 (2): 494–500.

Goldberg, P. K., A. K. Khandelwal, N. Pavcnik, and P. Topalova. 2010. Imported intermediate inputs and domestic product growth: Evidence from India. *The Quarterly Journal of Economics* 125 (4): 1727–1767. MIT Press.

Goldberg, Pinelope, Amit Khandelwal, Nina Pavcnik, and Petia Topalova. 2010. Imported intermediate inputs and domestic product growth: Evidence from India. *The Quarterly Journal of Economics* 125 (4): 1727–1767.

Goldberg, Pinelopi Koujianou, and Giovanni Maggi. 1999. Protection for sale: An empirical investigation. *American Economic Review* 89 (5): 1135–1155.

Goldberg, Pinelopi Koujianou, and Nina Pavcnik. 2007. The effects of the Colombian Trade liberalization on urban poverty: NBER chapters. In *Globalization and poverty*, 241–290.

Goldberg, Pinelopi, Amit Khandelwal, Nina Pavcnik, and Petia Topalova. 2010. Imported intermediate inputs and domestic product growth: Evidence from India. *Quarterly Journal of Economics* 125 (4): 1727–1767.

Gopinath, Gita, and Brent Neiman. 2014. Trade adjustment and productivity in large crises. *American Economic Review* 104 (3).

Gorlitz, Katja, and Joel Stiebale. 2011. The impact of product market competition on employers' training investments. Evidence from German establishment panel data. *De Economist* 159 (1): 1–23.

Gort, Michael, and Seong-Hoon Lee. 2003. Managerial efficiency, organizational capital and productivity. In *Working papers 03–08*. Center for Economic Studies, U.S. Census Bureau.

Greenstone, Michael, Richard Hornbeck, and Enrico Moretti. 2010. Identifying agglomeration spillovers: Evidence from winners and losers of large plant openings. *Journal of Political Economy* 118 (3): 536–598.

Griliches, Zvi, and Jacques Mairesse. 1995. Production functions: The search for identification. In *NBER working paper no. 5067*.

Groizard, Jose, Priya Ranjan, and Antonio Rodriguez-Lopez. 2014. Trade costs and job flows: Evidence from establishment-level data. *Economic Inquiry* 53 (1): 173–204.

Grossman, Gene, and Elhanan Helpman. 1994. Protection for sale. *American Economic Review* 84: 833–850.

Guo, M. X., L. Lu, L. G. Sheng, and M. J. Yu. 2018. The day after tomorrow: Evaluating the burden of Trump's trade war. *Asian Economic Papers* 17 (1): 101–20.

Hall, R. Alastair. 2004. *Generalized method of moments*. Oxford University Press.

Hallak, J. C. 2006. Product quality and the direction of trade. *Journal of International Economics* 68: 238–265.

Halpern, L., M. Koren, and A. Szeidl. 2011. Imported inputs and productivity. Center for firms in the global economy. In *Working paper 8*. Center for Firms in the Global Economy, Budapest, Hungary.

Halpern, Laszlo, Miklos Koren, and Adam Szeidl. 2015. Imported inputs and productivity. *American Economic Review* 105 (12): 3660–3703.

Han, Jun, Runjuan Liu, and Junsen Zhang. 2012. Globalization and wage inequality: Evidence from urban China. *Journal of International Economics* 87: 288–297.

Hanson, Gordon H., Raymond J. Mataloni, Jr., and Matthew J. Slaughter. 2005. Vertical production networks in multinational firms. *Review of Economics and Statistics* 87 (4): 664–678.

Harrigan, James. 1997. Technology, factor supplies, and international specialization: Estimating the neoclassical model. *American Economic Review* 87: 475–494.

Head, Keith, and John Ries. 1996. Inter-city competition for foreign investment: Static and dynamic effects of China's incentive areas. *Journal of Urban Economics* 40 (1): 38–60.

Heckman, James, and Edward Vytlacil. 1998. Instrumental variables methods for the correlated random coefficient model: Estimating the average rates of return to schooling when the return is correlated with schooling. *Journal of Human Resources* 33 (4): 974–987.

Helen Simpson et al. 2015. Place-based policies. In *Handbook of regional and urban economics*, vol. 5, 1197–1287.

Helpman, Elhanan. 1987. Imperfect competition and international trade: Evidence from fourteen industrial countries. *Journal of the Japanese and International Economics* 1: 62–81.

Helpman, Elhanan, Oleg Itskhoki, and Stephen Redding. 2010. Inequality and unemployment in a global economy. *Econometrica* 78: 1239–1283.

Helpman, Elhanan, Oleg Itskhoki, Marc-Andreas Muendler, and Stephen Redding. 2017. Trade and inequality: From theory to estimation. *Review of Economic Studies* (forthcoming).

Hsieh, Chang-Tai, and Peter Klenow. 2009. Misallocation and manufacturing TFP in China and India. *Quarterly Journal of Economics* 124 (4): 1403–1448.

Hu, C. 2014. Comparison of trade effects of China–ASEAN import customs clearance time: An empirical analysis based on different time-intensive agricultural products. *Guoji Maoyi Wenti (journal of International Trade)* 380 (8): 58–67.

Hunt, J., and M. Gauthier-Loiselle. 2010. How much does immigration boost innovation? *American Economic Journal: Macroeconomics* 2 (2): 31–56.

Iacovone, Leonardo, and Beata Javorcik. 2010. Multi-product exporters: Product churning, uncertainty and export discoveries. *Economic Journal* 120 (544): 481–499.

IMF (International Monetary Fund). 2017. *World economic outlook*. Washington, DC: IMF.

Javorcik, B.S. 2004. Does foreign direct investment increase the productivity of domestic firms? In search of spillovers through backward linkages. *American Economic Review* 94 (3): 605–627.

Johnson, George, and Frank Stafford. 1993. International competition and real wages. *American Economic Review* 83 (2): 127–130.

Jones, Derek C, Li Cheng et al. 2003. Growth and regional inequality in China during the reform era. *China Economic Review* 14 (2): 186–200.

Jonson, Justin, and David Myatt. 2003. Multiproduct quality competition: Fighting brands and product line pruning. *American Economic Review* 93 (3): 748–774.

Karabarbounis, Loukas, and Brent Neiman. 2014. The global decline of the labor share. *Quarterly Journal of Economics* 129 (1): 61–103.

Kasahara, H., and J. Rodrigue. 2008. Does the use of imported intermediates increase productivity? Plant-level evidence. *Journal of Development Economics* 87: 106–118.

Kasahara, H., and B. Lapham. 2013. Productivity and the decision to import and export: Theory and evidence. *Journal of International Economics* 89 (2): 297–316.

Kehoe, Timothy J., and Kim J. Ruhl. 2013. How important is the new goods margin in international trade? *Journal of Political Economy* 121 (2): 358–392.

Keller, W. 2002. Trade and the transmission of technology. *Journal of Economic Growth* 1: 5–24.

Keller, Wolfgang, and Stephen Yeaple. 2009. Multinational enterprises, international trade, and productivity growth: Firm-level evidence from the United States. *Review of Economics and Statistics* 91 (4): 821–831.

Kerr, W.R., and W.F. Lincoln. 2010. The supply side of innovation: H-1B visa reforms and US ethnic invention. *Journal of Labor Economics* 28 (3): 473–508.

Khan, Azizur Rahman, and Carl Riskin. 1998. Income and inequality in China: Composition, distribution and growth of household income, 1988 to 1995. *China Quarterly* 154: 221–253.

Khandelwal, A. 2010. The long and short (of) quality ladders. *The Review of Economic Studies* 77 (4): 1450–1476.

Khandelwal, Amit, and Petia Topalova. 2011. Trade liberalization and firm productivity: The case of India. *The Review of Economics and Statistics* 93 (3): 995–1009.

Kishore Gawande, and Usree Bandyopadhyay. 2000. Is protection for sale? Evidence on the grossman-helpman theory of endogenous protection? *The Review of Economics and Statistics* 82 (1): 139–152.

Klenow, P., and A. Rodriguez-Clare. 1997. *Quantifying variety gains from trade liberalization* (unpublished manuscript).

Kline, Patrick, and Enrico Moretti. 2014. Local economic development, agglomeration economies, and the big push: 100 years of evidence from the Tennessee Valley Authority. *The Quarterly Journal of Economics* 129 (1): 275–331; People, places, and public policy: Some simple welfare economics of local economic development programs. *Annual Review Economics* 6: 29–31.

Knight, John. 1995. Price scissors and intersectional resource transfers: Who paid for industrialization in China? *Oxford Economic Papers* 47 (1): 117–135.

Knight, John, and Lina Song. 1999. *The rural-urban divide. Economic disparities and interactions in China*. Oxford: Oxford University Press.

Kohli, Ulrich. 1990. Price and quantities elasticities in foreign trade. *Economics Letters* 33: 277–281.

Kohli, Ulrich. 1991. *Technology, duality, and foreign trade: The GNP function approach to modeling imports and exports*. Ann Arbor: University of Michigan Press/London: Harvester Wheatsheaf.

Lai, Tat-kei, and Travis Ng. 2014. The impact of product market competition on training provision: Evidence from Canada. *Canadian Journal of Economics* 47: 856–888.

Laird, Sam, and Alexander Yeats. 1990. *Quantitative methods for trade-barrier analysis*. Basingstoke, Hants: Macmillan Press.

Lardy, Nicholas. 1983. *Agriculture in Chinaís modern economic development*. New York: Cambridge University Press.

Latorre, M.C., H. Yonezawa, and J. Zhou. 2017. A general equilibrium analysis of FDI growth in Chinese services sectors. *China Economic Review* 47 (12): 172–188.

Lawrence, Robert, and Matthew Slaughter. 1993. International trade and american wages in the 1980s: Giant sucking sound or small hiccup? In *Brookings papers on economic activity: Microeconomics*, 161–226.

Leamer, Edward. 1993. Measurement errors and the convergence hypothesis. In *Open-economy macroeconomics*, eds. Helmut Frisch and Andreas Wöorgöotter, 241–256. London: MacMillan Press, Ltd.

Leamer, Edward. 1996. The effects of trade in services, technology transfer and delocalization on local and global income inequality. *Asia-Pacific Economic Review* 2: 44–60.

Learmer, E. Edward. 1984. *Sources of international comparative advantage: Theory and evidence*. Cambridge, MA: MIT Press.

Lev, Baruch, and Suresh Radhakrishnan. 2005. The valuation of organization capital. In *Measuring capital in the new economy*, eds. Carol Corrado John Haltiwanger, and Dan Sichel, 73–110. University of Chicago Press.

Levinsohn, James, and Amil Petrin. 2003. Estimating production functions using inputs to control for unobservable. *Review of Economic Studies* 70 (2): 317–341.

Li, Dominic, and Kai Y. Tsui. 1990. The generalized efficiency wage hypothesis and the scissors problem. *Canadian Journal of Economics* 23 (1): 144–158.

Li, H-C. 2009. Import competition and company training: Evidence from the US microdata on individuals. In *Working paper.* University of Southern California.

Lileeva, Alla, and Daniel Trefler. 2010. Improved access to foreign markets raises plant-level productivity...for some plants. *Quarterly Journal of Economics* 125 (3): 1052–1099.

Lileeva, Alla, and Daniel Trefelr. 2010. Improved access to foreign markets raises plant-level productivity...for some plants. *Quarterly Journal of Economics* 1051–1095.

Lileeva, Alla, and Daniel Trefler. 2010. Improved access to foreign markets raises plant-level productivity ... for some plants. *Quarterly Journal of Economics* CXXV (3): 1051–1100.

Lim, K., Trefler, D., and M. Yu. 2018. *Trade and innovation: The role of scale and competition effects*. University of Toronto (unpublished manuscript).

Limao, N., and A. J. Venables. 2001. Infrastructure, geographical disadvantage, transport costs, and trade. *World Bank Economic Review* 15 (3): 451–479.

Lin, J., F. Cai, and Z. Li. 1996. *The China miracle: Development strategy and economic reform*. The Chinese University Press.

Lin, Justin Yifu. 2003. Development strategy, viability, and economic convergence. *Economic Development and Cultural Change* 51 (2): 277–308.

Lin, Justin Yifu. 2005. Viability, economic transition and reáection on neoclassical economics. *Kyklos* 58 (2): 239–264.

Lin, Justin Yifu. 2007. Development and transition: Idea, strategy, and viability, marshall lectures. Cambridge University (forthcoming).

Liu, Dan, Sheng Liugang, and Yu Miaojie. 2017. Highways and firm productivity: Evidence from China. In *Working paper*.

Liu, Q., and L. Qiu. 2016. Intermediate input imports and innovations: Evidence from Chinese firms' patent filings. *Journal of International Economics* 103: 166–183.

Liu, Runjuan. 2010. Import competition and firm refocusing. *Canadian Journal of Economics* 43 (2): 440–466.

Long, Ngo Van, Raymond Riezman, and Antoine Soubeyran. 2007. Trade, wage gap, and specific human capital accumulation. *Review of International Economics* 15: 75–92.

Lu, Yi, Jin Wang, and Lianming Zhu, Do place-based policies work? Micro-Level evidence from China's economic zone program. In *Working paper*.

Lucas, Robert E. 1988. On the mechanics of economic development. *Journal of Monetary Economics* 22, 3–42.

Manova, Kalina, and Zhihong Yu. 2017. Multi-product firms and product quality. *Journal of International Economics* (forthcoming).

Manova, Kalina, Shang-Jin. Wei, and Zhiwei Zhang. 2015. Firm exports and multinational activity under credit constraints. *Review of Economics and Statistics* 97 (3): 574–588.

Marschak, J., and W. Andrews. 1944. Random simultaneous equations and the theory of production. *Econometrica* 12 (4): 143–205.

Martin, Philippe, Thierry Mayer, and Florian Mayneris. 2011. Public support to clusters: A firm level study of French local productive systems. *Regional Science and Urban Economics* 41 (2): 108–123.

Martin, Phillipe, Thierry Mayer. and Florian Mayneris. 2013. Are clusters more resilient in crises? Evidence from French exporters in 2008–2009. In *Working papaer*.

Mayer, Thierry, Marc Melitz, and Gianmarco Ottaviano. 2014. Market size, competition and the product mix of exporters. *American Economic Review* 104 (2): 495–536.

McKay, L., D. Lawrence, and C. Valstuin. 1983. Profit, output supply and input demand functions for multiproduct firms: The case of australian agriculture. *International Economic Review* 24: 323–339.

Melitz, Marc. 2003. The impact of trade on intra-industry reallocations and aggregate industry productivity. *Econometrica* 71 (6): 1695–1725.

Melitz, Marc, and Daniel Trefler. 2012. Gains from trade when firms matter. *Journal of Economic Perspectives* 26 (2): 91–118.

Melitz, Marc, and Gianmarco Ottaviano. 2008. Market size, trade, and productivity. *Review of Economic Studies* 75: 295–316.

Melitz, Marc J. 2003. The impact of trade on intra-industry reallocations and aggregate industry productivity. *Econometrica* 71 (6): 1695–1725.

Mendelson, Haim, and Ali Parlakturk. 2008. Product-line competition: Customization versus proliferation. *Management Science* 54 (12): 2039–2050.

Miller, Jefferey, and Thomas Vollmann. 1985. The hidden factory. *Harvard Business Review* 63 (5): 142–150.

Mincer, Jacob. 1974. *Schooling, experience, and earnings*. New York: Columbia University Press for the National Bureau of Economic Research.

Mullahy, John. 1997. Instrumental-variable estimation of count data models: Applications to models of cigarette smoking behavior. *Review of Economics and Statistics* 79 (4): 586–593.

Murat Seker Daniel Rodriguez-Delgado, and Mehmet Fatih Ulu. 2015. Imported intermediate goods and product innovation: Evidence from India. In *Central Bank of the Republic of Turkey working paper*.

National Bureau of Statistics of China (NBS). 2011a. *China statistical yearbook*. Beijing: China Statistics Press.

National Bureau of Statistics of China (NBS). 2011b. *China trade and external economic statistical yearbook*. Beijing: China Statistics Press.

Naughton, B. J. 2018. *The Chinese economy: Adaptation and growth*, 2nd ed. Cambridge, MA: MIT Press.

Naughton, Barry. 2005. The Chinese economy: Transitions and growth. The MIT Press.

Navas, A., Serti, F., and Tomasi, C. 2013. Intermediate inputs and the export gravity equation. In *Working papers 2013014*. The University of Sheffield, Department of Economics.

Neumark, David, and Jed Kolko. 2010. Do enterprise zones create jobs? Evidence from Californias enterprise zone program. *Journal of Urban Economics* 68 (1): 1–19.

Nocke, Volker, and Stephen Yeaple. 2014. Globalization and multiproduct firms. *International Economic Review* 55 (4): 993–1018.

OECD. 1993. Enterprise tenure, labour turnover and skill training. In *OECD employment outlook, Chapter 4*. Paris.

OECD. 2010. *Measuring globalisation: OECD economic globalization indicators*. Paris: OECD. www.oecd.org/sti/measuring-globalisation.

Olley, G Steven, and Ariel Pakes. 1996. The dynamics of productivity in the telecommunications equipment industry. *Econometrica* 64 (6): 1263–1297

Pavcnik, N. 2002. Trade liberalization, exit, and productivity improvements: Evidence from Chilean plants. *Review of Economic Studies* 69 (1): 245–276.

Pierce, J. R., and P. K. Schott. 2016. The surprisingly swift decline of US manufacturing employment. *American Economic Review* 106 (7): 1632–1662.

Preobrazhensky, Evgeny. 1926. *The new economics*. Oxford: Clarendon Press, 1965.

Qiu D. Larry, and Miaojie Yu. 2013. Multiproduct firms, export product scope, and trade liberalization: The role of managerial efficiency. In *Working paper*. Hong Kong Institute for Monetary Research.

Qiu, D. L., and Yu, M. 2012. Exporter scope, productivity, and trade liberalization: Theory and evidence from China. Beijing: Mimeo, Peking University.

Qiu, D. Larry., and Wen Zhou. 2013. Multiproduct firms and scope adjustment in globalization. *Journal of International Economics* 91: 142–153.

Restuccia, Diego, and Richard Rogerson. 2017. The causes and costs of misallocation. *Journal of Economic Perspectives, Summer* 31 (3): 151–174.

Roberts, Mark J., and James R. Tybout. 1997. The decision to export in Colombia: An empirical model of entry with sunk costs. *American Economic Review* 87 (4): 545–564.

Rodriguez-Lopez, Antonio, and Miaojie Yu. 2017. All-around trade liberalization and firm-level employment: Theory and evidence from China. Irvine: Mimeo, University of California

Rosenthal, S.S., and W.C. Strange. 2008. The attenuation of human capital spillovers. *Journal of Urban Economics* 64 (2): 373–389.

Rumbaugh, T., and N. Blancher. 2004. China: International trade and WTO accession. *IMF Working Paper* No. 4–36. International Monetary Fund, Washington, DC.

Sah, R. Kumar., and Joseph Stiglitz. 1984. The economics of price scissors. *American Economic Review* 74: 125–138.

Sah, R. Kumar., and Joseph Stiglitz. 1986. Price scissors and the structure of the economy. *Quarterly Journal of Economics* 102 (1): 109–134.

Sah, R. Kumar., and Joseph Stiglitz. 1986. The economics of price scissors: Reply. *American Economic Review* 76: 1195–1199.

Seker, Murat, and Daniel Rodriguez-Delgado, Jose. 2019. *Imported intermediate goods and product innovation: Evidence from India*.

Sheng, Liugang, and Dennis Tao Yang. 2016. Offshoring and wage inequality: Theory and evidence from China. *Journal of Development Economics* 118: 45–58.

Shorrocks, Anthony F. 1980. The class of additively decomposable inequality measures. *Econometrica* 48 (3): 613–625.

Stock, James H., and Motohiro Yogo. 2005. Testing for weak instruments in linear IV regression. In *Identification and inference for econometric models: Essays in honor of thomas rothenberg*, eds. Donald W. K. Andrews and James H. Stock, 80–108. New York: Cambridge University Press.

Tian, W., and Yu, M. forthcoming. A trade tale of two countries: China and India. *Journal of China and Global Economics*.

Tian, Wei, and Miaojie. Yu. 2015. Firm R&D, processing trade and input trade liberalisation: Evidence from Chinese firms. *The World Economy*, 297–313.

Tian, Wei and Miaojie Yu. 2016. Processing trade, export intensity, and input trade liberalization: Evidence from Chinese firms. *Journal of the Asia Pacific Economy* 20 (3): 444–464.

Tong, J. D., D. Y. Xie, Q. Bao, Q. H. Huang, X. Y. Li, Z. B. Liu, B. Jin, M. J. Yu, and X. S. Wang. 2017. The talks on paper of the deglobalization and transformation and upgrading of real economy. *Zhongguo Gongye Jingji* (*China Industrial Economics*) 351 (6): 5–59; Xiang, H. J., and K. He. 2016. The impact of free trade zone and capital flows—A natural experimental study of Shanghai. *Guoji Maoyi Wenti* (*Journal of International Trade*) 404 (8): 3–15.

Topalova, Petia, and Amit Khandelwal. 2011. Trade liberalization and firm productivity: The case of India. *Review of Economics and Statistics* 93 (3): 995–1009.

Trefler, Daniel. 2004. The long and short of the Canada-U. S. Free trade agreement. *American Economic Review, American Economic Association* 94 (4): 870–895.

Trefler, Daniel. 1993. trade liberalization and the theory of endogenous protection: An econometric study of U.S. Import policy. *Journal of Political Economy* 101: 138–160.

Tybout, J. 2003. Plant and firm-level evidence on "new" trade theories. In *Handbook of international trade*, ed. J. Harrigan and K. Choi, 388–415. New York: Blackwell.

UNCTAD (United Nations Conference on Trade and Development). 2009.

Van Biesebroeck, J. 2005. Exporting raises productivity in sub-Saharan African manufacturing firms. *Journal of International Economics* 67 (2): 373–391.

Verhoogen, Eric. 2008. Trade, quality upgrading and wage inequality in the Mexican manufacturing sector. *Quarterly Journal of Economics* 123 (2): 489–530.

Voss, H., P. J. Buckley, and A. R. Cross. 2008. Thirty years of Chinese outward foreign direct investment. In *Paper presented at the nineteenth chinese economic association conference, China's three decades of economic reform (1978–2008).* Cambridge.

Wang, Jin. 2013. The economic impact of special economic zones: Evidence from Chinese municipalities. *Journal of Development Economics* 101: 133–147.

Wang, Zheng, and Zhihong Yu. 2012. Trade partners, products, and firm performance of China™s exporter-importers: Does processing trade make a difference? *The World Economy* 35 (12): 1795–1824.

Wei, Shang-Jin. 1995. The open door policy and China's rapid growth: Evidence from city-level data. In *Growth theories in light of the East Asian experience, NBER-EASE*, vol. 4, 73–104. University of Chicago Press.

Wooldridge, Jeffery. 2002. *Econometric analysis of cross section and panel data.* Cambridge, MA: MIT Press.

Wooldridge, Jeffrey. 2008. Instrumental variables estimation of the average treatment effect in the correlated random coefficient model. In *Modelling and evaluating treatment effects in econometrics (Advances in Econometrics),* vol. 21, eds. Tom Fomby, R. Carter Hill, Daniel L. Millimet, Jeffrey A. Smith, Edward J. Vytlacil, 93–116. Emerald Group Publishing Limited.

World Investment Report. *Transnational corporations, agricultural production and development.* New York: United Nations.

Yu, M.J. 2018. Three tasks for building an all-around opening-up strategy. *China Economic Transition* 1 (1): 118–123.

Yu, M. 2011a. Moving up the value chain in manufacturing for China'. In *Can China avoid the middle-income trap?*, eds. H. Yiping and J. Zhuang. Asian Development Bank Institute, Tokyo.

Yu, M. 2011b. *Processing exports, firms' productivity and tariff reductions: Evidence from Chinese products.*. Beijing: Mimeo, Peking University.

Yu, Miaojie. 2015. Processing trade, firm productivity, and tariff reductions: Evidence from Chinese firms. *Economic Journal*, 125 (585): 943–988.

Yu, Miaojie, and Wei Tian. 2012. China's processing trade: A firm-level analysis. In *Rebalancing and sustaining growth in China*, eds. Huw McMay and Ligang Song, 111–148. Australian National University E-press.

Zellner, Arnold. 1962. An efficient method of estimating seemingly unrelated regression equations and tests for aggregation bias. *Journal of the American Statistical Association* 57: 348–368.

Zhao, Lex, and Kenji Kondoh. 2007. Temporary and permanent immigration under unionization. *Review of Development Economics* 11: 346–358.